Scandal and Survival in Nineteenth-Century Scotland

Scandal and Survival in Nineteenth-Century Scotland

The Life of Jane Cumming

Frances B. Singh

University of Rochester Press

Copyright © 2020 by Frances B. Singh

All rights reserved. Except as permitted under current legislation, no part of this work may be photocopied, stored in a retrieval system, published, performed in public, adapted, broadcast, transmitted, recorded, or reproduced in any form or by any means, without the prior permission of the copyright owner.

First published 2020
Reprinted in paperback 2022

University of Rochester Press
668 Mt. Hope Avenue, Rochester, NY 14620, USA
www.urpress.com
and Boydell & Brewer Limited
PO Box 9, Woodbridge, Suffolk IP12 3DF, UK
www.boydellandbrewer.com

ISBN-13: 978-1-58046-955-5 (hardcover)
ISBN-13: 978-1-58046-989-0 (paperback)

Library of Congress Cataloging-in-Publication Data

Names: Singh, Frances B., 1947– author.
Title: Scandal and survival in nineteenth-century Scotland : the life of Jane Cumming / Frances B. Singh.
Description: [Rochester, NY] : University of Rochester Press, [2020] | Includes bibliographical references and index.
Identifiers: LCCN 2019036826 | ISBN 9781580469555 (hardback) | ISBN 9781787444850 (pdf)
Subjects: LCSH: Cumming, Jane, 1795 or 1796–1844. | Racially mixed women—Scotland—Biography. | Racially mixed women—Scotland—Social conditions—History—19th century. | Trials (Libel)—Scotland—History—19th century. | Divorced women—Scotland—Social conditions—19th century. | Scotland—Social conditions—19th century.
Classification: LCC DA816.C86 S56 2020 | DDC 941.107/4092 [B]—dc23
LC record available at https://lccn.loc.gov/2019036826

My tongue will tell the anger of my heart, or else my heart concealing it will break.
> —Kate, in Shakespeare's *The Taming of the Shrew* (act 4, scene 3, ll. 82–83)

CONTENTS

Dramatis Personae	ix
Author's Note	xxvii
Explanatory Notes	xxxv
Introduction: Placing Jane	1
1 Ante Jane	28
2 Educating Jane (1)	54
3 Educating Jane (2)	81
4 Jane and the Lords of the Law (1)	106
5 Jane and the Lords of the Law (2)	136
6 Jane and William Tulloch	165
7 Jane, Posthumously	196
Conclusion: Assessing Jane	219
Acknowledgments	231
Appendix A: Marianne Woods, Jane Pirie, and Romantic Friendship	237
Appendix B: What Really Happened to Miss Marianne Woods and Miss Jane Pirie?	243
Appendix C: "Corinna, A Ballad"	247
Appendix D: Richard Rose's Letter to Sir William Written from the Kinnedar Manse, Dated January 12, 1835	249
Appendix E: Jane's Letter to Sir William Written from the Dallas Manse, Dated February 15, 1836, Regarding Wood Stealing at Dallas	251
Notes	253
Bibliography	285
Index	303

DRAMATIS PERSONAE

Caveat lector: This section gives an idea of the personalities and histories of many of the figures in *Scandal and Survival*, but it also reveals much of Jane's story.

Well over a hundred characters make appearances in this biography. What follows is a partial list of these figures arrived at through much pencil-gnawing. They were chosen for at least one of three reasons. First, they had a stronger effect than other people on Jane Cumming's life, or, conversely, she on theirs. Second, their lives, attitudes, or behavior, and/or their writing, offer a significant perspective on her life. Third, they reflect not just the borders Jane crossed (some more indeterminate and permeable than others) and the overlapping and intersecting social and political circles of the world in which her years ran their course, but the wide sweep of her life in space, in time, in ideology.

BRUCE, JOHN (1748–1826). Professor of logic and metaphysic at the University of Edinburgh and historiographer to the East India Company, John Bruce was at first unwilling to bring his brother's first-born biracial daughter from India to Scotland. However, he not only brought up his brother's second biracial daughter, Margaret Stuart, in the Bruce family's Princes Street home but bequeathed her his estate.

BRUCE, MARGARET STUART (later Tyndall Bruce) (1781–1869). Born in India to Colonel Robert Bruce and an unnamed Indian woman, Margaret was brought to Britain in early childhood and carefully introduced into the Bruce family home. Much loved by her father's family, she inherited substantial monies from her father and her uncle, made a love marriage with Onesiphorus Tyndall, and endowed scholarships at the University of Edinburgh and at St. Andrews. Her complexion was probably somewhat darker than her portraits make it out to be.

CHARLES, CHRISTIAN (1750?–1826). A lifelong resident of Elgin, Miss Christian Charles was the well-respected governess to all of Helen Cumming's children. By the time Jane arrived from India, Miss Charles had set up her own school in her home in Elgin. Jane spent six years under her tutelage there. After Jane gave testimony, she was again boarded with Miss Charles. The teacher left nothing to Jane in her will.

CLERK, JOHN (1752–1832). Fiery John Clerk was the lead advocate in court for Marianne Woods and Jane Pirie. In his summation speech, he used Jonathan Swift's poem "Corinna" to suggest that Jane might have been the victim of childhood, perhaps even infant, neglect and sexual abuse in Calcutta and to foresee a future for her that would include further sexual scandal. Clerk's set of case proceedings was purchased by William Roughead, and is now at the Signet Library in Edinburgh.

CLIVE, ROBERT (1725–74). A bully and an extortionist in his youth, Clive was shipped out to India at the age of eighteen. His victory over Indian forces at the Battle of Plassey (1757) ensured British control of India and garnered him the titles of 1st Baron Clive and Major-General the Right Honourable Lord Clive. Clive became a multimillionaire in India and was commended by Parliament for his great service to his country. He died the day Jane's father George was born.

COONGEE (?–?). When Jane boarded the *Bengal* bound for Britain in 1802, she was accompanied by a personal servant identified in the passenger list as Coongee. Coongee had been her ayah (Anglo-Indian, from the Portuguese: nursemaid) in Calcutta, one of her three local guardians. After the ship docked in London, Coongee accompanied Jane and Jane's brother Yorrick to Scotland; she was sent away about six months after they arrived. I have not been able to find out more about her.

CRANSTOUN, GEORGE (?–1850). Tall, elegant, and mellifluous George Cranstoun was, along with Henry Erskine and James Mackenzie, a member of Helen's defense team. Together with Erskine, he presented Jane's education in India as respectable and argued for the existence of same-sex passion between women.

CUMINE, ADAM (1767–1841). In 1791 Adam Cumine was an officer on the *Fort William*, among whose passengers was Jane's father, George Cumming. In 1802 Cumine would be captain of the *Bengal*, among whose passengers were Jane and Yorrick.

Dramatis Personae

CUMMING, ALEXANDER PENROSE (called Penrose) (after 1804, Sir Alexander Penrose Cumming Gordon, 1st Baronet of Altyre and Gordounstoun) (1749–1806). Penrose, Jane's grandfather, was ambitious, aggressive, stubborn, ill-tempered, and greatly devoted to his wife, Helen. In farming his estate, he employed progressive methods. The death of his son George in 1800, his forced vacating of his seat in Parliament in 1803, and his daughter Charlotte's ultimately fatal illness probably played their part in the strokes that killed him.

CUMMING, CHARLES LENNOX (later Cumming-Bruce) (1790–1875). Charles Lennox, Jane's uncle, was the youngest of the three sons of Penrose and Helen Cumming Gordon who lived to adulthood. He and his brother William split the costs of the case, the settlement the teachers received, and Jane's marriage settlement. Jane appointed him a co-executor of her estate, but he refused to serve in that capacity.

CUMMING, CHARLOTTE (1792?–1806). The youngest child of Penrose and Helen Cumming Gordon, Charlotte was placed in a Doncaster seminary around 1805. She fell sick there and died in early 1806, shortly after her father's demise.

CUMMING, GEORGE (1752–1834). Jane's great-uncle George Cumming was one of Penrose Cumming Gordon's younger brothers. He went into service with the East India Company, amassing a fortune. On returning to Britain, he settled in London. He helped get many young men from the Moray area of northeast Scotland, including his nephew George, positions in the East India Company. Jane stayed at his house for some two weeks after arriving from India.

CUMMING, GEORGE (1774–1800). George Cumming, Jane's father, was Penrose and Helen Cumming Gordon's firstborn child. He received a gentleman's education in Scotland and London. By his late teens, he had a reputation as a dandy; his uncle also considered him fiscally irresponsible. He was dispatched in 1793 to India, where he ran up huge debts and fathered two children before dying at the age of twenty-six.

CUMMING, HELEN (née Grant) (after 1804, Lady Helen Cumming Gordon, called "Dame" in the lawsuit) (1754–1832). Jane's grandmother Helen was child-centered, anxious, impulsive, manipulative, and imperious. Mother to sixteen children, of whom ten were girls, Helen was a believer in female education. She seems to have pressured her husband into sending for Jane from India. Soon after the girl arrived at the Cumming estate of Altyre, near Forres, Helen boarded her with Miss Charles, who was running a school in nearby Elgin. Helen's original intention was for Jane to become a milliner or dressmaker, but six years later, Helen transferred Jane to an Edinburgh boarding school and gave her to understand that if she did well she would be introduced to society as a member of the family. Within a year, when Jane informed her that two teachers at the school were engaged in a sexual relationship, Helen found herself the defendant in an 1811 defamation of character lawsuit, *Miss Marianne Woods and Miss Jane Pirie Against Dame Helen Cumming Gordon*. Helen arranged for Jane's marriage in 1818 to the schoolmaster William Tulloch.

CUMMING, MARY (?–1835). Yet another of Jane's aunts, Mary was living at Charlotte Square while Jane was a student at the Woods-Pirie School. When Woods and Pirie did not receive an explanation from Helen as to why she had turned against them, they wrote to Mary, begging her to tell them what Jane had accused them of. Mary did not respond to the teachers' note.

CUMMING, YORRICK (later George) (?–1812). Jane's father, George Cumming, mentioned in his will that she had a sibling but did not identify the child by name. On the passenger list of the ship that brought them to Scotland, Jane's sibling is identified as Yorrick Cumming, age seven. Soon after arrival, his name was changed to George. He was receiving a gentleman's education when his untimely death occurred.

CUNYNGHAME, MARY (1758–1846). Called Dame Mary Cunynghame in the case proceedings, she was the mother of Mary Cunynghame, a pupil at the Woods-Pirie School. Helen Cumming Gordon recommended the school to her, but Cunynghame did not enroll her daughter until she had done her own investigation into the teachers' moral character and professional competence. When Helen told her, without giving a reason, that she must withdraw her daughter from the school, Cunynghame told Helen to her face that she would not take her daughter out. She then visited the school and offered to try to extricate Woods and Pirie from the situation they found themselves in. However, when she subsequently heard the story that the teachers had

Dramatis Personae xiii

been sexually intimate, she withdrew her daughter from the school and had no more to do with Woods and Pirie.

CUNYNGHAME, MARY (1796–1867). Daughter of Dame Mary Cunynghame, Mary attended the Woods-Pirie School and was the other girl left with the teachers over the summer of 1810. She was not called as a witness in the lawsuit, however. Cunynghame settled in London and never married. At her death her estate was valued at £30,000.

DARWIN, ERASMUS (1731–1802). Erasmus Darwin, grandfather of Charles Darwin, was a physician, botanist, natural philosopher, and proponent of abolition of the slave trade. He had a number of illegitimate children, two of whom established a boarding school for young women at the end of the eighteenth century. Darwin outlined his theory of female education in the 1798 pamphlet *A Plan for the Conduct of Female Education in Boarding Schools, Private Families, and Public Seminaries.*

DE LA TORRE, LILLIAN (1902–93). Lillian de la Torre was an American writer of historical mysteries, many of which were set in the eighteenth century. While doing research in Edinburgh, she met William Roughead, who told her about Jane Cumming. After Roughead's death, de la Torre wrote a letter to the editor of *The New Republic* in which she interpreted Jane's story as the consequence of the race hatred to which she had been subjected.

EDMONSTONE, NEIL BENJAMIN (1765–1841). Neil Benjamin Edmonstone distinguished himself in his thirty-four years of service with the East India Company. He started as a writer, became a Persian translator, and was made secretary in the foreign, political, and secret department. His treatment of the children he fathered during his many years in India was far less distinguished.

ERSKINE, HENRY (1746–1817). In addition to supporting the points made by his legal colleague George Cranstoun in court, Henry Erskine argued that moral character and sexual preference were independent of each other. He presented Jane as a whistleblower who alerted her grandmother to the teachers' inappropriate behavior.

EWING, W. W. (1857–1932). W. W. Ewing was a Free Church minister and a historian. Some seventy years after the Disruption, he published an account of how the event played out in every parish in Scotland. In his book, Ewing celebrates all the women who joined the Free Church, with the exception of Jane.

FLETCHER, ELIZABETH (née Dawson) (1770–1858). One of Edinburgh's elite, Elizabeth attended the Manor House Boarding School in York in the 1780s. Decades later, Anne Lister and Eliza Raine attended the same school. In later life, Fletcher rued employing a governess recommended to her by Elizabeth Hamilton.

FORBES, LOUISA (née Cumming) (1778–1845). A daughter of Penrose and Helen Cumming Gordon, Louisa was educated at boarding schools in London and Edinburgh. She proved to be an unpretentious, level-headed woman who raised a large family and remained devoted to her mother. Helen asked Louisa to look after Jane after she herself left Edinburgh for Altyre in May 1810.

FORSYTH, AMY SURWEN (née Fraser, aka Young) (1818–1901). Amy was the daughter of William Fraser and his *bibi* (Urdu, from the Persian, a respectful term for a woman; in Anglo-Indian usage, it connoted a native mistress) Amiban. Under the surname Young, she was sent to Scotland in 1828. In 1835 she married a merchant, who divorced her many years later. Amy lived very comfortably and had many children. Though Amy was proud of her Fraser blood, her paternal grandmother never accepted her.

FORSYTH, ISAAC (1768–1859). Isaac Forsyth was the Elgin-based bookseller who kept northeastern Scotland supplied with books, magazines, and writing materials. Between 1806 and 1809 Helen Cumming Gordon and her son Sir William bought sermons, magazines, and novels from him, as well as copy books for Helen's granddaughter Jane. His corner shop on Elgin's High Street was very near Miss Charles's residence.

FRASER, WILLIAM (1784–1835). One of five brothers sent out to India by their cash-strapped father, William Fraser had a distinguished career with the East India Company. Something of a white mogul, he became a patron of the arts and established a conjugal relationship with a native woman. He fathered at least two children, one of whom, Amy, was sent to Scotland. He commissioned an album now known as the *Fraser Album*; one of the paintings depicts Amy and her mother, Amiban, in a village setting.

GILLIES, ADAM (Lord Gillies) (1760–1842). Lord Gillies presented Jane Cumming as an intellectually weak young woman filled with a degree of malice approaching the pathological. It was his opinion that she used excessive means to achieve a paltry end—namely, being taken out of school.

GORDON CUMMING, CONSTANCE FREDERICA ("Eka") (1837–1924). One of the youngest children of Sir William G. Gordon Cumming, Constance traveled the world and published many books about her experiences in foreign parts. Jane was her first cousin but is not mentioned in her autobiography. In later years, Constance befriended her niece Eleanora, an illegitimate daughter of one of her brothers, but got involved in a lawsuit with her in the early twentieth century.

GORDON CUMMING, WILLIAM GORDON (formerly Cumming and Cumming Gordon) (1787–1854). William, Jane's paternal uncle, became the 2nd Baronet of Altyre and Gordonstoun after the death of his father, Penrose. He ensured that Jane's husband, William Tulloch, became the minister at Dallas, historically part of the Gordonstoun estate. Jane referred to him as her "worthy uncle" in her will, but there was no love lost between the two. By refusing to increase her marriage settlement, he forced Jane to stay with Tulloch, whose behavior seems to have precipitated her nervous breakdown. At the time of Jane's death, Sir William refused to serve as an executor of her estate. He reversed the order of the family surnames from "Cumming Gordon" to "Gordon Cumming," so that his full name became William Gordon Gordon Cumming. His descendants kept that order.

GRANT, ANNE (of Laggan) (1755–1838). Though born in Scotland, Anne Grant spent a substantial portion of her childhood in upstate New York, where she got to know Dutch settlers, English soldiers, and even some Mohawks. A poet and memoirist, Grant was part of Edinburgh's lively social and literary network, along with Elizabeth Fletcher and Elizabeth Hamilton. When her son Duncan was in East India Company service, Grant let him know that if he formed a connection with an Indian lady, she would welcome her as his wife.

GRANT, ANNIE (later Need) (1781–1869). Annie Grant, an illegitimate daughter of one of Elizabeth Grant's relations, received an education from a Gordon Cumming relative. She became Elizabeth Grant's governess; in her memoirs, Elizabeth described Annie as caring, understanding, and sensitive, unlike all the other "wanting in wisdom" teachers she knew, who punished and tortured their students in the name of education. Annie went to India, where she married Major-General Samuel Need in 1815. Need's *bibi* had recently died, leaving him with four young children. The antithesis of the wicked stepmother stereotype, Annie was deeply involved with these children throughout her life. When Annie and Need returned to England, the four came with them. She raised them on an equal footing with the children she had with Need.

GRANT, ELIZABETH (of Rothiemurchus) (1797–1885). Elizabeth Grant knew quite a few of the Gordon Cummings and thought every member of the family odd. In her *Memoirs,* Grant not only strongly criticized teachers who hurt children's feelings but praised women who acted the mother's part toward illegitimate children, pointing out that such children did very well in life. She chose not to mention, however, that her beloved governess Annie Grant raised Annie's husband's biracial children alongside their own children.

GRANT, JAMES (Sir James Grant of Grant, 8th Baronet) (1738–1811). Sir James Grant, MP, was Helen Cumming Gordon's brother. He exerted pressure to get his son James Thomas into East India Company service. After James Thomas's death in India, he attempted to get his son's two biracial children sent to Scotland, but the effort was unsuccessful.

GRANT, JAMES THOMAS (1776–1804). James Thomas Grant and George Cumming, Jane's father, were first cousins. James Thomas preceded George in joining the East India Company, as a writer in the geographically huge and profitable administrative area known as the Bengal Establishment. He rose to the level of magistrate, and by the time of his death had set himself up as a laird (Scots: owner of an estate) on the banks of the Ganges. While on a visit to James Thomas, George seems to have met the woman who became the mother of his two children. James Thomas maintained a respectful and strait-laced manner in letters to his parents, but he, like his cousin, was the father of two illegitimate, biracial children, and he did not comply with his father's wish that he return to Scotland. George appointed his cousin one of Jane's guardians, but as James Thomas was stationed hundreds of miles from Calcutta, it is unlikely he had any close contact with her.

HAMILTON, ELIZABETH (1756?–1816). Novelist, philosopher, and pedagogue, Elizabeth Hamilton lost her parents early in life and was raised lovingly by an aunt. She was very close to her brother, a highly regarded Orientalist in the employ of the East India Company. While her *Translation of the Letters of a Hindoo Rajah* offers a generally positive view of Indian men, she suggests in the same work that Indian mothers make poor nurturers. In her educational treatises, she implies that children who were poorly nurtured in infancy have little chance of overcoming their deficits. Hamilton chose Jane Pirie to work under her when she was engaged to supervise the education of the Earl of Lucan's daughter. Called as a witness during *Miss Marianne Woods and Miss Jane Pirie Against Dame Helen Cumming Gordon*, Hamilton, uncomfortable under questioning, acknowledged her protégé's temper but claimed that it did no damage to children and Pirie was always able to regain their affection.

HELLMAN, LILLIAN (1905–84). Lillian Hellman was an American dramatist and memoirist whose first play, *The Children's* Hour (1934), was inspired by William Roughead's account in *Bad Companions* (1930). Hellman did not acknowledge Roughead as her source, and he nearly sued her for literary theft. In 1979, the American novelist and critic Mary McCarthy accused Hellman of lying and fabricating. Hellman responded with a libel suit.

HOPE, CHARLES (Lord Hope) (1763–1851). Charles Hope became lord justice-clerk of the Court of Session in Edinburgh in 1804 and Lord President of the court in 1811. The first time the case *Miss Marianne Woods and Miss Jane Pirie Against Dame Helen Cumming Gordon* came up for a verdict, he voted in favor of Helen, but the second time he determined in favor of the teachers. After a brutal interrogation of Jane, he concluded that she had acquired much sexual information, that she was still a virgin, and that she was intensely bitter.

INNES, WILLIAM (1775–1841). William Innes and James Mackenzie were the founders of the law firm Mackenzie & Innes, which handled all the legal business of the Gordon Cumming family. It was Innes who informed Sir William Gordon Cumming that the firm had settled with the teachers after the House of Parliament's law lords determined against his mother, Helen.

KETT, HENRY (1761–1825). Henry Kett was an English clergyman, academic, and writer. Helen Cumming Gordon bought his *Emily: A Moral Tale* (1809), which deals with the successful raising of a daughter by her father after the mother dies.

THE LADIES OF LLANGOLLEN, Eleanor Butler (1739–1829) and Sarah Pononsby (1755–1831). Butler and Pononsby ran away together from their families in Ireland and lived as a couple for over fifty years in Llangollen, Wales. Elizabeth Hamilton, Anne Lister, and William Wordsworth all visited them. Their living arrangement raised eyebrows; to this day, scholars are divided as to how to describe their relationship. Where were they on the spectrum, anchored on the one side by deeply devoted, affectionate, but platonic same sex romantic friends and on the other by a lesbian couple in a conjugal relationship?

"LADY IN THE NORTH" (?–?). While visiting his cousin stationed in northern India, George Cumming met a young Indian woman with whom he soon established a conjugal relationship and then had two children, Jane and Yorrick. In 1796 he referred to her as his "wife," and in 1799 as "the Lady in the North"; in his 1800 will, however, he called her "the most evil-intentioned of all women." In keeping with East India Company practice, the two children were taken from their mother at an early age. I have not been able to find out anything about her background, or about what happened to her after she was separated from Jane and Yorrick.

LISTER, ANNE (1791–1840). Anne Lister was born into a Yorkshire landowning family. She knew from an early age that she was attracted to women only. She was sent to the Manor House Boarding School in York, where the biracial Eliza Raine was also a pupil. The two became friends, then lovers. Lister's leaving of Raine contributed to Raine's mental breakdown. Lister was a prolific diarist who recorded her sexual life in graphic detail, in code.

MACKENZIE, COLIN (1770–1830). Principal clerk to the Court of Session during the time the case was being heard, Colin MacKenzie subsequently, albeit privately, criticized Lord Woodhouselee for persuading the other judges that "poor black Jeannie had a polluted imagination."

MACKENZIE, HENRY (1745–1831). Also known as The Man of Feeling after his sentimental novel of the same name, Henry Mackenzie was a tax lawyer and Penrose Cumming Gordon's brother-in-law. Mackenzie's second son, Lewis, was a writer in East India Company service at the same time as George Cumming, while his thirdborn son, James, was a lawyer and co-founder and owner of a law firm.

MACKENZIE, JAMES (1780–1870). James Mackenzie's law firm handled the legal affairs of the Gordon Cummings. After Helen was served with a summons in the lawsuit, Mackenzie & Innes hired the advocates who would defend her, conducted interviews, took care of all the paperwork, and sent the statements to Sir William.

MACKENZIE, LEWIS (1779–1800). The second son of Henry Mackenzie, Lewis joined the East India Company as a writer. He arrived in Calcutta in 1798, showed great promise, but died two years later. He is memorialized on a wall plaque in Edinburgh's Greyfriar's Cemetery.

MACONOCHIE, ALLAN (Lord Meadowbank) (1748–1816). In his university days, Allan Maconochie was a friend of Henry Mackenzie. He assumed the title of Lord Meadowbank on his appointment to the Court of Session in 1796. Of all the judges involved in *Miss Marianne Woods and Miss Jane Pirie Against Dame Helen Cumming Gordon*, he was the most familiar with the case. Though he was deeply affected by the personal element in it, he determined in favor of the teachers. His personal copy of the case proceedings is now at the National Library of Medicine in Bethesda, Maryland.

MILLER, HUGH (1802–56). Hugh Miller was a self-taught geologist. One of his early schoolmasters exhibited the kind of inappropriate behavior William Tulloch, Jane's husband, was later accused of. Miller worked for some years as a stonemason, and in this capacity met the illegitimate son of the Earl of Crawford. In *My Schools and Schoolmasters*, Miller trained a sympathetic lens on this young man, whose father had cast him out.

MONCREIFF, JAMES (1776–1851). Together with John Clerk, James Moncreiff represented Woods and Pirie in their lawsuit. Moncreiff's set of case proceedings has been at the Law Library of the Faculty of Advocates in Edinburgh since the latter part of the nineteenth century. Roughead consulted this volume when writing up the case.

MOORHOUSE, SUSAN (née Cochrane) (1808–67). The illegitimate, biracial daughter of Peter Cochrane, an East India Company surgeon, Susan was educated at a fashionable boarding school in London. Sent to India to "catch" a husband, she met Henry Moorhouse. They married there on the strength of her presumed inheritance and returned to England, but the inheritance eluded her.

MORE, HANNAH (1745–1833). An English writer on moral and religious subjects and friend to leading abolitionists, Hannah More as a young woman taught at her father's boarding school for females in Bristol. She is the author of two books relating to female education and character formation.

MUNRO, JANET (b. 1795, m. 1816–?). As an adolescent, Janet Munro was considered pretty and gullible. The most junior girl at the Woods-Pirie School, she swore that she too was aware that Woods and Pirie had been sexually intimate. When Jane attempted to get Janet to sleep with her, Janet told Miss Pirie about Jane's harassment. Munro married in 1816, but I have not been able to find out anything more about her post-case life.

MUNRO, MARY (178?–?, m. 1804?). No relation to Janet Munro, Mary Munro was the illegitimate, biracial daughter of Alexander Munro, an indigo planter in India. Mary was ensconced in her grandfather's Glasgow residence by 1796. She met with race prejudice initially, but over time the family took to her. Her relatives pressured her absent father into sending money so she could make a "respectable" marriage.

NAKESKA, ELEANORA (née Gordon Cumming) (18??–1929). Eleanora was an illegitimate daughter of the big game hunter Roualyen Gordon Cumming, son of Sir William G. Gordon Cumming and brother of Constance Frederica Gordon Cumming. The Gordon Cummings paid for Eleanora's art education but then forgot about her. Many years later Eleanora got in touch with Constance, who helped her financially. Eleanora, however, subsequently alleged that the Gordon Cummings had not given her a fair share of the proceeds from her father's estate. She started a lawsuit and claimed that she would leak a dark secret about the Gordon Cummings to the press. Was she bluffing, or had she stumbled across the story of Jane Cumming? The damaging material was never disclosed, and the case was resolved in favor of the Gordon Cummings.

OBERON, MERLE (1911–79). Born Estelle Merle O'Brien Thompson to an Indian mother and an Irish father in India, Merle Oberon became a movie star in England and Hollywood. She masked her biracial identity, claiming that she was born in Tasmania and that the dark-skinned woman who lived with her was her maid rather than the woman who had brought her up, either her mother or her grandmother. Samuel Goldwyn Meyer cast her for the role of the teacher Karen Wright in *These Three*, the first film adaptation of *The Children's Hour*.

OPIE, AMELIA (1769–1853). Amelia Opie was a successful English writer who was for a time a neighbor of Jane's great-uncle George Cumming on Berners Street in London. She wrote "The Poor Hindoo," a song about the anguish an Indian woman feels when her white partner abandons her, as well as *The Father and Daughter*. That novella deals with the need for parents to love and accept their children, even if they have formed an attachment outside of marriage, and to provide for the children born of those unions. Helen Cumming Gordon bought the book in 1809.

PALMER, JOHN (1767–1836). At one time, Calcutta-based John Palmer was the richest merchant in India. His father's second marriage was to an Indian, and Palmer was close to his biracial half-brother. He was also very aware of the politics of racism, and told his brother not to send his biracial children to England unless they could "pass" as white. Palmer was kind and helpful to East India Company men who found themselves in dire straits, including Jane's father, George Cumming. Palmer served as one of Jane's local guardians in Calcutta before she was sent to Scotland in 1802.

PHILLIPS, KATHERINE ("Kitty") (née Kirkpatrick) (1802–89). Born Sahib Begum to Colonel Achilles Kirkpatrick and Begum Khair-un-Nissa in India, Kitty was raised from an early age in her grandfather's London home, where one of her tutors was Thomas Carlyle. She made a happy marriage to Captain James Phillips. Late in life, she established a connection with her mother's mother, still living in India, and wrote poignantly and in detail about being virtually torn from her mother's arms and forcibly separated from the Indian milieu.

PIRIE, JANE (1779–1835). A protégé of the pedagogue Elizabeth Hamilton, Jane Pirie was employed as a governess by a number of well-connected families. She was highly qualified and zealous in the discharge of her duties, but had an irritable disposition and a violent temper. She and Marianne Woods were partners in a short-lived female boarding school in Edinburgh when they brought their lawsuit for defamation of character against Helen Cumming Gordon. The two acknowledged that they were romantic friends, but Pirie's attachment was so strong that it suggested to some sexual desire rather than friendship. During the case, Jane Cumming presented Pirie as the sexually needy one. When Woods and Pirie separated, Pirie was devastated. She died a broken woman, emotionally, physically, and financially.

PIRIE, MARGARET (1780–?). Margaret was Jane Pirie's sister and, like her, a governess. After marrying Thomas Ferguson, a Glasgow lawyer, Margaret gave up that work. The sisters had a falling-out in the second decade of the nineteenth century over a property in Edinburgh's Old Town.

RAINE, ELIZA (1788?–1860). Along with her sister Elizabeth Jane, Eliza Raine was sent to York from India in the last years of the eighteenth century. She attended the Manor House Boarding School, where she became friends with, and later the beloved of, Anne Lister, whose diaries, written in code, document their lesbian relationships, often graphically. By the time Lister left her, Eliza had already lost mother, father, and native country. Psychiatrists believe the breakdown she suffered was the result of these cumulative losses. Eliza never recovered, and spent the rest of her life in various mental institutions.

RAINE, JANE ELIZABETH (1790–?). Not yet of age, Elizabeth Jane married a cadet about to be sent out to India. The marriage did not last; she returned to England pregnant with another man's child. She and the child died young.

ROSE, RICHARD (1769–1853). Richard Rose was a highly respected clergyman who got along well with the Gordon Cummings and was also William Tulloch's mentor. Though he officiated at Jane Cumming's marriage to Tulloch, Rose came to regard him as a vicious bully and the marriage itself as a mistake.

ROUGHEAD, WILLIAM (1870–1952). William Roughead was a lawyer who devoted himself to writing about "matters criminous." He owned John Clerk's set of proceedings from *Miss Marianne Woods and Miss Jane Pirie Against Dame Helen Cumming Gordon*. Based on Clerk's and James Moncreiff's sets, he wrote up the case in his book *Bad Companions* (1930). He recognized but refused to touch on the psychosexual element in the teachers' relationship, and he regarded Jane Cumming as an embodiment of evil because her mother was Indian and Jane was dark-skinned and had spent her younger years in India. When he learned Lillian Hellman hadn't acknowledged his essay as the source of *The Children's Hour*, he considered suing her for literary theft.

SANDFORD, DANIEL (1766–1830). An Anglican clergyman who served in the Scottish Episcopal Church, Daniel Sandford was bishop of Edinburgh from 1806 to 1830. He placed his daughter as a day-scholar at the Woods-Pirie School, and was very pleased with her "improvement" under the tutelage of Miss Woods. Once he was told that Helen Cumming Gordon was absolutely certain the teachers had committed sexual improprieties, he withdrew his daughter from the school.

SHERWOOD, MARY MARTHA (née Butts) (1775–1851). In her youth, Mary attended a boarding school whose principal styled herself Mrs. La Tournelle though she couldn't speak French. Later, Sherwood spent eleven years in India, where she founded schools and orphanages for Indian children. While she adopted two special-needs Indian girls, she also had the race prejudices common in her age.

SOLLEY, JOHN B. (1872–1947). John Solley was a medical doctor practicing in Manhattan who read about Jane Cumming in Roughead's *Bad Companions*. He subsequently sent Roughead a letter in which he offered a reading of Jane and her allegations based on the writings of Sigmund Freud, Havelock Ellis, and Margaret Mead.

TULLOCH, WILLIAM (1777–1845). William Tulloch, who worked for a long time as a schoolteacher, held an M.A. from Marischal College, Aberdeen, and was licensed to preach the Gospel. He may have been the "Mr. Tulloch" who shepherded Jane Cumming, her brother, and Coongee from London to Altyre. Some years before his marriage, his ecclesiastical brethren cautioned Tulloch to be circumspect in every aspect of his conduct. In 1818 he and Jane were married. He was appointed parish minister at Dallas in 1822. Tulloch turned out to be a womanizer. At the time of the Disruption, he stayed with the Established Church, while Jane and their three children joined the Free Church.

TYTLER, ALEXANDER FRASER (Lord Woodhouselee) (1747–1813). Lord Woodhouselee, a Court of Session judge, was not involved with the case when it first came before the body, but he went through the proceedings minutely when it came up on appeal. He thought Jane a rebellious adolescent, but also felt her story derived from the "Eastern climate" in which she was raised. In his private life, Woodhouselee helped raise William Fraser, who later went to India in the employ of the East India Company. A sociable man, Woodhouselee often hosted gatherings at which Elizabeth Hamilton, Henry Mackenzie, and Lord Meadowbank were guests.

WHIFFIN, CHARLOTTE (1792–18??). For as long as the school was in existence, Woods and Pirie employed Charlotte Whiffin as a servant. She came from Kent, and was just a few years older than Jane. Charlotte talked to the girls, and Jane claimed she told them that the teachers were having sexual relations and she had seen them "at it." Charlotte denied this. I have not been able to trace her after she gave testimony in 1811.

WILLIAMSON, THOMAS (?–1817). Captain Thomas Williamson served with a British regiment in Bengal for over twenty years. The result of his acquired knowledge was published in 1810 as the two-volume *The East-West Vade Mecum*.

WOLLSTONECRAFT, MARY (1759–97). Writer, philosopher, and spokesperson for women's rights, Mary Wollstonecraft had a deep romantic friendship with Frances ("Fanny") Blood. The two, together with Mary's sisters, started a female boarding school in London. In her 1792 *Vindication of the Rights of Women*, Wollstonecraft decried the practice of bedsharing.

WOODS, ANN (?–after 1820). Ann Woods was the aunt of Marianne Woods, one of the accused teachers. In 1809 Jane Pirie was still under contract as a governess, so the aunt and niece opened the boarding school for girls in Edinburgh that Marianne and Pirie had dreamed about. Ann Woods had no formal position at the school, but in its initial days she handled the business accounts. When Pirie joined the school and reviewed Ann's account book, it looked to her as though Ann was presenting herself as Pirie's superior and Pirie as the subordinate. Pirie's obsession with that drove a wedge between her and Marianne.

WOODS, MARIANNE (1781–1870). Marianne Woods was a cofounder of what was formally called the Mrs. Woods and Miss Woods Boarding School for females but is generally known as the Woods-Pirie or Drumsheugh School. Marianne was English, but was raised in Scotland by her thespian uncle William Woods and his wife Ann. The pleasant-mannered Marianne and her high-strung romantic friend Jane Pirie dreamed of running a boarding school for girls in Edinburgh. The dream became a reality in 1809, when the school opened in a house within walking distance of Helen Cumming Gordon's residence on Charlotte Square. Jane Cumming arrived as a pupil, and though initially prejudiced against her on account of her race and illegitimacy, Marianne came to treat her no differently from the other students. Cumming developed a crush on Marianne, who did not take it seriously. That rejection, combined with other factors, led Cumming to tell her grandmother that Woods and Pirie were in a sexual relationship. The teachers then initiated the lawsuit *Miss Marianne Woods and Miss Jane Pirie Against Dame Helen Cumming Gordon*. The school, however, soon went out of business, its students having been withdrawn by parents and guardians. After a decade in the courts, the case was decided in favor of the teachers, but they received very little by way of compensation from the Gordon Cummings. Marianne left Edinburgh for London and then Brighton, where she died.

AUTHOR'S NOTE

I came to Jane Cumming when I decided to teach Lillian Hellman's play *The Children's Hour* (1934) in an advanced expository writing class. I found Mary Tilford, the character based on Jane Cumming, enigmatic, and thought that if I learned more about Jane I would understand Mary better. Secondary literature gave me to understand that Jane had disappeared from history after the sensational case turning on her allegations of a lesbian relationship between teachers at her Edinburgh boarding school in the early nineteenth century. Irritated, surprised, and also a tad delighted to discover, in the age of online catalogues, genealogical databases, and easy access to research specialists, nobody had already decided to search for her, I decided that finding Jane would be my next project. Internet browsing confirmed that the National Records of Scotland held letters written by Jane's father, grandfather, and grandmother, and that the National Library of Scotland housed the Gordon Cumming Depository. Might Jane be lurking in some file in one of those libraries?

I spent parts of three summers poring over this material in Edinburgh. I also became a willing prisoner of the British Library. Back in New York, glued to a chair in my study, I examined digitized census returns and wills on Findmypast.com, Ancestry.co.uk, and other databases. I found the site of the Woods-Pirie School on a map digitized by the National Library. From this physical and virtual research Jane began to emerge—as did her short-lived brother, her husband, her husband's mentor, her children, and her descendants.

I shared my growing knowledge of Jane at conferences. Kindred souls came up to me, encouraging me to write this book. Set the record straight, they said. Put the case in context. Tell the early history of this transplanted individual whose "punishment" for alleging that her schoolmistresses Miss Marianne Woods and Miss Jane Pirie were sexually intimate was to be confined within the racially and sexually inflected construct of the wily Indian seductress. Could you give the reader an idea of what she looked like? Tell her later history as the wife of a flirtatious minister? Is there any way we could hear her voice as well as hear how she got talked about? They were happy when I told them I was going to be taking into account the losses and separations Jane experienced, the psychological consequences of having a rash and imperious grandmother, a grandfather who referred to her as an "encumbrance," an insensitive uncle, and a bullying, womanizing husband. Others wondered how I would handle those special friends Woods and Pirie whose friendship did not survive. Would I be able to tell what happened to them? And would I tackle the "were they or weren't they, did they or didn't they" questions?

However, because the life of Jane Cumming raises issues not limited to parent-child relationships, domestic abuse, international adoption and the integration of ethnically different children into the population, education, friendship, sex within and outside marriage, sexual orientation, and resilience, I have always thought her story would resonate with many today. Since this second audience would not necessarily be familiar with information the scholarly audience knew, I added explanations for them. That material may slow down the reading for the scholars, but I felt, in this case, more was better.

The making of this book has been a bumpy journey. The four cats who started it with me are all in that snug corner of heaven where cats who sit on your desk, offering uncritical companionship, go. My computer (but not the external hard drive) was stolen, a basement flood derailed me for an entire semester. I would imagine that all academics have faced such challenges and then gritted their teeth and gone back to their self-appointed task.

Of all the sections of this book, the introduction was the most difficult to write. Even before the narrative gets under way, the reader learns something of the pre-case plot and the case itself, and about Jane's life after the case concluded. To avoid repetition, and to whet readers' interest in Jane's complex life, I have tried to give just enough information as I go along—but bearing in mind the knowledge level of my two audiences, maintaining the delicate balance between exposing and keeping in reserve has been challenging.

The second problem also has to do with balance, in this case between the Jane material and the Woods-Pirie relationship. Scholars have been more interested in romantic friendship and how the two teachers fit into that category than in the historical Jane Cumming.[1] I was more interested in Jane Cumming than in the teachers, and in Jane's forty-seven-year life Woods and Pirie's romantic friendship occupied less than two years. The Jane I was writing about had a long, fraught relationship with her uncle William Gordon Cumming. There is evidence that her grandmother continued to play a role in her life through about 1822. Jane's twenty-six-year marriage was marked by difficulties and declined into mutual hostility. Her life was impacted by the death of a brother, the disastrous Moray floods of

1829, and the 1843 Disruption that split the Scottish Presbyterian Church. So, yes, I had to talk about the teachers, but as Jane's biographer, I see them as just one of a number of shaping influences. At the same time, I wanted to satisfy readers coming to *Scandal and Survival* because of an interest in romantic friendship and the Misses Woods and Pirie. My solution was to dedicate two appendixes to the teachers: one looking at them in the context of romantic female friendship (the "did they or didn't they, were they or weren't they" questions) and one providing as much closure as I could find to their lives after the case.

The third challenge was more prosaic: it had to do with the dating. Lord Meadowbank determined against Helen in 1811 and 1812 but the formal 1811 determination no longer exists. What exists are undated notes, notes from 1811 and 1812, and the 1812 formal determination, which is a revision of the 1811 determination. So exactly what Lord Meadowbank added, subtracted, or modified from 1811 is unknowable. Since the decision itself was unchanged, I granted myself license to date the undated notes to 1811 and to discuss the written determination in the part of chapter 5 where I deal with the 1812 appeal.

In order to contextualize and make sense of Jane's life, I found myself traveling paths not taken by other scholars. A long-standing interest in medicine and the medical humanities made me wonder if research in those areas could shed light on Jane's behavior. It was obvious that there was no dearth of stress in her life, but was stress, built up to toxic levels, in some way connected to her extreme responses? The book's conclusion, subtitled "Assessing Jane," presents the results of that foray. The attempt to unpack Jane's story led me into fictional, psychological, and legal studies of what might be called keyhole witnessing.

Indeed, at one point the subtitle of this book was *A Keyhole History of Jane Cumming*. Though that was discarded, this biography explores the various keyholes through which those around Jane viewed the workings of her mind and attempted to prognosticate her future. The lawyers and judges alluded to the Bible, nodded to John Locke's 1693 *Some Thoughts Concerning Education and of the Conduct of the Understanding*, referenced Shakespeare's Iago and Swift's "Corinna, A Ballad." Lord Woodhouselee constructed Jane using a well-known keyhole: adolescent rebelliousness against school and authority figures. Lord Gillies peered at her through what I call the "disreputable servant" keyhole. In the end, the racist Orientalist keyhole of the "lewd and contriving Indian woman" prevailed.

I too looked to Shakespeare, particularly *The Taming of the Shrew*. I regard William Tulloch, Jane's husband, as a Petrucchio figure, to some extent chosen to reform her. To me, Kate's declaration "My tongue will tell the anger of my heart, or else my heart concealing it will break," offers such insight into Jane's emotional state when in crisis that I chose it for the epigraph.[2] I also see my subject through apertures such as "female passenger on board a cramped ship," "dependent of an emotional, headstrong, impetuous, easily-stressed, and imperious grandmother," "maltreated child," "the testifying female," "the minister's wife," and the "later-adopted international child" and "hypervigilant individual." I also borrowed terms from Elizabeth Hamilton. Her explication of the "ardent temperament" in young persons and adults elucidated the behavior of the two Janes, as did her "contact zone" allegory telling how two individuals occupying the same social space, both ego-threatened but one more socially empowered than the other, and both desiring the same object, would strike at each other.

While the subtitle went, the dependence on keyholes stayed. In using controlling frameworks, so necessary and sometimes so unreliable, I acknowledge my kinship with those lords of the law who read Jane "orientally," seeing in her a personification of "the Eastern woman." As a popular song of the late twentieth century puts it, "we are all just prisoners here of our own device." That said, I do believe that when the sightings of Jane I obtained through the apertures I used are strung together, they add up to something greater than themselves: the life of a complex and sometimes unstable woman.

As I wrote this biography, long-buried memories surfaced. I remembered my contact with the Presbyterian Church in the 1970s when my husband and I moved to Shillong, a city in northeastern India, many of whose residents had been converted to that faith in the previous century. In my first year there, I fell sick with jaundice and spent a week at the local Presbyterian hospital. A minister making his pastoral rounds came to see me and inquired about my spiritual health. I think I told him something to the effect that I was focused on regaining my physical health. In response, I received a hellfire and brimstone sermon. I was amazed rather than intimidated by this performance, but in general the local people, regular attendees of Bible study classes and church services, feared the local church governance. I heard of cases where neighbors informed the minister and the elders who advised him that their neighbors were acting improperly, and soon the accused neighbors found their names cut from the church rolls, themselves pilloried by the community.

The autobiographical substratum runs deeper. Readers will sense that my presentation of Jane is sympathetic though not uncritical. That's because she got under my skin. The more immersed I became in her, the more I started to see bits and pieces of her narrative in people dear to me. The personal became yet another keyhole through which I came to read Jane.

Both of my parents came to the United States as adults, with strong memories of lives lived elsewhere and the knowledge that they could never go back again. My father lost his mother at age ten. His father remarried when he was fourteen, and he had a lifelong testy relationship with his stepmother, each regarding the other as an encumbrance. When Hitler came to power, my father fled his natal country, Austria. He boarded a New York bound ship in Cherbourg, but his father stayed behind in Europe. He never saw him again. My father had a business relationship with his brother-in-law, and this strained his ties with his sister. Though he became an American citizen and could deploy English with the accuracy of a smart bomb, he always felt he never really belonged. I think what he longed for his whole life was an attachment bond—a desire for physical closeness with a person he could trust, who he felt understood him and to whom he could turn for emotional support.

In later life my father suffered from depression and paranoia. There was a period when he stayed up all night keeping tabs on the neighbors' nocturnal habits. He would on occasion talk back to his superiors and not follow orders; his rebellious streak cost him his chevrons a couple of times when he was in the army. He was quick to act, which sometimes led to wrong decisions, and he always stood up for the underdog. There was, he once told me, only one four-letter word in the English language: hate. He wasn't able to overcome his negativity toward his family, but he made sure it wasn't passed on. In 1969, he had me spend an entire summer with his stepmother, who had arrived in Ecuador in 1943 and was then living in Chile. During this time, I also began to bond with his sister and brother, who had survived the war and were also living in Chile.

There are parallels as well between my mother's story and Jane's. My mother's mother married young in Russia, for the wrong reasons, and when she realized her mistake she divorced her husband. By then she was living in China and had a small daughter. This was at a time when divorce was still considered a shameful act. Her well-to-do elder sister took her and her daughter in but made my grandmother feel she had disgraced the family's reputation. However, the rich relative allowed my mother to get a decent education. From the time she was eight until she was about eighteen, the woman who became my mother felt herself to be an unwanted resident in a close relation's house. She never forgot, never forgave: *she* could hate.

The experience left her with a permanent distrust of the motives and values of family members with money and status, and the conviction that a woman's salvation lay through education.

My mother told me that when she turned eighteen, she climbed the tallest hill in town. She had recently read Margaret Mitchell's novel *Gone with the Wind*, she said, and Scarlett O'Hara's words "I will never be hungry again" had impressed her hugely. Shaking her fist at the town below, my mother uttered the same vow. However, since the book wasn't published until three years after her fist-shaking, it's obvious that my mother so identified with Scarlett's will to survive and triumph—her determination, resilience, and defiance—that she read her into her own story and came to believe in a statement that was factually impossible but emotionally true. Shortly after that, she and her mother moved to a big city in China, where my mother learned English, found employment, and did well.

Years later, my mother came to the United States, where she gave talks on China to people who considered themselves educated; tired of audience members asking her how a person from China came to have blue eyes and dirty-blond hair, she told them, "I am a freak." There was always a note of boastful pride in her voice when she recounted the effect her words had on her interlocutors: *I shocked them into silence*. Decades later, during a transit strike in New York City, she told another outrageous lie. Unable to get to work, she asked a neighbor who always drove into Manhattan if he would give her a lift. He refused, and she found somebody else. After the strike was over, the neighbor asked if she had been able to get to work. Of course, she said, looking him straight in the eye, the company sent a helicopter. She got her revenge in the form of his popped-out eyes and dropped jaw. Like the opera singers she adored, she enjoyed being the center of attention.

After World War II, these two survivors of stressful, unhappy childhoods found each other and married. They were helpmeets and complemented each other; he was hot-tempered and sometimes impulsive, while she was a planner who kept her emotions under control and would always, as she said, "sit on" her decisions for at least twenty-four hours. For many years they worked together, and my father depended on her to execute the hard decisions. Later on, she rose through the ranks of nonprofit organizations to become a personnel director. She had managerial talent, absolutely, but there was a ceiling for women in those days, and it wasn't made of glass.

Their child-rearing styles were quite different. My father was the softy, wanting me to experience the happy life he had led before his mother died. My mother was the tough one, afraid that if I didn't do well in school I wouldn't be able to survive. For her, it was more important for a girl to be able to put the letters "PhD" after her name than a "Mrs." before it, and she pushed me to do well in school. As a reader, I was always delighted by the books she introduced me to, but if she had also picked up a lipstick and taken me shopping for some stylish shoes, my adolescent years would have been happier. Her intentions were honorable, but her obsession with high academic success drove a wedge between us. My anger has subsided, replaced by the sad understanding that there was no outlet at the time for her executive capability other than me.

My parents were savers rather than splurgers, but there were at least two notable exceptions to this pattern. My mother had minor musical talent and was convinced I was musical too. The result was that a quality piano ended up in our living room and I had weekly lessons for five years. It turned out that I was not musical at all. The piano teacher was nice, but because of my lack of talent the lessons were a torture. In my fifth year, my father heard me praying for a robber to break into the house and steal the piano, and the next day the lessons stopped. The piano remains with me as a symbol of high hopes not realized, a reminder of the misery one person can inflict on another, with the best of intentions.

The other exception involved a special holiday. The eldest of my Chilean cousins had been sent to New York to get to know us, and to celebrate the occasion we took a trip to Washington D.C. I was seven or eight and thrilled, he was sixteen and miserable, because he was pining for his girlfriend back in Chile as only an adolescent whose father wanted him to break up with a girl can pine. I remember the Chesapeake Bay Bridge and the wide sweep of water below; the basket of fruit on my bed at the Statler Hilton; the coolness of the Jefferson Memorial inside. It was a very special trip for me, but for my besotted cousin, it was a trying one. Unable to be rude in speech, he expressed his unhappiness in body language, sleeping the whole way there in the car, occasionally moaning, "Liliana!" At the time, I regarded him as a spoilsport who put a damper on the vacation. I suspect my parents, my mother especially, thought him an ingrate. Now that both the cousin and I are much older, and he, after several other relationships, is finally together with Liliana, I have another view of his behavior. Together with my parents' history, I suspect my sympathy for the plight of the adolescent Jane Cumming, separated from the person she loved, has its roots in a mid-1950s road trip.

This book acknowledges that Jane was, at times, motivated by a slew of malignant passions—anger, malice, bitterness, jealousy, a desire to take revenge and inflict hurt and even to go in for the kill. While I saw that destructive energy, I kept thinking about Linda Loman's speech in Arthur Miller's *Death of a Salesman*. "He's not the finest character that ever lived," she says of her husband Willy. "But he's a human being, and a terrible thing is happening to him. So attention must be paid."[3] I acknowledge that my heart went out to this woman who was maltreated as a child in Calcutta, kept at arm's length as a girl in Scotland, and married to a man who turned out to be a sycophant, a bully, and a womanizer—even as I recognize that she too had serious flaws.

Scandal and Survival recovers Jane and offers a recuperative reading of a woman who had very few options at her disposal for making people pay attention to her. Many critics, knowing her only from her testimony during the case, have loved to hate her, as the sly, spiteful, contriving adolescent who destroyed the lives of two tender friends. My hope is that with more information, their response to her will become more nuanced.

EXPLANATORY NOTES

Orthography

The documents from which I quote are orthographically diverse. To make the quotations more accessible, I have, in general, used modern spelling and followed present-day conventions regarding punctuation and capitalization.

Language

Latin phrases, words from Hindi/Urdu, and Scots expressions and legal language are sprinkled through *Scandal and Survival*. I have translated the Latin phrases and put definitions in parentheses following Scots words and legal terminology and words from Hindi/Urdu.

The term "writer" appears frequently in this book, and it refers to two distinct careers. A man who applied for a position with the East India Company submitted a Writer's Petition, asking to be appointed to a post that would require him to record all aspects of the company's operations, such as decisions taken, accounting details, and minutes. In Scots usage, on the other hand, a writer was a lawyer; today he would be called a solicitor. These writers did not have the privilege of pleading or arguing in either civil or criminal court, but rather did chamber work, giving legal advice and providing legal services, such as drawing up wills and preparing contracts or claims.

"Illegitimate" also appears frequently in this book, because in the long eighteenth century in Jane's part of Scotland, irregular unions were common and the number of children born out of wedlock high. Words such as "bastard," "illegitimate," "acknowledged," "accidental," and "natural" were used at the time to describe them. Contemporary scholars who study sexual behavior frequently refer to these children as "illegitimate." I have followed suit.

The Case

The printed proceedings of *Miss Marianne Woods and Miss Jane Cumming Against Dame Helen Cumming Gordon* were supposed to have been destroyed by the lawyers and judges who received copies. However, some of the proceedings survived. The standard "text" is comprised of the numerous sets of proceedings that Lord Meadowbank had bound. Since each set is numbered from page 1 onward, I have entered the page reference followed by the name of the set so that readers who wish to check the quotation will know, for example, which "page 1" to turn to.

Nomenclature

Place Names in India

Calcutta is now known as Kolkata, but I have chosen to use the older name. On the other hand, I use the more recent Moorshidabad for Moorshadabad, as the city is easier to locate under that name.

The Ill-Fated School

The school Woods and Pirie ran was listed in the 1809 Postal Directory as "Mrs. and Miss Woods Female Boarding School," with the address given as "Drumsheugh." In the proceedings, this name was never used. Rather, the school was variously called an establishment, a seminary, or was referred by its address. As academics generally call it the Woods-Pirie School, I tend to refer to it by that name.

Personal and Family Names

There are many Georges, Janes, Elizabeths, Alexanders, Margarets, and Williams who figure in this book, as well as many people with the same last name—for instance, Cumming or Grant. I have tried to avoid confusion by using a number of techniques: referring to them by their full names, referring to them only by a last name, referring to them by a middle name, using or not using an honorific before their name or a place name afterward. Women who married are generally referred to by their married name; a major exception is Elizabeth Grant of Rothiemurchus. Elizabeth Hamilton, who never married, referred to herself as Mrs. Hamilton, and I have honored her choice. For Marianne Woods and Jane Pirie, I have at various times used their first names, their full names, or only their last names.

When Alexander Penrose Cumming succeeded to the estate of Gordonstoun, he became Sir Alexander Penrose Cumming Gordon. Though the official name of the case was *Miss Marianne Woods and Miss Jane Pirie Against Dame Helen Cumming Gordon*, the formally correct way to refer to Helen is Lady Cumming Gordon. I have mostly called her Helen or Helen Cumming Gordon. Helen's son William Gordon reversed the order of the surnames, becoming Sir William G. Gordon Cumming. His descendants kept that order.

The Structure of the Church of Scotland

The Church of Scotland accepted the Presbyterian faith in the sixteenth century. Structurally, the Presbyterian church (in Scotland as elsewhere) has four levels of government. From lowest to highest, they are: session, presbytery, synod, and General Assembly. While the minister is responsible for conducting church services, each individual church is governed by a body of elders, referred to as the session. This group polices the behavior of the congregation. The clerk of session takes minutes when the elders meet and maintains all the church's ledgers. In Jane's day, presbyteries were composed of the ministers from a local area. They discussed issues of general concern such as their housing and dealt with cases sent to them from congregational sessions. In addition, they liaised with the heritors (Scots: large landowners) in the area and carried out visitations to individual churches. Presbyteries are grouped into synods. A synod has the power to appeal verdicts from the lower levels. Presbyteries and synods send delegates to the General Assembly, which is the highest court of appeal. At General Assembly meetings, significant theological issues are debated and decided on. In 1843, at a meeting of the General Assembly, the Church of Scotland split over the issue of outside interference by heritors in church governance, and those opposed to it formed the Free Church; this is known as the Disruption.

Currency Conversion

In the long eighteenth century, ten Indian rupees were worth one British pound. When George Cumming died in 1800, his debt amounted to

45,000 rupees, or £4,500. To give readers an idea of how much estates were worth or how much people spent or made, I have used the historical currency converter measuringworth.com, which computes "real value" over time, and takes inflation into account. In today's terms, George saddled his father with a debt of $567,000. I have not converted all amounts mentioned in this book to their present-day equivalents, only those I felt were historically or socially significant or especially revealing of character.

INTRODUCTION

Placing Jane

Jane Cumming's allegation that her teachers had been sexually intimate led to a racially inflected early nineteenth-century defamation of character lawsuit, *Miss Marianne Woods and Miss Jane Pirie Against Dame Helen Cumming Gordon*. Jane was born in Patna, India, in 1795 or 1796; by 1803 she was being brought up in Scotland. Her father was Scots, her mother Indian, and she was of color. From the case documents, we know Jane was a well-developed adolescent, bigger than the average Scottish girl her age—and if she wasn't more knowledgeable about sexual matters than the gentry girls who were her classmates, she was certainly less coy about describing them to men in a public space. The absence of any remark in the case documents about her speech suggests that the English she spoke was free of any Indian accent. She was, according to various accounts, a bully, a ringleader, a mediocre student, something of a drama queen. At times she was malicious or manipulative. She brooded over slights and plotted revenge. Despair gave her courage. She was also reflective, observant, grateful, and affectionate. She developed a crush on one of her teachers and made sexual overtures to a classmate. She was compared both to a famous victimizer (Iago) and to a victim (a sexually abused infant).

These details suggest a complicated person, and they whetted my curiosity to know more about her. I ended up writing this biography because I couldn't find out what happened to her after she stepped down from the witness stand in March 1811. Drawing on many sources, some never tapped before, *Scandal and Survival* recovers, reconstructs, and contextualizes Jane Cumming's life.

Chapter 1, which begins before she was born, sets the stage. It introduces the Cumming family, which traced its roots back to the twelfth century, and family members including Jane's ambitious but choleric grandfather, her emotional and impulsive grandmother, the uncle who made a fortune in East India Company service, and a father who stopped his ears whenever the subject of prudence was broached. Jane's great-uncle Henry Mackenzie, better known as The Man of Feeling (after his 1771 novel by that name), makes a cameo appearance. The chapter ends with her arrival in Scotland, accompanied by a personal servant and a younger brother. Chapters 2 and 3 examine the education Jane and, to a lesser extent, her brother received in Scotland. Using both the printed case transcripts and the judges' handwritten notes, chapters 4 and 5 deal with the case spawned by her allegation that her teachers had been sexually intimate, and in particular, with how the judges viewed Jane.

Jane's brother dies in chapter 6, but the bulk of the chapter deals with her marriage to the lubricious William Tulloch, a schoolteacher who became a minister thanks to Gordon Cumming's patronage. The chapter's climax is what I call, after the Scottish village in which it took place, *l'affaire Dallas*. In the 1830s, Tulloch was openly flirting with village girls; eyewitnesses to his easy familiarity were divided as to whether he was also sleeping with them. A rejected, jealous, and very unhappy Jane was convinced he was unchaste and decided to destroy his reputation. The Reverend Doctor Richard Rose emerges as the hero of the chapter because he saw that Tulloch had made Jane miserable and begged Sir William to increase her marriage settlement and give his blessing to a separation. While I present *l'affaire Dallas* as a reprise of the situation that inspired Jane to take action against her schoolmistresses, I also place her marital woes in the context of the Ten Year's Conflict (1834–43), which ended in 1843 with the Disruption, the splitting of the Presbyterian Church into the Established Church and the Free Church. Jane dies at the end of the sixth chapter, but she had an afterlife in the twentieth century. In chapter 7, she crosses the Atlantic when Lillian Hellman, inspired by an account of the case, reincarnates her as the malicious youth Mary Tilford in *The Children's Hour*.

Jane Cumming's parents were George Cumming and an Indian woman whose name is unknown; he acknowledged his paternity in his 1800 will and referred to his daughter as "natural." George was the firstborn son of Alexander Penrose and Helen Cumming, landed gentry living near the town of Forres in northeastern Scotland. He had been sent to India as a writer in East India Company service in the hope that he would shape up and, like his namesake uncle, amass a fortune, but all he amassed were debts. Within six months of her arrival in Scotland, Jane had become a boarder at a school in Elgin, also fairly close her grandfather's estate. Helen's idea at this time was that after receiving a modicum of education, her granddaughter would be able to take up a respectable, albeit inferior, place in society as a milliner (hatmaker) or mantua-maker (dressmaker).

Six years later, Helen changed her mind, deciding that Jane should occupy a higher social position. To this end, in 1809 she placed her in a boarding school for girls in Edinburgh run by Marianne Woods and Jane Pirie. The two women, who were romantic friends and business partners, had contrasting teaching styles. Woods was kind to Jane while Pirie picked on Jane and was verbally abusive to her. Jane developed a crush on Miss Woods, which the teacher brushed off. In 1810 Jane told her grandmother that the teachers were sexually intimate. Without investigating the story, Helen took Jane out of the school and convinced the other parents and guardians to withdraw their daughters.

The school collapsed, and the now ruined teachers filed a defamation of character suit against Helen. In 1811 Jane was called as a witness and spent about twenty-four hours, over four days, testifying at the Court of Session She described the teachers' lovemaking and was grilled by the advocates and judges. These men came up with five lines of questioning to help them develop explanations for the content of her story.

First, was Jane telling the truth about the teachers? Second, since she didn't want to remain at the school and had already ascertained that nothing shocks better than a tale of deviant sex, was hers simply an adolescent invention designed to get her guardian to withdraw her from the seminary? Third, since she had problems with her teachers, was this payback? Was a spiteful Jane taking revenge on Miss Pirie, who spoke harshly to her, and Miss Woods, who had brushed off her overtures of affection? Fourth, did Jane's attention-grabbing story point to a history of child abuse and chronic neglect? Fifth, since the opinion in Britain at the time was that Indian women were licentious and talked only of sex, and Jane had spent her early years in their company, had they impressed on her notions about sexual proclivities unknown in the West? Had her time in a brothel-like environment unavoidably polluted her mind? *Scandal and Survival* appraises these five proposed explanations. It speculates as well about whether Jane had acquired some knowledge from reading lewd literature, and whether she was projecting sexual fantasies of her own.

Jane's life continued to be eventful, even scandal-tinged, after 1811.her appearance in the Court of Session. As already mentioned, she was married in 1818 to the womanizing William Tulloch, whom she later accused of not being sexually chaste. She lived through the catastrophic Moray floods of 1829. Prevented from obtaining a separation, she made a will effectively cutting her husband out of her estate. She then had a breakdown from which she emerged unhealthily suspicious. In 1843, when the Disruption took place, Tulloch stayed with the Established Church while Jane adhered to the Free Church. Apparently she was the only minister's wife in Scotland not to stand by her husband at that juncture. The Free Church was so shocked by her mini-disruption that the minister who wrote the account of what happened in every parish at the time couldn't bring himself to mention her by name. Even Jane's afterlife was eventful, for her story inspired an American dramatist to write a play subsequently made into two movies. Every time the play is performed or one of the movies seen, the story of the biracial adolescent who alleged her teachers were sexually involved with each other comes back into view.

The complex strands we call race, class, and sex/gender choreographed Jane's life and world. The chapters that follow trace those strands' movements over time. Here, I offer an overview of each of the three elements, with examples to show how they combined and recombined, sometimes performed solo, and always shaped events during the period covered by the book.

Race is associated with color consciousness, through the use of such laden words as white, dark, black, and tinged; and with geographical regions, through such terms as European, Asiatic, Eastern, Oriental, and Indian—the latter four essentially interchangeable. Certain sexual customs and behaviors were associated with those geographic areas and ascribed to their inhabitants. The Western prejudice ran in favor of white and European, so Helen attempted to downplay Jane's color by saying there was only the slightest tinge to her complexion. However, Miss Pirie was so disgusted by Jane's color, she demanded that her pupil never look her in the face. Perhaps she thought that color argued for Jane Cumming being a devolved specimen of humanity; as will be discussed shortly, it was not an unknown reaction to a darker individual. It seems reasonable to assume that Miss Pirie's race prejudice helped provoke Jane's hatred of her, the refractory behavior she displayed, and the charge she leveled, but did Jane also internalize this prejudice? As the minister's wife in the 1830s she held an important position in her local society, but she comes across in surviving accounts from the time as a troubled woman. In the conclusion, I consider to what extent internalized race prejudice could be responsible for her anxieties and insecurities, her breakdown, and her incomplete recovery.

In the essentially racially homogeneous society that Jane was transported to, her status as a biracial individual who looked "other" raised concerns for the family who brought her over from India. They had to work out what she should be called, where she should be kept, how she should be educated. Then they had to find a man willing to marry a girl with an "Asiatic" complexion and decide how much money should be settled on her at the time of her marriage. The Cumming Gordons come off pretty well on the first set of concerns. Jane was acknowledged as a Cumming, she spent her holidays at Altyre, and though she was originally destined to earn her living making hats or dresses, she came to receive a gentry girl's education in social accomplishments. The family scores less well in their choice of mate for Jane, for they knew Tulloch was not of stellar moral character and was so ill-paid that he would be happy to take whatever they gave him in the marriage settlement. When Tulloch revealed his true nature, Sir William made Jane's life more miserable by refusing to increase her marriage settlement, frowning upon the idea of her separating from her husband.

Class, then, followed on the coattails of race, but it also danced with sex. In Jane's world, a common prejudice held that female domestic servants (irrespective of race) were sexually loose, mendacious, untrustworthy, and bad influences on the young. As an adolescent, Jane attempted to exploit this prejudice by ascribing the tale she told about the teachers to Charlotte, the school servant. Two decades later, as a minister's wife, she fired her female servants one after the other, claiming that they had no morals, sexual or otherwise.

Jane died in 1844, and class conflict particularly shaped the last decade of Jane's life, which coincided almost exactly with the decade-long struggle (1834–43) in the Church of Scotland. The confrontation had begun in earnest with the 1711 Church Patronage (Scotland) Act, in which Parliament restored to heritors the right to appoint ministers. It was a highly unpopular piece of legislation, and between 1834 and 1843 two parties arose in response to it. The Moderates espoused the right of heritorial involvement; the Evangelicals challenged it, maintaining that secular figures should not be involved in spiritual matters. Most ministers and congregants were opposed to the influence wielded by heritors, whose ranks included Jane's uncle Sir William Gordon Cumming. In 1843 the Church split over the issue. Tulloch stayed with the Established Church, while Jane, together with her children and most of the congregation at Tulloch's parish of Dallas, joined the Free Church. Sir William was very unhappy with this loss of power and did his utmost to harass adherents of the Free Church. He must have been particularly annoyed with Jane, who by joining the Free Church symbolically repudiated his power over her life, obtaining a spiritual separation from Tulloch when her uncle had put a legal one out of her reach. As for Tulloch, by taking herself, their children, and his congregation out from under his control, Jane symbolically emasculated him as husband, father, and minister.

Sex as it relates to gender conduct—behavior appropriate to or conventionally associated with the male or the female sex—receives considerable attention throughout the book. If there were a prize in the category "most egregious example of conduct unbecoming a man," it would be awarded to William Tulloch. Long before he married, he was accused of sexual misconduct. During the 1830s he attempted to get his hands on Jane's marriage settlement, though he had renounced his *jus mariti* (the right of a husband, especially the right he acquires to his wife's moveable estate by virtue of marriage) before they wed, and even though his lawyers told him it would be an ungentlemanly thing to do. His emotional cruelty to Jane was obvious to the Reverend Richard Rose, the clear-eyed minister respected by both Tulloch and Sir William Gordon Cumming for his skills, knowledge, and expertise in handling delicate situations. Appalled by Jane's misery, Rose implored Sir William to increase his niece's marriage settlement and not put obstacles in the way of her obtaining a separation.

The prize for "most egregious example of conduct unbecoming a woman" would go to Jane Pirie. Her violent temper marked her as an "unwomanly woman," a negative role model. When Pirie was still a governess, one of her employers said that when Pirie was venting her anger, she (the employer) took the girls out of earshot. Much of chapter 2 is devoted to female boarding schools, where self-control, obedience, and submission to authority, understood as the behaviors that made for a happy and fruitful marriage, were inculcated though an education in social accomplishments. Female teachers, particularly in British boarding schools, were supposed to be maternal. This did not imply that they shouldn't criticize or punish, but that the relationship between student and teacher should remain warm, the teacher always able to regain the affection of the pupil after correcting her.[1] Miss Pirie, unfortunately, could only criticize harshly, and she never realized how her lack of sensitivity led to Jane's revenge. A sad commentary on the limited opportunities available to single women at the time, and a sad irony of the present book, is that Jane Pirie didn't have the temperament to model the qualities she was supposed to be instilling at the boarding school she co-ran.

Because she was imperious, manipulative, and stubborn and destroyed the lives of two other women, Helen Cumming Gordon has gone down in the history books as one whose conduct was unbecoming of a woman. Though she was faulted for being too much of a "take-charge woman" for the sensibilities of her day, Helen was also a "very womanly woman" who lived by her marriage vows and believed motherhood was the *summum bonum*. Her union with Penrose was marked by mutual fidelity, tender goodwill, esteem, respect, and obedience.[2] A caring mother, she worried over the health of her numerous offspring and was particularly concerned with her daughters' education. There is also evidence from about a decade before Jane was sent to Scotland that Helen was moved by the plight of four orphaned, homeless sisters to ask her sister-in-law to take the eldest into domestic service. It is hard not to believe that when Penrose and Helen learned their son was asking them to look after his soon-to-be orphaned natural children, the maternal Helen saw them primarily as vulnerable youngsters and herself as their protector.

Sex, race, and class intersected when Helen decided that, despite her granddaughter's illegitimacy and compromised racial identity, she would use her own aristocratic status to enable Jane's introduction to gentry society, leading to a proposal from a man with social status and a companionate marriage. It seems that Helen's desire for a "good" match for Jane trumped any discomfort with the girl's origins and complexion, if indeed Helen ever felt any. So Lady Cumming Gordon struck a deal with the financially struggling business partners and romantic friends Marianne Woods and Jane Pirie. If they would put aside their prejudice against an illegitimate, darker-skinned child, she promised to find them pupils among her gentry connections.

There is no evidence that in 1809, when Helen successfully pushed for Jane's admission to the Woods-Pirie School, the teachers' physically demonstrative behavior toward each other struck anybody as erotically undecipherable, a challenge to heterosexual norms, or laden with same-sex sexual desire. In retrospect, it is easy to say that their kissing and hand-holding was not appropriate for a workplace, but at the time, having two such schoolmistresses prepare an adolescent girl for marriage seemed to Helen a perfectly logical way to proceed. Since intimacy in marriage was thought to be the product of a wife's fulfillment of her duties to her husband, what better way to make her granddaughter a good wife than by sending her to a school where she would learn to submit to the rules established by a pair of mutually affectionate authority figures?[3]

The plan backfired. When Jane's fellow student Janet Munro informed Miss Pirie that Jane had propositioned her, the teacher reacted with her customary harshness. Miss Woods's recent rebuff of Jane's overtures made Miss Pirie's tongue-lashing even harder for the girl to bear. Scorned by one teacher and humiliated by the other, Jane not only played class against sex but also set off a class war when she informed her grandmother that Woods and Pire had been intimate. Helen never expected that the middle-class teachers, beholden to her for getting their school on a solid financial footing, would charge her with defamation of character. The ensuing legal battle reduced them to the level of indigent gentlewomen.

As the advocates and judges tried to understand where Jane's allegation about the teachers' sexuality came from, the case became an excursion into the issue of female same-sex attraction and the racist perspective we call Orientalism. Critics such as Emma Donoghue, Valerie Traub, and Susan Lanser provide substantial evidence that passions between women were the subject of many British works in the long eighteenth century. Jonathan Swift, muse of the teachers' lawyer John Clerk, referenced Delarivier Manley's text about a lesbian community, *The New Atalantis*. Arthur Maynwaring's 1708 poem "A New Ballad: To the Tune of Fair Rosamond," written at the behest of Sarah Churchill, Duchess of Marlborough, insinuated that Queen Anne and her then favorite, Abigail Masham, were in a lesbian relationship. A sapphic spotlight was shone on Sarah Pononsby and Eleanor Butler, who lived together in the Welsh village of Llangollen, in various London periodicals of the 1790s.[4] In the case, Helen's defense team did not bring up the Ladies or any of the above-mentioned works, but they did present a bibliography of respectable books that offered evidence for the existence of lesbianism in the West. They also "lesbianized" the teachers.[5] Adapting a common anti-Catholic bias to their purposes, they insinuated that Woods and Pirie were like nuns who chose to live in an all-female environment so they could engage in sapphic practices.

The task of the pursuers' (Scots: plaintiffs') lawyers, John Clerk and James Moncreiff, was made easier by the fact that Jane was not white. Her biracial origins allowed them to typecast her as an Oriental woman, lewd and lacking any notion of sexual propriety. In their argument, Clerk and Moncreiff stated that in the school Jane had attended in Calcutta, the only topic of conversation among the non-European staff was sex, and that she was continually exposed to couples, homosexual as well as heterosexual, engaging in sexual activity. Jane's story, therefore, could be explained by the "nurturing" she received in India.

If an Eastern upbringing accounted for Jane's sexualized thinking, why hadn't any of the many other biracial girls educated in Indian institutions and brought over at about her age shown signs of that mindset? Edinburgh's New Town was a sociable world where nothing seemed to stay behind closed doors; such girls would surely have been topics of conversation. The absence of other reports indicates that Jane's story was a singular one that grew out of something that had happened to her personally.

Despite the speciousness of the Orientalist keyhole, many of the judges continued to ascribe Jane's allegation to the way she was brought up. Indeed, the deeper they bit into the Orientalist apple, the more they denied the existence of consummated sexual passion between women in

Europe. Lord Woodhouselee dismissed sexual congress between European women as "a thing perhaps impossible" and Lord Meadowbank stated categorically that "*venus nefanda* [was] unknown in this country."[6] The Orientalist approach was affirmed by the Law Lords of Parliament's House of Lords: Jane, the product of an Eastern upbringing, had carried a tale to her grandmother that could not apply to Western women.

Since Helen's defense lawyers also described sixteen-year-old Jane as having one of those extremely sensitive dispositions in which slights others considered insignificant rankled and festered, they implied that the story she told was due to other factors as well. Those factors were the nature she was born with, and the period of life she was going through: adolescence. Viewing Jane through the keyhole of adolescence—that time of emotional instability when youths experience sudden mood changes, seem totally different people than they used to be, rebel against authority, discover and explore their sexuality, and want passionately to experience intimacy—opens up the possibility that the effect of the Misses Woods and Pirie's affectionate behavior, including their bedsharing, was to sexually awaken Jane.[7]

Jane's sexual behavior at the school, and perhaps the discussion of female sexuality in the Indian context during the case's lengthy life, may have made Helen wonder about her grandchild's sexual orientation. Perhaps there *was* something deviant about her. Possibly she could be "fixed" by being fixed up with a husband who would reorient her. Even if Helen's mind wasn't running in that direction, it was time, once the case was behind them, to start thinking seriously about a suitable husband for Jane. In keeping with her take-charge character, Helen had her son William, now the second baronet, strike a deal with a schoolmaster, some twenty years older than Jane but university-educated, who was living on a meager salary and waiting for a heritor to appoint him as a minister. In 1818, the twenty-two- or twenty-three-year-old Jane was married to William Tulloch. Jane's marriage settlement was small by Gordon Cumming standards. Tulloch must have been given to understand that Sir William would use his clout to enable Tulloch's transition from schoolmaster to parish minister in a timely fashion.

Thanks to Gordon Cumming patronage, Tulloch did indeed become a minister at the parish kirk (Scots: church) in the village of Dallas near Elgin, and as the minister's wife, Jane was supposed to set the standard for obedience and compliance in a marriage. Ideally, she would show the obedience to authority that had not been a hallmark of her disposition. Ideally, too, she would love, trust, and respect her husband and be a companionate wife and a good mother to the children they had together. Ideally, Tulloch would love, protect, and provide for her.

The solution didn't work. One reason was that Tulloch's sexual drive was too robust. One would think that as a married minister with a reputation to uphold he would at least be discreet, but he was openly flirtatious. In the 1830s, he paraded around the parish with local women, humiliating his wife and scandalizing the villagers, his easy familiarity with women making a mockery of his marriage vows.

Another reason the solution failed was that neither Jane nor Tulloch was willing to follow the other rules of marriage. Tulloch tried to get his hands on Jane's portion of the marriage settlement. And Jane wasn't willing to play the role of obedient, submissive wife, keeping quiet and avoiding confrontation. She reported her husband to the presbytery for sexual misconduct and screamed at him in public. Her most dramatic conjugal disruption was leaving the Established Church, their children and the bulk of Tulloch's parishioners in tow.

Race, sex, class—even after her death, these elements continued to shape how Jane was presented. Transgressive behavior didn't faze Lillian Hellman, though the Hays Production Code forced her to turn the lesbian-ish dynamic between the teachers in her play into a heterosexual love triangle when she wrote the filmscript for *These Three*. For Hellman, race was more the issue. She blocked a director from staging the play with a biracial cast and cut words connoting dark or black in an attempt to restrict her play's message to "Lies have the power to damage lives irrevocably."

Ironically, the attempt to foreground this message revealed the power of race- and class-based prejudice to damage lives irrevocably. Samuel Goldwyn chose Merle Oberon to play the character of the teacher Miss Wright in *These Three*. Oberon, as was suspected then but is widely known now, was half-Indian, and both her Indian mother and her British father came from the lower social strata. She grew up in Calcutta and Bombay (now called Mumbai), and didn't get to England until she was in her twenties. For her acting career to take off, she had to hide the truth of her origins. She was forced to pass off the dark-skinned woman she lived with, either her mother or grandmother, as her maid, and to deny the social class in which she was raised. She fabricated numerous stories that emphasized her whiteness and high status on the surface and reveal anxieties simmering just below around abandonment, adoption, and her reception in a second homeland.[8]

In one of Oberon's fictions, a highly placed British Army officer from the upper echelons of society found her as a child dancing on a Tasmanian beach. He brought her back to India, where he was posted. In another fiction, her parents belonged to the white Tasmanian colonial elite. After her father died in a hunting accident, she and her mother moved to India, where she was raised by titled British godparents. In yet a third fiction, she was an unwanted Tasmanian child who was brought to India at the age of seven in a deal made by her father, then living in Tasmania. In 1978 she visited Tasmania but hardly ventured out of her hotel room. It was given out that she was sick—which she was, but the source of the illness was anxiety.

Oberon's stories show the shame and self-hatred she had internalized. To feel good about herself and attempt to make others sympathetic to her, she told preposterous lies and spun self-dramatizing stories that were ultimately self-justifying performances. Unlike Jane's, her stories never hurt anyone besides herself. But like Jane's, they reveal strong survival instincts in the face of a history of abandonment. Underneath the successful movie star is a woman who feels apprehensive, threatened, so gripped by anxiety that she becomes ill when she faces the stressor of Tasmania. In Oberon, we see the psychological damage caused by race- and class-based prejudice; we realize Jane was not only one who needed to spin fantasies in order to cope.

I now turn to one particular movement in the dance of race, sex, and class. I first encountered it in studies dealing with illegitimacy in Scotland in the long eighteenth century.

In the Western imagination, the East or Orient, that vast area stretching from North Africa through Turkey, southeast to the Gulf of Aden, across the Indian subcontinent and south Asia, then as far as the South China Sea, has always been considered, among other things, a destination for refractory sons. Out of the way there, they would be less of an embarrassment; if they didn't die, they might shape up.

Some years before the wayward George Cumming was bundled off, Richard Clive, a Shropshire lawyer, got his terror of a firstborn son sent out to India as a writer with the East India Company. Eighteen years old at the time, the youth continued to get into trouble in India, but when he traded the civil service for the army he found his métier. As a soldier, he rose through the ranks to become a major-general and commander-in-chief in India. He amassed a fortune so mind-boggling that in 1772, two years before the birth of George Cumming, Parliament questioned him to ascertain if he had acquired his wealth by improper means. This was the arc of Robert Clive, whose victory over Indian forces at Plassey in 1757 ensured Britain would have access to India's riches for two hundred years.

Clive died the day Jane's father George was born, so the memory of his transformation from delinquent youth to national hero might have had special resonance for Penrose. Be that as it may, foppish, feckless, firstborn George was nineteen years old when his boat docked in Calcutta.

Sending an undisciplined son to India was risky. India was hot, and the climate was accounted one of the lesser dangers the land posed to young white men.[9] Many Europeans believed that the heat had stunted the development of Indian women's reasoning powers even as it enhanced their artfulness and their sex appeal. Those who took this position regarded it as a fact that Indian women were endowed with enormous, irresistible, and indiscriminate sexual appetites that no man, even if he were made of "iron or steele," could resist.[10] The number of children born to East India Company fathers and native women, as recorded in the parish registers of Madras and Calcutta, could be taken as evidence supporting this claim.[11]

Two months shy of his twenty-sixth birthday, George Cumming lay on his deathbed. He had not turned out to be a second Clive or to be made of anything remotely resembling iron or steel. In his will, he confessed his very substantial debts and informed his father that he was also leaving behind two children. He described them as "natural" and referred to the elder one as "my daughter Jane."[12] In the same document, he implied that their Indian mother had captivated him, held him in thrall, and affected his judgment. George begged his father to take care of the children.

"Caelum non animum qui trans mare current" (They change their sky, not their soul, who rush across the sea): George's cousin James Thomas Grant, also in East India Company employ, quoted Horace's dictum in a letter to his father, Sir James Grant, dated August 1, 1793. The purpose was to reassure his parent that he was stronger than iron or steel. Though only seventeen at the time, he was the kind of man who could stand fast against the sexual charms of Indian women. Though he was lonely, viewing himself as "a solitary figure on the banks of the Ganges," he informed his father that he possessed the "resources" necessary "to stay morally insulated from everything of interest in his new environment."[13]

Somewhat later, another Scotsman took the moral high road. This was twenty-two-year-old William Fraser, who in 1806 wrote a letter to his parents in Inverness in which he criticized other Scotsmen who had started families with Indian women. He did not think himself impervious to the women, but felt that the ensuing children, particularly girls, would cause problems. "What a care is that to provide for, and if they are girls, how much more difficult to bring them up in the paths of virtue and honor."[14] He then looked askance at Neil Benjamin Edmonstone, distinguished as a civil servant but, as will be discussed shortly, a heartless father to his biracial children.

These protestations notwithstanding, across all levels of society in northeastern Scotland, irregular connections and the children born from them were almost the new normal. Ministers fulminated against fornication and bastardy but the general public treated the "sinners" and their offspring less censoriously. Some said the parents were only following the dictates of nature. Elizabeth Grant of Rothiemurchus, who moved in the same social circles as the Cummings and Grants and was about the same age as Jane Cumming, remarked that the appearance of such children was such a frequent occurrence that nobody batted an eye, punished the child, or stigmatized either parent.[15]

Among the rural poor of northeast Scotland, it was common for maternal grandparents to extend a safety net for their daughters' children. Taking the place of absent fathers, they looked after the children and provided emotional stability while their daughters went back to work and supplied the income that supported the household. As the grandparents aged, the children whom they had taken in took care of them, and the old folk were proud that they had brought them up with good values. This multigenerational family structure provided an alternative to the conventional family structure growing out of marriage. Andrew Blaikie has called it "a kind of loving."[16]

In the higher social echelons, the mechanisms for accommodating illegitimate children included their being raised with their father's second, lawful family, maintained at schools with all expenses paid, and groomed for respectable positions—"respectable" being a euphemism for "a reputable but inferior station in life."[17] So while George Lindsay, twenty-second Earl of Crawford, refused to recognize his illegitimate son Robert, it was far more common for children born to propertied or prosperous fathers and poor lower-class mothers to be acknowledged and receive "a kind of loving." In 1799, a few years before Jane and Yorrick arrived at Altyre, a Mr. Baillie of Douchfour appointed Jane's grandfather Penrose the manager of a substantial trust fund set aside for the benefit of his natural son Alexander. Penrose took this responsibility seriously but impersonally. Until 1806, the year of his death, Penrose looked after the boy's material needs, withdrawing from the trust to pay for Alexander's educational expenses at boarding school and all other items appropriate to a young gentleman. Money from the fund even paid for Alexander's fifty-day trip to London. Thanks to his father's trust fund and its trustee, Alexander was maintained comfortably and, it appears, received the kind of education that would allow him to choose and follow a socially acceptable path; on a personal level, Penrose seems to have stayed aloof and maintained distance from the boy.

What path this Alexander took and whether he grew up well-adjusted despite the absence of personal involvement on his trustee's part is unknown, but as Stana Nenadic has shown, many children born in Scotland to gentry fathers and lower-class mothers were successfully integrated. Some males became factors (Scots: estate managers), a position that carried considerable social status. Others were guided toward the law and the army or received an education that enabled them to follow potentially lucrative commercial careers in cities. As for females, they often entered the millinery trade or managed small retail shops—genteel, if precarious, positions.[18]

Elizabeth Grant reserved her praise for women who did more than their duty for such children. One of the most moving stories she recounts in her autobiography, *Memoirs of a Highland Lady*, deals with a boy named Sandy Duncan. Sandy's father had social standing; his mother, Mary, was a cook. According to Grant, Sandy's conception was inevitable because his father was left alone in a "wild isolated place with no companion for the whole winter . . . but Mary." His father had no love for the child, regarding him as an encumbrance, but his lawful wife raised him with and as one of her own. At the time of her marriage, she "brought little Sandy home . . . and as much as lay in her power acted a mother's part by him."[19] The result of her love and assiduous attention was that Sandy Duncan grew up to become a respected factor and a good son.

Another story she tells is that of an illegitimate girl named Annie Grant. Annie was the daughter of Elizabeth's great-granduncle and his very good-looking housekeeper. Lady Logie, a Cumming kinswoman, surprised her relatives by taking a personal interest in Annie. She not only provided her with a solid education in Forres but apparently made her feel wanted and secure. Annie became a milliner, then a governess, then a lady's companion. In this last capacity she went out to India, where she met and married a general. As the governess of Elizabeth and her sisters, she was warm and nurturing, giving each exactly what she needed—encouraging one, coaxing another, soothing the future writer. Elizabeth Grant tells how Annie's "gentle, steady rule" undid the psychological damage done to her and her sisters by previous governesses, and how Annie's presence in the household made everybody "happier."[20] By singling out the nurturing role played by Mrs. Duncan and Lady Logie in Sandy Duncan's and Annie Grant's lives, Elizabeth Grant made a larger point—namely, that, in her view, all children, but particularly those who might be at a disadvantage, needed more than mere acknowledgement, more than what duty demands, more than "a kind of loving" if they are to do well in life.

For the young Scottish men who rushed across the sea thinking that riches would fall into their laps, harsh reality soon replaced magical thinking when they found themselves alone and lonely in a very un-Scottish environment. India was "far from fertile fields," as George Cumming put it in a poem he wrote in 1794, a place where he found himself working "beneath the burning ray where rolls the fiery bar of day."[21] Sandy Duncan's father would not only have understood their predicament completely but been baffled by James Thomas Grant's and William Fraser's rejection of a sexual relationship with a local woman. Judging from Elizabeth Grant's remarks, under the circumstances in which young men in India found themselves, seeking solace with a woman there and having children by her was seen as an inevitable consequence even more than as a behavior tolerated under the norms of the culture they had grown up in.

Robert Malcolm's life presents the best possible ending for the question "How's a single young man in a hostile environment supposed to manage?" Malcolm, who entered East India Company service in the 1770s, became a judge based in insalubrious Mausalipatnam, a town in southern India that "only a Dutchman, a frog or an alligator would have chosen as an abode."[22] Alcohol and gambling nearly ruined him; cohabiting with a Muslim woman named Nancy Moor Noman, with whom he had six children, made his life a comfortable and happy one.[23]

In the end, James Thomas Grant and William Fraser capitulated. By the time Grant died in 1804, he was the father of two half-Indian children, whom his father unsuccessfully attempted to bring to Scotland.[24] By 1815 moral high-roader William Fraser was maintaining a *bibi* and two or three children in Rania, a village near Delhi. There may have been more children. The French botanist Victor Jacquemont, who met Fraser on several occasions, wrote in an 1832 letter that "he must have as many children as the King of Persia."[25] Around 1795, George Cumming established a conjugal relationship with a woman he referred to respectfully, poetically, and geographically in a 1799 letter to his paternal uncle George as "the Lady in the North."[26]

Despite the tolerant attitude of Scottish society toward its own population of children born out of wedlock, color complicated the response to the illegitimate children of British fathers and Indian mothers. Maria Graham, daughter of the head of the naval works at the East India Company's

Bombay dockyards and wife of a Scottish naval officer in India, thought they shouldn't be sent to Scotland, as "their complexion must subject them to perpetual mortification."[27] When in the early 1780s Colonel Robert Bruce wanted to send his firstborn daughter to Scotland, to be raised in the family home on Edinburgh's Princes Street, his brother John denied his request. John insisted that it would be impossible for her to be introduced into the city's polite society as a member of the family.[28]

John Palmer, at one time the richest merchant in Calcutta and one of Jane's guardians before she left India, was a kind and concerned man. He went out of his way to improve the lives of biracial children, finding them jobs, providing them with music and dancing lessons, and even securing their marriages. However, he counseled his own brother William in 1802 not to send his biracial children to Britain unless they were fair-skinned enough to "pass" as white. William Palmer took his brother's advice and only sent his son William Fitzjulius, but the child met with prejudice nonetheless. Initially, Fitzjulius stayed with Warren Hastings, the retired Governor-General of India, but something unpleasant must have happened because Hastings put Fitzjulius into boarding school and kept him there over the holidays. The child obviously felt unwanted, since he informed family members that he couldn't wait to return to India.[29]

John Palmer helped many a biracial child in India find a place in society, but the prognosis for most biracial children who stayed, girls particularly, was dire. One of the schools set up to care for them boasted that during a cholera outbreak only five girls died in three days.[30] Captain Thomas Williamson, a contemporary observer of the Indian scene, noted that if such girls were lucky, they became ayahs (Anglo-Indian, from the Portuguese: nursemaids), ladies' maids, or children's nurses, but if not, they might have to accept a position as a "housekeeper to a single gentleman"—possibly a euphemism for mistress or concubine.[31] Williamson thought many of these girls "became insane" in adolescence once they realized the uncertainty of their future; their fate, he wrote, was "truly lamentable."[32]

Scottish fathers of means serving in India could choose between sending the children they had had with native women to Scotland, where they would be exposed to race prejudice, or keeping them in India, where their future might be bleak. Since Scotland had a tradition of integrating illegitimate children into the social fabric, the former might have looked like the better choice. George Cumming apparently subscribed to this view, for though he had enlisted the kindly John Palmer as Jane's local guardian, in his will he asked his father to send for his children.

Helen's first plan for Jane, to establish her in a reputable but inferior station in life, seems more typical of the future meted out to illegitimate, rather than biracial, Scottish children. Had *l'affaire Drumsheugh* never happened, perhaps her second plan, which involved introducing Jane to society as a Cumming girl, might have translated, as it did for other biracial girls, into a marriage with a miller owner, merchant, manufacturer, banker or Army officer, even an East India Company employee, which would have taken her back to India.

How many "Janes" came to Britain, and what happened to them? To get some idea of the number of half-Indian children who were transplanted, I asked a London-based researcher to go through the passenger lists of the 139 ships that plied the "Coast and Bay" route between 1785 and 1805. I began with 1785 because around that year the East India Company stopped paying for the passage of biracial children born in India. I ended with 1805, a few years after Jane arrived, on the assumption that that many ships over the twenty years would have brought in a substantial number of children. I chose the route because Jane traveled by it and because ships stopped at Madras and Calcutta, the two major ports of India at that time.

Not all captains were so considerate as to produce passenger lists, however, let alone passenger lists with children's names and ages at the time of embarkation, or their "racial origins." Some of the captains generated lists but had execrable handwriting. Unless a captain identified a child or children accompanying an adult with a phrase such as "by a native woman," there was no way of knowing if they were European or biracial. Thus, though there were definitely more than 150 children carried on those 139 ships, my researcher could only count 150, and with the help of wills, the genealogical databases FamilySearch and Findmypast, and other online sources, I could identify only about fifty of these children as of mixed race and trace, to some degree, the trajectories of the lives. However, additional sources provided me with data about the lives of other children who were sent from India to Britain, so my time frame came to end in the 1820s. Because this is a biography of a woman and the fathers were more concerned for their daughters, I have largely focused on transplanted girls.

The fates of these Janes varied tremendously. Their biographies confirm that race, class, and sex, in varying combinations and permutations, choreographed their lives as well as hers. Race awareness was a factor for all of them. The fathers and individuals who stood in loco parentis ran the gamut of human nature, from despicably heartless to involved-from-a-distance to caring. The children were educated, some at posher boarding schools than the ones Jane attended. The emphasis placed on girls' education speaks to the belief that Helen shared—that a solid grounding in principles and accomplishments would not only improve their chances in the marriage market but make them a credit to their sex. Family money helped secure these unions, and the marriages guaranteed the young women a position in society. As in Jane's case, these children's stories also show the limits of money in ensuring happiness and well-being. I now turn to their lives.

Mary and Juliana Crommelin, both of whom arrived in 1796 aboard the *Marquis of Lansdown*, married a senior merchant and a surgeon, respectively, both with the East India Company. Eliza Breithaupt, nine years old when she arrived in Britain in 1798 on the *Lord Hawkesbury*, was the granddaughter of a Danish missionary and a Tamil convert. She returned to the East with her husband, John Palmer Keasberry, who rose to the rank of Lieutenant-Colonel. John Carnie, a surgeon with the East India Company, and his six-year-old biracial son Alexander were fellow travelers with Jane on the homeward-bound voyage of the *Bengal*. Alexander returned to India, got married, and at the time of his death was head assistant at the Government Lithographic Press in Calcutta. Diana Denton and Samuel Charles, the natural children of Samuel Turner, a sea captain in the employ of the East India Company, were raised in the London house of the captain's good friend George Nesbit Thompson, formerly the private secretary to the governor of Bengal.[33] The Thompson connection no doubt helped secure Samuel Charles a military appointment in India. Thompson must also have been behind Matilda's marriage in Bombay to Henry Diggle, a judge and senior merchant with the East India Company; the couple's daughter married the son of a distinguished Edinburgh physician in Calcutta.

The two orphaned daughters of George Bogle, the first British man to visit Tibet, arrived in 1785 at the Bogle estate of Daldowie, where they were received with open arms by their father's sisters and brother.[34] Family lore has it that they grew up happy and well loved, that they had their own maid and carriage, and that they enjoyed, as any young girl who has ever walked around in her mother's high-heeled shoes will immediately understand, dressing up in the old brocade dresses they found in boxes in the attic.[35] Both daughters married Glasgow manufacturers.

Born in 1781, Margaret Stuart, later Margaret Stuart Bruce and finally Margaret Stuart Bruce Tyndall, was the younger biracial daughter of Colonel Robert Bruce. Margaret and her father arrived from India in 1786, and he kept her in England for two years, occasionally bringing her to visit his bookish bachelor brother John, their unmarried sister Peggy, and their widowed mother, who lived together in Edinburgh. He told his family Margaret was the daughter of a deceased friend, and it was only after they had gotten used to her and he was about to return to India alone that he informed them the child, now about seven years old, was his.[36] Once back in India, he did not answer the letters she wrote him. However, the multigenerational household into which Margaret had been inserted provided her with attentive care, financial security, and affection. She came to fill the void left in the family home after her father died in India in 1796, and grew up much loved in the house on Princes Street.

On her deathbed, her grandmother commanded John and Peggy to be kind to Margaret. Peggy acted as a mother to her, nursing her through illnesses and worrying, for example when Margaret started to develop black hair on her upper lip, that she would become the butt of hurtful remarks when she went out. (Peggy's solution in that case was to look for depilatories.) Uncle John played an invaluable, more "masculine" role with his niece, arranging for Margaret to be tutored by the best masters available in Edinburgh and ensuring that the substantial money and properties in India her father bequeathed her passed smoothly to her when she turned twenty-one.[37] John and Peggy left their estates to her as well. An heiress by 1826, she married for love the impecunious Onesiphorus Tyndall, ten years her junior, in 1828. Proud of her Bruce connection, she insisted that he change his name to Tyndall Bruce. She paid off his debts and Onesiphorus was made Keeper of Falkland Palace.

Margaret and Onesiphorus stayed happily married and led a very public existence. In her will, she left £10,000, or $1,170,000 in today's money, to found and fund the Tyndall Bruce fellowships and scholarships at Edinburgh and Saint Andrews universities. Her oversize portrait hangs in the stairwell of the Playfair Library of Edinburgh University. In the painting, her clothes and the furnishings of the room she is sitting in bespeak wealth and taste. She has dark hair and a sallow complexion that contrasts sharply with the ruddy faces of the men whose portraits also hang in the stairwell. If, as a contemporary archly remarked, she was "lively and agreeable but of colour," then the artist who gave her an off-white complexion outed her "racial impurity."[38] It was a stain that her fortune, education, accomplishments, and family acceptance bleached but could never quite wash away. Nonetheless, she is the only woman honored by a portrait in the stairwell.

Colonel Bruce's best friend in India was William Denby. Denby, an army officer, entered his son, also a William, into a tontine (a life insurance scheme in which the beneficiaries are the survivors who maintain a policy to the end of a given period) that would assure him of a substantial amount if he married, £2,000 on his eighteenth birthday, and all the money in the tontine if the other person whose name was entered predeceased him. Denby boarded his son in a Yorkshire school under the name Jackson and gave the boy to understand that he was merely his guardian. When the son found out the truth, he quarreled with his father and became a deckhand on a slaving ship, where he was maltreated. The younger William considered himself, and rightly so, "a poor unfortunate orphan (and cast off)." When he died in Jamaica at the age of twenty, his father attempted to keep his death a secret so that he could collect his son's share of the tontine.[39]

Upon her arrival from India in 1796, Mary Munro, the daughter of the indigo planter Alexander ("Sandy") Munro, was received into her grandfather's Glasgow house. He found her "woefully dark" and almost considered her a devolved specimen of humanity.[40] Despite the girl's sweet disposition, Sandy's sister thought her niece would never be able to get married. As the family got to know Mary, they warmed to her and cooled toward racially prejudiced friends who refused to visit them on account of the girl' complexion. They were upset with Mary's father because he never sent money for her upkeep. When in 1804 a "miracle" occurred and the under-manager of a local cotton mill proposed to the penniless Mary, members of the Munro family, from grandparents down to uncles, aunts, and in-laws, made sure the match would not fall through. They barraged Sandy with letters, arm-twisting him into providing Mary with money that would enable her husband to set up his own mill. Sandy's grudgingly given £1,000 allowed Mary to become middle class and assume a place in British society.[41]

Eliza Raine and her younger sister Jane Elizabeth arrived in England in 1798 after a long voyage on the *King George*. Unlike the six lawful children of Colonel William Cuppage who sailed on the *King George*, the captain did not put the honorific Miss in front of their names. Though he entered their ages as six and five, they were closer to nine and eight, so they would have understood and remembered who and what they were being separated from. Their father, William Raine, a surgeon with the East India Company, left them heiresses, but did not accompany them on the voyage; they never saw him again.[42] Did they ever come to know that he boarded the *Asia* in 1800 with an infant male child referred to as "Jno. Raine, Dr. W. Raine's son (Native)" on the passenger list? Did they ever learn that their father died on board the ship or that they had a brother? There are no letters in the Calderdale Archives (which hold the papers of Eliza Raine) that mention her father's death or her baby brother, but it is not unreasonable to assume that the sisters at least came to know about their father's death, and that it added to their sense of loss and separation.[43]

It is generally believed that Raine's friend William Duffin, a retired East India Company surgeon living in York, returned to India to chaperone them, but he is not on the passenger list. Duffin did, however, serve as their local guardian once they arrived. Eliza was placed in the Manor House Boarding School, where she met Anne Lister, from a gentry family. The two were considered deeply attached friends; it has since been revealed that Eliza was Anne's first lover. Anne was Eliza's anchor, and Eliza was fearful of losing her—understandably, since she had already lost her father and her homeland. Friendship with the Listers and money notwithstanding, Eliza may well have been anxious about her position in York society.

Duffin and Eliza were the witnesses to younger sister Jane Elizabeth's 1808 underage marriage to Henry Boulton, a cadet about to be shipped out to India. The marriage didn't last; she separated from him and returned to England alone, pregnant with another man's child, and with a reputation for criminal conduct.[44] In letters Anne Lister and Eliza exchanged, the two make passing references to the returned Elizabeth Jane's shameful and pitiable existence. When Anne left Eliza for another lover, this blow, coming on top of those Eliza had already suffered, was too much for her to bear. She had a breakdown from which she never recovered, and spent the rest of her life in mental asylums, where she was treated with great kindness.

Alexander Read, the son of a customs-sloop officer from Dundee, spent decades in south India, where he helped develop a system for collecting land revenue. In the 1790s he sent his two older biracial children, William Alexander and Helena, to London, where they were enrolled in expensive boarding schools; the youngest child, Harriet, arrived on the *Marquis Wellesley* in 1801. Read left India not long after Harriet departed. Unable to tolerate cold, damp England, he relocated to warm, sunny Malta.

In his 1804 will made in Malta, Read outlined the futures of the children. He knew education alone couldn't guarantee a happy or successful future; to the best of his ability, he tried to micromanage a life that would be both for the three children. Son William Alexander was in school with a few years remaining, but Read arranged for him, on completion of his studies, to be placed first in a counting house, then apprenticed after two years at a bigger counting house in London, and after seven years, to be given £10,000, the equivalent of $1,160,000, so that he could start his own business, go into partnership in London, or consider going to India and parlaying his inheritance into a fortune there. Read's elder daughter,

Helena, was to be maintained at a London boarding school through 1806. He regularly paid £106 a year for her schooling, but as he now wanted her to learn geography, astronomy, experimental philosophy, and drawing and be a parlor boarder, he laid out an additional £625 to cover the expense. His third and youngest child, Harriet, presently maintained at another London seminary, was to receive education in English grammar, writing, accounts, geography, astronomy, a little history, some polite literature, dancing, music, and needlework, and in her final school year was also to become a parlor boarder. To cover her educational outlays through 1806, he set aside £400.

Apparently aware that, despite their accomplishments and money, their complexions would be a drawback when they came to be of marriageable age, he thought the girls would have better luck finding a husband in India, where accomplished women were scare, standards lower, and young men not only less picky but, if they were lowly officers with the East India Company, hard up for cash. Rather than state the truth so baldly, he conceptualized India as an embracing mother, writing in his will that the girls, "having a predilection for India as their native country," were to return to Madras no later than 1807. He set aside funds so that they could live in high style. They would have their own establishment, wear clothes of the finest muslin and calico, maintain a carriage and horses, and inherit £5,000 apiece when they reached the age of twenty-one.[45]

But did Read's careful planning fructify? Genealogical databases are constantly adding data, but when I last looked on Findmypast, I found nothing about Harriet. If the William Alexander Read who testified at the Old Bailey in 1820 that he had been robbed of a coat and was accused of being inebriated was Read's son, then his father's high hopes were not realized. Only Helena's 1813 wedding in London to Richard Richards Ternan, a military officer in East India Company employ with a distinguished pedigree, suggests that Read's strategy worked.

In 1801 Neil Benjamin Edmonstone sent his four children to Britain under the name of Elmore. He barely wrote to them, kept their existence hidden from his legitimate children, and didn't want them getting "above their station."[46] Of the two males who reached adulthood, one, prevented from attending a university, joined an army regiment, and the other entered the manufacturing business. However, while the Edmonstone boys seemed to have been forced into undistinguished lives, daughter Eliza led a very comfortable life. Remembering William Fraser's letter about biracial girls needing more care because they were more vulnerable, could it be that Edmonstone's response to his children was gendered? As a civil servant in the East India Company, Edmonstone was admired for being a skillful behind-the-scenes negotiator. At a time when marriages were orchestrated by parents, it is not a leap to think he might have had a hand in Eliza's marriage to John Barker Plumb. Eliza and John went to India, where he was in banking in Calcutta. They had a number of children, who did well. On returning from India, they lived in affluent Notting Hill.

Colonel James Achilles Kirkpatrick and Begum Khair-un-Nissa were that rare thing, a devoted couple married according to Muslim rites and together raising their children: Sahib Allum, born in 1801, and Sahib Begum, born the next year. Following Kirkpatrick's death in 1805, however, the children were separated from their mother and sent to Britain. Shortly after they were ensconced in their grandfather's London residence, they were baptized William George and Katherine Aurora ("Kitty") Kirkpatrick. Their father had amply provided for them, and they were treated as family members. But they were not allowed to write their mother or their grandmother in India, and they missed their homeland horribly. William George's life was sad, for he lost one of his limbs in an accident and died in his late twenties.

Despite being emotionally and physically separated from India, Kitty thrived. She was tutored by Thomas Carlyle, who immortalized her in *Sartor Resartus* as Blumine: an exotic beauty, "a many-tinted radiant Aurora . . . fairest of Orient Light-bringers." She made a happy marriage to Captain James Phillips, with whom she had a number of children. Well into the Victorian era, she confided that her father's description of her in his will as a natural child pained her, but on the plus side, she established a connection with her grandmother, still living in India. Though she had been only three when she arrived in Britain, in her first letter to her grandmother Kitty wrote, "I often think of you and remember you and my dear mother. I often dream that I am with you in India and that I see you both in the room you used to sit in. I can remember the verandah and the place where the tailors worked. . . . When I dream of my mother I am in such joy to have found her again that I awake, or else am pained in finding that she cannot understand the English I speak. I well recollect her cries when we left her. . . ."[47] Since she was only three, the memory may be a reconstructed one, but the anguish that inspired it is real enough.

Around 1804, Anne Malcolm, a daughter of Robert Malcolm, the judge who had settled down in swampy Mausalipatnam with Nancy Moor Noman, was brought to Bombay by an uncle. By 1805 she had met and married a very rich businessman named Robert Leckie. Not long thereafter the Leckies and their infant son, Robert Lindsay, sailed for England.

Robert Lindsay was subsequently sent to Charterhouse, the prestigious London public school.[48]

Perhaps his parents imbued him with the positive idea that India offered scope for career advancement, social acceptance, and emotional and psychological security—that there, he could amass a fortune, while finding his niche and people like himself.[49] Perhaps he also imbibed the negative feeling that in a race-conscious society like Britain, his ancestry could stigmatize him despite his father's wealth and his own fine education, for he returned to Bombay, where he prospered as a banker or merchant. The appearance of his name on the rolls of the Bombay Geographical Society suggests that he was socially accepted and enjoyed the companionship and respect of the resident British educated elite. There was a social ceiling, though, even in India: on account of his mixed blood, he would not have been "invited to those assemblies given by the governor on public occasions."[50]

Robert Lindsay Leckie might not have cared about the ceiling. The notice in the 1841 issue of *The Gentleman's Magazine* announcing his marriage in Bombay to Eliza Ann Tanner, a daughter of Captain Thomas Tanner, argues strongly that, like his father, he found marital happiness in India; genealogical records suggest that Eliza Ann's bloodlines were similar to those of his mother.[51] On their return to London, Robert and Eliza Ann lived in Pimlico, a neighborhood of grand houses populated by well-to-do professional families.

Susan Cochrane, the daughter of Peter Cochrane, a surgeon with the East India Company in Bengal, and a woman identified as Raheem Bibi was born in Bengal around 1807. In 1818 Peter was still in Calcutta, but in the will he drew up, he mentioned that Susan was presently at a London boarding school, where she was receiving instruction in social accomplishments that would make her amiable and, he hoped, lead to a good marriage. Fond father that he was, he was concerned that attention be paid to "the study and knowledge of letters" so that "her [Susan's] morals [would be] strengthened and improved." In the will, he also tasked his lawful wife, Margaret, who was in Britain with their two sons, to take a benevolent interest in Susan and take the role of mother with her. In addition, he left Susan £12,500—$1,110,000.

Peter returned to Edinburgh soon thereafter. In 1825, thinking that Susan would be able to find a husband in India, he sent her to Calcutta, where she stayed with people known to him, and he gave these people to understand that should she find a husband, the man would be given a handsome settlement too. Susan met Henry Moorhouse, an army ensign, and they married on the strength of her fortune and the promised settlement. After the wedding, Peter Cochrane crossed out "Susan Cochrane" and penciled in "Susan Moorhouse" on a copy of this will. Susan and Henry returned to Britain in 1829 and were received affectionately by Susan's father in Edinburgh, though it appears Henry did not get the settlement.

Also in 1829, unbeknownst to Susan and Henry, now domiciled in London, Peter Cochrane made a will in Edinburgh. That will acknowledged Susan's existence but bypassed her entirely, as he left all his assets to his wife and their children; if these legitimate children died without issue, the estate would pass to Susan's children. Peter died in 1835, but the problems began when his wife Margaret followed him to the grave. Their sons had died young and without issue, and none of the children from Susan and Henry's marriage had survived either. Susan and Henry fought in court for years to lay claim to the estate, which by 1860 had grown to a whopping £48,408, in today's terms, $5,680,000. They said that Peter had regarded Susan, to all intents and purposes, as a legitimate daughter. They even argued that Susan was not illegitimate because Peter had married Raheem Bibi.

In 1860 the courts finally decided against Susan and Henry. They found that the evidence Susan and Henry had presented to establish that Peter and Raheem Bibi had been lawfully married was insufficient, and that, though Peter Cochrane had left his daughter a substantial sum in his first will and penciled in her married name after her wedding, the first will had no legal standing on account of the more recent one. In their determination, the judges expressed sympathy for Susan, whose marriage had been predicated on the assumption that she would inherit a fortune, but said that the wording of her father's later will was clear and she could not claim a penny.[52]

One can apply the lesson of Dickens's *Bleak House* to this case. The protracted, costly, all-consuming, maddening, embittering, wasteful legal battle was not worth the fighting. It took a toll on Susan's physical and mental health. In 1864, three years after the court ruled, Susan died; the death record gives "brain disease" as the cause. Her father's money passed to descendants of his wife Margaret who had no personal or biological connection with Peter Cochrane.

Around 1814, Elizabeth Grant's sensitive governess Annie Grant, now Mrs. General Samuel Need, returned from India with her husband and his three surviving children by his recently deceased *bibi*; she allowed the three to bring back a pair of embroidered Indian slippers that had probably belonged to their mother.[53] They settled down at the Need family estate, Fountain Dale in Nottinghamshire. Annie played the mother's part with these children. All were "warmly included within the second family of Samuel Need and Annie Grant."[54]

The boys, Johnstone and Walter, were sent to boarding school. Daughter Caroline married into the local gentry. Johnstone married in England, and he and his wife moved to Tasmania in the 1830s. He became a schoolteacher; his descendants still have the slippers. Walter returned to India, became a merchant, and was killed in crossfire during the 1857 Mutiny, now known as the First War of Indian Independence. Throughout their lives, Annie, her biological children, and her stepchildren stayed in touch. Annie's goodness is memorialized in the number of Need descendants named Annie.[55]

William Fraser's sons stayed in India, but around 1814 he sent his daughter Amy to Scotland, where she was maintained under the name of Young. Her paternal grandmother, Jane Fraser, dismissed her as a "plain black lassie" albeit an amiable one, and did not allow her into the Fraser home. However, Amy's darker complexion apparently garnered her many beaus in Keith, and in 1835 she married one of them, a leather merchant named John Forsyth. They employed servants and had a dozen children.[56] She and Forsyth divorced after being married for twenty-five years. The breakup appears unrelated to her racial identity, and she seems to have lived comfortably afterward. Over time the grandmother softened and met Amy's children.[57] Amy was not ashamed of her Indian roots, for she sometimes styled herself Amy Surwen Fraser Forsyth, Surwen being one of the names by which her Indian mother was known.[58]

In his 1992 memoir, the transplant surgeon Thomas Starzl noted that how individuals responded to organ transplants varied from person to person. Nothing could be predicted, since the transplant was just the beginning of a process by which the recipients had to reassemble themselves, psychologically as well as physically. The gift of a new life did not always lead to a better existence for these "puzzle people," as he called them: "Many died. Some found the world a better and kinder place than they had ever known before. Others encountered a cruel swamp in which their vulnerability was turned against them in ways they could not have imagined."[59]

The distinctions Starzl draws are useful for thinking about the biracial people who were brought from India to Britain. On that continuum, it would appear that quite a number of Indian transplants found the transplanting worked to their advantage. The Bogle girls and Caroline Need, for example, seem to have melded seamlessly into local society. Margaret

Stuart Bruce Tyndall's transformation from a social embarrassment kept under wraps to academic benefactress gladdens the heart. On the other hand, for William "Jackson" Denby, life was extremely cruel. From the little we know of the biography of William Alexander Read, it seems that his father's big investment didn't pay off. Though the Raine sisters were monied and were socially accepted in York, their vulnerability led to their different but catastrophic ends.

Most of the others about whom we have more than a quantum of information fall somewhere between the two extremes. For Kitty Kirkpatrick, transplantation was a blessing tinged with sadness. We can be fairly sure that the race prejudice exhibited by Munro family acquaintances pained Mary, and surer that when her aunt and other relatives championed her cause she felt better. The absence of any information about her life as a married woman suggests that she lived a normal, unremarkable existence. Eliza Edmonstone (Elmore) was one of the many girls whose marriages took them back to India, where they lived comfortably; they lived comfortably in England on their return as well. Robert Lindsay Leckie left Britain for India to advance his career. His professional life there was successful and he found a wife whose racial identity was also mixed; the two later settled back in London.

Some of the transplants relocated permanently, including the sons of General Need, Johnstone and Walter; Johnstone went to Tasmania and Walter to India. Transplantation may have made little or no difference in the life of Alexander Carnie, since mid-level administrative positions in the printing trade were filled almost exclusively by people of mixed race.[60] Amy Surwen Fraser Forsyth received only "a kind of loving," but many men found her darker skin attractive. Her marriage lasted a long time and she always lived comfortably, her divorce was unrelated to her biracial identity, and her children got to know their Indian great-grandmother. Susan Cochrane Moorhouse's British life started out well but came to be dominated by the unsuccessful lawsuit that may have hastened her demise. On the other hand, her marriage, premised on an inheritance that never happened, withstood that blow, and the judges who ruled against her were upset that the law forced them to make that determination.

By the end of this book, readers will be able to place the puzzle person who is the subject of this biography on the continuum anchored by those other puzzle people, Margaret Stuart Bruce Tyndall and Kitty Kirkpatrick (despite her later longing) on the one end, and the Raine sisters on the other.

Chapter One

ANTE JANE

The life of Jane Cumming's great-grandfather Alexander Cumming is the stuff of which boys' adventure stories are made. As the eldest son, Altyre should have been his birthright, but his father ensured that the lairdship passed laterally to his own brother George. Legally precluded from succeeding to the estate and bitter toward his father and his uncle, Alexander entered military service at the age of fifteen. On the voyage out to Jamaica in 1739, he fought a duel with a superior officer. On the island, he signed away rights to valuable property and nearly died of a tropical fever.

Returning from Jamaica in 1748, he was shipwrecked off the coast of Cornwall. The sea-swallowed Alexander was rescued and introduced to the local gentry. After meeting him, Grace Pearce, a Cornish heiress, called him "that ugly Scotchman," but she ended up marrying the stranger who stood "upwards of six feet."[1] Through the marriage, Alexander succeeded to income-generating estates in Cornwall. The first of his and Grace's children, Alexander Penrose, was born in Cornwall on May 19, 1749.

At the beginning of a family history that he never completed, Penrose described his bitter, energetic, impulsive, hot-tempered, and persistently incredibly lucky father as a man of "much vivacity, great natural parts, undaunted courage, and a degree of sarcastic humor that did not tend to heal the natural or unnatural rivalry that early showed itself between him and his uncle George, and which terminated only with his death."[2] Penrose definitely inherited the hot temper, the obsessive determination to trounce rivals, the vivacity, the undaunted courage, and the sarcastic humor, which in his case did not tend to heal the tensions that developed between him and *his* eldest son, George.

Penrose and two of his brothers, William and George, were impressed by the trajectory of their father's life. The wheel of fortune rose quickly from the bottom and stayed for a long time at the apex. Pluck guaranteed luck. Penrose inferred that risky behavior and odds-defying actions would be capped by a happy, strategic, fruitful marriage to a woman of status and wealth. A life that started unpromisingly and followed a bumpy path would have a fairy-tale ending, with luster added to the family name and lucre to its coffers. High hopes were in order.

Younger brothers William and George went into the East India Company's civil service in the Bengal Establishment, and fortune favored them. Though the odds of surviving in the hostile environment of India were grim, both did well there.[3] William prospered professionally, achieving the rank of Senior Merchant. George, who arrived in the late 1770s, spent seven years in an office in Calcutta where the work was tedious and the perks nonexistent, survived a near-fatal illness, then was appointed to a collectorship. Collectorships were prized positions. A collector's task was to collect taxes imposed on farmers' land by the East India Company. However, the job gave them the opportunity to line their own pockets, probably by extorting money from the farmers. Brother George "collected" so well that by 1784 he was able to return permanently to London. There, he engaged in financial speculation and served in Parliament and on East India Company committees. His clout with the Court of Directors of the East India Company enabled him to get many men from the Moray area into company service, including Penrose's eldest son. George, who died in 1834 in his eighth decade, left an estate valued at over £36,000, equivalent to $4,120,000 today.

Firstborn Penrose followed in his father's footsteps and joined the army. Regimental duties were apparently light in 1770 because he took two years off to travel through Italy and France. All of twenty-one when he began his Grand Tour, overwhelmed and perhaps intimidated by the masterpieces in the galleries he visited, Penrose copied whole chunks of material from guidebooks into his diary. Nights, he hinted, were given over to debauchery and wild carousing. Nonetheless, despite the orgy of the previous night and the morning hangover, he was able to stay focused the following day on the scenes unfolding in front of him.

When he trusted his judgment, he dispensed with the copying altogether and arrived at his own conclusions. He was underwhelmed by the king of Naples, finding his dogs and his appetite at table more remarkable than his person. On viewing a statue of a hermaphrodite, he wrote in his travel diary that "the sexual organs were strongly marked." Of an allegorical painting by Rubens where Hercules is positioned between Virtue (represented by Minerva) and Vice (represented by Venus), he wrote, "people say that he [Hercules] intends to follow the Path of Virtue but he seemed to me to have a great inclination to have a tête-à-tête with Venus."[4] Frank curiosity, a hedonistic approach to life, and an eye for the physical and sexual are characteristics of Penrose the young sojourner and diary-keeper, as are dry humor and an ability to step back, reflect, and critique.

Back in London, Penrose continued enjoying life's pleasures to the full. He spent time in Bath, a town synonymous with high-stakes gambling, and in the company of the Duke of Dorset, a notorious seducer. However, even as he was living in the fast lane and enjoying the sowing of wild oats, he realized that this was just a stage. Unlike his father, Penrose was not locked with George Cumming, the current laird of Altyre, in an implacable rivalry. Nor was George dead set against his nephew. In 1772 George was both childless and in the twilight of his life. He and Penrose had come to an understanding that, on George's demise, Penrose would succeed to the estate denied his father. The agreement made it possible for Penrose to formalize his bond with Helen Grant, a sister of Sir James Grant of Grant, eighth baronet and Grant clan chief. If it had involved waiting, the match also came loaded with promise. According to the historical novelist John Prebble, for Penrose this strategic marriage "weigh[ed] like heavy gold with hopes of success."[5] Penrose told an Elgin friend that once he was married, he would happily put dalliance behind him and take to sowing the right kind of oats.

Penrose was true to his word. The twenty-year-old Helen became his in 1773; not long after, saying that their union was a source of complete personal happiness, Penrose recommended the married state to one of his friends from his rakish past. A year later, on November 22, 1774, Helen gave birth to their first child, whom they named George. Fifteen more children would follow, and of these, most lived to adulthood.

A woman of intense feeling, Helen worried herself sick over her children's boils, fevers, sore throats, joint pains, and progress in acquiring social accomplishments. She was extremely sensitive and responsive to a child's emotional distress. Believing that London boarding schools provided children with the best education, she sent three daughters to London but then sent a fourth because, as she informed her sister-in-law Lady Grant, the girl's "heart was so soar [sic] at the idea of parting" from three of her older sisters. Her children always came home for the summer holidays, even when they were studying in London, and even though the journey by boat north consumed a good portion of the vacation period.[6]

Her fear that a child's life, particularly a girl's life, would be filled with greater suffering if her needs weren't met extended beyond her own children. In an undated but pre-1800 letter to her sister-in-law Lady Grant, she expressed her anxiety over the condition of "four helpless girls, the youngest about eight," the father dead, the mother dying. She asked Lady Grant if she could give one of these soon-to-be orphaned girls a position. "There are so many objects of distress in this town," Helen wrote, "that anything that can be done to lessen it is an object of attention."[7] Why she chose to ask Lady Grant to help out instead of accommodating one of these children in her own establishment is not known, but it does suggest a character trait that would become more visible later on: readiness to delegate responsibility.

Penrose was devoted to his emotional Helen, whom he referred to as Nelly, Mrs. C., and, after 1804, Lady C. in his letters, and he wanted her to feel happy as Altyre's new mistress. On the walls of Castle Grant, where she had grown up, hung paintings by Rubens, van Dyke, and Poussin, as well as the Scottish artist Gavin Hamilton. In London in 1775 Penrose bought an enormous painting by Hamilton titled *Andromache Lamenting the Death of Hector*. Destroyed during World War II, it was notable for its depiction of a statuesque Helen of Troy, who is the central character in the tableau.[8] As the painting made its way north to Altyre, Penrose must have been glowing in anticipation of his Helen's delight. Having grown up in the company of Gavin Hamilton paintings, she would know to take this monumental and striking Helen as a witty compliment to her own ascendancy. Since he died in 1806, Penrose never knew that his Helen, like her legendary counterpart, would bring costly and long-lasting trouble to her family.

When Penrose succeeded to the estate of Altyre in 1776, he began making improvements almost immediately. He shifted from planting bere, a kind of barley, to oats, a higher-yielding crop. He introduced potatoes, asparagus, and artichokes, cultivated turnips, and planted grass seed imported from England. To beautify the place, he filled one hundred acres with oak, spruce, and larix, another variety of conifer. He bought harrows and ploughs, and drill barrows for planting turnips; he employed blacksmiths, saddlers, and wrights to keep the horses and agricultural equipment in good shape. He also purchased varieties of ryegrass and red and white clover seeds from a merchant in Forres to improve the diet, health, and marketability of his livestock.[9]

There were mishaps along the way. In 1780 a wind-driven fire consumed the young trees he had planted to beautify the estate. "It has hurt me so much that I don't know what to say or think, it even deprives me of my sleep and has almost made me forswear planting," he wrote Sir James after assessing the damage.[10] A foray into animal husbandry didn't go according to plan. Penrose had bought English steer and fed them on the imported clover with a view to mating them with the Scottish cows he already owned so as to improve the herd, but in 1784 he had to sell to the local butcher a young steer that had died from overindulging on the clover.

Despite these mishaps, Penrose did not forswear farming, and Altyre consistently ran a profit during his years as laird.[11] Penrose's brother George in London kept him abreast of high-yielding investment opportunities and advised him on how to make his profits generate further income. This financial advice was solid; at the time of Penrose's death in 1806, the estate was valued at over £17,000, or $1,820,000 in today's terms.

Helen was emotional, but Penrose saw intelligence and executive capability in her. While he was away from Altyre, he entrusted her with handling estate business. She wrote to the factor about money to be collected, payments to be made, farm implements that had been ordered, and so forth. For her husband, Helen, combining as she did sound business sense with warm family-centeredness, was the beating heart of Altyre.

Penrose's confidence in his wife's business ability was surpassed only by his concern for her happiness and well-being. On one occasion, in 1795, hearing that Helen had fallen "dangerously sick" in London, he rushed to be with her, not thinking of his own safety or comfort, starting out from Forres almost at midnight. Seven weeks later, Helen was better and back in Scotland, but Penrose delayed leaving Edinburgh for Forres because the road wasn't clear. "Mrs. C. can't stand either stress or cold," he told his factor."[12] Knowing Helen wanted her girls to have the best education money could buy, Penrose had four of them studying at boarding schools in London, which might have cost him £400 in total a year, or in today's terms,$54,000.[13]

Penrose also did his best to shield his wife from bad news. In the 1780s he served as a captain in the Northern Fencibles, a militia of local youth who were being trained at Fort George to guard Scotland's border. Either accidentally or deliberately, in 1782 he received from one of these men "a shot from a wad of cannon which most providentially did not kill me, but which gave me such a contusion on the left groin and testicle as was very alarming." Concerned about how Helen would react, he communicated the news to Sir William, Duke of Gordon, the distant kinsman whose estate, Gordonstoun, he would later inherit, telling him, "I have hitherto blinded Mrs. C. about it and hope to do so till I get home."[14] The Cumming luck held this time too. Penrose and Helen went on to add many children to the brood already living at Altyre.

Helen herself recognized that Penrose treated her every wish as his command. As she wrote her brother Sir James after Penrose's death in 1806 at the age of fifty-seven, "in my lamented and beloved husband . . . I [have lost] one whose every thought was ever occupied for my advantage and happiness."[15]

Despite his tender domestic side, Penrose the laird was ambitious and litigious. In the 1770s and 1780s he sat on the Forres Town Council, serving as its provost twice. Not content with local politicking, he stood for election in the 1780s as an MP. His loss to the incumbent did not quench his desire to sit in Parliament. In 1792 he expressed interest in the parliamentary seat about to be vacated by Sir James Grant's ailing son, Lewis Alexander. Penrose withdrew his name from consideration when he realized he didn't have enough political backing to win, but in 1802 his ambition was realized when he was elected to Parliament from Inverness. The election was challenged, however. Rather than fight the challenge, Penrose vacated the seat and returned to Scotland in 1803. By then, he had already succeeded to the estate of Gordonstoun. In 1804 he was created a baronet, elevated to the peerage as Sir Alexander Penrose Cumming Gordon, 1st Baronet of Altyre and Gordonstoun. Helen became Lady Cumming Gordon.

The parliamentary defeat must have rankled, though. Penrose's anger manifested itself as a desire to punish anybody he thought stood in his way. In 1804 he locked horns with a very small man—the Reverend John Macdonnell, minister at Forres. Penrose claimed Macdonnell was hunting and killing game on his property. The prosecutor warned him that the compensation he would be awarded would be slight, if he got any at all. Penrose, who had recently had a stroke, continued with the case. The letter he wrote to his factor showed he was his father's son, a man of "great vivacity" and "undaunted courage," but also unreasonable, unrealistic, uncompromising, and overbearing, with an unhealthy "degree of sarcastic humor," recklessly brave and certainly self-injuring. "I have much pleasure in informing you," he wrote the factor on September 19, 1804, "as I am sure you will have in hearing that notwithstanding the manifest injustice I met with at the court of Monday last, the shameful partiality of the bench, and the unexampled imprudence and falsehood of the culprit Macdonnell I have every reason to believe that I shall still prevail and will laugh them to scorn."[16] Penrose did not win the case and soon had a second stroke.

Penrose took his responsibilities as a father seriously throughout his life. When his children were young and living at home, the local doctor was called in for check-ups on a regular basis, not just when a child fell sick. When his adolescent daughters were in boarding school in Edinburgh in the late 1790s, Penrose paid for their lessons in French, music, and the millinery arts and also for quarterly visits from "John the dentist" to clean their teeth.[17]

Penrose also took legal steps to protect his offspring. In 1787 he was in the prime of life and his son George—his only son at that point—was thirteen years old. Perhaps remembering how his father had been prevented from inheriting Altyre, Penrose made sure that history would not repeat itself. He drew up a testamentary document in which he left his entire estate to his only son George Cumming, "out of the love and affection which I bear to him."[18] By 1794 Penrose was the father of two other thriving male children, William and Charles, so the 1787 document was canceled and replaced by a trust disposition. William was named next in line to inherit all the entailed lands should anything happen to George, for whom Penrose again expressed great love and affection. His wife and daughters were also amply provided for in various testamentary documents.

Befitting his status as heir to a considerable estate, George's future was plotted out for him. He needed to be made capable of running the estate for a profit, and of course become a gentleman, well turned out, able to dance, appreciative of music and literature, knowledgeable in geography, accomplished in the classics, but also possessing self-control, able to enjoy the good life without being seduced by its luxuries and pleasures. In 1785, when George was eleven, Penrose received a note from his son's tutor in Inchdrewer stating that George was reading Ovid, Plato's *Phaedrus*, and *Robinson Crusoe*, studying geography and Latin grammar, and attending dancing classes; included was a bill for nearly £30 for hairdressing, clothing, dancing lessons, and books. George was then sent to tutors in Edinburgh and London, who presented Penrose with bills for outlays on music and dancing lessons, and for coats, jackets, breeches, and the bending of a hat.

A Grant family member who met George in Edinburgh on his return from London in 1793 seems to have thought Penrose had received a good return on his investment in his son's social development. He pronounced George refined, amiable, socially accomplished, fashionably attired, well-groomed—a young man with great potential. "I always thought Mr. George was made of good stuff, his appearance and manner exceeds my expectations, and if he has days, no doubt remains with me that he will add luster to your family," Ludovic Grant wrote Penrose about his "à la mode" son.[19]

Penrose was not so sure. In 1792 he had told Sir James Grant that the real reason he was interested in filling parliamentary seat held by Grant's sick son was "to improve the chances of procuring a passage to India for his son [George]."[20] Penrose's brother George did not agree with Ludovic's assessment at all. His nephew had stayed with him while in London and had exhausted his patience. Uncle George thought the young man had a long way to go before he could be considered worthy of Altyre. He would have seconded William Cowper's description in book 3 of *The Task* (1785) of the essential fop: "Well-dress'd, well-bred, / Well-equipaged, is ticket good enough / To pass us readily through every door." Nephew George was spoiled, demanding, and self-centered, a pleasure-seeker and an unrepentant spendthrift so drawn to the temptations of city life that Uncle George determined that the sooner he was out of London, the safer he would be. In letters to his brother, Uncle George described the young man as fashionably melancholy and unmotivated. His fear was that unless his nephew was given something to do and forced to become independent, he would spend his father's money on whatever caught his fancy, and his time waiting for Penrose to die.

To shape up this wayward son hurtling down the path to perdition in London, and bring "the good stuff" within him to the fore, Penrose and his brother decided that son and heir George should follow in his uncle's footsteps and go into the most lucrative branch of the civil service of the East India Company, the Bengal Establishment. As India was more often the destination of portionless younger sons and the mortality rate there was very high, theirs was an unusual decision. They were certainly taking a risk. But the Cummings had historically been lucky, and the brothers hoped that shipping nineteen-year-old George out to India as a writer would "cure" him of his bad behavior and habits. Perhaps he would do as spectacularly well as that other very troublesome firstborn son, Robert Clive. Even if George didn't return a nabob, service in India would force him to grow up and think and act responsibly so that when the time came he would have acquired the experience needed to make Altyre an even more profitable concern.

Perhaps Uncle George was thinking of how he had survived a near-fatal illness in India, how seven years of laborious office work had led to a position in which he amassed a fortune, and how his status now gave him clout with the company's Court of Directors. Perhaps Penrose at this point remembered his Grand Tour; he had been exposed to frank expressions of sexuality and indulged in vice and debauchery in foreign lands without any ill effects. Perhaps at the back of both their minds was the trajectory of their father's life. He had acted irresponsibly, even stupidly, as a young man, fighting with a superior officer and signing away rights to property. But he was also lucky: he survived a shipwreck to marry an heiress, have children, and live happily ever after. If this eldest son was cut from the same cloth as his father, uncle, and grandfather, George would enjoy life's pleasures, emerge stronger from brushes with death, mature, and acquire a fortune. Once back in Scotland, he would follow in his father's steps. He would make a strategic marriage, find love and happiness within that marriage, have a large family, and manage the Cumming estate wisely and well.

But it wasn't at all clear that George was cut from the same cloth. Penrose seized an opportunity and went on a Grand Tour; George was being pushed into East India Company service by his worried father and uncle. On December 20, 1792, while George's petition for a writership was still being reviewed by the Court of Directors and after Penrose's trial balloon for the parliamentary seat had been punctured, Penrose told his brother-in-law Sir James Grant, then the sitting MP from Banffshire, that he believed his expectations "relative to George . . . were justly raised," but also requested him to "help him [George] forward" in case "adverse fortune should disappoint me."[21] The language leaves no doubt that Penrose realized his eldest son might need further support.

As a writer in East India Company service, George would be recording all aspects of the company's business operations. George returned from London to study bookkeeping and arithmetic with the rector of the local grammar school at Forres, Mr. Shand. George's 1793 *Writer's Petition* includes a letter from Mr. Shand, who considered that George had achieved "a suitable and very laudable proficiency. . . . In my opinion he is well qualified for entering upon the practice of keeping accounts in real business."[22] Uncle George shepherded George's application through the process, and he was able to write Penrose in April 1793, before the Court of Directors formally announced it, that the petition had been successful. Nevertheless, Uncle George was aware that his nephew was different from other sons of the Scottish landed gentry who applied for a writership, and that the power brokers at Leadenhall Street were aware of it as well. George told his brother that the appointment was a stroke of "luck." "Had it not been for a variety of circumstances," he wrote Penrose, "we never should have accomplished our wishes" with respect to the pleasure-seeking young man who closed his ears whenever "the subject of oeconomy was broached."[23]

After young George received his appointment, his uncle noted that he didn't seem very grateful for the string-pulling done on his behalf and appeared far from keen to embark on his employment. He resisted being outfitted for the journey to India, then forced his uncle to lay out more than £300 or $46,000 for clothing and books—a shocking amount at a time when the East India Company deemed that a sea chest, a case of bottles, Castile soap, some shirts, velvet jockey caps, and three pounds of books were all that was "necessary . . . for a lad heading out to the East Indies."[24]

George would be sailing on the *Fort William*, presently at anchor in Portsmouth. Its captain, Adam Cumine, and most of its officers were still in London, and in the same letter in which he shared the news of the appointment, Uncle George told Penrose that he had spoken to the captain. Cumine had promised to give young George "a good berth . . . and to show him every power of attention in his power." The uncle then packed his nephew off to Portsmouth. He laid out the hundred guineas for the youth's passage; two securities for £500 apiece, required by the East India Company for all successful candidates, were also furnished. But he could not resist saying he was glad to wash his hands of his nephew. "A more troublesome and a more unthankful office never fell to my lot," he wrote Penrose on May 26, 1793, adding, "I thank my lucky stars there is no probability of a repetition of it."[25]

The *Fort William* docked in Calcutta in April 1794, and the first test in the experiment to transform George came immediately. Boats such as the *Fort William* were met by *dubashes* (money agents). They "spoke knowingly . . . and with all the insinuation of the world [offered] their services to the passengers on board." For just a trifling amount, they told callow youths like George, "if the master should have occasion for a little money, the dubashes purses shall always be devoted for his convenience."[26]

Calcutta was an expensive city. Captain Williamson estimated that to live simply in Calcutta a bachelor would require £600 a year, while a writer's salary would only reach £500 after three years. If he wanted a garden house to which he could repair when the weather turned humid and a carriage for visiting friends, going to parties, and taking drives, if he wanted to maintain a concubine, he would need much more. The access to ready money melted whatever resolve George might have possessed, and the writer soon began spending above his salary. Contrary to the directive of the Court of Directors, who wanted their employees to live humbly, George began making expensive purchases of household objects made of silver, including a pie dish, candlesticks, and a set for eleven of spoons and forks.[27] He furnished his accommodations with carpets, curtains, and commodes with china pans.[28]

By October George was serving as a lowly assistant in the office of the secretary of the Board of Trade in Calcutta. In December he was appointed Commissioner of the Court of Requests. Four months later, in April 1794, he was given another low-level position in Calcutta, that of assistant to the president of the Board of Revenue. In October 1794 he had a stroke of luck. His uncle William Cumming, a senior merchant with the East India

Company, died in Calcutta. In his will, William bequeathed his young nephew a windfall—six thousand rupees in cash.[29] Six thousand rupees was equivalent to £600, and in today's terms, the senior merchant left the young writer $87,000. George put up a marker in the South Street Burial Ground at the spot of his uncle's interment and squandered the rest. He accumulated more silver objects and house furnishings. He bought history books and geographies. Always attentive to personal appearance, he bought hanging mirrors and clothes horses as well as a curling iron and powder puffs of swans' down, the latter two quite useful in the humid Calcutta climate. He purchased a cavalry cocked hat and a ceremonial sword. He also owned a palanquin carpet and riding gear: jockey boots, jockey whips, and a jockey cap. He must have cut a dashing figure as he moved around Calcutta on foot, on horseback, or in a palanquin. Cowper's description of the metropolitan fop fit him even more snugly now. George became more and more indebted to moneylenders.[30]

George's seven years in the employ of the East India Company occupy nine lines in the 1839 *Alphabetical List of the Honourable East India Bengal Civil Servants, from the Year 1780 to the Year 1838*, and fourteen in the 1844 *A General Register of the Hon'ble East India Company's Civil Servants of the Bengal Establishment from 1790–1842*. After the initial positions in Calcutta, George applied for and obtained postings in Bihar. Between February 1796 and February 1797 he served as registrar of the *zilla adawlut* (district court) in both Ramghur and Shahabad. In February 1797 he returned to the environs of Calcutta, where he again served as the registrar in a *zillah adawlut*. In March 1799 he was appointed registrar at Comilla (now in Bangladesh), but about eighteen months later he was back in Calcutta. In a letter to Uncle George from Calcutta, dated November 10, 1799, he explained that for the past two years he had not been well, that he had become "reasonably stout," that is, strong and healthy, only since leaving Comilla, that he was dissatisfied with the lack of opportunities for promotion in the Bengal Establishment, and that he was thinking of trying his luck either in Bombay or at the cape of Good Hope.[31] On September 20, 1800, he drew up his last will and testament. He boarded the homeward-bound *Anna* on October 10, 1800. The twenty-six-year old's death at sea on December 23, 1800, and the fact that his effects were left at the Cape and then put on an India-bound Danish ship the following day, were noted by the captain in the ship's log.[32]

George's career was an undistinguished one. The position he held for most of it, registrar in a district court, was the lowest official grade. James Cumming (no relation), head of the Revenue and Judicial Department at

East India House in the 1820s, described the position as soul-killing. The individual appointed to it was "confined to the drudgery of expounding the regulations and settling the petty cases which arise among the traders, chiefly of the town in which the court is situated. . . . He goes in the morning to the court house to carry on the court business agreeably to the seven folios of Regulations. . . . His mind gets contracted, too often completely sickened and disgusted against the natives from the disputes, falsehoods, prevarications and crimes which are the only matters brought before him."[33]

Unlike for his uncles who had preceded him in East India Company service, India had not worked out for George. He had moved laterally from one dull, laborious position to another; in the course of seven a few years, he ran through rather than amassed substantial sums of money. As an experiment to breed bad values and attitudes out of him and bring the good stuff in him to the fore, East India Company service was an expensive failure, for George never learned fiscal responsibility. Indeed, in his last will and testament, George acknowledged that starting with his early days in Calcutta, "through a degree of the most culpable thoughtlessness and extravagance," he had "contracted several debts, which from the accumulated interest do amount to a considerable sum," that sum being Rs. 45,000 (£4,500, or $567,000).[34] George had lived grandly, but when the house furnishings, books, and personal items that comprised his estate were sold, the inventory of his estate indicates that they brought in only Rs. 1,700 (£170, about $20,000). Penrose, who was responsible for paying off the remaining debt, was livid and dressed his anger in heavy sarcasm. "From every account I can get and new ones are coming to me daily," he wrote Sir James on March 28, 1802, "he seemed for the last three years to be running the race of ruin, in which at last he completely succeeded."[35] The absence of letters from George to his father in the National Library of Scotland or the National Records of Scotland suggests that Penrose burned them.

Penrose's rage speaks to his dashed hopes, yet there were strong signs before George left that his eldest son would not be able to live up to expectations. India revealed that the young man who impressed the Grant family kinsman in Edinburgh in 1793 had a literary persona that matched his sartorial affectations. On August 11, 1794, George wrote Sir James Grant in London. Not quite twenty years old at the time, he was determined to impress his maternal uncle with his worldly wisdom and *savoir faire*. He climaxes a disquisition on the violence of the French Revolution by adapting Hamlet's lines from the "to be or not to be" soliloquy to the contemporary

European political scene. "I hope," he wrote, "that France will . . . serve as a dreadful warning to surrounding nations, to use Hamlet's words, 'make them' rather fear those ills 'they have than fly to others' which 'they know not of.'"[36]

However, the sensibility George assumes in this long letter, while obviously indebted to that character of many postures, Hamlet, is also derived from another figure whose existence is inextricably linked to Hamlet's. This is Laurence Sterne's Reverend Mr. Yorick, who in Sterne's extremely popular *A Sentimental Journey* (1768) shares his subjective and emotional impressions to establish his persona.

Knowing that Sir James wants to have "satisfying" news of his eighteen-year-old son James Thomas, also a writer with the East India Company, George begins his letter by informing him that James Thomas does not have a good chance of being appointed to a much-desired position, that of registrar in the city court of appeals in Benares. After throwing his uncle this crumb, with its seasoning of *schadenfreude*, George describes a recent trip of his to the ruined imperial city of Moorshadabad (now spelled Moorshidabad). The city is located on the eastern bank of the Bhagirathi, a branch of the Ganges. Today it is a six-hour drive from Calcutta on highways and expressways, but it would have taken George considerably longer to reach, for his route was fluvial, along the Hoogly, the Ganges, and the Bhagirathi. He would have gone by budgerow, a kind of barge driven by sails if there was enough wind, but in the absence of wind, either towed by men on the riverbank or propelled by boatmen on board using long poles. He would have passed cloth factories and indigo plantations, perhaps seen the *shikaras* (Sanskrit: tall towers) of Hindu temples in the distance.[37]

It was a scenic enough route, but for anyone in East India Company service in 1794, the destination, Moorshidabad, held special interest. Until 1757, when Robert Clive bested the nawab (Urdu: governor) of Bengal at the Battle of Plassey, a victory that signaled the beginning of British rule over India, Moorshidabad was an imperial capital, the administrative and financial hub of West Bengal. Clive recollected that it was "as extensive, populous and rich as the City of London" and full of individuals "possessing infinitely greater prosperity than any" in London.[38] Its mint held gold and silver plate, jewels, and rich goods in addition to the equivalent of £1.5 million in rupees, the equivalent of at least $15,400,000.

Moorshidabad, only thirty miles from Plassey, was Clive's first port of call after winning the battle. He plundered the treasury, taking with him the equivalent of £160,000. In the course of his career in India, Clive multiplied that sum many times over. His country rewarded him; subsequently he was appointed Commander-in-Chief of India. Though his wealth led to parliamentary inquiries, he successfully defended himself in the House of Commons and left his descendants very well off indeed.[39] Truly, for those who believed India was the way to fame and fortune, Moorshidabad was a pilgrimage destination.

However, the Moorshidabad that George Cumming visited in 1794 was much changed from the city Clive had entered almost four decades earlier. Following Clive's victory, Calcutta replaced Moorshidabad as the administrative hub of West Bengal, growing at the latter's expense. In 1769 Moorshidabad was struck by famine. A year later a smallpox epidemic claimed 63,000 lives. The city was nowhere near recovery in 1794.

In his letter, George employs sentimental rhetoric to call attention to the city's ruinous state, and to construct a rationale for foreign governance of India. He reflects that imperial Moorshidabad, once full of life and excitement, had become a site of abject misery and squalor, for all his eye perceives is "two hundred thousand straw huts" along the river. George takes delight in Moorshidabad's misery because it allows him to recall and apply Gibbon's phrase "a dead uniformity of abject misery" to the Moorshidabad situation.

Gibbon used the phrase in *The History of the Decline and Fall of the Roman Empire* (1776) to scorn the subjects of the Byzantine Empire and honor the Greeks and Romans. George does not empathize with the residents of Moorshidabad, either, seeing in their condition "melancholy proof of the never failing ravages of tyranny and despotism." This "proof" allows him to "that such will ever be the fate of governments whose fundamental laws are subversive of the first principles of justice and the natural privileges of men in society, who are bound to respect the authority of a first magistrate, and in return for that respect have a claim on his protection and to his best success in promoting the general welfare of the community."[40] In holding that their own rulers brought them to this miserable state and that it is now the duty of a superior "first magistrate" to uplift and protect the residents of Moorshidabad—and, by extension, all Indians—George justifies and reveals his commitment to an understanding of the East India Company as a superior ruling power and of its scheme of governance as benevolent.[41] The people of Moorshidabad would be saved, but by external agency.

In addition to putting on a politically correct (for late eighteenth-century Britain) performance for his uncle, George was also acting out a contemporary understanding of Hamlet's character. In many eighteenth-century texts the act three "to be or not to be" soliloquy was yoked with the act five graveyard scene in which Hamlet addresses the skull of Yorick, to suggest Hamlet's changing spiritual and emotional state.[42] Like Hamlet as he contemplates the skull of Yorick, a figure who in life was very special to him, George's responses to Moorshidabad seem to alter. Initially, the city excites him; it is a place he had been keen to visit, since it was associated with Clive's rise to prominence and wealth. Then its condition disgusts him, as the skull disgusts Hamlet. However, when Hamlet moves beyond the skull and begins to consider "the noble dust of Alexander" and whether Yorick's dust might now be part of a sheltering wall, Hamlet turns from disgust toward pity and compassion for those in need.[43] Sentimental George adapts Hamlet's change of direction. Instead of thinking about himself, he now considers the plight of the almost-homeless residents of Moorshidabad and suggests that the mighty wall that will keep them safe and secure is the East India Company.

The George who adopted the persona of a sentimental figure of empire in writing to Sir James was in reality a twenty-year-old burning with sexual desire. On September 7, 1794, just three weeks after returning from Moorshidabad, George addressed a poem to a Colonel Lawtie stationed in Calcutta in which the first-person speaker described his situation in terms that might suggest the author's personal response to the allure of his new environment. Though removed "far from fertile fields" and now found "beneath the burning ray where rolls the fiery bar of Day," the "I" is happy because in this hostile land it is also possible to "taste the sweets of love." "Where'er by Fate ordained to roam, / The sweetly talking Nymph I'll love, the Nymph who sweetly smiles," the poem concludes.[44] On November 1, slightly less than two months later, George sent another poem to Lawtie, in which he finds the antidote to a harsh environment where death lurked everywhere in the embraces of a Nymph. With mounting excitement, the "I" of this poem tells the Nymph to "haste to th'inviting shade," bringing her "toilet and perfume" so that "while Fortune, youth and Fate approve," the two of them can "taste the sweets of Love."[45]

In 1795 George travelled to Patna, some four hundred miles northwest of Calcutta, to spend time with his cousin James Thomas, who, as George had predicted, did not get the Benares posting. In Patna, James Thomas distracted himself with work and books so as keep his mind off the interesting things in his environment, but George ran toward its attractions. In a March 1796 letter to his mother, James Thomas mentioned that George had had such a lovely time in Patna that he had "applied to his friends in Calcutta to pressure for him an appointment in the country."[46] The transfer came through: George was sent to his Uncle George's old posting,

Ramghur. Unlike his uncle, though, who was appointed to a collectorship, George obtained only tedious, unremunerative low-level positions which, as James Cumming put it, sickened and contracted the mind. Yet by August 1796 James Thomas reported to his father that George had found health and happiness the country.

What happened in Patna in 1795 that transformed George into a happy person? In 1811 in Edinburgh, George's biracial daughter Jane Cumming affirmed that she had been born "at Patnah . . . about the end of 1795, or beginning of 1796."[47] Not long after, George became the father of a second child. A letter dated October 31, 1796, written by his uncle Henry Mackenzie to Lady Grant, says that George has "a wife." In a letter to Uncle George dated November 19, 1799, George refers to the Indian woman who became his partner and his children's mother romantically, respectfully, poetically, and geographically as "the Lady in the North."[48]

Lending credence to the notion that in Patna George was turning himself into a responsible, involved father and a concerned husband who found happiness within a conjugal relationship, just like his own father, are two shards of evidence. Like Penrose, who drew up a trust disposition when George was still a minor, George bought a share in a tontine for the benefit of children in Jane's name just after she was born and deposited his title to the share with his Calcutta attorneys. And then, mixed in with the works of history and geography he left behind when he boarded the *Anna* is a book called *Mrs. Cole's Cookery*, part compendium of British recipes adapted to the Indian climate and part family medical manual offering remedies for common illnesses. It does appear that in upcountry India George found something far better than the classical nymph his mind had conjured up in the poems of 1794—the personal happiness that his father had found decades earlier in taking care of his wife and children.

Penrose had hoped that in India George would become a man in his own image, but he did not appreciate the way in which his son fulfilled this wish. Back in Scotland, Penrose saw George's conjugality and his Indian children as recklessly endangering the line of succession to Altyre. The son who had formed a union with a native woman and the pugnacious father with conventional sexual mores clashed over who should inherit Altyre. In the already-mentioned late 1796 letter in which Henry Mackenzie referred to the Lady in the North as George's wife, Mackenzie shared with Lady Grant his sorrow over the predicament of "poor George," whose father had put him "in that state of suspense which may distress him more than any imperfect intelligence"; he also indicated that he was willing to discuss a plan with the "Barons" (titled landowners) to "quiet George's anxiety."

Mackenzie's oblique wording suggests that Penrose was thinking about disinheriting his eldest son. This was not an empty threat, as Scots law allowed for a proprietied father to "alter the destination, even perhaps to the extent of totally disinheriting his heir [on account of] riotous and extravagant" behavior.[49] Mackenzie's reference to George's anxiety suggests, too, that George was aware of this proviso and afraid his father would use it to punish him. Mackenzie, a kindly man, was willing to try to get Penrose's peers to talk him down, but his efforts came to naught. In October 1800 Penrose revised his deed of settlement. It was highly unlikely that British courts would have viewed George and the Lady in the North's connection as constituting a legitimate marriage, but litigious Penrose wasn't taking a chance of his property passing to the biracial grandson. In this revised deed of settlement, he dropped George's claim to the entailed property behind that of his younger brothers and their male offspring, making it virtually impossible for his eldest son or his eldest son's son to inherit.

As Mackenzie noted, George was now only too aware that his behavior had put him in harm's way, and to make matters worse, around 1797, with his second child either recently arrived or expected soon, his health began to decline. The anxiety and anguish George was going through are encapsulated in the name he gave his son: Yorrick. Indeed, and as might be anticipated from his earlier nod to the play, it is *Hamlet*, a work obsessed with father-son relationships, paternal expectations, death, and dynastic succession, that seems to hold the key to George's perception of himself in the late 1790s as he challenged his father's authority to control his life.

At the simplest level, since Yorrick (more commonly spelled Yorick) is a cognate of George, in choosing it for his son's name, George might not only have been slyly acknowledging his paternity but implying that his days were numbered, that the happiness he had hoped to find in the Indian countryside had proved elusive. Going deeper, because Yorick was the kind and gentle father figure in Hamlet's life, George may have chosen the name to indicate how he had hoped to be with his son. In other words, through the name Yorrick, George was setting himself up against his own father, who cared for his children but reserved his deepest feelings for his wife. Unlike him, George would be, like Yorick to Hamlet, a man of play and affection. However, Hamlet lost his Yorick when he was a child—which, if the parallel holds, suggested that George would not be there for his child.

Continuing his disquisition on mortality, Hamlet takes up the fate of Alexander the Great. Hamlet connects Yorick with Alexander, asking

Horatio if he thinks Alexander's body, like Yorick's, has become dust of the earth. When Horatio answers in the affirmative, Hamlet considers whether the dust of Alexander's body might now perform the homely and humane function of "stop[ping] a hole to keep the wind away" or "patch[ing] a wall t'expel the winter's flaw."[50] Horatio thinks Hamlet overingenious, but George's father's first name was Alexander, and George had shown familiarity with the play. He seems to have had this scene in the back of his mind when describing the situation of the abject residents of Moorshidabad and implying that their salvation lay in the benevolent East India Company. Now posturing George was using the famous scene again, not only to revenge himself on his powerful father by picturing him dead but also to catch the conscience of his father. By stressing the affinity between Alexander Penrose and Yorick, and pointing out how mighty Alexander's nature had changed over time, the sick but artful George was using the graveyard scene to ask his father to move beyond indignation, to show compassion and pity, to be kindly disposed toward this grandson who would be needing protection when still a child. As the East India Company would protect the people of Moorshidabad, so, George hoped, would Alexander Penrose prove to be the external agent who would offer a soon-to-be fatherless child a sheltering wall.

In an attempt to move his father and regain his affection, George worked the vein of guilt. In the same 1799 letter in which he informed Uncle George about his attachment to the Lady in the North, he drew a parallel between himself and one John Harris who had just died in Calcutta from a "vile fever." John Harris was "the eldest and indeed the only son . . . a very fine young man who was really the support of the declining hours of his parents."[51] At a time when letters were shared, George could be confident that this sad information would be transmitted to his furious father.[52] The descriptors George used for the late John Harris, a dearly beloved "eldest son," "a very fine young man" and "the support of . . . his parents," suggest that the sick George hoped his father would reconsider him in those terms before it was too late. Though they have not survived, this letter was followed by a slew of others in which George attempted to conciliate his father. However, Uncle George advised his brother to wash his hands of his prodigal George, as he himself had done. "My dear Sandy," he wrote on April 29, 1800, "I have urged George not to come home . . . how as things have turned out and it would be very imprudent indeed."[53] Penrose took his brother's advice and signed the October deed that effectively disinherited George.

George was prepared for this outcome. In September, a month before Penrose drew up the new deed, George put his signature to his last will and testament. Now that he was dying, he knew exactly what he wanted: the lairdship of Altyre. To achieve that goal, in his will he declared his children to be natural: his father could rest assured that Yorrick would not inherit. Abandoning love and attachment, he referred in the document to his children's mother as "the most artful and evil-intentioned of all women," from whose snares he had finally, perhaps too late, freed himself.[54] George had given out that he was thinking of trying his luck in Bombay or at the Cape of Good Hope, but when he boarded the homeward-bound *Anna* on October 20, 1800, he had already separated his children from their mother and put them into institutions in Calcutta. He could well have been thinking about returning to Scotland, challenging his father's deed, and reclaiming his birthright once his health improved.

Having suddenly grown into a man like his father, contentious, determined and purposeful, a man who strategized and left nothing to chance in matters of succession, this prodigal son also prepared for the possibility that he might not realize his goal. However, by working the rich vein of guilt once more in his will, George ensured that his seed would be sent to Altyre where his father could stand as a protecting wall to them. After itemizing the debts Penrose would have to pay off, George entreated his father to take care of the children. At present they were placed at "Mrs. Bolts School."

In 1802 James Thomas informed his father Sir James that he, an ayah, and John Palmer were looking after George's children, but as James Thomas was by then posted in Furruckabad, hundreds of miles northwest of Calcutta, that responsibility actually was borne by the ayah and Mr. Palmer. George had mentioned in his will that he had set aside money that would "save them [his children] from want," but as he was dying in debt, how much he had set aside is moot. George then added that Penrose's "sense of duty to his own family" would make it unnecessary for those funds to be used. As he wrote, "from my knowledge of his kind heart, I assure myself that he will protect them."[55] George boarded the *Anna* on October 10. Six weeks later he was dead, and his body committed to the deep.

The *Anna* docked at Gravesend on March 15, 1801, and soon after *The Aberdeen Journal* carried a notice of George's death at sea. Now that George was no longer an embarrassment or a threat to his father, his death could be announced openly, in the manner befitting the scion of a gentry family. The obituary notice in the *Aberdeen Journal* was followed by others in the *Gentleman's Magazine*, the *Edinburgh Magazine*, and the *European Magazine and London Review*. Never one to waste time, in April 1801 Penrose drew up yet another deed of settlement in which he appointed his second son William as his successor. The document begins on a resurgent note: "I Alexander Penrose Cumming Gordon of Altyre and Gordonstoun being lately advised of the death of my eldest son George on his way home from India...."[56]

Penrose's satisfaction was short-lived. By March 1802 he had been made aware of the extent of George's indebtedness and the contents of the will. The sale of George's goods at public auction came nowhere near to balancing out his debts. But George's testamentary document achieved its purpose. After raging, getting the children transferred to a less expensive institution, and arranging for his son's debts to be paid off, he orchestrated their passage. In the already quoted March 1802 letter to Sir James, he mentioned that he had "directions for having the children properly sent home." He was doing this out of duty; the other word he used in the letter for the children was "incumbrances." George had bested him in the end. His son was returning home, albeit in the form of these children.

But behind these "directions" must also have been child-centered Helen, that looming presence in Penrose's life to whom he was devoted, whose judgment he trusted, and who also couldn't tolerate stress. As his helpmeet at Altyre, she could well have presented to her farmer husband an agricultural argument, much applied in Scottish circles to human improvement: "transplantation into a more kindly group improves a plant, and unwearied culture increases these improvements."[57] She could argue the children's illegitimacy was not an issue; they would not inherit, and Scottish society had structures for accommodating them, one of which was grandparents. As a motherly mother, she was sensitive to the suffering of children. All children's pain moved her deeply, and she did her utmost to alleviate it; she also knew that Penrose feared for her health and strove to keep her happy. What would have been of utmost importance to Helen at this point was that young Jane, and younger Yorrick, now about five, should be treated as orphans, "objects of distress," and assisted. Though the children had local guardians in India, it would have been completely in character for Helen to have pressured her husband to have them brought to their grandparents' estate, where they could receive, if not loving, then "a kind of loving."

George had appropriated *Hamlet* for his purposes, but his easily stressed mother, blessed with a Scottish sensibility, executive capability, a maternal nature, and an uxorious husband, took her cues, so to speak, from *Macbeth* and *King Lear*. She had lost her son and, like Macduff, could not help but remember her loss. If she didn't fight for her son's children, she might lose these little ones as well. Feeling like a man but acting like a woman, she now emulated Edmund by standing up for the bastards. She stayed offstage while Penrose organized the children's transplantation.

Before George had boarded the *Fort William* in Portsmouth in 1793, Uncle George had introduced him to one of its officers, Adam Cumine. Now Cumine was the captain of an East Indiaman, the *Bengal*, a new vessel launched in 1799. The *Bengal* had three decks, was 146 feet long, and weighed 818 tons. The roundhouse or uppermost room on the ship was six feet six inches in diameter; smallish ships such as the *Bengal* generally had cabins for passengers in back of it. On September 13, 1802, it stopped in Calcutta, where it picked up Jane and Yorrick Cumming, and the ayah, listed on the manifest as "Coongee, Miss Cumming's Black female servant."[58] Though Cumine entered their ages on the passenger list as nine and seven, respectively, they were more likely younger; Helen would later state that Jane left India "some months before she attained the age of eight."[59] Their great-grandfather, the sea-swallowed man who had been pulled from the water, was a tall man; perhaps they took after him.

There were around ten other children on board, so Jane and Yorrick would not have lacked for playmates—although the ship was so packed that there wasn't much space for playing. In addition to the civilian passengers and the crew, the ship also took on a detachment of the Ceylon Native Infantry comprised of six privates, one officer, and four prisoners. Unquestionably, conditions on vessels such as the *Bengal* could be disagreeable. Writing in 1845, when one might expect improvement since 1802, Emma Roberts counseled women to take an upper cabin to avoid

> all the disagreeables attending upon encountering persons engaged in the duties of the ship. It may seem fastidious to object to meeting sailors employed in getting up different stores from the hold, or to pass and repass other cabins, or the neighbourhood of the steward's pantry; nevertheless, if ladies have the opportunity of avoiding these things, they will do well to embrace it; for, however, trivial they may be in a well-regulated ship, very offensive circumstances may arise from them.[60]

Emma Roberts did not specify what these "disagreeables" were, but they might well have included seeing men expose themselves, hearing them utter sexually crude or derogatory insults, or finding oneself the recipient of unsolicited touches. The heading "disagreeables" could also extend to glimpsing men engaged in homoerotic practices, including solicitation; nonpenetrative emissive sexual activities like masturbation, including mutual masturbation; and penetrative anal sex (sodomy). On British navy, British East India Company, and Dutch East India Company vessels, the latter two types of offenses were punishable. They connoted a breakdown of law and order on the ship. If the penetrative sex was nonconsensual, it was regarded as rape. Non-penetrative (emissive) offenses were regarded as misdemeanors, while penetrative (ejaculatory) offenses were punishable by death.[61]

At sea, captains investigated the cases brought to their attention, interviewed the individuals involved along with those who might have witnessed it, then imposed punishment. Notations in ships' logbooks indicate that crew members proved to have committed a sexual misdemeanor (sometimes referred to as "indecent conduct" or "uncleanliness"), were flogged.[62] A case involving two Dutch soldiers caught engaging in sodomitical practices in Cape Town could well have happened to any two sailors flying under the Union Jack or the East India Company's colors. In 1759 these two soldiers were confined to a hospital in Cape Town, where a third soldier, spying on them through a hole in a lavatory wall, saw them masturbating each other. The Cape Town court sentenced them to whipping and banishment to the Netherlands.[63] Though captains had the right to conduct trials on board their ships, records suggest that since sodomy cases involving penetration carried a death sentence, captains preferred to offload the offender at the first available port or to have him tried stateside by a navy court.[64] Whether accused men were exonerated or found guilty, their reputations and careers were destroyed.[65] So many such cases were prosecuted that Sir Charles Philip Yorke, appointed First Lord of the Admiralty in 1818, described homosexuality as "unhappily too frequent in the navy."[66]

While the *Bengal's* journal makes no mention of men caught *in flagrante delicto*, the absence of such a notation doesn't mean that officers or crew members didn't harass the female passengers. Nor does it mean Jane didn't see nakedness and the kind of sexual behavior that could have led her to tell the Edinburgh judges in 1811 she was absolutely certain Miss Woods had put an unidentified something (but presumed not to have been a tool) "in" and not "on" what Miss Pirie said was "the wrong place," making Lord Hope ask whether she saw any wetness on the sheets.[67]

Leaving aside this suggestive line of inquiry into the long-term effect of sexual behaviors Jane could have seen on the *Bengal*, disagreeable things did happen during the voyage. The ship's journal indicates that four crew members died. About three months into the trip, evidence of misbehavior starts appearing in the journal. Seaman William Oakes was punished with two dozen lashes for "attempting to strike the 4th Mate" and Thomas Smith with a dozen lashes for "drunkenness and riotous behavior." The ship's cook Noel Peligan got off lightly with six lashes for "riotous behavior and insolence." Fourth Officer George Gerrard was suspended from his station "for ungentlemanly conduct," an eyebrow-raising phrase; within a day, however, the ungentlemanly Gerrard was "returned to his station from alleviating circumstances appearing in his conduct and from his former good behavior."[68] Even if she did not witness the floggings, information and rumors would have circulated on the boat and sunk into Jane's mind.

There was hardly any privacy on the ship, and very little space in the cabins once the standard furniture—cots described as "shallow wooden coffin[s] suspended at each end from the deck beams above," tables, a washstand—and personal possessions were put in place.[69] The cabins off the roundhouse were partitioned from each other only by screens or light wood panels. There were probably two latrines on the whole ship. On long voyages people went unwashed, as water was in scarce supply. It was only too common to fall sick from the "flux," an intestinal disease that caused severe diarrhea and blood loss. The smell was stomach-churning, even when the porthole windows were open. Then there was the noise. In addition to that made by the ship's machinery, there was the constant pecking and clucking of the poultry kept in coops above the cabins. As for food, there was never enough and the quality deteriorated over time.[70]

The *Bengal*'s journal indicates that the weather was mainly squally, so the porthole windows were probably kept closed a good deal of the time. Three days after Jane boarded, a heavy swell "made the ship roll deep"; fourteen inches of water were pumped out. It is hard not to think that Jane wouldn't have been frightened that day, or when the storms and waves were so severe that Captain Cumine couldn't conduct church services on Sundays.

Since she was probably seven when she boarded the ship, she was old enough to have memories, but when in 1811 Jane was asked about her years in India, she was not questioned about the long voyage that brought her to Britain. What we do know is that Jane and Yorrick disembarked on May 24, 1803, at London, and Coongee two days later, at Gravesend.

Unaware that the children were already on the high seas, James Thomas, mindful of Penrose's dangerous temper and fearful that his anger would be visited on Jane and Yorrick, wrote his father on October 5, 1802, asking him to "use [his] good offices on Mr. Cumming to be charitable to his offspring."[71] He even suggested a cost-effective yet caring solution to the problem posed by the children: they could be maintained, out of sight and almost out of mind, in the north of England until they could fend for themselves. James Thomas's advice was not quite followed.

After disembarking, the children spent about two weeks in London with Uncle George (their great-uncle), then living on Berners Street, a fashionable thoroughfare branching off from Oxford Street. Its spacious, well-appointed houses were considered quite new, having gone up only in the past forty years.[72] Varying in size and detail, they represented the range of mid-Georgian terrace house types. Almost all possessed a frontage of twenty to thirty feet, and had an external stone staircase with iron railings, plasterwork on ceilings and over doors, and bay windows looking out on a garden. In general, the internal staircase was at the back, on the side. Also at the back was the mews where people could stable their horses.[73] Having known only the interiors of institutions and a cramped East Indiaman, being ensconced in one of these grand houses must have made a huge impression on Jane.

Uncle George's neighbors on Berners Street included John and Amelia Opie. The Opies were a companionate and unusual pair—John, a successful portrait painter, was the son of a carpenter whose first wife was Jewish, and Amelia, his second wife, was the talented daughter of a respected physician. Her very popular tale *Father and Daughter* (1800) was written on Berners Street, as was her well-known, tender song "The Poor Hindoo" (1802). In contrast to the conventional depiction of Indian women as licentious, treacherous females who used sex to capture and control white men, Opie gives us the powerless and desolate Lola. Abandoned by her white partner for a "British fair," Lola voices her emotional suffering over the course of several stanzas. The Opies were also members of the Wollstonecraft-Godwin circle, and thus open to other kinds of sexual unions.[74] There is no evidence that the Opies knew their neighbor was harboring his nephew's biracial children, but one would like to think this unconventional couple would not have looked harshly on them, understanding their father's feelings for his Lady in the North and the Lady in the North's feelings upon on being separated from her children and then jettisoned by the man who once called her his "wife."

What Uncle George thought of these children he was minding or how he looked after them in the brief period they were his responsibility is also unknown. In the mid-1790s, when Penrose sent four of his daughters to London boarding schools, Uncle George looked after them until they joined their school. Playing the role of fond uncle, he told Helen that

"George's carriage would be at the young ladies' service" and that Louisa was so delighted at seeing the regiments of horse guards for the first time that he was "scarcely . . . able to keep her in the carriage."[75] But how would he have treated his brother's grandchildren? Would he have taken Jane and Yorrick out in his carriage, or kept them as sequestered as possible, as Margaret Stuart Bruce was initially maintained?

After about a fortnight, George was relieved of his responsibility. Jane and Yorrick were brought to Scotland by a Mr. Tulloch. This Mr. Tulloch must have been deemed a respectable, trustworthy person, one able to handle the journey north, probably by sea, with two young children in tow.[76] Fifteen years later Jane would marry a Mr. Tulloch, a schoolmaster with a licentiate to preach the Gospel, and about eighteen or twenty years older than herself. Were the two Tullochs one and the same? Circumstantial evidence, discussed in chapter 5, connects them.

On August 17, 1803, Adam Cumine and Penrose met in Aberdeen, where the captain signed a receipt on which he acknowledged receiving £259 11s 3d, or $31,000, for "the childrens passage and expenses."[77] At the respective ages of fifty-four and forty-nine, Penrose and Helen acknowledged themselves in loco parentis to their son's children. Yorrick's outrageous name was soon changed to its respectable English cognate, George. Initially Jane and Yorrick/George resided at Altyre under Helen's eye, but their presence may have been too much for Penrose to handle. In addition to George's death and the ignominious end of his political ambitions, his youngest daughter Charlotte fell seriously ill shortly after being placed in a Doncaster boarding school in 1803. Toward the end of that year Coongee was sent away. In March 1804 Penrose had a stroke.

We know from the same letter of September 1804 in which Penrose made mincemeat of the Forres minister John Macdonnell that the children by this time had already been placed in boarding establishments in Elgin about eighteen miles from Forres. Receipts for their education and clothes indicate Jane was boarded with Miss Christian Charles, the governess who had educated all of Helen's children, and her brother with Elgin's Episcopalian minister, the Reverend Hugh Buchan. However, because of the proximity of Elgin to Altyre, Helen saw her grandchildren frequently, or at least whenever she was around, which probably wasn't much because she was attending to her daughter Charlotte dying in England. Perhaps other family members dropped in to see Jane when they were passing through Elgin. The children always spent their holidays at Altyre.

When Penrose died in 1806, the children were provided with articles of mourning and shoes. Penrose's son William, now Sir William, succeeded to the estate—and the care of Jane and Yorrick/George. As for Helen, Penrose's death seems to have invigorated her. Her machinations on behalf of her brother-in-law George Cumming when he was a candidate for the parliamentary seat of Inverness were so open that the *History of Parliament* entry on Cumming refers to them.

She next challenged the trustees and representatives of her late husband's estate. A month after Penrose died, Charlotte passed away. Helen requested reimbursement for the "upwards of £1,000" in expenses she had incurred during Charlotte's illness, the reimbursement to come from the £2,000 Penrose had left Charlotte in his last testamentary document. The trustees and representatives were rather shocked by Helen's claim. "Imperiously called upon to attend her" was how these men phrased a mother's decision to run to the bedside of her dying youngest daughter without first consulting anyone.[78] In a determination that would prefigure a later case in which she was involved, one in which a (grand)daughter and ducats were also mixed up, the trustees and representatives denied the request of this woman whose sensibility moved her to take actions that were construed as imperious, impulsive, bold, challenging, confrontational—in a word, wrong for a member of the female sex.

Chapter Two

EDUCATING JANE (1)

In the eighteenth century, a girl raised with the values of gentry society was expected to behave according to well-established norms. In practice, this meant she had to subordinate herself to male authority and appear amiable, accomplished, graceful, dignified, modest, and refined in social situations. Over her emotions and feelings she exercised control. It was drilled into her that any charge of vulgarity or inappropriate behavior, any breach of etiquette, could destroy her reputation.[1] A woman who "talks loud, contradicts bluntly, looks sullen, contests pertinaciously, and instead of yielding, challenges submission" was, according to James Fordyce, author of *The Character and Conduct of the Female Sex* (1776), lacking in virtue.[1] It was taken as a given that her realm was the domestic sphere, that her marriage had as much (if not more) to do with negotiations between families than with personal choice, and that the duty she performed within that intimate relationship called marriage was to obey and submit.[3]

Education was key in the inculcation and deep-rooting of these qualities and ideas, and during the course of the century, academies, seminaries, and boarding schools for females were established all over Britain. Their advertisements proclaimed that they offered instruction in the polite arts of dancing, music, French, and drawing, as well as needlework (ornamental and useful) and writing. The theory was that through obedience to teachers and school rules and a disciplined, structured education in these subjects, girls born into families of good repute, thus well-bred by birth, would be improved: turned into feminine women, a credit to their sex.[4] They would become well-behaved ladies, companionable, amiable, gracious women who knew how to speak with restraint and conduct themselves as members of the female sex—well-bred through proper nurturing. Education, therefore, would not only teach women to conform to social expectations and know their place in society but to value and be comfortable with their lesser status.[5]

The hope was that this methodology would lead to a good marriage in a refined home in which they would perform their duties as wives submissively, respectfully, virtuously, and graciously, in full awareness of *Ephesians*

5:22–23 ("Wives, submit yourself unto your husbands, as unto the Lord, for the husband is the head of the wife, even as Christ is the head of the church").[6] As mothers, they would pay careful attention to the education of the children, transmitting from infancy onward the values impressed on them during their own education. If marriage eluded them, they would be cheerful, useful women who would know how to pass the time at home in a productive manner.[7]

The mission of these schools thus was in keeping with the spirit of the times and its desire to improve the breed, so while Penrose focused on improving Altyre by feeding his cattle special grasses and seeds and mating Scottish steer with English cows, Helen busied herself with improving her nine daughters.[8] By the time Jane arrived in 1803, all her daughters had received a basic education in reading, writing, spelling, needlework, French, and arithmetic from the family governess, Miss Christian Charles. After placing four of them in a London boarding school in the early 1790s, Helen realized she was taking a gamble. "I hope it will be of advantage," she wrote Lady Grant shortly afterward, then confided her anxieties over their lack of progress in music and dance.[9] In 1803, her youngest daughter Charlotte, born in 1792 and thus no more than three or four years older than Jane, was also about to be placed at a boarding school at Doncaster, where there was a ready supply of potential husbands in the form of young army officers.[10]

In 1803 Helen's wish that a boarding school education would be of advantage to her daughters was being fulfilled. Two daughters had already made good marriages, Helen to Sir Archibald Dunbar of Northfield, Margaret to Samuel Madden, an army captain; negotiations for a third marriage, that of Louisa to John Hay Forbes, a well-known, civic-minded Edinburgh lawyer, were probably also underway. Helen's unmarried daughter Sophia played the pianoforte exquisitely, much to the delight of her family and circle of acquaintances.[11] Sending Charlotte to a Doncaster seminary looked like a strategic move, since even if she didn't snare one of the officers stationed there, she would end up, like her sister Sophia, with skills that would enable her to be a cheerful and amiable woman.

Though Helen believed deeply in female education, boarding schools in general enjoyed an indifferent reputation, with the worst tagged either as "seminaries of vice and insignificance" or "ante-chambers of death."[12] French instructors were a particular source of anxiety. The language enjoyed cachet and parents wanted their daughters to acquire it, but the credentials of the instructors were often dubious. Mary Wollstonecraft, who ran a female boarding school for a few years, acknowledged her inadequate command of the language. John Burgoyne satirized the teachers as deserters from Dunkirk. Furthermore, the behavior of male instructors of the French language was considered rude, almost lewd. It was also feared that they might that they might make Catholics of the students.[13]

At the Reading Ladies' Boarding School or Abbey School, which Jane and Cassandra Austen attended in 1785–86, informally known as Mrs. La Tournelle's School after its owner, the owner had no command of the French language. Her name at birth was Esther Hackett. She changed the first to Sarah and the latter to La Tournelle when, early in life, she found a position as a French teacher. After she died in 1797, the truth came out. Her obituary in the "Obituary of Remarkable Persons; with Biographical Anecdotes" section of *The Gentleman's Magazine* states that "her employers thought it right to introduce her to the school under a foreign name. She accordingly took that of La Tournelle, and her real name was known only to a few of her numerous friends."[14] According to another of the school's distinguished alumnae, Mrs. Mary Sherwood (née Mary Martha Butts), Mrs. La Tournelle's strength lay in making tea and ordering dinner.

That these schools bred inflated notions of self was taken as a donnée. Elizabeth Hamilton could have counted on agreement when in her *The Cottagers of Glenburnie* (1808), a tale about a lower-class Scottish community that improves itself without help from the gentry, the generic female boarding school is presented as a "nursery of folly and impertinence, where [a girl] learned nothing but vanity and idleness."[15] Similarly, in *Pride and Prejudice* (1813), Jane Austen ascribed the pretentiousness, vanity, unpleasantness, bad manners, and economic folly of the Bingley sisters to their having been educated in a London seminary. In her *Autobiography*, Mrs. Elizabeth Dawson Fletcher, a sensitive writer, literary patron, supporter of parliamentary reform, founder of Scotland's first female friendly society, and subscriber to societies whose goal was to improve the lives of the poor and the disabled, looked back at her four years (1781–85) at the highly regarded Manor House Boarding School in York. She remembered that reading and breadth of knowledge were held in low esteem, whereas a "graceful curtsey was [considered] the chief end of human existence and . . . an awkward gait was worse than a bad action."[16]

Another frequently discussed problem in boarding schools was lax supervision. While Elizabeth Fletcher was a pupil at Manor House, servants routinely brought in forbidden "dainties" while "mischief of every kind (short of actual vice)" went on, unsuspected by the governess who ran the school.[17] In his 1785 *Female Tuition: or an address to mothers, on the education of daughters*, John Moir noted that at boarding schools "many melancholy and desperate elopements [were] constantly happening."[18] Even at the very strict boarding school established by Jacob More, the father of the English writer Hannah More, a fourteen-year-old "heiress [was] trepanned away from school" and "all . . . efforts proved fruitless" to bring her back."[19]

Mary Wollstonecraft wasn't so sure that the mischief stopped short of actual vice. She decried the sexually dubious consequences of the moral standards obtaining in boarding schools. In her *Vindication of the Rights of Women* (1792), she stated that schoolmistresses ignored pupils' talking to those purveyors of sexual information, the servants. She also called attention to a common practice of the time: bedsharing.[20] She stated that dormitory arrangements where the close placement of beds encouraged sexual experimentation boded no good for the girls' later conjugal life. In her opinion, these sleeping arrangements led girls to develop "immodest habits" and learn "nasty tricks." This "pigging together" or "gross familiarity," she argued, "frequently renders the marriage state unhappy."[21]

J. L. Chirol, identified as "one of his Majesty's chaplains at the French Royal Chapel, St. James' Palace" on his book's title page, seconded Wollstonecraft, referring to the "disgusting and indecent practice" of bedsharing and pointing out that the intimate proximity also increased the chances of a healthy girl contracting a disease.[22] As for hygiene in these schools, Chirol remarked that in many of them the bed linen was changed at most three times a year and the girls washed only their hands, faces, and mouths on a daily basis.[23]

Erasmus Darwin implicitly pointed to the lack of proper ventilation throughout schools and specifically argued for the installation of ventilators in bedrooms to prevent disease; he advised prospective parents to inspect the beds and bedrooms before enrolling their daughters, "as their future health and sometimes their lives depend of this attention." He also implied that the girls did not get enough physical exercise. While others saw dancing as a social accomplishment, he saw it as a physical activity, and he advocated that more forms of bodily movement be added to the daily regimen. As activities to be considered, he listed ball games, ice skating, swimming, and swinging light dumbbells, or a bell with resistance supplied by a flywheel "to prevent its too hasty descent," to extend the spine and strengthen chest and arm muscles.[24]

To this list of problems contributing to the girls' ill health, others added inadequate food, the insufficient warmth and the smokiness of the rooms, and the practice of strait-lacing.[25] Helen herself learned that "oft expectation fails where most it promises" when her daughter Charlotte died of the unspecified but protracted illness she contracted at her Doncaster boarding school.[26]

If the boarding schools in Britain raised concerns, the institutions in India set up in the long eighteenth century to provide for the many abandoned or orphaned children of indigent European fathers and Indian mothers were also worrisome. At Calcutta's overcrowded, insalubrious United Charity and Free School, the children received a basic education that was intended to make them productive members of the colonial state. Girls were instructed in needlework. Boys often became bandsmen in the army or were steered toward the printing trades.[27] But since they left school by the age of twelve, and there were more children than positions, the fear was that the boys would become vagabonds and the girls would be forced into prostitution.[28]

Because Jane's father had set aside funds for her education and the fee-paying wing of the United Free and Charity School did not exist until 1817, that establishment was not her destination. Captain Williamson noted that fathers in East India Company service with some means usually put their biracial daughters, while still very young, in private fostering. Mrs. Bolts School, where George placed Jane sometime in 1800, may have been such an arrangement. The outcome for children in privately run operations was as uncertain as those of the girls educated at the United Free and Charity School. So even though one of Jane's local guardians was the compassionate John Palmer, she would become increasingly vulnerable as she matured.

By the middle of the century, it was recognized that these early nineteenth-century fostering arrangements, euphemistically called schools, had a culture of neglect. An anonymous 1850 article in the *Calcutta Review* dealing with the early educational establishments of Calcutta indicates that those who ran the schools had no educational training and the schools themselves were really "*make-shifts*—mere plans, like other domestic plans, which men contrive for augmenting their subsistence . . . until fortune smiled propitious."[29] Focused on their own straitened circumstances, the owner-teachers pay little attention to their wards' learning and emotional needs, though they do provide shelter and they do feed them, for the children are described as "chubby."[30] In the latter part of the nineteenth century, the diet reflected the children's bloodlines: boiled beef, carrots, and potatoes on Monday, curry, dal, and rice on Tuesday.[31] The author shows us a widow smoking a hookah and daydreaming while the girls go through their spelling and reading exercises. In another tableau, a half-asleep former veteran, surrounded by boys doing arithmetic exercises, is just waiting for his wife to summon him and them to dinner; he is oblivious to some pupils' eyes red from weeping. So convinced is the author of the accuracy of this picture that he or she dares readers to challenge its presentation of institutionally abandoned children, fed and housed in a setting something like a home but emotionally neglected by the people who should be standing in for parents with them.

What these proprietary schools charged for education, room, board, and other items is unknown, but Penrose thought Mrs. Bolts School's fees outrageous. He instructed Mr. Palmer to transfer George's children to another institution where they could be maintained just as well for less. In 1811 Jane recollected she had been a boarder at a large school in Calcutta where there were native women servants and acknowledged that she was "acquainted with many girls of her own age" there, so it is possible that Palmer pulled strings sometime in 1801 and had her admitted to the United Free and Charity School until she left for Britain.[32] Actually, it is difficult to imagine that a charity school always suffering from "an insufficiency of funds" would not readily accept two fee-paying pupils.[33]

By the time she left India, Jane, by her own account, had learned to read English but did not feel comfortable speaking it, and used the vernacular with her ayah Coongee. In the eight months she spent on board the *Bengal*, however, she would have picked up more English. Perhaps Mrs. Eliza Nixon Barbut, the wife of Lieutenant-Colonel B. G. Barbut, Commandant and Collector of Jaffna in Ceylon, who was traveling by herself on the *Bengal* and was known for "her desire to diffuse happiness among those in less favourable circumstances than herself," used some of her leisure time to instruct Jane and the other children in reading and writing; it was common practice for women to do so.[34]

The concern in India for the plight of orphaned, abandoned, poor biracial children was genuine. Without parents or protectors, they were vulnerable to sexual exploitation. The founders of institutions such as the United Free and Charity School felt they were doing their utmost to save these young people, but recognized that the odds were against the children, particularly the girls. They were discharged too young, and there were few ways they could be decently integrated into the social fabric. Since the founders also believed that before being placed at school these children had been raised in environments where they had been "constantly exposed to the corrupting influence of scenes of profligacy," to some extent they felt their mission was doomed from the start.[35]

In conceiving of their task in Sisyphean terms, they were following John Locke. In *Some Thoughts Concerning Education,* Locke notes that even "almost insensible impressions" can have "important and lasting consequences" on children's characters. Some pages later, he gives his opinion that "men's minds may perhaps be a little mended but cannot be totally altered and transformed into the contrary."[36] Those statements suggest a good deal of skepticism about attempts at amelioration. Once a child's mind has been stamped, later education will not be hugely successful in undoing damage caused by the initial set of experiences.[37] For as Locke also points out, if a dog finds it difficult to give up "the ill and restive tricks . . . learned when young," it is far more difficult for a child "at seven," by nature more willful than a dog, to be retrained.[38]

Furthermore, European doctors generally held that underage sex was common in India, particularly among Indian women who submitted to "domestic drudgery," like the women employed by a school such as the one Jane attended.[39] Only the slightest stretch was required for those of an even more pessimistic cast of mind than Locke's to state categorically that outside and inside the walls of the Calcutta educational establishments there were many sexually unrestrained native women who exposed children to all manner of sexual behaviors and irrevocably corrupted them. And that is exactly what lawyers and judges in Jane's case did. They presented as fact that Indian girls commonly got married and had consensual sexual relations by the time they were seven or eight. Native servant women were construed as lewd in speech and behavior, more so than the most lowminded European servants.

Those who accepted this construct of the lower-class Indian female would believe that by the age of eight the mind of a child placed in such an institution would have been indelibly impressed by the sexual conversations and practices she had heard and seen. Such a girl, it was felt, who conversed with natives in the vernacular, must "daily and hourly see objects, calculated to convey notions, which would not occur to a European . . . ; and in conversing with them, she must have these notions excited and confirmed. . . . Habituated to conversations concerning all manner of indecencies. . . . Hearing and seeing the most abominable scenes of lewdness . . . exposed to lascivious conversations, and lascivious practices generally, [such a girl would have] impressions and conceptions on the subject of venereal intercourse altogether different from, and much more lively than, the mere imperfect instincts which young women carefully educated in this country possess."[40] To summarize, boarding schools in Calcutta were "such masses of pollution [that they were] . . . honored by a comparison to a brothel," and any child, however innocent she was at birth, was, by the time she was extracted some years later, mentally corrupted, her every thought turning to sex or triggering a sexual response.[41]

The only way to save the poor creatures was to remove them from India as soon as possible. Captain Williamson pointed out that "few Europeans' children were kept beyond their third or fourth year."[42] In a country of fatal fevers and moral pollution, it was too dangerous for their health to stay longer. Those with systems already assumed to have been compromised by their Indian mothers' blood were believed most at risk.

Helen deemed such thinking "founded in absurdity and falsehood," but her bold and confident assertion may have masked fear as she had no evidence to back it up.[43] How could she be sure that there wasn't truth in the Western consensus position? What had been impressed on her granddaughter's mind before she was placed at her schools? Helen knew nothing good about the Indian woman who was Jane's mother, and may have held her responsible for bewitching her son."[44] People of the time also believed breast milk transmitted a mother's qualities, so despite her surface confidence, Helen have been worrying about that elemental source of contamination too.[45] She knew nothing about Jane's ayah, either, and Captain Williamson maintained that ayahs were moral corrupters. They not only made their "young charges crafty, proud and unmannerly . . . but initiated [them] in many practices . . . such as must require infinite assiduity to subdue."

And if Jane stayed in India, how would the anxious Helen be able to trust that there would be someone to protect her when she grew up? Her nephew James Thomas was posted in Furruckabad and so involved in building his career and setting himself up as a laird with an estate on the banks of the Ganges that he wasn't paying much attention to his own two illegitimate children. How could such a man be trusted with the care of the offspring of his late cousin? The best that John Palmer could have done for Helen's granddaughter would be to marry her off to a rajah or nawab.[46] So the grim fate outlined by Captain Williamson for biracial girls could not be discounted.

Jane was already past Williamson's cut-off age; she was being looked after by an ayah; and the consensus held that by the age of seven or eight a child's mind held impressions and notions that a second set of preceptors might not be able to completely redirect, let alone extirpate. This was the background that propelled Helen to act. Penrose gave orders; Jane and her brother were sent for. Accompanying them would be Jane's personal servant Coongee. According to Helen, Jane was still a few months shy of her eighth birthday when she left India in September 1802.[47] Even though Helen believed Jane had not been exposed to anything improper, she emphasized Jane's age so as to stress that she had saved her granddaughter from the conversations and practices she had not yet been exposed to just in time. The biases that had not been stamped on her could be straightened out; her "good" Cumming blood could trump the "bad blood" of her Indian mother.[48] At the very least, Jane could be mended. If the Cumming luck held, her thoughts could be rechanneled, her mind reprogrammed.

Saved or not, pure or impure, Jane was likely in her eighth year when she arrived in Scotland. By any standard, she was a later-adopted child from a foreign land with memories and experiences, and a personality stamped by the people who had brought her up. In addition, she had just spent eight months on a crowded ship where very little happened in private. Helen could hope that transplanting Jane would improve her human stock, but as the wife of a farmer, she also knew that experiments in animal husbandry sometimes went awry.

We do not know what Jane looked like on her arrival at Altyre, other than (probably) being tall. However, later accounts indicate that she had a "non-passing" complexion. Her grandmother described her as a girl with a barely noticeable "tinge" to her complexion, while another observer archly stated that she was "wanting in the advantages of . . . a European complexion."[49]

Helen did not seem to know what to do with the girl she had "saved." Her first and quite unoriginal intention was "that she should be bred to business as a mantua maker or milliner."[50] Such a career would have involved some outlay by the family, for anybody in the apparel business needed a modicum of educational skills and social accomplishments and had to go through an apprenticeship.[51] Even then, Jane would have led a marginal and precarious existence. Of such a future, Jane's contemporary and Helen's neighbor on Charlotte Square in the second decade of the nineteenth century, Elizabeth Grant, dryly noted that for portionless girls, legitimate as well as natural like Jane, "there was nothing dreamed of but the dressmaking, a trade never overstocked, its victims dying off quite as quickly as the vacant places were demanded."[52]

By 1803, Miss Charles, who had served as governess for all Helen's daughters and was now in her sixties, was the proprietress of a boarding school for girls in Elgin. Located on Elgin's High Street was the shop of Isaac Forsyth, the bookseller who kept northeast Scotland supplied with writing materials, books, and magazines. The ruins of the once majestic thirteenth-century Elgin Cathedral were much visited and sketched, even though its interior was piled high with the rubble and rubbish of centuries. An 1822 map of Elgin indicates that Miss Charles owned a substantial piece of property between High Street and Back Street (or Passage).[53] Surviving receipts from 1806 onward indicate that Sir William paid Miss Charles £25 a year for Jane's board and education in two half-yearly installments; in today's terms, $2,680. The sum, did not include outlays for washing and mending of clothes, coals and candles, and school supplies like copybooks and quills. Compared to what Penrose spent on his own daughters' London education, Miss Charles's fees were modest. Nevertheless, Miss Charles once had to remind Penrose's son to pay an installment.

Though Jane was maintained at Miss Charles' establishment, Helen claimed that she was not forgotten. The girl always spent the summer holidays at Altyre, and Helen, making light over the months when she was attending to her daughter Charlotte in Doncaster and putting immense trust in the good hearts and free schedules of family members, maintained that since Elgin was "in the near neighbourhood of Altyre," whenever she or a family member was in the country, there were "constant and almost daily opportunities of seeing her."[54]

Jane said that during the six years she was with Miss Charles she studied "reading, writing, spelling and arithmetic, French, music and [needle]work."[55] Receipts from 1806 through early 1810 found in DEP 175/111, "Household Accounts, 1801–1819," which holds many receipts for the domestic expenditures the Gordon Cummings made in that timeframe, including for the children, corroborate her statement, except with regard to music. Jane had a reading and writing master plus a dancing master for whose services the factor of Gordonstoun regularly disbursed ten and twelve shillings, respectively. In June 1808 the factor reimbursed Miss Charles £5 16s for six months of fees for Jane's English and French teachers. Between September 1808 and July 1809 Jane received four hours a week of tutoring in English and arithmetic from one Alexander Reid, who was paid a guinea for his services. Miss Charles billed Sir William one pound for "canvas and worsteds for two footstools," which Jane presumably embroidered. In 1809 Miss Charles bought Jane a chest of drawers and sent Sir William a bill for £2 5s. Based on the tradesmen's bills, her clothing was of calico, muslin, and silk.

Judging from the receipts for the outlays for Yorrick/George's education, he was being raised as a gentleman. Like his father, he received instruction in Latin, geography, and dancing. His Elgin guardian the

Reverend Hugh Buchan regularly disbursed £14 10s every six months for such items as school fees; books, paper, and quills; repair of a watch; shoes, a penknife, a toothbrush, a pocket hair comb; and school subscription balls. In 1809 Sir William paid £5 10s for "furnishings" for the lad; these included a "fine" belt and buckle, stockings, handkerchiefs, a hat cover, worsted gloves, and gilt, pearl, and metal buttons and many hanks of silk thread to sew them on with. Between November 1809 and August 1810 Helen personally spent £4 10s on "articles" for Yorrick/George; these included new vests and trousers, including a pair of nankeen trousers. All in all, the Gordonstoun factor calculated that Sir William disbursed about £60 annually for the boy's educational, social, and clothing expenses; the factor consistently paid out more money for Yorrick/George than for Jane.

The transplanted children thrived in their new surroundings. Yorrick/George was always needing new shoes. By 1806, when she about ten, Jane was using stays. Since the purpose of these boned bodices was to raise and support the bust, she may have been showing signs of developing into a buxom woman. A doctor was called in for Jane only once, on June 22, 1809. The problem couldn't have been serious, for on the "State of Payments" for Jane's board and education prepared by the Gordonstoun factor, the ailment isn't specified and the doctor's fee is given no more importance than the money paid to the shoemaker.

Miss Charles did not keep Jane at her books constantly. Every afternoon Jane and the other boarders were allotted two hours to play outside, sometimes unchaperoned, but near the back of the house so Miss Charles could keep an eye on them. Miss Charles's concern for her pupils' safety, physical and moral, also manifested itself in her not allowing them to mix with children of the town, and imposing a curfew. Thus, in summer, after the writing master left at seven, they were allowed to walk about but had to be in before nine. Personal hygiene, on the other hand, was not given much attention. Though her clothes were washed regularly, just two years after she left the school Jane recollected that she never bathed while there.

Miss Charles, who over the years had closer contact with Jane than her own grandmother, reported to Helen that while Jane was not academically distinguished, she possessed "an innocent, amiable and upright character," and Helen, based largely on that report, thought her granddaughter "simple, innocent, veracious."[56] Miss Charles's assessment must have pleased Helen, but as a paid caregiver, could her judgment be trusted? Helen decided to do some research to learn more about the effect of upbringing on a young person's development. Between 1807 and 1809 she bought two works of fiction from Isaac Forsyth. These were *The Father and Daughter*, the 1801 novel by Amelia Opie, the Berners Street neighbor of her brother-in-law George, and Henry Kett's *Emily, A Moral Tale, Including Letters from a Father to His Daughter, Upon the Most Important Subjects* (1809).

Both Kett's *Emily* and Opie's *Father and Daughter* deal with widowed parents on whom devolves the task of bringing up a young girl. In *Emily*, the widowed Colonel Lawton, bound by love for his late wife, a sense of responsibility for his now motherless daughter, and desire to honor his dying wife's request that he raise Emily to be of good moral character, instructs her on such topics as the forgiveness of injuries. To this end, he uses the parable of the Prodigal Son because "the lesson of duty it inculcates is so congenial with the most generous and noble feelings of our hearts."[57] Over the course of two volumes, Colonel Lawton cautions his daughter about scandal-mongering and the need to inquire before judging and destroying a person's reputation. He spends much time on the importance of self-command, pointing out that people with violent tempers, in addition to being impolite and undignified, cannot ever know happiness. Unable to regulate themselves, they act in a rash but unrelenting manner that ultimately brings them no satisfaction. Responsive to her father's educational ministrations, which involved her being "kept in a constant state of control . . . where no fault was suffered to pass unnoticed" but any such faults were corrected with sensitivity, Emily grows up with a sweet disposition that enables her to stand fast against the tribulations of life.[58] She is rewarded with a long, happy marriage to the gentleman she has always loved. Not content with being a caring mother and a companionate wife, she establishes a "school for the education of the indigent girls of the parish."[59]

The widowed Helen could easily have identified with Colonel Lawton, since both came to be preceptors through the untimely deaths of loved ones. Since her own eldest son was very much in the mold of the Prodigal Son, this anxious mother would have found in Kett's exposition of the parable a most pleasing validation for bringing Jane from India. Going further, she would have found advice about how to discipline a young girl so that she grew up with a pleasing temperament, able to appreciate criticism meant for her improvement, and be a credit to her family. In addition to assuring Helen she had done the right thing by sending for Jane, Kett's book might well have made Helen feel hopeful that her efforts on Jane's behalf would make an Emily of her granddaughter: a well-bred woman, happy, sweet-tempered, emotionally stable and strong, a doer of the kind of good deeds that Helen wanted to accomplish, and one who gets to enjoy a long and loving marriage.

In Opie's *The Father and Daughter*, the daughter, Agnes, is being brought up by her devoted widowed father, Fitzhenry. Agnes repays her father's love, however, by eloping with a man with whom she has a son, Edward. Agnes's sexual behavior tips Fitzhenry into madness. When the prodigal daughter finally returns home with her son, she puts her energies into curing her father and distances herself from Edward. Opie criticizes both father and daughter, the former for his extreme response and the latter for neglecting her son. However, the author shows Edward growing up happy and secure because others take good care of him and show him much love. She also structures the plot so that Edward's life follows the trajectory of a fairy tale. Thus, though Edward's biological father plays no part in his son's infancy, after Agnes dies he takes responsibility for him, raising him in comfort and bequeathing him a large fortune. Edward's successful nurturance by a caregiver would have reassured Helen that she had done the right thing in handing Jane over to Miss Charles. In addition, Helen could have seized on the parallels between her son George and Agnes, between Jane and Edward, between Fitzhenry and Penrose, and above all, between herself and Edward's late-on-the-scene biological father, and believed she could ensure Jane's life had a happily-ever-after ending.

But these were works of fiction. To see if the promise they held out was realistically achievable, Helen also bought two books on education by Elizabeth Hamilton. These were the 1801–2 *Letters on the Elementary Principles of Education* and the 1806 *Letters Addressed to the Daughter of a Nobleman on the Formation of the Religious and Moral Principle*. Both deal with the crucial role of the mother in directing the child's "native passions and affections of the heart" during the "most important period of [her] existence, that is, infancy."[60]

As a person, Hamilton tried to avoid being judgmental, understood the importance of a caring home in a child's development (particularly for one who had been adopted, as she herself was), and was known to go out of her way to help others.[61] In addition, Hamilton's late brother Charles, like Helen's late son, had been in East India Company service. Charles had "whetted Elizabeth's appetite for factual as opposed to apocryphal or fantastical information about the East."[62] Hamilton's first work, the political novel *Translation of the Letters of a Hindoo Rajah* (1796), was composed as a memorial to her beloved brother and dedicated to Warren Hastings, the late Governor-General of Bengal who had had a mixed reaction to William Palmer's biracial son Fitzjulius. However, the book shows some distancing from the Orientalist paradigm of the Indian male, voiced by Robert Clive in 1772 when he defended his rapacity to the House of Commons. "The inhabitants of Bengal," he told its members, "in inferior positions are servile, mean, submissive.... In superior positions, they are luxurious, effeminate, tyrannical, treacherous, cruel."[63] One of the novel's distinguishing characteristics is the degree of respect and sympathy it evinces for non-British characters. Readers meet an Indian male who is strong and humane as well as gentle; moreover, he seems able to mix with people in England on even terms. Hamilton also takes the important position that love and Christianity demand a woman's concern for her immediate family be extended to people outside it, including those of different races and origins.[64] But the respect that the author has for her Indian characters is, of course, relative.

In accordance with the ideas of the age on improvement through cultivation, Hamilton also speaks up for women's education, but she points out that a Western education focused on the cultivation of showy, ornamental accomplishments, ironically, produces women no better than, and possibly morally worse than, Indian women. According to her, a Western woman's devotion to card playing is a form of "poujah" (Hindi: the act of worshipping the deities).[65] A better goal of education, Hamilton maintains, would be to enable women to use their talents for the good of society, or at least to set their sights higher than on mere husband-catching.

Among the educated and benevolent-minded women of Edinburgh who met socially, had an extensive network of friends and acquaintances, analyzed the latest books, talked about politics, and also had sons in East India Company service, it is hard to imagine that the ideas of *Letters of a Hindoo Rajah* would not have been discussed.[66] Leaving aside the possibility that a boarding school education could make Indians out of Scots girls, Hamilton addressed Helen's concerns in a relatively positive way. In conveying a notion of (male) Indians as humane, the novel could have helped Helen overcome her hostility and resentment toward the Lady in the North. It could also have provided confirmation that her decision to send for Jane was the right one not only for the girl but for herself, establishing that Helen was a loving mother figure and a good Christian. The novel's thoughts on education might have disturbed her a bit. Helen had fretted over her daughters' underwhelming performance in the ornamental aspects of their schooling. They had not come to harm, but if an education in social accomplishments could facilitate the transformation of a Scottish woman into a Hindu idol worshipper, the only half-Scottish Jane was at high risk for regressing to that state. Luckily, Helen had decided that Jane would enter the dressmaking business, in which she would have to present as an amiable, submissive, well-spoken lady if she hoped to have a stream of clients.

When Helen turned her attention to the books by Hamilton on education that she had bought, she would have had a shock. Hamilton's 1801–2 *Letters* neither endorsed the actions she had taken with Jane nor provided a sympathetic, respectful view of Eastern women as mothers. Indeed, it offered a prognosis that oscillated between guarded and hopeless. Helen's experiment was hopeless because history has proved that when a child is taken from her parents at an early age for purposes of education, "the sympathetic affections . . . become extinct." Such a child will grow up with a "tendency to hatred and ill-will, which may continue to rankle in the heart for ever." On the guarded side, Hamilton asserted that it was one's duty to "rescue the children" of "foolish, idle and profligate parents" in order "to make up to them for the neglect they have experienced," but warned it was a fraught enterprise. She pointed out that the children's early neglect rendered "those faculties defective, upon which every species of intellectual improvement ultimately depends."[67] Consequently, their dispositions were bent toward the selfish and the malevolent.

Hamilton would have agreed with John Locke's position, adumbrated in *Some Thoughts Concerning Education*, that the right education might mitigate the consequences of early experiences but could go only so far in effecting positive change. A person damaged by neglect will never be cured or make a full recovery; if treated correctly, however, she might acquire what a modern psychologist would call resilience, that is, the ability to maintain equilibrium for substantial periods.[68] An Emily Lawton outcome would be an unreasonable to expect, but a damaged person who developed or was taught strategies for leading a psychologically healthy life could have a decent future. For Hamilton, everything hinged on the nature of the attention a child received from her mother very early in life. Thus, a child who in later life is fearful, confused, cruel, selfish, malevolent, self-willed, bitter, angry, sullen, proud, slothful, resentful, or obstinate, or who manifests a combination of these passions, is the product of a mother who didn't pay proper attention to her in her earliest years.

According to Hamilton, among the women who make the worst mothers, either because they neglect or indulge their children, were Eastern women. Unfortunately, the authority she turned to for knowledge of Eastern women was John Milton, whose lines from book 11 of *Paradise Lost* (1667) characterizing the Oriental female as "empty of all good, wherein consists / Women's domestic honour and chief praise" she quotes in *Letters on the Elementary Principles of Education*.[69] Expounding along those lines, she calls Eastern women "degraded."[70]

"Degraded" was a term much used later in the nineteenth century by Scottish missionaries to India, for whom it connoted cruel, victimizing practices that Indian women were subjected to. Those included *sati*, or immolation of a widow along with her husband's corpse; child marriage; concubinage; and a life as a slave to men's sexual appetites or as a domestic drudge living in poverty.[71] However, Indian women could be lifted from their degradation through Christianity as it was not commonly practiced back in Scotland. Forgetting about the high number of irregular unions and illegitimate births there, the missionaries painted marriage in Scotland as a state where chastity and fidelity prevailed and wives—despite much evidence in the kirk session and court records of marriages terminating in separation and divorce occasioned by adultery and abuse—were construed as helpmates, partners, companions, and comforters.[72]

Hamilton's understanding of "degraded" was quite different. She saw Eastern women as victimizers of the young, writing that moral depravity, sloth, ignorance, pride, and self-importance as well as "every species of corruption become the inheritance of children committed to their care."[73] Consequently, there was only a "very small chance" that a European school education could rectify any child's "wayward humours" or extirpate the biological mother's "baleful influence on [her] moral character."[74] By the end of the second volume of her *Letters on the Elementary Principles*, even that hope is gone. Her conclusion is that "the education of the heart is the work of domestic life, and where this preliminary is neglected, all the endeavours of the school-master will be fruitless."[75]

Hamilton's slightly later *Letters Addressed to the Daughter of a Nobleman* (1806) was a little less pessimistic, offering a possible solution to the challenge posed by the child who had either received no attention or too much of the wrong kind. In this book, Hamilton opines that if such a child applies herself, she might make up for her deficits. For that to happen, however, the person in loco parentis needs to make the child both cognizant of her faults and capable of overcoming them. Hamilton identifies two figures who could function in this capacity. One is a "grandmamma, a lady of great age and experience, and of excellent good sense, and who, notwithstanding her extreme fondness for her grandchild, sees and points out her faults." The second is a governess who with "disinterested zeal" and "undivided attention" promotes the moral and religious development of the child so that over time she conquers "the wayward inclination to disobedience," deals constructively with disappointment, learns to appreciate the value of self-denial and the "wholesome discipline of restraint," and "attain[s] a complete control over every passion."[76]

Hamilton's qualifier "disinterested" is noteworthy in that it implicitly references Robert Burton's early seventeenth-century *Anatomy of Melancholy*, in which he placed zeal, along with anger (defined as the desire for revenge), hatred (defined as inveterate anger), and what we call schadenfreude among the bad inclinations conducive, at the very least, to savage indignation.[77] A favorite of Samuel Johnson, in 1800 Burton's tome was in its ninth edition, and it is likely that the well-read Hamilton was familiar with it. By adjectivally modifying "zeal," Hamilton suggested that under certain circumstances, as when it wasn't personal, when it wasn't focused on an individual, zeal could be a fountainhead of positive transformative energy.

The anonymous reviewer of Calcutta's early educational establishments was convinced that the children placed in these schools were neglected in every way except the physical. Since the proprietors' one purpose was to provide them with a steady stream of income, they made no effort to foster their pupils' moral and emotional development into sympathetic, generous, amiable, equable, obedient, disciplined, reflective, and self-controlled people. It seems probable that Jane had been at such a school. If Hamilton was right, any attempt to extirpate her assumed malignant passions—pride, resentment, stubbornness, sullenness, bitterness, anger, etc.—and imbue her with good qualities at this late stage would have little expectation of success. On the other hand, if a child who had been neglected was provided the right support, by a fond but critical grandmamma, or by a governess whose zeal was disinterested and attention to the moral development of the child steady, the child's deficits might be remedied. If grandmother and governess shared the commitment to improvement through constructive discipline, it was just possible that the experiment in retraining could work. Of course, as Hamilton pointed out, the child had to apply herself to the task: she must "conquer the wayward inclination to disobedience" and "acquire a habit of self-control."[78]

Much could go wrong when breeding wayward humors out of a child. If a teacher didn't understand the disposition of a student or was herself self-centered and lacking in empathy, or zealous as Burton defined the passion, she would cause further damage. In *Letters Addressed to the Daughter of a Nobleman*, Hamilton warned, for example, that children with "ardent feelings" were prone to experiencing "the keenest misery" if separated from "the objects of their tenderness . . . that had called forth the fondness of the heart."[79] Caught up in her own misery, such a child would be impervious to all efforts to improve her. The worst thing a teacher could do in that trying situation would be to discipline the unhappy child harshly. Hamilton counseled self-reflection. If a teacher did not first practice self-reflection, "cautiously examin[ing] her own opinions and carefully distinguish[ing] between those which have received the sanction of reason and judgment, and such as have been implicitly adopted from the family of prejudice . . . reflect[ing] upon the motives . . . and on the tempers and dispositions of her own mind," she could be "guilty of inflicting a wound in [a child's] bosom," further injuring an already wounded soul.[80] As we shall see, Hamilton's words on the psychology of a child with an ardent temperament described the behavior of Jane Cumming and the effect of Jane Pirie on her.

Hamilton offered no guarantees, and Helen, who had been involved in decision-making at Altyre, knew that some breeding experiments could only be described as costly mistakes. Despite the evidence of the steer that had to be slaughtered, the failure of East India Company service to turn George into a responsible man, and Charlotte's death at boarding school, Helen was willing to take a risk again. She had done research. Hamilton was skeptical, but Helen could cull from her books hope and expectations, positive ideas, and a set of conditions and procedures. Helen was, by nature and nurture, ardent, hopeful, imperious, and self-confident. She was desirous to help a child victim, and disposed to believe in the ameliorating powers of education. Once she had accepted Miss Charles's assessment of Jane as an innocent, amiable, and upright child, Helen scrapped the idea of her granddaughter entering the apparel business. She decided that, the stigma of her birth and tinge of her complexion notwithstanding, Jane would "be introduced into the world as a daughter of the family."[81]

Helen was raising the ante. Would it be possible to breed out of her half-Indian granddaughter any (as yet invisible) traces of her mother's (maybe nonexistent) artful and evil-intentioned nature, and retrain her out of any (as yet invisible) lascivious sexual notions and behaviors and disgraceful values impressed on her in Calcutta, through an education in the polite arts? Helen decided that Jane should be treated just as her own daughters had been, receiving the same kind of boarding school education, with the same future in view. After two years at such an establishment, Jane would be introduced to polite society. Helen did not specify when that introduction would take place, but if Jane was born about the end of 1795 or beginning of 1796, she would reach her majority sometime in 1817, after which marriage would follow. But before she could be introduced to society, let alone marry, there were educational steps to be mastered.

Implementing Hamilton's precepts, Helen made it clear to Jane that if she didn't apply herself during the two years at school, if she showed signs of disobedience or lack of self-control, she would be "return[ed] to her original destination," meaning that she could yet become a mantua maker or milliner.[82] According to Helen, Jane understood the stakes and accepted the terms of the agreement.

Basically, Helen was conducting an experiment to test the effectiveness of a particular kind of education in reforming her biracial granddaughter. She knew that environmental interventions could go wrong, but she hoped this particular one would extirpate Asiatic "degradation" and replace it with Western, specifically Scottish, goodness. But she also made it clear to Jane that her future lay essentially in her own hands. The future she got, dressmaking or gentry marriage, depended on how she applied herself at school to the business of self-improvement. It was, as Elizabeth Hamilton would have said, not so much about the acquisition of refinement and social accomplishments as about how well she accepted discipline and living under obedience to school rules and authority figures, and acquiring self-control over such wayward passions as might be deeply rooted in her.

The last payment the Gordonstoun factor made to Miss Charles for Jane's board and education in Elgin, covering the period November 1808 through May 1809, was on June 22, 1809. Jane would have been about fourteen at this point, an adolescent going through that stage in life when even properly brought up children can exhibit some of the extreme behaviors Hamilton associated with children neglected from infancy onwards. However, there is no evidence that the adolescent girl whom Helen brought to Edinburgh in late 1810 was willful, stubborn, disobedient, angry, mendacious, malicious, accusatory, jealous, defiant, aggressive, overly sensitive, insecure, confused, bitter, or vengeful, or, despite being well-developed physically, that she was manifesting an unseemly interest in sex.

According to Helen, Jane had no regrets about leaving Elgin and Miss Charles's establishment after six years there. Indeed, she was quite excited in November 1810 because she was about to embark on the next, and critically necessary, stage of her journey toward social acceptance as a lady of an illustrious Highland family.

The Old Town of Edinburgh sits high on a hill. Its main thoroughfare is the High Street, also known as the Royal Mile, connecting Edinburgh Castle and the Palace of Holyroodhouse. Off the High Street are steep narrow lanes and gated alleyways; Jane Pirie grew up in one of these. Topography prevented the city from sprawling, so it grew vertically, with multistory apartment houses lining the High Street. Below the hill was a polluted and smelly body of water known as the North Loch (Scots: lake). The city fathers, realizing that the loch was loathsome and the Old Town congested, decided that a new Edinburgh needed to be built. The draining of the loch began in 1759. In 1767 James Craig won a design competition for a new town, to be constructed down the hill and across the loch. A bridge connecting the High Street with Princes Street on the "new town" side of the loch was built. A map published in 1768 shows a street plan in which two end squares are joined by a straight street, with equally straight streets running parallel to it. Streets running vertically divided these straight streets into uniform blocks. Each end square was to have its own church. Other areas, such as Leith Street, where Marianne Woods grew up, would be developed along similar rational principles, but these planned streets ending in the two squares would become the heart of Edinburgh's New Town.

The western square, later renamed Charlotte Square, would become one of the most valuable pieces of real estate in Edinburgh. Initially, construction in the neighborhood proceeded slowly because of the Napoleonic wars, but once the threat of invasion receded, the market for houses improved. Spacious, elegant stone residences with neoclassical lines were rising on the square's west side by 1803 and on the east side by 1810. Helen had been settled at her residence, No. 22, by 1807, but construction continued all around her. Jane's new school was a short walk away, in Drumsheugh.[83]

The seminary Helen chose for her granddaughter was Mrs. and Miss Woods Boarding School, a very new school, having opened on Whitsunday (May 15) that year of 1809.[84] Drumsheugh is the older name for Queensferry, one of Edinburgh's arterial roads, as well as the general name for the area just to the southwest of Charlotte Square. The school itself occupied a long, narrow house, about 60 feet by 14 feet. It was a two-story structure with a sunken story or basement as well, faced south, and had a small, roughly triangular garden in front. A house of such proportions and with such an orientation just off the Drumsheugh road, is clearly visible on Ainslie's 1804 town plan, "*View: Old and New Town of Edinburgh and Leith and with the proposed docks.*"[85] It was only a short walk from Helen's town residence.[86]

Despite its official name, the school was owned and run by Miss Marianne Woods, a teacher who had trained in London, and her friend Miss Jane Pirie, who had considerable experience as a governess and provided the start-up money for the venture. The Mrs. Woods in the school's name was Marianne's aunt Ann Woods, who had spent over £160 (more than

$15,300) of Pirie's savings on quality items that would bespeak the genteel character of the establishment.

To make the school seem homelike, Mrs. Woods had bought such items as chairs, fire irons, plates, dishes, tea jugs, wineglasses, soup plates, and a looking glass. The living room was furnished with a sofa and a piano.[87] In addition to making the school cozy, the outwardly familial character was supposed to mirror the relations obtaining in the ideal family, where the children were treated as "members of one family . . . governed by the same rules . . . treated with equal attention" by the teachers who stood in the place of parents to them.[88] Money was also spent on educational items. The globes from which the students would learn geography came from London. Two pairs of dumbbells and two drawing stands, plus an atlas and books deemed delightful and instructive for young persons of quality, were also purchased.

The books included Mrs. Trimmer's *Sacred History*, Hort's *Mythology*, and Paley's *Natural Theology; or Evidences of the Existence and Attributes of the Deity*. While it is unlikely that William Paley's treatise would have been taught to girls who ranged between the ages of eight and sixteen or so, the other two choices speak to the teachers' informed conservative pedagogical values and teaching style. Sarah Trimmer's *Sacred History* was a multivolume collection of Biblical passages whose subtitle, "Annotations and reflections particularly calculated to facilitate the study of the Holy Scriptures in schools and families," set forth its purpose. These "annotations and reflections" were geared to young people's comprehension. The passages were selective (none had explicit sexual content), and the explications and commentary stressed respect for authority, particularly in times of trouble. Since they grew out of material Mrs. Trimmer had developed to inculcate religious knowledge and belief and, most importantly, religious understanding in her own children, the author herself became an object lesson in how the good mother behaves, carries out her responsibilities, and uses her influence and power.[89]

William Hort's *Mythology* was a compilation of classical mythology in question and answer format. Another useful if not delightful purchase was Dr. R. Gray's widely used *Memoria Technica*, which offered a system for memorizing historical dates and figures. Compared with the amount spent on the domestic furnishings, the school's educational expenditures were light.

This domestic model was typical of English boarding schools for girls in the early nineteenth century, but Woods-Pirie's emphasis on strict adherence to rules, a daily regimen of highly structured and supervised activities with a heavy dose of religious instruction, and close oversight to safeguard the girls' virginity, suggests that it also resembled a French boarding school, itself derived from the European convent model.[90] The use of books like Hort's *Mythology* and the *Memoria Technica* indicates that learning was by rote.

The day was full, with no time wasted, leaving the girls few moments free or alone. To teach compliance and submission to a higher authority, religious instruction in the form of daily prayers and reading of Scripture framed the day. During breakfast, the pupils recited their lessons. The writing-master came at nine and left at ten; one of the teachers was always present while he was teaching. At one, the girls were taken for a walk by Jane Pirie, and during their time outdoors got part of their geography lesson; they may have walked as far as the Water of Leith. Dinner was served at two.

Then the Misses Woods and Pirie sat with their scholars and worked with them individually. Miss Pirie was particularly concerned with the girls' religious education, and once, when worried about a pupil's lack of understanding, turned to Elizabeth Hamilton for advice. The girls also practiced music during this period. On some days the dancing master came in after dinner. Until eight or nine p.m., the two teachers "were constantly employed in severally teaching the different branches of education to the young ladies."[91] Before the nightly reading from Scripture, the girls played with dumbbells for a short while, presumably under supervision.

The girls' sleeping arrangements were tight and there wasn't much privacy. The teachers functioned as superintendents in the bedrooms to make sure pupils did not engage in sexual experimentation. Woods and Pirie also read the girls' letters before posting them. On Sundays Miss Woods took the Episcopalian girls to church while Miss Pirie chaperoned the Church of Scotland girls to their house of worship. The week before Jane was confirmed, she was taken to the Melville Street house of Bishop Daniel Sandford for tea.

Elizabeth Fletcher had noted that at her boarding school, in addition to all the other "negative evils" she encountered, she was unfortunate enough to have "as daily associates some girls of thoroughly depraved character"; unfortunately for us, she did not mention what the girls did to earn them this dubious distinction.[92] No doubt aware that they could unknowingly enroll "girls of thoroughly depraved character," Woods and Pirie strove to nip in the bud bad behaviors they saw their pupils exhibiting. Discipline at Drumsheugh was formally codified in a book that set down the penalties for infractions and the penalties for them. This book has not survived, but we know from the case proceedings its penalties were psychological rather than physical, and strictly enforced.

A student who didn't follow the rules was in some way disgraced, singled out, ostracized, made to sit apart, or given an extra task that cut into recreation time. A girl who talked during the lesson got a noise card and one who broke a rule might get a decorum card or be made to sit separately at a "disgrace table" at mealtimes. Sometimes pupils were scolded. Jane's classmate Janet Munro was given a substantial number of lines to learn from *A New History of England; from the Earliest Period of The Present Time*.[93] But students were not locked in a room, or starved, or forced to eat something unpalatable.

The girls at the Woods-Pirie School may well have chafed at the tight supervision, the emphasis on memorization and regurgitation, the religious indoctrination, and the "discipline and punish" philosophy. Looking back on her years at Manor House, Elizabeth Fletcher found the approach counterproductive:

> During the four years I was at [Manor House], two chapters of the Bible were read every morning by two of the young ladies as a reading lesson. Prayers were regularly drawled out by the husband of our governess, a choleric old man, who thumped our fingers so often for bad writing, with his mahogany ferrule, that we listened to his prayers with any feelings but those of love or devotion. I do not remember to have received a single religious impression at this school, though creeds were repeated, and catechisms taught, and all the formalities of religious service regularly performed.[94]

From Helen's perspective, the Woods-Pirie School was the perfect one for her granddaughter. The religious instruction would inculcate the bedrock values of marriage: obedience and submission. The secular curriculum would teach Jane all the accomplishments that defined a gentlewoman and made her an adornment. An outside French instructor would not impart lewd notions because the subject was being taught by the regular teachers, two women deeply concerned for the spiritual well-being of their pupils. The strict regimen, constant surveillance, and system of punishments would have allayed any anxieties Helen had about Jane being an adolescent who might have been educated by women "bred only and completed to the taste of lustful appetence," as John Milton said, and possibly exposed to sexual practices during her formative years in India or on the ship coming to Britain.[95] The Misses Woods and Pirie also had a solution to the problem posed by bedsharing.

The teacher-partners were exemplars of organization. The innovations of dumbbells and outdoor lessons suggested that they were familiar with Erasmus Darwin's 1798 treatise *A Plan for the Conduct of Female Education*, in which he argued that a little physical exercise would produce healthy girls. And the use of psychological rather than physical punishment to achieve compliance seemed to show that the teachers were progressive and understood how to correct behavior through the good use of authority.

The person who convinced Helen to choose the school was Margaret Ferguson (née Pirie), formerly governess to the Misses Dunbar, the daughters of Helen's eldest daughter—and underneath Margaret's extolling of the school was desperation. Jane Pirie was her sister, and five months after opening, the school in which Jane had invested her savings was not doing well. The problem was that the school had only two pupils before Helen materialized. Bankruptcy loomed.

Helen responded to distress, but Margaret had a supremely persuasive piece of information that she no doubt shared with Helen—namely, that around 1804 her sister had been chosen by Elizabeth Hamilton to work as governess "under her direction" and had served in that capacity for six months.[96] Once Helen knew Jane Pirie was a protégé of Elizabeth Hamilton she could not doubt the quality of the moral education her granddaughter would receive at the new boarding school. No one could be more expert than a teacher trained by Hamilton in dealing with a girl with Jane's history. It was as if the grandmamma had found the perfect governess to bring the breeding experiment to a successful conclusion. Helen was sure Jane would apply herself, since the girl had promised and knew a golden future awaited her if she behaved well.

Had Helen done more investigating, she might not have chosen this particular school. Though Hamilton was highly respected, her desire to foster the ambition of young, single women who wanted to earn their own living by teaching sometimes clouded her judgment.

Living not far from Helen's residence in Edinburgh was Elizabeth Dawson Fletcher, who was a friend and admirer of Elizabeth Hamilton, and highly critical of her own boarding school education. Mrs. Fletcher had recently moved to the house at 51 North Castle Street house because it had a "larger back green as play ground" for her children.[97] Around 1804, Fletcher, needing a governess for her daughters, had turned to Hamilton for advice. Hamilton strongly recommended a Miss Rattray. As Fletcher recounts in her autobiography, Miss Rattray was "truthful, pious, considerate of the poor, and very industrious." But she also had "a sternness and want of sympathy, a harshness of nature which made the schoolhouse irksome, and which was alike unfavourable to the temper and happiness of my daughters."

In later life, Fletcher realized that "it was a great mistake to inflict on them [the daughters] this unnecessary discipline" and "bitterly regretted" tolerating a governess who made her children so unhappy.[98] It is possible Mrs. Fletcher chose, out of embarrassment, or to avoid sullying Mrs. Hamilton's reputation or straining her relationship with her esteemed friend, to keep silent about Miss Rattray. But stories had a way of spreading in Edinburgh.

If the story about the bad recommendation came to Helen's attention, she chose not to factor it into her decision to send Jane to a boarding school co-owned and -run by another of Hamilton's protégées. Certainly Mrs. Hamilton engaged in a bit of cover-up at this time. When other parents asked her about Jane Pirie, she did not tell them what she would reluctantly admit two years later: that Pirie was pious, industrious, stern, harsh by nature, and wanting in sympathy, not to mention, possessed of a temper.

Placing Jane at the school was not that easy. Even though Margaret Pirie had recommended the establishment, Marianne Woods and Jane Pirie "hesitated to receive" Jane as a pupil because she was illegitimate and "a girl of colour."[99] The first objection was minor, and Helen countered the display of racist sentiment in the second by haughtily reminding the teachers that she was not only placing Jane at the school but two other granddaughters, Jane's first cousins the Dunbar girls, so she was doing the near-bankrupt teachers a "favor of the greatest magnitude." Woods gave in gracefully; Pirie had to be "induced to receive her."[100] Their initial denial of admission to Jane Cumming on racial grounds may be seen as an aborted attempt to prevent depravity from taking root at their establishment.

Jane joined the school as a boarder in December 1809. The Dunbar cousins joined shortly thereafter, but as day-scholars. Though Jane had been received with reservations, Helen was satisfied with the arrangement, which would give Jane the same kind of education as her lawful cousins yet keep her at a distance, a reminder that she was not yet equal to them.

In her short time at the school, Jane was an academically unremarkable student who was more often than not in her teachers' bad books. She got many scoldings from her teachers, often over trivial matters: for neglecting to put all her dirty things in the laundry bag for the washerwoman, for forgetting her gloves in the schoolroom, for leaving the school without telling a teacher she was going to take tea with her aunt Louisa Forbes, for inferior recitation of the French catechism. She was threatened with expulsion for taking an unauthorized walk around Castlehill one Sunday evening; both teachers were so upset with her after she returned that they told her "she would never sleep another night at Drumsheugh, if the same happened again."[101]

Miss Pirie never overcame her antipathy to Jane, and her rebukes were more in the nature of verbal lacerations. The tongue lashings put Jane in a "perpetual state of subjection and humiliation," and she started to manifest many of the malignant passions and refractory behaviors that Elizabeth Hamilton identified.[102]

Helen repaid the teachers further for admitting Jane by pressuring a number of parents or caregivers she knew to send their girls as well. Before placing them at the school, some of these people made inquiries about the teachers. Once they received a "satisfactory account" from Elizabeth Hamilton of Jane Pirie, they followed Helen's example.[103] All told, Helen was responsible for the addition of seven or eight pupils to the school. Thanks to her, the foundering school was now such a thriving concern that the teachers expected more boarders and day pupils to enroll.

Helen had rescued Jane and given her an education in Elgin with the woman who had educated her own daughters. By her own account, she had visited her whenever she was in Elgin, made her feel welcome at Altyre during the school holidays, and grown fond of her. She had broken down the resistance of Woods and Pirie to Jane's admission as a pupil. Her granddaughter was now receiving the kind of schooling that would stamp her as a well-bred gentlewoman and give her the knowledge, accomplishments, values, and manners she needed to be introduced to society as a scion of an old family.

From Helen's perspective, she had done all she could to help Jane; now everything rested with Jane. If Hamilton was right, what was required of Jane in this final stage of the breeding experiment was attention, application, self-discipline, and obedience. These were (and are) difficult to achieve at the best of times, particularly for an adolescent, but Helen believed that the future she held out was the stimulus Jane needed. What was required of Jane's teachers was disinterested zeal and close attention to her social, moral, and religious development, but that Woods and Pirie possessed these qualities Helen was certain. Helen's touting of the school in the circle of gentry families she knew proved she entertained the highest regard for the teachers with whom she had placed her three granddaughters.

Then Helen did something out of character. Satisfied that Jane was "as safe under their protection as her own," in May 1810 she left Edinburgh for Altyre—and Jane with her teachers for the summer holidays.[104] Before departing, Helen appointed her daughter Louisa Forbes Jane's local guardian during her absence. Despite having received a boarding school education in London, Louisa was unpretentious and unaffected. A mother of three and pregnant with a fourth, she was familiar with children. With her daughter and the teachers watching Jane, Helen felt sure nothing bad would befall the girl. Though Helen had never boarded her own children with their teachers during their summer holidays and Jane had always spent her summers at Altyre before, it now seemed to Helen that this kind of loving was good enough. Helen would not return to Edinburgh until November, six months later.

Chapter Three

EDUCATING JANE (2)

Marianne Woods was born in London in 1781 to George Woods, a successful merchant tailor, and his wife, Hannah. George and Hannah had two other children, Martha and William. Martha married George Tindall, an engraver who became well-to-do. William, later Sir William, had an illustrious career at the College of Arms, which deals with all matters of heraldry, and whose officers are appointed by the sovereign, William always maintained that his biological father was Charles Howard, 11th Duke of Norfolk, and his appointment to the College of Arms suggests that he was right.

The Woods's marriage may have been damaged by Hannah's extramarital affair, for while her siblings stayed in London, Marianne was sent to Edinburgh when she was about seven and a half—approximately the same age that Jane was when sent from India to Altyre—to be brought up by her paternal uncle William Woods and his wife, Ann. William Woods was an extremely popular actor on the Edinburgh stage who in 1800, when past his prime, commanded the top salary of two guineas a week. The three must have lived comfortably, for the *Edinburgh and Leith Directory to July 1801* lists William Woods as occupying one of the new terraced houses on Leith Street, like Charlotte Square, a New Town development.[1]

Elizabeth Hamilton would have approved of the upbringing Marianne received from her second parents. Aunt and uncle took it upon themselves to instill moral principles in their niece so she would grow up "well-disposed and well-principled."[2] So that she would be able to live by her own means, she was taught skills and social accomplishments. Her uncle "spent many hours a day with her, in reading with her and pointing out the beauties of the English language, so as to qualify her for earning her own bread as a teacher or governess"; as she grew older, she assisted him "in teaching reading and elocution to private pupils."[3] Subsequently, with her uncle's approval, she began teaching on her own. Despite William Woods's connection with the stage, she "was not permitted to frequent the theatre." The result of this model upbringing was that she was adjudged a "remarkably modest, well-behaved young woman."[4]

Marianne was rather plain in appearance but seems to have had a self-deprecating sense of humor. In August 1810, after spending time at the seaside town of Portobello outside Edinburgh, she described herself to her London-based sister Martha as "black and yellow as an old boiled bean, and as thin as an empty purse."[5]

Elocution lessons had been wildly popular in Edinburgh since the middle of the eighteenth century, when the Irishman Thomas Sheridan not only lectured to the men and women of the city on the connection between "court" pronunciation and gentility but offered elocution lessons to reduce their accents.[6] Two residents who did not buy into this were John Clerk, the teachers' future brilliant, fiery lead lawyer, who spoke with a strong Scottish accent, and Louisa Forbes, who took pride in her Scotticisms.[7] Many others, however, felt that accent reduction was essential. Tradespeople who wanted to attract an affluent clientele and aspiring but self-conscious elites flocked to the lessons offered by Sheridan's successors, or sent their children. The hope was that these lessons would not only "facilitate their reading, writing and speaking the English language, with elegance and propriety" but also "eradicate vulgar prejudices and rusticity of manners, improve the understanding, rectify the will, purify the passions, [and] direct the minds of youth to the pursuit of proper objects."[8]

As a Londoner by birth and the niece of Edinburgh's popular actor, Marianne Woods would have been much in demand as an elocution teacher. She charged two guineas for a course of twelve lessons, a moderately high fee that reflected her talent and reputation as well as the solid economic status of her clients. As an elocution teacher, however, she lived her life on a treadmill, working twelve-hour days in order to stay in place. There might well have been anxious periods, too, if a client was slow in paying or there were no clients. When her uncle died in 1802 and left his entire moveable estate to her father, money became an issue, as she now had to support herself and her aunt. To improve her marketability, in 1802 she took a drawing class in Edinburgh with a Mr. Dallaway, as well as lessons in Latin. She made a little money giving private lessons in reading aloud to Jane Pirie, who was also in the art and the Latin classes.

Jane Pirie was from the middle class. Her mother was a surgeon's daughter while her father was a writer (Scots: lawyer).[9] James Pirie's sister owned an apartment in nearby Gladstone's Land, a seventeenth-century tenement, now a tourist attraction and then home to wealthy tenants, but her own family lived nearby in Lady Stair's Close (Scots: gated alleyway) in the

Old Town, just off the High Street. The address suggests the fiscal health and social respectability of the Piries, for in the late eighteenth century the descendants of Lady Elizabeth, Dowager Countess of Stair, lived in the close as well, in an elegant townhouse built in 1622. Jane knew, however, that after her father died, she would have to support herself. Jane seems to have been close to her younger sister Margaret, who, before her marriage to Thomas Ferguson, a writer in Glasgow, served as governess to the Misses Dunbar, the daughters of Helen's eldest daughter and namesake, and had acquitted herself well. Born in 1779, so a shade older than Marianne, Jane also "determined to go into the profession of a governess," so as to be financially independent.[10]

Like Marianne, Jane was plain in appearance. By the time she was in her late twenties, she was already afflicted with rheumatism. If her irascible disposition was not caused by the back pain she endured, the pain may have made her crosser and more snappish. Unlike the well-behaved Marianne, who was blessed with a sense of humor, Jane Pirie was high-strung and easily provoked. Trifles agitated her, and she worried them obsessively.

Mrs. Helen Campbell, a former employer who had the highest regard for Miss Pirie as a teacher, said she had an "ardent temper." When aroused, she "express[ed] herself with a keenness that every woman had better let alone." Whenever the governess's temper was in the ascendant, Mrs. Campbell did all she could to prevent her girls from "imbibing any of it."[11] Thus, Jane Pirie was not only lacking in the gracious manners and self-control that characterized the well-bred woman; her conduct was considered unwomanly. Even though Mrs. Campbell respected Pirie's dedication and declared that her wards improved under her tutelage, she also declared that when upset, Pirie's behavior set an example so bad that it posed a threat to the well-being of other females. Elizabeth Hamilton, author of many books on educating children and also, briefly, Jane Pirie's employer, once wrote that people who are guided strongly by their emotions have "ardent likings and . . . hatreds [that] are not always free from malignity," and as we shall see, this description fits her well (and also Jane Cumming, but that is to get ahead of the story).[12]

Despite her fierce temper, Jane Pirie was able to focus on professional advancement. She took the art and Latin classes that Marianne was also attending, and then she took classes and private lessons with Marianne to improve her oral reading skills, presumably to reduce her Scottish accent. Marianne seems to have regarded Jane as a friend, though she was not averse to kissing, cuddling with, and fondling her. But if Jane's taking lessons from Marianne is a bellwether, from the outset Jane's feelings were those of a smitten lover toward a beloved she had placed on a high pedestal. She told Elizabeth Hamilton in 1810 that she had "loved [Marianne] for eight years with sincere and ardent affection . . . contemplate[d] her as the model of every virtue," and would never have been able to "conquer" her affection even if Marianne had spurned her.[13]

The two friends, both in their twenties, seem to have decided around 1802 that running a boarding school for young ladies was a better way to achieve financial stability than governessing. They felt that school administration would require "far less labour" and produce "comparatively little anxiety."[14] Once they were more credentialed, they would jointly open a boarding school. To prepare herself for such a future, Marianne Woods spent 1807–8 in London at the Camden House Boarding School learning about school administration. Jane Pirie picked up a number of well-paid teaching positions with good families and saved her earnings.

It was not unknown in the seventeenth and eighteenth centuries for female friends to go into business together, and a number of those ventures were successful.[15] That said, it was a gamble, just like any other business venture established with a friend. A well-known example of a business between female friends that was sustained by deep affection is that of Elizabeth Carter and Elizabeth Hatchett. These two Elizabeths were married women who operated a pawnbroking business in London about a century before Woods and Pirie opened their school in Edinburgh. A contemporary of the women said the pair "'had a greater love and kindness to and for each other than one sister could have for another.'"[16] Even though their relationship was more meaningful than their marital ties for their emotional well-being, no taint of sexual irregularity ever hovered over them. Despite their attachment, however, the two eventually fell out, with Carter denouncing Hatchett as a thief and bringing a case against her at the Old Bailey.[17]

There is considerable evidence that female relatives, as opposed to female friends, ran educational establishments. Sister-sister and mother-daughter combinations were common.[18] For a while, the Reading Ladies' Boarding School was run by Lydia Bell and her sister or half-sister Sarah Hackett.[19] Mary Wollstonecraft's first romantic friend, Jane Arden, set up a school, which she operated with her sister. Wollstonecraft, her two sisters, and Mary's second romantic friend, Frances Blood, ran a boarding school in Newington Green in north London in the 1780s. Erasmus Darwin wrote his 1798 *Plan for the Conduct of Female Education in Boarding Schools* as a blueprint for the Derbyshire school he set up for his two illegitimate daughters, the Misses Parker, whom he prepared for a teaching career; the school took off and operated for years.

An article titled "Female Boarding Schools" in *The Female Preceptor, Essays on the Duties of the Female Sex, Conducted by a Lady in the Years 1813 and 1814*, lists a number of schools run as a family business, either by two sisters or by a mother and daughter(s), but only three that seem to have been run by people unrelated by blood. There is an establishment in Hungerford, Berkshire, "conducted by Mrs. and Miss Pocock and Miss Price," "a seminary for young ladies . . . in Keynsham, near Bristol . . . established by Mrs. M. Geary, but since her decease . . . conducted by Mrs. Singer and Miss Ford," and a third school in Hickley, Leicestershire, run by the Misses Musson and Bannister. The use of the second "and" in the description of the Pocock-Price school suggests that Miss Price was the equal of the Pococks, but was she friend or family, perhaps a cousin, niece, or stepsister? The description of the school run by Singer and Ford indicates that they took it over after Mrs. Geary's death. Because of the difference in names, it is unlikely that Miss Ford was Mrs. Geary's daughter, though it is possible Mrs. Singer was a married daughter of the late proprietress, which could suggest that the daughter roped in a friend to continue the business. Interestingly, the author of "Female Boarding Schools" is a bit skeptical of Singer and Ford's ability to keep the school going.[20] Of the three schools, the one run by the Misses Musson and Bannister is the most likely to have been run by female friends, but whether they were romantic friends is unknown.

Female boarding schools tended to have a short life span, but Marianne and Jane had high hopes for theirs. If a common vision and work ethic are predictors of business success, Woods and Pirie started off right. As mentioned earlier, to learn about running a school as a business, Woods spent time at the Camden Boarding School in London. Pirie got extremely lucky, for in 1804 or 1805 she came to the attention of Elizabeth Hamilton. Hamilton, who took pleasure in "foster[ing] unprotected talent," particularly that of a woman entering teaching, must have seen potential in her, for when Hamilton accepted the 1804 offer of the Earl of Lucan to supervise the education of his daughter, she chose Jane Pirie as the governess "on whom was to devolve the subordinate office of tuition."[21] Pirie spent six months under Hamilton's direction as they worked to improve the Earl's lovely daughter Lady Elizabeth Bingham—who needed very little improving, since she was, in Hamilton's opinion, "the most amiable and engaging of children" she had ever met.[22]

Jane Pirie's stint with Hamilton gained her entry into gentry households. Mrs. Macdowall Grant, who employed her from 1805 to 1807, commented favorably on her teaching of flower drawing, French, writing, arithmetic, geography, and music to her daughters. Mrs. Grant highlighted the "constant and unwearied exertions for her pupils' instruction and improvement" and the "proper authority" Jane maintained over her children. Pirie's next employer, Mrs. Helen Campbell, called her "the most indefatigable teacher I ever met with."[23] At a time when governesses generally earned no more than £40 per year, Mrs. Campbell paid Pirie £80, or $8,560.

Though Mrs. Campbell rewarded Jane Pirie's efforts to impart skills and accomplishments to her wards, girls ages thirteen and fifteen, she was cognizant of her main character flaw—the "ardent temper" that led her, when provoked, to express herself with unwomanly sharpness. Because she cared for Pirie and respected her strictness and the sense of dedication she brought to improving the girls, Mrs. Campbell tried to correct her governess' violent temper, but made no headway. She was equally unsuccessful in reasoning Jane out of her attachment to Marianne. The descriptors she used for it, "folly" and "nonsense," suggest that she considered it excessive.[24] Perhaps she was implying that there was something nonnormative about her governess's feelings for Woods. But in calling attention to Jane's not even wanting to listen to her employer on the subject, the well-meaning Mrs. Campbell was also pointing to a more common, more "normal," and, in our day and age as well, a greater problem—her stubbornness or inflexibility, a refusal to listen to others.

Despite having chosen her as the governess who would do the actual instructing while she did the supervising of the education of the Earl of Lucan's daughter, Elizabeth Hamilton acknowledged (rather belatedly and awkwardly, under pressure) that she had the same mixed reaction to Jane Pirie. Her "great propriety of moral conduct" was a strength, but Hamilton found fault with her manners ("not of the most polished") and with her manner of instilling knowledge ("too fervent"). By saying that she was possessed of "uncommon zeal to perform her duty to her pupils," she implied that Pirie's zeal, being a form of ego, was anything but disinterested and impersonal.[25] It was of the kind that potentially led to anger, indignation, hatred, malice, and a desire for revenge from the recipient of her zeal.

In mid-May 1809, seven years after Marianne and Jane had met in the art class, their school opened. They had not put anything in writing, but they considered themselves the sole proprietors and schoolmistresses. However, as Jane was still under contract to Mrs. Campbell and would not be released until November and Marianne had her beloved aunt Ann Woods living with her in the house and helping her, the school was readied and opened to students by Marianne and Ann. They would have paid to have it listed in the 1809–10 Edinburgh postal directory as "Mrs. and Miss Woods Boarding School." While "Mrs. and Miss Woods" might have given the impression it was a family-run operation, more maternal and domestic on that account, and aunt and niece might even have rationalized the combination as more likely to attract parents, Jane Pirie was furious when she found out. In return for giving her best friend the start-up capital, that best friend had cut her out of the school's name and put in her aunt's name. Pirie's anger only escalated over time.

The ground floor consisted of a schoolroom, a drawing room, and a small room. The schoolroom was long and had a fireplace. A door separated the schoolroom from the drawing room; its lock was brass and did not have a keyhole. The sofa, the expensive piano, the globes that had come from London—fine items that had been bought with Miss Pirie's money—were placed in the drawing room.

Upstairs, there were three bedrooms, a dressing room, and a closet. Two of the three bedrooms were full of beds placed close together, some no more than a foot or eighteen inches apart. Five boarders were packed into one bedroom and four into the other. Each girl had her own bed, except Jane Cumming, who shared a bed with Jane Pirie, and the last girl to be admitted to the school, Janet Munro, who slept in Miss Woods's bed. Mrs. Woods occupied the third bedroom. As already mentioned, to make sure that the girls did not engage in sexual experimentation, each teacher functioned as a bedroom superintendent. Two servants, one of whom was pregnant, kept the house tidy, a job made somewhat easier because at least one of the beds was on castors.

Giving a school a cozy, domestic look was relatively easy. Keeping discontent and discord out of a school was, however, virtually impossible. Conflict must have been rife at the school Elizabeth Hamilton attended in her youth, for when she returned home for the Christmas holidays, she wrote a poem in which she described her home as "Dear home! Abode of love and heartfelt bliss / Temple of peace, where discord never entered / with jarring note, to untune domestic harmony."[26]

The first jarring note in the domestic harmony of Mrs. and Miss Woods Boarding School sounded when the school was given a name that suggested it was run by the Woods family. The dissonant tones increased in volume and number once Jane Pirie reviewed the accounts, which had been handled by Ann Woods before her arrival. It looked to Pirie as though Mrs. Woods had used Pirie's money to present herself as the proprietor of the school and Pirie as the governess working under her; worse still, it appeared to Jane Pirie that Marianne had gone along with this misrepresentation.

Jane did not hold back in expressing her irritation to Marianne. Today, female friends who run profitable businesses say that a secret to the longevity of their relationship and ventures, in addition to a shared vision, is honesty, even brutal honesty, with each other when differences arise.[27] However, with Woods and Pirie, Jane's venting had the opposite effect, probably because she became extremely agitated and expressed herself too strongly. Her jealousy and resentment of Ann Woods's hold on her niece (or Marianne's attachment to her aunt), and her perception that she and Marianne no longer shared a vision or objective, led the two teachers to quarrel loudly with each other about Mrs. Woods's position at the school within earshot and in sight of the pupils. However, because they still cared for each other, the two would make up afterward like lovers after a spat, kissing, caressing, and fondling each other; one of the pupils noted that "they particularly caressed each other" after a fight.[28] But when pushed to it, Marianne chose the aunt over the ardent friend.

In hindsight, their relationship was doomed to failure because it lacked the all-important characteristic in any relationship between consensually partnering adults: mutuality.[29] By August 1810 Marianne and her aunt were supping together while Jane ate alone in the schoolroom. However, on occasion Jane Pirie would stop at Marianne's bedside on her way back from supper to talk, and when one of them was indisposed, they still rubbed each other's backs.

Feeling deceived as a business partner and spurned as a best friend made Pirie miserable. Even after it was officially arranged that Mrs. Woods would leave the school by Martinmas (November 11) 1810, just six days before her scheduled departure Jane wrote angrily to Elizabeth Hamilton about how her beloved Marianne had attempted to "establish *her* [Ann Woods; italics Jane Pirie's] as head of this concern."[30]

For all that Jane Pirie idolized Marianne and was cursed with an irritable disposition, her sense that the two Woods women were in collusion was not wrong. In a letter Marianne wrote her sister Martha Tindall in September 1810, she mentioned that she and her aunt had rejected an offer that would allow them to "keep the concern themselves and let Miss Pirie go" only because it would make them look bad. As Marianne realized, she and her aunt "would have been charged with reports . . . [that they] had made use of her [Miss Pirie] the first year of school when money was wanted, but as soon as the scheme was becoming profitable, she was turned out" (144).

In early October 1810, unable to tolerate a situation in which she knew she had been double-crossed and was unwanted, Jane told Marianne that she considered herself "selfishly, disrespectfully and unkindly treated" (142) and, against the advice of her sister Margaret Ferguson, proposed that the school be dissolved. However, the document that was drawn up, probably in late October, increased Jane's misery and anger. While it was acknowledged that Mrs. Woods had misrepresented Jane as the governess and herself as the head or mistress of the school, and settled that the school would be dissolved in May 1811, Jane paid a heavy price. Under the terms of the document, Mrs. Woods would "retire with a third of [the] profits" (152). The arrangement dealt Jane Pirie a substantial financial blow without delivering peace of mind.

Nonetheless, as she told Elizabeth Hamilton in that early November letter, even though she believed that Marianne had sacrificed her for her aunt, she was still romantically attached to. On Marianne's birthday in October, Jane gave her a Bible. The book was accompanied by a fervent note that mixes or melds spiritual love for God with unrequited longing for the physical Marianne and a desire for an intimate relationship. "Accept, my beloved, of that Book, which can give consolation in every situation; and dearest *earthly* friend, never open it, without thinking of her, who would forego all friendships, but her God's, to possess yours," Pirie wrote (139). She might not have recognized her sexual desire as such, but identifying with the Bible that can be opened and absorbed, she takes joy in thinking that when Marianne opens the book, it will be as if her special friend, fingers and eyes sanctioned to rove, is exploring her (Pirie's) body. Jane Cumming saw the letter to Hamilton but claimed that she did not read this note. However, for a girl who was considered "officious" (94), meddling with another's papers would not be out of character.

Having Ann Woods there was galling for Jane Pirie, and Jane Cumming's presence was provocative and intensified her distress. Unlike Marianne, who had bowed gracefully to Helen's pressure and came to treat Jane Cumming just as she did the other girls, as part of a family, Pirie's aversion grew. As long as the school was in existence, the two Janes shared a bed, but whenever possible, Pirie "never slept with Miss Cumming when it was in her power to avoid it" (43). On the days when she couldn't avoid it, the maid who made the beds in the morning "observed a considerable swell in the middle, indicating that the two persons had slept at a distance from each other" (106). During the day, the teacher adjured the pupil to turn her face away from her on all occasions. Her prejudicial treatment was so obvious that Marianne had to remind her it could only produce bad results. "All the pupils," she told her, "should be governed by the same rules,—served with the same accommodation,—treated with equal attention, and in every respect taught to consider themselves as members of one family, since discord and discontent must be the consequences of different treatment" (140).

Elizabeth Hamilton had been Pirie's mentor, but her idea that the good teacher goes about her work with "disinterested zeal" had not impressed itself on Miss Pirie's consciousness. Exemplifying overzealousness or "uncommon zeal," Pirie came to pick on Jane Cumming. She herself acknowledged that on one occasion she told Jane, in the presence of the other girls, that "she [Jane] had no heart . . . [or] a bad heart" and that "Miss Cunningham [a classmate] was too good to speak to her."[31] In the school's final three months, Jane Cumming kept a book in which she brooded over Miss Pirie. A humiliated and mortified Jane was obviously burning with anger when she committed her feelings to paper. Those who read the book at the time agreed that she had taken Pirie's remarks to heart; if the teacher's remarks were also tinged with racism, Jane's pain would have been the greater. With becoming understatement, the lawyers all agreed that the "things set down [in the book] evidently indicat[ed] a certain degree of spite towards Miss Pirie in particular."[32]

These scalding scoldings seem to have been at their worst between late September and early November 1810, when Pirie's misery was at its height. So upset was she with Marianne's preference for her aunt that she flailed out in all directions. In addition to attacking Jane Cumming, Pirie proposed the school be dissolved, told Marianne she had made her life a misery, called her "my beloved," vented to her sister Margaret Ferguson, and told Elizabeth Hamilton that no matter what, she would always love and worship Marianne.

The sequence of events strongly implies that the extremely unhappy and lovesick Jane Pirie transferred her frustration, a mixture of emotions such as anger, hostility, jealousy, and wounded, blinding pride, to the girl, showering her with the verbal barbs she could not inflict on the Woods women who were outraging her own feelings and torturing her affections. In essence, Pirie was sacrificing the girl to secure a degree of personal comfort—exactly what she was accusing Marianne of doing to her by favoring her aunt. But Pirie was too wrapped up in herself to see this, or to reflect on Marianne's observation that the pupils should be treated equally, or to realize or care that she could be inflicting deep pain on Jane Cumming. In November, she told one of Helen's daughters she had done nothing to Jane Cumming that might explain why the girl told her grandmother the two teachers had been sleeping with each other—that is, "excepting too rigidly discharging [her] duty and too freely telling her of her faults."[33]

Elizabeth Grant would have understood how the behavior of a Miss Pirie could devastate and negatively transform any girl, particularly one who didn't conform to her expectations. Reflecting as an adult on her personal experiences with teachers who used psychological punishment to enforce compliance, she concluded that the zealous, self-righteous type was the worst; "want[ing] in wisdom," in the name of duty and improvement, they did great harm to the dispositions of sensitive children. Overly assiduous teachers had humiliated her, an emotionally fragile girl, with "unkind cutting rebukes" all because she did not fit in.[34] Such teachers could not understand that underneath the badly behaved girl might be an unhappy one, separated from those she held dear, and about whom they knew nothing. Their rebukes turned shy, high-strung, or ardent children into sly, sullen, insolent ones.

Grant concluded that these teachers' inability to enter into the feelings of their pupils planted and nurtured "seeds of evil" within such girls that ineluctably "grew to bear their bitter fruit."[35] The "bitter fruit" might lead them to commit suicide or take the form of physical aggressiveness; it might also be reflected in a personality change. Elizabeth remarked that under the tutelage of such teachers she herself, a loved child with beloved siblings from a loving family, became stealthy, withdrawn, and mendacious.

Elizabeth subsequently had a sensitive governess well suited to her, in the form of the soothing and encouraging Annie Grant, and recovered from the teacher-induced psychological damage, but her conclusions were to prove only too true for her transplanted contemporary Jane Cumming. Jane was already familiar with instability, loss, emotional distancing, and institutional consignment before she was placed in the Woods-Pirie School, where she encountered two teachers, each, in different ways, unwise, and together, so openly affectionate (when they weren't fighting) that they inflamed her adolescent imagination. Within a year of her admission to Woods-Pirie, she became a bully, a sexual aggressor, a ringleader, a hate-filled plotter seeking revenge, the fabricator of a salacious story.

But from December 1809, when she joined the school, through May 1810, the period when Helen was still in Edinburgh, Jane did not find the school's conservative ethos, or the teachers' strictly enforced set of humiliating chastisements, or even Miss Pirie's undisguised race hatred, bothersome, or at least that is what she claimed some months later. Whether or not we give credence to this claim, Helen's decision to keep Jane with the teachers during the 1810 summer holidays must have come as an unwelcome surprise to the girl. Helen had always sent for her own children, and Jane had always spent time at Altyre when she was boarded in Elgin. But there is evidence of one other occasion on which Helen asked another person to take care of a child who excited her sympathy. As mentioned earlier, instead of taking care of some poor parentless children she had come across, Helen had delegated the responsibility for these "objects of distress" to her sister-in-law Lady Grant. Was Helen saying that, while she cared about Jane, love from a distance was good enough? Were her heart or her intentions toward her granddaughter changing?

So Jane and another "left-behind" pupil, Mary Cunynghame, plus the school servant Charlotte Whiffin, spent the summer holidays of 1810 at Drumsheugh, except for the week, probably in the latter half of July, they all went to the fashionable seaside resort of Portobello on Edinburgh's outskirts. The approximately five-mile journey from the school in New Town to Portobello's High Street would have taken them along Edinburgh's High Street. They would have skirted the fourteenth-century Tolbooth, a multi-story jail. In the past, prisoners had been tortured there; the days of torture were now past, but those presently incarcerated lived in filth. At Holyrood Castle, the road divided, the right fork leading straight into Portobello. It was not a complicated or time-consuming journey; within a few hours, the five of them would have been ensconced at their lodgings, which Jane later described as a bedroom within a drawing room. According to Jane, both rooms had doors that could be locked so those in the bedroom could doubly barricade themselves in for protection from intruders; considering the number of burglaries, attacks, and rapes that took place in lodgings, the two women responsible for three younger women might well have thought an extra lock made their living arrangement safer.[36] The bedroom held a double bed and a cot, the latter positioned at the foot of the double bed.

Portobello, described in 1886 as the "favourite bathing quarter of the citizens" of Edinburgh, was, by the summer of 1810, something of an "it" place, thanks to Sir Walter Scott.[37] In 1801, he had cut quite a figure furiously riding a big black horse along the Portobello sands, racing in and out of the surf. The following year, a kick from the horse curtailed his riding but gave him the opportunity to complete the first canto of *The Lay of the Last Minstrel* in his Portobello lodgings. The poem, published in 1805, was an immediate success. Scott became famous and Portobello developed rapidly. Soon the streets leading directly to the beach were lined with summer cottages. Some belonged to well-to-do Edinburgh families, while others were rented out to those, like the teachers, who could afford a brief change of scenery.

Portobello offered much to see and do in the summer of 1810. On the half-mile-long sandy beach the regiment posted at Musselburgh drilled daily in full tartan regalia. Visitors could gawk at the octagonal folly on Beach Lane known as the Tower. Built in 1785, it had fragments of medieval stone carvings and other incongruous material embedded in its walls.[38] For those who didn't want to sample the bracing waters of the firth (Scots: an inlet of the sea, an estuary) directly, there were the recently completed hot and cold water baths by the beach. Cold though the water was, Miss Woods regretted that she only went into the sea twice during her week in Portobello; back in Edinburgh, her sunburned skin proclaimed she had been on a seaside holiday. The zealous Miss Pirie may well have found pleasure in employing the tower for an on-the-spot history lesson for Jane and Miss Cunynghame. On Sunday she probably took them to the parish church, which had opened that year, but on the whole the teachers allowed their pupils some leeway in Portobello.

Jane later recollected that the teachers sent her and Mary Cunynghame out of the house on a walk multiple times while they stayed behind in the lodgings, and that on returning, the girls found themselves locked out. Security, or a desire for privacy? Some months later, Jane inclined toward the latter explanation. What Miss Cunynghame thought is unknown.

The week in Portobello had momentous consequences for the teachers and Jane Cumming. Without the irritating presence of Ann Woods, Marianne Woods and Jane Pirie apparently reclaimed the trust and the pleasure in each other's company. At night the two shared the double bed. Jane slept in the cot at the foot of the bed. Where the servant and Miss Cunynghame slept is not known.

Despite Wollstonecraft and Chirol's critique of bedsharing at boarding schools, when practiced properly by adult same-sex friends, it connoted their mutual affection, trust, and comfort. Bedsharing could also provide a sense of security. When husbands were absent, fearful wives often sent for a (female) friend to share their bed or requested their maidservants to sleep with them. But as Sasha Handley points out, this consensual bedfellowship was governed by unwritten rules. These rules dictated that the same-sex bedsharers avoid engaging in pillow talk, lest they cross the line separating the emotional from the sexual.[39] In March 1811, eight months later, Jane, now in her mid-teens, recollected that she had been disturbed on a few early mornings by a low, moaning, wet kind of noise and by the teachers' "kissing and speaking and shaking the bed," but that at the time she had not considered any of this indicative of indecent or improper behavior.[40]

There are two inferences we can draw from Jane's subsequent presentation of the teachers as a couple at Portobello. First, what she constructed was a scene in which a couple is engaging in sexual play. Second, Jane described the scene from the viewpoint of the party left out of the action.

The child left with teachers during the holidays is an icon of rejection and abandonment. The despair, anger, bitterness, and loneliness of a boarding school child whose family doesn't want her or him is well documented, as is the child's common externalized response, a display of refractory behaviors.[41] And Jane had a history of separation. If she interpreted Helen's leaving her with the teachers to mean that she was not to consider Altyre her home anymore, the teachers' newfound fondness and happiness in each other's company would have aggravated her misery. If Jane analyzed Helen's decision further, she might infer that her grandmother, in not treating her as she had her own children when school was out, was reneging on her promise to bring Jane out into society as a Cumming girl. Such an inference was not off the mark, for when the case was being reviewed by the Law Lords of the House of Lords in 1816, Helen claimed that she "never intended to bring her out into the world on the same footing as her own daughters."[42] If Jane felt she was being rejected once again, an encumbrance of no account, that could well account for her recollection of the Portobello bedroom as a space in which two people were pleasuring themselves and one was not just left out, but considered of so little significance that the teachers apparently forgot she was there.

It is now accepted that eyewitness testimony is not particularly reliable or accurate from a factual perspective, but Jane's recollection of the teachers' behavior in the bedroom at Portobello and her perception of herself as the outsider, observing but excluded from what was going on, was psychologically real and very intense for Jane. Once school resumed, she was an extremely bad-behaving girl on the outside and a deeply unhappy one on the inside.

The teachers' happiness in each other's company was not to last. Once school started up again, the situation at Drumsheugh declined precipitously. Pirie's nemesis Ann Woods was still there. It had been agreed that she would leave in November, but Marianne was unhappy about it. Bound by duty and affection to Mrs. Woods, Marianne felt that when her aunt left, people would say she had acted cruelly and meanly toward her. Both

Marianne and Jane wrote letters to their sisters in which they confided their unhappiness. In her letter, Marianne said that Jane Pirie was placing her in a false light. Marianne's sister Martha Tindall sympathized with her and advised her to start afresh in London once the school was dissolved. Martha's husband, George, offered his unconditional support to his sister-in-law. "Come to London," he wrote Marianne, "where I doubt not but fortune will smile upon you, and where we shall have an opportunity of proving, more than we can at present, that we are, and ever shall be yours most unfeignedly."[43] Knowing her family supported her, Marianne sent Jane a "break-up" letter in October 1811, about the same time that Pirie sent her the erotically charged birthday note.

On the other side, Jane Pirie's sister Margaret Ferguson counseled her sibling not to be ruled by her emotions. The best way to frustrate Marianne in her attempt to make her partner so miserable that she would leave was "to be steady and stick by the school . . . and for Godsake do not give it up after you are so well established."[44] Jane did not follow her sister's reasonable advice; she proposed that the school be formally dissolved. Marianne agreed to this. The document that was hammered out was a victory for Marianne in that it recognized Ann Woods as equal to her and Jane. Thus Jane would lose a lot of money, since two-thirds of the establishment's assets would go to the Woodses upon the school's dissolution in May 1811. Having been hurt by her own proposal, Jane Pirie was particularly distraught in September and October 1810. The only happy moment appears to have been the birthday party organized for Marianne. The tight controls were briefly lifted that evening when a maidservant entertained the girls and teachers by dressing up as a man.

Portobello had affected Jane Cumming profoundly. The new term found her bullying the younger pupils, on whom she attempted to foist her decorum cards. It also found her longing to attract the attention, or win the affection, of someone nice, caring, and even-keeled in temperament. Jane developed something much more than a schoolgirl crush on Miss Woods, who did not have a wicked temper, treated all the girls equally, and once helped Jane make a card-box.[45] So needy and possessive was Jane in her attachment that she put herself in situations where she could have Marianne's undivided attention and be as physically close to her as possible. Thus, "out of affection," as she said, she was always wanting to hand Marianne "bread, tea &c." She felt "anxious" unless she was walking next to her beloved teacher.[46] In the 1830s, Charlotte Brontë, at that point a teacher in a boarding school, wrote in her journal how much she hated the clinging affection of pupils.[47] Marianne Woods's response was less extreme: She brushed Jane off and called her "selfish."[48]

Undaunted by the criticism, Jane expressed her fondness for Miss Woods more boldly. Miss Woods's bedmate was Janet Munro, and Jane asked if she could sleep with Miss Woods on days Janet was absent from the school. That desire was not granted, so Jane then asked Janet to sleep with her. Munro, who, as Miss Woods's bedmate, stood proxy for her, was pretty, possibly deaf in one ear, not terribly good at her lessons, in the habit of receiving extra lines to learn from the teachers, and the newest girl at the school. Jane, who, being the third pupil to be admitted, had considerable seniority there, probably thought she could bully Janet into acceding to her proposal, but she was mistaken. Janet recognized Jane's proposition as sexual harassment, called her invitation "nonsense," and reported it to Miss Pirie. The gist of her words as recorded in the case proceedings was "that she did not know what to say to Miss Cumming herself, but that she did not want to sleep with her."[49]

Miss Pirie no doubt vetoed Jane's proposal with the sensitivity she was noted for not having at the best of times, and these were the worst of times for the Janes. The teacher must have perceived Jane Cumming's desire to sleep with Marianne as a muscling in, an attempt to displace her as the object of Marianne's affections, and she reacted with a hostility fueled by jealousy that melded with her hatred of Mrs. Woods, who had also, successfully, come between her and Marianne. Totally insensitive to anyone's feelings but her own, filled with a self-justifying pride that she was doing her duty, the rebukes Jane Pirie directed toward Jane Cumming became harsher and more humiliating. At first the girl dealt with her pain by confiding her feelings to a notebook.

Those who read the notebook somewhat later commented on Jane Cumming's temperament, so similar to that of Pirie. Cumming, they said, belonged to that class of people who took things to heart, obsessing over comments that others might brush off, magnifying remarks into affronts mortifying to their pride and self-esteem. Mrs. Hamilton, who would not have read the notebook, would also have understood the dynamic between the two Janes who each wanted Woods for herself. Indeed, she foresaw how it would play out. In 1806 she had theorized in allegorical terms about what would happen when two people, both ardent, both filled with a "relentless propensity to extend the idea of self," came into contact:

> This propensity leads every man to create around himself a sort of circle, which, in imagination, he completely fills and which he perpetually

endeavours to enlarge, by carefully stuffing into it as many objects as he can possibly find means, to appropriate. Pride having once adopted as its own all that has been identified with self, is bound to defend the possessions thus acquired from being intruded on by the pride of his neighbor. When the two circles come near each other, Pride instantly assumes the form of Jealousy. When they come in contact, Pride sends Anger to the post of danger; and if the enemy is so strong as to occasion Fear, Malice mounts perpetual guard.[50]

In Hamilton's allegory, when the self-involved person is threatened, she responds with anger because such is the nature she was born with. Adapting the allegory to the situation at hand, when an individual with such an emotional disposition was a teacher, that person, threatened and fearful of losing something valuable to her, and probably also filled with hate, would strike back. She could hurt a pupil, born with the same temperament, to her core without realizing the damage done. The wound would be even deeper if the person was sensitive and had been separated from the object of her affections. And the ensuing retaliation by the pupil would be vicious and malicious, too, because she had provoked her charge's anger and fear. This is exactly what happened, though because Jane wasn't white, the majority came to conclude that her response stemmed from the type of nurturing she received in India. If the story Jane developed had been the creation of a Scots lass named Jane, in all respects exactly like her except for racial background, the men involved in the case would not have looked into doppelgänger Jane's upbringing. They would have ascribed her behavior to her inborn nature.

Jane's attempt at catharsis was a failure, for by early October 1810 she had made a sexual overture to one classmate and was bullying other classmates and developing a plot to bring both teachers down—Miss Woods for rejecting her attentions, Miss Pirie for her outrageous attacks. She roped in two classmates, Janet Munro and Eliza Christian Stirling, neither of whom liked Miss Pirie. She coached them in the early mornings before breakfast, "in the little garden in front of the house," on the particulars of the teachers' lovemaking. When Janet Munro told her old nurse, Mary Brown, about it, she learned from her that the prevailing sentiment was that women who preferred women as sexual partners were "worse than beasts and deserve to be burnt."[51] Janet subsequently shared this with Jane.

At times, the teachers did stand by the other's bedside at night and talk. Marianne did rub Jane's rheumatic back, and once, when Marianne was feeling unwell, Jane rubbed her back. When they weren't quarreling they were very physically affectionate. Jane Cumming had seen them in bed together during the summer holidays. Though she did not find such behavior improper, she had also learned more recently (or received confirmation) that women who loved women were considered an abomination. Independent of what happened at Portobello, being a female of a certain age she possessed some knowledge about sexual intercourse. She had also most likely read Jane Pirie's erotically worshipful note, from which she could infer Pirie's attachment and sexual neediness and see that Pirie considered herself subordinate to Marianne. If the Woods-Pirie School was anything like Elizabeth Dawson Fletcher's school, perhaps the occasional tidbit of a smutty chapbook, a ribald ballad, a lubricious novel, was smuggled in. Acquaintance with that sort of literature could have provided Jane with the coarse dialogue she subsequently put into the mouths of her proper teachers.

Jane's revenge was also fueled by an adolescent's sexual desire, and frustration and deep unhappiness. Her crush on Miss Woods had been brushed off; Janet Munro had reported her for sexual harassment. Helen had left her with the teachers. Her first cousins the Dunbar girls were going to be leaving the school in mid-November, while she was to be kept another term. Miss Pirie's chastisements were mortifying. Helen's leaving her with the teachers during the holidays suggested to Jane that she was a plaything of her grandmother's caprices. Some years before, the old India hand Captain Williamson had noted that biracial girls often became insecure, anxious, even unhinged, when they realized in adolescence that they were totally dependent on people whose trustworthiness was not to be relied on. In 1810, Jane, in Scotland and now in her teens, seems to have begun experiencing similar feelings, for the same reason. Her account of the holiday at Portobello, which she developed months after the trip took place, reveals that she perceived herself as excluded, irrelevant, an invisible or unwanted presence. To redress the balance, she took what she had intuited about the relationship between the teachers, what her mind reconstructed from what she saw and heard, what she knew or had picked up about sexual congress, and what she fantasized about it. She spun it into a hot tale of lesbian love that would ruin the teachers, force Helen to pay attention to her, reclaim a sense of self-worth, and make herself important.

Set at the Drumsheugh school, the story that Jane Cumming developed was that Marianne Woods, the dominant partner, came into the bed that she shared with Jane Pirie on numerous occasions and had sex with Miss Pirie while she, Jane Cumming, was also in the bed. According to her, they kissed, whispered, touched, panted, and made the bed shake. Woods was the self-controlled and aggressive partner who found satisfaction in toying with Pirie's self-abasing affection and abject sexual neediness. Jane seems to have taken vicarious delight in the sexual power she gave Miss Woods, revenging herself in this way on the woman who was actually being emotionally abusive to her: Miss Pirie. By positioning herself as the unwanted third party in the bed, however, Jane Cumming revealed the depth of her misery—and the truth, that neither of the teachers was paying attention to her needs.

To provide backup for her story, Jane fed it to Eliza Christian Stirling and Janet Munro. Janet was more under Jane's influence; Eliza, a reasonable and cautious girl, counseled her classmate to talk about the teachers' sexual behavior only if were true; but if it were true, Eliza said, she would have nothing to fear from those who heard her. Feeling betrayed by both Helen and Marianne, her sexual desire aroused yet frustrated, maddened by Miss Pirie's treatment, Jane was beyond caring about what would happen to her and the teachers if the story became known. To Eliza, she simply said, "I don't care who hears me"—fighting words, but also those of someone who has lost hope and shouts in desperation.[52]

The end came swiftly. In early November Miss Pirie told Jane, who had been in a fight with Mary Cunynghame over a despised decorum card, that she either had a bad heart or was heartless. Helen returned to Edinburgh on November 9. The Dunbar girls were scheduled to leave two days later, as was Mrs. Woods. On November 12, a clear, crisp day, Jane took leave from the school and went to visit her grandmother, to whom she confided the story about the teachers' congresses. It was a very short distance she had to walk, only 425 feet if she took the diagonal shortcut that went north and east from Drumsheugh and ended at the back of the plot set aside for St. George's Church, just four buildings to the left of 22 Charlotte Square.[53]

Helen was settled at her residence, but Charlotte Square was a construction site. Rubbish was everywhere. As Jane approached Charlotte Square that day, she would have seen workmen on scaffolding using ropes or cables, or operating pulleys and cranes, that carried sheet glass to the top of the building, skilled laborers using the latest technology—tools such as the line gauge, the spirit level, the drafting compass—and less skilled workers clearing away earth and debris. She might have seen ramps for hauling loads up.[54] Though the walk was short, her shoes might have gotten scuffed and the hem of her dress muddied or slightly ripped. What exactly she communicated to Helen is unclear, but Helen understood that the teachers were sexually suspect and that Charlotte the maid and some of the other girls could vouch for the truth of the report.

It was as if one of the panes of glass being hoisted or one of the loads of debris being hauled away had suddenly dropped right in front of Helen. Jane's grandmother was imperious, meddlesome, easily stressed, and perhaps too quickly roused to action, but she was also sincerely concerned with the plight of children, and her reaction to Jane's story was consistent with her disposition. The strictures expressed in Kett's *Emily* about the ruinous consequences of scandal-mongering and acting without self-command seem not to have made an impression on her—or, to be charitable, when presented with this crisis she did not act as rationally as she should have. Convinced of the story's truth on first hearing, Helen determined at once to withdraw Jane from the school and kept her at home that night. On November 13, she spoke to her daughter Louisa about the matter, "minutely interrogated [Jane] with regard to all the circumstances," and summoned Miss Dunbar, one of her other granddaughters. Younger than Jane, and a day scholar, Miss Dunbar said "she had seen nothing herself, but had heard the stories of Miss Munro and Charlotte Whiffin."[55] Even if she wasn't familiar with that proviso of Scottish libel law according to which the slandered individual has the right to demand proof from the one making the accusation, a reasonable person would have given the two adults the opportunity to make their case, but Helen was not thinking reasonably.[56] She decided that two pupils' statements were proof enough of the teachers' misconduct.

So, as she had once before, she stood up for her son's daughter, again deemed in need of rescue. On November 14, Helen sent a haughty note to Miss Woods telling her to "send her a statement of the Miss Dunbars and Miss Jane Cumming's accounts" as well as "Miss Cumming's clothes."[57] She wrote cards to all the parents telling them to withdraw their children immediately from the Drumsheugh establishment without specifying why, and roped in Louisa Forbes and her husband John Hay Forbes to disseminate the particulars of the story to everyone who had children at the school. That her daughter complied is not surprising, but the son-in-law was an advocate who had been admitted to the bar some ten years earlier. One can only imagine the strength of Helen's character, convincing an established lawyer to do her bidding in this legally dubious business.

Upon receiving Helen's note, the teachers sent a card begging her to "candidly state to them every particular circumstance which has occasioned her Ladyship's disapprobation."[58] When it went unanswered, Miss Pirie sent an emotional note to Helen's daughter Mary, dated November 16, 1810. In it, Pirie begged Mary to tell what your niece has said to injure two innocent persons, who have labored for nearly twelve months to improve her in every religious and moral virtue, and who are thus cruelly repaid by her. We never did anything to offend her, excepting too rigidly discharging our duty towards her, and too freely telling her of her faults. You are again implored, for the sake of that God from whom you hope for mercy, to tell us of what she accused us, as the calumny has been traced to her, and she appears to be the sole author of it. If ever Christian mercy or pity had a place in your heart, do not delay to state *all* she says against us, as every hour's delay increases the misery she has already occasioned.[59]

That note also went unanswered. To her credit, Mary Cunynghame's mother, Lady Mary Cunynghame, was not swayed by the card she received from Helen. She paid a call on her to find out her objections to the school, and when Helen refused to divulge them, was even more determined to keep her daughter with Woods and Pirie. She then visited the school and spoke to Miss Woods, telling her that she was most "grateful for the kindness and attention" [Miss Woods] had shown to [her] daughter" and would do whatever she could to help them out of any "imprudent . . . scrape."[60] But when she heard that they had been guilty of sexual improprieties, she withdrew her daughter and severed her connection with Woods and Pirie. The school was quickly emptied of its pupils. Overwhelmed by "obloquy and disgrace," the teachers found themselves "compel[led] to abandon their establishment."[61]

Jane reacted to the collapse of the school with exultation. When she went back for the last time say goodbye to her teachers, her body language expressed her feelings: when she saw Janet Munro being taken away, she clapped for joy. If she couldn't have Miss Woods as a partner in bed, she could at least feel happy that Janet Munro couldn't either. Somewhat later, she reconstructed this last day at school as dumb show theater. She averred she saw Charlotte surreptitiously stick out her tongue at Miss Woods. When it was Jane's turn to part from the teachers, Miss Pirie was not around, but Jane planted a kiss on Miss Woods's cheek. The daily readings from Scripture had at least taught her that the sign of love was also the sign of betrayal. Jane revealed with her kiss that in the end the teacher she hated more deeply was the one who had scorned her in love: Miss Woods.

Initially, it was presumed that bankruptcy had brought the school down, but the tale of sapphic love first poured in Helen's ear spread quickly among the gentry of New Town. The mother of one ex-pupil made it known that only with difficulty had she gotten her daughter accepted into another boarding school. Two other girls were less lucky when their parents tried to place them at other seminaries; they were refused admission on the grounds they might bring Drumsheugh's contagion with them.

Somewhat later the story may have reached Anne Grant of Laggan, who moved in the same social circles as Elizabeth Hamilton. Without mentioning names or giving specifics, on October 25, 1811, ten days after the teachers' lawyers asked the court to review its narrow determination in favor of Helen, Mrs. Grant wrote from Edinburgh to her Bombay-based son Duncan, saying that she understood why "men destined to spend their lives in India" might form relationships with native women. Sympathetic to the plight of these men and of the opinion that the women they settled down with were "often innocent and even amiable," she felt compassion for the children born of their unions. Once the fathers decided to return, she lamented, these former "objects of paternal fondness" were "thrown off . . . rejected . . . forsaken." Anne Grant told her son that if he formed a connection with an Indian woman, she and her daughter would welcome her into the family; presumably they would be welcoming any children from the relationship. She assured Duncan that "difference of nation, or even of religion, would not alienate us from any wife that you would choose. . . . We would far rather make room in our hearts for a stranger . . . than see you in the predicament I have described."[62]

Was Anne Grant's decision to broach this topic at this moment with her son a response to one facet of the case? Might Anne Grant be implying that the Gordon Cummings reaped the bitter fruit from the seeds of evil they themselves had planted? If they had welcomed George's Lady in the North as his son's wife and treated their daughter Jane with greater warmth, perhaps this scandal would never have happened. It is, of course, also possible that the position Anne Grant adopted owes something to the view expressed by her friend Elizabeth Hamilton in *Translation of the Letters of a Hindoo Rajah* about it being incumbent on a woman to show kindness to others, including those of other races and religions. In addition, the sensitivity that Anne Grant showed was already in the public domain in the form of the popular song composed by Uncle George's Berners Street neighbor Amelia Opie in 1802. In the absence of evidence, we will never know what motivated Anne Grant to write about interracial relationships, but the timing of her letter seems to support the possibility that the case was a factor.

Elizabeth Grant, who would write many years later about Sandy Duncan and the bitter fruit reaped from seeds of evil, would have concurred on the importance of personal attention in the lives of unwanted children.

The moral the author drew from her story about Duncan is that for an unwanted child to become a good child, he or she must be brought up with love and personal attention by a mother figure. So in addition to holding Jane's teachers responsible for her transformation into a trouble-making girl, Elizabeth Grant would also have held Helen accountable.

The factors that led to Jane's bringing down of the school were more complex than Elizabeth Hamilton, Anne Grant, or Elizabeth Grant imagined, but while these women might have been shocked by the particulars of her accusations, none would have been particularly surprised that her personality had undergone a sea change before she made them. They understood that a child who received only a "kind of loving" could become a defiant hurtful, even malicious one.

The teachers too regarded Helen as the cause of their ruin. Though she refused to meet with them, they had quickly come to understand that she was accusing them of "of lewd and indecent behavior towards each other . . . kissing and caressing each other before the young ladies in a wanton manner."[63] In 1790s Amsterdam, such behavior was deemed criminal, and the Amsterdam municipal archives hold the records of thirteen women, referred to as "tribades" by one judge, who were arrested, tried, and found guilty of engaging in "caresses and filthy things"; the sentences ranged from a lenient two years of jail time to execution.[64] Not so in Britain, where such behavior was criminal only with respect to men. In 1790, the Ladies of Llangollen, Eleanor Butler and Sarah Pononsby, were the subject of a waspish article that appeared in the *St. James Chronicle* and reprinted almost verbatim in the *General Evening Post* and the *London Chronicle*. Entitled "Extraordinary Female Affection," the anonymous author's purpose in insinuating that they were tribades was strictly to disparage their character; they responded by asking Edmund Burke if they should sue for defamation of character. (He advised them against taking this step, and they followed his counsel.) Twenty years later, Woods and Pire decided to sue. They engaged John Clerk and James Moncreiff, two of Edinburgh's leading lawyers, to initiate a civil defamation of character suit against Jane's grandmother. *Miss Marianne Woods and Miss Jane Pirie Against Dame Helen Cumming Gordon* was the result.

John Clerk was known for his broad Scots accent, his limp, his caustic wit, passionate perorations, and unswerving commitment to his clients. James Moncreiff cut a less flamboyant figure but possessed great legal knowledge; working through thorny issues of law was his cure for migraine.

Clerk and Moncreiff got to work immediately. On November 27, 1810, just sixteen days after Jane informed her about the teachers' trysts, Helen was served with a summons. The summons stated that the teachers considered themselves to "have been unjustly and cruelly defamed and injured . . . by means of false, injurious and defamatory allegations and insinuations . . . which allegations, insinuations and reports were to the effect that [they] had been guilty of some very improper or criminal conduct."[65] The two teachers whose praises she had sung just twelve months back were now her "pursuers" (Scots: plaintiffs). To compensate for the loss of their reputations and careers, they demanded £10,000, $938,000 in today's money. This broke down to £2,000 for *solatium*, or recompense for personal suffering or grief, £7,500 for damages, and £500 for legal expenses.

The summons would have forced Helen to confess to her son Sir William what she had brought into being, since he would be the one paying the bills for her defense. Whatever words and looks passed in private between the two or between Sir William and his brother Charles, with whom he generally split such legal expenses as the family incurred, is unknown, but in public Sir William stood by his mother. He contacted the family law firm of Mackenzie & Innes—family in two senses of the word. Its lawyers handled the Gordon Cummings' legal affairs, but the Mackenzie of Mackenzie & Innes was also Sir William's maternal first cousin James, whose father, Henry, some years back, had tried to intercede with Penrose on behalf of George. The firm engaged two fine lawyers, George Cranstoun, classical scholar, friend of Sir Walter Scott, and gentle satirist of the style of two of the judges hearing the case, and tall, elegant, vivacious Henry Erskine, whom they brought out of retirement to defend Helen.

Erskine and Clerk had met in court before. In the notorious Deacon Brodie trial of 1788, Erskine had defended Brodie while Clerk represented George Smith, Brodie's locksmith accomplice.[66] Both Brodie and Smith were convicted, but Clerk's audacious defense made him famous. Now Clerk and Erskine were on opposing sides.

From the teachers' perspective, Helen had revealed herself to be an unwomanly woman—unsympathetic, harsh, and imperious and challenging. From Helen's perspective, the teachers were unwomanly and the breeding experiment a dreadful failure. As for the now sixteen-year-old Jane, she generated a set of vexing questions for the learned judges and lawyers involved in the case. Why did her problems with the teachers start during the summer holidays, specifically at Portobello? If her story was a fiction, where did its raunchy details come from? What was the nature of her mind? Was she the victim of her early years in India among licentious native women who had impressed all manner of sexual notions on her, or was she poisonous and remorseless by nature, rather like "the cobra Capello of her native Ganges"?[67] Alternatively, was this adolescent akin to Swift's Corinna, a hypersexualized child rumormonger about whom it could be predicted that as an adult she would produce "of scandal . . . a cornucopia?"[68] In the triangle formed by the two teachers, who kissed and caressed each other and on occasion slept in the same bed, and the disaffected, observant, sexually hungry Jane, was she the "real" lesbian?

The Edinburgh world Jane knew was small. Between November 1809, when she was formally enrolled at the Drumsheugh establishment, and the school's collapse a year later, her social contacts were family and school-connected. She had paid visits to her aunt Louisa Forbes's house on Princes Street, taken tea at Bishop Sandford's home on Melville Street, gone to church, stayed at 22 Charlotte Square. She had walked as far as Castlehill, the western end of the High Street, gone down to the Water of Leith, spent a holiday at Portobello. Jane's social and geographical world would now include the Court of Session at Parliament Square. Like Charlotte Square, Parliament Square was a construction site, and Jane would get far more muddied there than she ever did walking to and from her former school and her grandmother's house, as the pursuers' counsel and the judges analyzed and interrogated her on the tale of the amorous teachers.

Chapter Four

JANE AND THE LORDS OF THE LAW (1)

The bicameral Court of Session is Scotland's highest court for civil cases. Cases are first heard in the Outer House and, if they are not resolved there, recommended to the Inner House. In 1810, as now, the Court of Session sat at Parliament Square in Edinburgh, but in 1810 the square was a work in progress. The equestrian statue of Charles II was in place, but neither the shell of the Library Block nor the severe neoclassical refronting of Parliament House was complete. On the inside, while the arched roof was made of oak, "its cross beams, struts, and straining posts, rising from carved stone grotesque corbels (brackets) so as to form a five-segmented plan," had been in place for well over a century; there were only a few paintings hanging on the walls and some statuary on the sides, so the hall itself did not have the appearance of an art gallery, as it does today. Where today there is a central fireplace there was then a large stove. Windows on the southwest and east sides of the hall provided light, but the portion of the facade that had been put up made the place dark. The big stained-glass window of the south wall was more than fifty years in the future.

While the Inner House had its own rooms, the Outer House conducted business in the alcoves of Parliament Hall. Though the booksellers, toy shops, jewelers, and coffee shop that had also conducted business in the hall in the eighteenth century were gone by 1810, it was still a noisy, bustling place, with advocates conversing with each other and their clients and first-instance judges (the judges of the Outer House) holding court. As occasion demanded, the all-important macer would make himself visible to the people below. Sticking head and shoulders out of a window cut out from the east wall and framed by two of the oak beams that supported the high ceiling, he would, in his stentorian voice, call out the case numbers.[1]

The atmosphere of the Inner House courtrooms stood in stark contrast to this liveliness. So that the judges, the advocates who appeared before them, and the other legal figures in the room would elicit "reverence and regard" for them personally, for the offices they held, and for the law in general, in 1610 James VI issued a set of sumptuary laws that decreed what Court of Session judges and advocates were to wear. The judges donned splendid gowns of red crimson satin lined in white. The wrist-length bell sleeves of the gown were voluminous. Over time the gowns became more ornate. Three rows of ribbon added textural contrast to the monochromatic front. The bell sleeves developed blue insets. A tippet or mantle edged in satin or ermine was placed over the gown. Exposed between the edges of the gown and covering the chest was a wide white neckpiece called a fall.

Less colorful but also majestic in their severity were the advocates' black silk gowns with elbow-length slashed sleeves and the black gowns faced with velvet worn by the other functionaries in the courtroom. In the course of two centuries the advocates' gowns had acquired rows of "frogs," bows made of ribbon, that ran down the front and the sleeves.[2] The symmetry enhanced the lawyers' already imposing appearance. Anyone entering an Inner House courtroom and seeing the judges sitting together at their curved bench, the advocates standing and pleading the cases, and agents and functionaries performing their clerkly duties, would have been impressed by the grandeur of the scene.

Born in 1748, Allan Maconochie, later Lord Meadowbank, studied law at the University of Edinburgh where he, along with Helen's future brother-in-law Henry Mackenzie and a few others, founded the Speculative Society. At university, he developed a reputation as an able public speaker. He spent several terms at Lincoln's Inn and lived in France to broaden his horizons. Over the years he developed a reputation for a thorough knowledge of law, both its statutes and its philosophy. In 1804 he was appointed a Lord Ordinary—that is, a first-instance or Outer House judge. In late 1810 Lord Meadowbank was sixty-two years old and had been married for thirty-six of those years. In addition to being the father of four grown children, he had raised a relative's son from the age of nine after the death of the boy's father. Lord Meadowbank seems to have made an excellent father substitute, for in 1810 the boy whom he raised was a lieutenant in the British navy.[3]

Because of his position as a judge of the Outer Court, *Miss Marianne Woods and Miss Jane Pirie Against Dame Helen Cumming Gordon* came to Meadowbank's attention on December 13, 1810. The weather in Edinburgh was nasty that day: *The Scots Magazine* records that both snow and rain fell. The floor of Parliament Hall must have been dirty and slippery, and the case being explained to Lord Meadowbank by Helen's legal team, led by George Cranstoun and Henry Erskine, was so dirty and slippery that it was heard, not in an alcove of Parliament Hall, but behind "shut doors."[4]

Lord Meadowbank was no stranger to slippery cases, or to offering subjective interpretations. He had recently dealt with an inheritance case in which the two parties were, respectively, the daughters of one John Cunningham, deceased, and on the other, Cunningham's niece. The niece asserted that Cunningham's estate should go to her because the daughters were illegitimate. Such hard evidence as could be produced supported the niece, for in letters Cunningham referred to his daughters as natural, and no marriage certificate was ever submitted to the court. Lord Meadowbank, however, ruled in favor of the daughters, because local society, in which Cunningham and his daughters' mother moved, visited and entertained them; this social acceptance by neighbors, acquaintances, even the village minister, Lord Meadowbank maintained, would not have been accorded had the couple not been deemed married.[5]

But the case that came before him at the end of 1810 was far more complex than the Cunningham case, as it pitted respected women from two social strata against each other and dealt with intimacy between women. One story belonged to Lady Helen Cumming Gordon, that caring, easily stressed, but domineering dowager. On the basis of shocking but unverified information provided to her by Jane, she accused the Misses Woods and Pirie of gross immorality and shameful indecency; more specifically, she had persuaded the parents of Jane's classmates that the women had been "guilty of an unnatural lust, of a species of *venus nefanda.*"[6] The other story belonged to the Misses Woods and Pirie, two hard-working schoolmistresses with excellent professional credentials whose livelihood had been taken away from them as a consequence of Helen's disseminated claim. The two were suing her for defamation of character. Would Lord Meadowbank be able to decide the case by himself, determining whose was the more credible story, or would he have to recommend the case to his Inner House brethren?

On January 19, 1811, Cranstoun and Erskine came before Lord Meadowbank. They presented a narrative of the events preceding Jane's unbosoming to her grandmother the previous November. From Helen the lawyers had garnered some facts about Jane's life before she was enrolled at the Drumsheugh establishment. They apprised Lord Meadowbank that Jane was Helen's granddaughter, that she had been born in India and placed when very young in a boarding school in Calcutta. Sent for at the age of seven, she arrived in 1803, accompanied by a "black" female attendant. The servant was sent away and Jane was then boarded with Miss Charles in Elgin. In 1810 she was placed at the boarding school run by the Misses

Woods and Pirie in Edinburgh, where she shared a bed with Miss Pirie. Lord Meadowbank was also informed that Helen had left Edinburgh at the beginning of May 1810 and that Jane became cognizant of the teachers' sexual relationship during the summer holidays in Portobello. The lawyers then said that they would go on to chronicle incidents that took place at the Drumsheugh seminary between the end of July and the beginning of November 1810.

Cranstoun and Erskine presented a careful, politic construction designed to establish the bona fides of their client and her granddaughter. It did not mention the length of time Jane was boarded with Miss Charles. It implied Jane had had no contact with her mother and emphasized the respectability of the schools the girl had attended in Calcutta. The lawyers made no mention of Miss Pirie's rebukes or Jane's punishments. They kept silent about Helen's absence from Edinburgh and Jane's emergence as a third-party presence at her teachers' lovemaking. They claimed that before the girl's charge the teachers spoke of Jane "in terms of the warmest approbation."[7]

The lawyers must also have spent considerable time with Jane taking notes, for the bulk of their condescendence (Scots: additional statement setting forth the allegations on which an action is founded) consisted of her recollections of the teachers' amorous congresses. No specific dates were attached to these assignations, the cumulative listing intended to imply that behind their respectable facade the teachers were lustful creatures. Cranstoun and Erskine recounted Jane's story about a night when even before Miss Woods came into the bed Jane shared with Miss Pirie, Miss Pirie was begging Miss Woods, "Do it, darling!" Once Miss Woods was in the bed with them, Miss Pirie lifted her shift and Jane "felt her naked skin." At this point, Woods, who lay above Pirie, said, "I would like better to have some one above me." Then, according to Jane, who was only pretending to be asleep, "Miss Woods put down her hand, and they made a noise, which was a wet kind of noise, attended with a shaking of the bed."

On a third reported occasion, a sleeping Jane was awakened by a noise and motion of the bed and became aware of Miss Woods lying above Miss Pirie. Then Jane heard Pirie say, "Oh, you are hurting me." On a fourth occasion, Helen's team said that Jane "felt them take up their shifts," after which "Miss Pirie said, 'Oh, you are in the wrong place!,'" to which Miss Woods said, "'I know.' Miss Pirie said, 'Why do you do it then?'" to which Miss Woods replied, 'For fun.'"[8]

Cranstoun and Erskine provided Lord Meadowbank with two more instances, complete with dialogue from the teachers' lovemaking, in which

Miss Woods came across as the hurtful, dominant partner who took pleasure in getting Miss Pirie to beg and admit her sexual neediness. According to Jane, Miss Woods asked Miss Pirie to promise not to embrace her or come into her bed until the holidays. Miss Pirie replied that she would not be able to keep the promise. In response, Woods engaged in some emotional torture, telling Pirie that although she wouldn't embrace her or go to bed with her, she would allow Pirie to kiss her and would deign to kiss her back. On these two particular occasions, as well on numerous others, Cranstoun and Erskine averred that "Miss Cumming was sensible of their being both in bed with her, lying the one on top of the other, kissing and embracing."[9] All told, Jane provided the lawyers with concrete details for six occasions and indicated that she had been privy to their sexual activity numerous other times as well.

Cranstoun and Erskine also reported that Jane was not the only witness to the teachers' lovemaking. Her cousins the Misses Dunbar, Eliza Christian Stirling, Janet Munro, and the servant Charlotte Whiffin had also observed them in compromising positions. Jane told the lawyers that after she told Janet about how the teachers were disturbing her, Janet told her that the same thing was happening to her, in the bed she shared with Miss Woods. One night, according to Jane, Janet became sensible of Miss Pirie's body in the bed and "observed the same motions and the same shaking of the bed" that Jane had. When Janet went home one day and told her nurse about the teachers' behavior, the nurse said that the teachers were worse than beasts. Jane also said that Charlotte told the girls she had seen the teachers making love on the sofa in the drawing room through a keyhole in the door to that room, as well as upstairs in bed, and that they were so well-known as sexual deviants that they "could not go out without their being hooted at" by people on the road to the Water of Leith. Jane also said that in the presence of the girls, Charlotte stuck out her tongue to indicate what the teachers were doing.[10]

On the basis of what was reported to him, Lord Meadowbank felt compelled to send the case to his brethren of the Inner Court: Lord-Justice Clerk Hope (the second most senior judge of the Court of Session) and Lords Boyle, Robertson, Glenlee, Newton, and Polkemmet. Cranstoun and Erskine's defense statements, with rejoinders from the pursuers' advocates, Clerk and Moncreiff, were also forwarded, so by the date the first witness was called, March 15, 1811, the judges had been supplied in a timely manner with documents from both sides. All parties agreed that all printed material generated by the case would be "destroyed or otherwise disposed of" at its conclusion.[11]

Voyeurism is the term used since the nineteenth century to describe the behavior of one who becomes sexually excited and aroused gazing at, observing, peeping at, or spying on people's sex acts or naked bodies, in the vast majority of cases without their consent or knowledge. This paraphilia includes eavesdropping or listening to the erotic conversations of others. There is no consensus on the etiology of voyeurism, but according to *The Gale Encyclopedia of Mental Health*, some experts think that childhood trauma or other childhood experiences, including sexual abuse, puts an individual at risk for exhibiting voyeuristic tendencies, generally before the age of fifteen.[12] The most recent edition of the *Diagnostic and Statistical Manual of Psychiatric Disorders* (*DSM*) continues to distinguish voyeurism, a sexual tendency or behavior on the part of individuals who otherwise do not display any psychological problems and whose legal and mental history does not indicate that they acted on their tendencies, from voyeuristic disorder. This is a pathological condition of at least six months' standing, one that causes the affected person significant emotional distress or impairment in everyday life, and is comorbid with anti-social behaviors and conduct and personality disorders.[13] The entry on voyeurism in the 2010 *Encyclopedia of Identity* adds the important detail that by watching, the voyeur becomes a participant in the sexual drama and acquires intimate knowledge or erotic insight.

However, while voyeurism as a term is relatively new, the behavior has a long history in literature and art. It appears in the Bible in the stories of Susanna and the Elders and David and Bathsheba. Mass-produced Roman ceramics from the Augustan era (27 BC–14 AD) document the voyeuristic dynamic of sexually engaged couple and interested watcher. These terracotta cups, bowls, and vases depict tableaus of heterosexual and homosexual couples making love. On these artworks, there are sexually aroused Hermes figures standing behind a couple, often shown in in a bed whose headboard sports carvings of satyrs' heads as finials. The Hermes figures are ready to join the action they are gazing at and the satyrs add four more leering eyes to the scene. When more than one copulating couple is depicted, the scenes are separated by another set of onlookers—statues of Eros.[14] This artware allowed its Roman buyers to gaze on explicit sexual encounters depicting various sexual postures and forms of desire and presented viewers as lustfully complicit with the lovemaking, all in the comfort of their own homes. Penrose may well have seen examples of these ceramics in the galleries he visited on his Grand Tour, though there is no evidence that he brought any back with him.

In the long eighteenth century, female voyeurs appear in many literary works. In Eliza Haywood's *Love in Excess* (1725), a wife spies on her husband through a keyhole. Maddened by the desire to possess him, she subsequently chases him and causes him to fall on an object suggesting the nature of her desire: his sword. Fielding's *Joseph Andrews* (1742), Smollett's *Roderick Random* (1748), and Sterne's *Tristram Shandy* (1768) all have scenes in which women (and servants) peep at men so as to collect private information, which is then spread publicly as rumors, for the purpose of damaging these men. These scenes are comic, yet they also reveal how limited were the means available to the socially inferior classes to make and press charges against those in positions of power.[15] In what is generally recognized as "the most famous example of scopic sodomy" in the eighteenth century, Fanny Hill, the protagonist of John Cleland's 1749 *Memoirs of a Woman of Pleasure*, describes an instance of male-male congress as seen through a peephole; the scene is brought to a conclusion when Fanny, jumping down from a chair, slips and falls, rendering herself unconscious.[16] From a psychoanalytic perspective, this state of unconsciousness itself suggests that the whole scene is a sexual fantasy on Fanny's part, one that offers a keyhole into Fanny's imagination (sexualized, as a result of her life experiences) but marketed as a real event.[17]

As this excursus into the workings of the sexual imagination indicates, the act of peeping at others was variously interpreted, presented, and used. It was a way to express one's desires, heighten sexual arousal, get sexual satisfaction, and indulge one's fantasies, but when it went on too long and began to have a negative impact on the voyeur's mental and emotional well-being and social behavior, it could be described as a disorder. Through reflection, contrast, or vicarious participation in the intimate scene being witnessed at a remove, voyeurs made a statement about how they construed themselves. It was, in addition, something far more unsavory, unsettling, and threatening, a way for those of lower status to acquire knowledge that could be exploited in blackmailing more powerful individuals or spread through gossip, rumor, or testimony so as to defame and destroy them. As Barbara Benedict pointed out in her analysis of William Godwin's *Caleb Williams* (1794), however, such stealthily acquired scandalous information could damage the reputation of the person who collected it as well as of the person it related to.[18] With the exception of falling unconscious after witnessing a sexual act between two members of the same sex, all the elements above—the gazing, the sexual desire and the desire to harm, the observer who lacks power, the vicarious enjoyment, the fantasizing, the smutty details—are found in the stories Jane told Cranstoun and Erskine about the Misses Woods and Pirie's lovemaking; the "falling unconscious" element came later, when Jane told her stories in court.

By virtue of their placement as outsiders looking at the lovemaking through a sexually suggestive aperture, voyeurs are themselves complicit with the scene, psychologically identifying with the couple even though they are physically separated from them, and even though they may say the situation is criminal or indecent.[19] In the literature of the period, voyeurs of homosexual lovemaking try to be factual in their descriptions and convey that they found the behavior indecent, but what they are really doing is giving formal shape to their desires and fantasies. For their delectation and an audience's, they are constructing graphic scenes featuring rumpled beds, shed clothing, body parts, and coarse language. By sharing their keyhole experiences, the onlookers can experience their pleasure once again. On the other hand, the voyeurs, aroused by the sexual activity they claim they are witnessing, are only able to enter into it through an act of imagination or storytelling. Consistently positioning themselves as gazers in the narrative, they present themselves as locked out. They are subordinate players in the drama, reporters rather than doers. As Michelle Bobker puts it, they reveal themselves as obsessed with the "gap between their second-hand experiences and the apparently authentic ones from which they have been excluded."[20]

In maintaining that she perceived the teachers making love in her bed but got the keyhole story from Kent-born Charlotte, Jane was both aligning herself with and distancing herself from another non-Scottish female. Her positioning of herself as a sentient presence in the bed was a reminder of the distance separating her from the teachers' passionate embraces, while the pleasure she took in replicating the story suggests both that she wanted to experience what she perceived they were enjoying and to get them in trouble.

Of all the details Jane communicated, the most serious related to the keyhole. The likelihood is strong that the judges now in possession of Cranstoun and Erskine's condescendence would have known that keyhole or eyewitness testimony offered in sodomy trials prosecuted in criminal or navy courts often led to conviction of the accused.[21] Because Jane said that Charlotte told her she watched the teacher making love through a keyhole in the drawing room door, they had to consider that the events Jane reported really happened and exemplified consensual sex.

On the other hand, as well-read men, they were probably familiar with the erotic dynamics of that staple of eighteenth-century fiction, a sexual fantasy seen through a keyhole. Jane's allegation could also be false because its descriptions of body parts and risqué dialogue sounded like they came from a piece of trashy erotica. Could *Fanny Hill* have been on the shelves of the Altyre library? Might she have read it or another book of that nature when nobody was paying attention? Actually, during 1808, while Jane was still with Miss Charles, Sir William bought a number of books from Isaac Forsyth, the Elgin bookseller. These included Radcliffe's *Mysteries of Udolpho*, a complete set of Sterne's *Works*, and the Arabian *Nights*.[22] All these contain sexually suggestive scenes, some transgressive and voyeuristic. Perhaps Jane dipped into these volumes and took away remembrances of racy lines and erotic scenes. Alternatively, Charlotte Whiffin, known to have talked to the girls, might have communicated the gist of some bawdy ballad she had heard.

The servant girl could even have brought in (and later taken out) some species of obscene fiction. Eighteenth-century flagellation narratives, in which much is made of the lifting of shifts and petticoats, the positioning of the body, and the revealing of certain body parts, were often set in boarding schools. Tribadism and submission are central to *Exhibition of Female Flagellants*, which bills itself as a collection of "authentic anecdotes . . . found in a Lady's closet."[23] The stories feature best female friends who whip each other, adolescent girls who are whipped by their schoolmistresses, and a maid glued to a keyhole who watches two women beat a man. Jane's stories about the affectionate teachers are set in a boarding school, feature same-sex activity viewed through a keyhole, and place great emphasis on body positioning, lifting of clothing, and feeling and touching of naked skin. Were her accounts based on literary sexual fantasies? While acknowledging the existence of pornographic literature and its arousing effects, the judges did not explore this route into her stories.[24]

Yet another possibility that might have occurred to the judges was that Jane's voyeuristic story was, to use a term that wouldn't be coined for more than two centuries, a primal scene, a memory of an early sexual encounter now reflected, refracted, reconstituted, converted, or transposed to another context and other players. Freud never came to a firm conclusion on whether these primal scenes were fantasies or historical events and acknowledged that not everyone's sexual development was affected by them, but either way, for those who *were* affected, they were perceived as real and a source of the individual's sexual issues in later life. If the judges were thinking along these lines, they could tie Jane's Scottish story to a postulated primal scene set in India. Jane's story, then, would not be about the teachers and their sexuality; it would offer the judges a psychosexual keyhole into her past.

In due course the Court of Session would speculate about Jane's past, but the first order of business was to assess the actual keyhole story. Did or didn't the drawing room have a keyhole with a line of sight to the sofa on which, Jane said, Charlotte told her she had seen the teachers going "at it?"[25] Not long after Cranstoun and Erskine's document was forwarded to the Inner House, the teachers' advocate James Moncreiff addressed the judges who would hear the case. He informed them that the keyhole story was a fabrication, because one drawing room door had no keyhole and the other had a keyhole that did not go all the way through to the opposite side.

Cranstoun and Erskine soon retracted, at a second pretrial hearing, the story Jane had ascribed to Charlotte about the teachers being hooted at by women near the Water of Leith. They also kept mum about the keyhole. Perhaps they had done some fact-checking in the interim and discovered that the drawing room door did not have a keyhole that permitted a gazer to see the sofa. They also offered tamer versions of earlier statements. For example, the detail about Jane being able to feel Miss Pirie's "naked skin" is gone. According to Lord Meadowbank, "nobody could be more convinced of [the] . . . truth of the facts" than Cranstoun, but these modifications indicate that even before the case went to trial, Cranstoun himself recognized that Jane's account contained material that appeared false, dubious, and damning.[26] He was already having to acknowledge that his leading witness's credibility was suspect, that she wasn't the truthful and well-bred young lady her grandmother thought her.

Even as Cranstoun backpedaled, the teachers' lead advocate, John Clerk, revealed an extraordinary sympathy for Jane. In early 1811, around the time of the second pretrial hearing, he and all the other lawyers met behind closed doors to discuss a specific issue: who could be called as witnesses. There was much debate about whether Jane could be called, and in this context, Clerk put before his peers the case of a girl brought up in a "bawdy house—not guilty herself but the recipient of impressions," implying that Jane was a victim of the environment in which she had lived in India.[27] It was his position that her voyeurism and sexualized imagination were the result of her having spent years in Indian institutions where she had been exposed to indecent practices at a very early age. Revealing race prejudice and yet thinking like a Lockean, Clerk implicitly opened up the possibility that Jane was a victim of child maltreatment. She had been exposed to sexual scenarios that subsequently affected her judgment, making her unable to distinguish between the innocently romantic and the wantonly sexual.

Clerk's partner, Moncreiff, made no such allowances at the pretrial hearing. He cast doubt on Jane's narrative, her behavior, and her memory.

If the teachers were engaging in such disturbing behavior, why hadn't she reported it to her aunt Louisa Forbes, whom Helen had appointed her guardian while away from Edinburgh? Since Miss Pirie went to bed wearing various articles of clothing, including a petticoat and stockings, why didn't Jane feel them? Why did she mention only the shift? He also provided reasonable explanations for the teachers' nighttime meetings: Miss Pirie's rheumatic back needed rubbing, Miss Woods stopped to chat with Miss Pirie after returning from supping with her aunt. In addition, he pointed out that the period from May through November 1810, when Jane said the teachers were sexually active, was a time when they were quarreling over the status of Ann Woods; those months were characterized by hostility rather than loving friendship. The last important thing Moncreiff did at this second pretrial hearing was gingerly introduce Miss Pirie as a jealous person.

Based as it was on *veritas convicii*, personal conviction of the truth as conveyed to her by one individual, Helen's case was always a weak one, and she may have compromised it from the very start. As previously mentioned, Scottish law dealing with this particular defense states that the slandered individual has the right to demand a proof of the truth from the one making the allegation, and Helen had refused to meet with the teachers and explain why she had spread the story. Realizing that testimony from independent witnesses would bolster their client's case, Cranstoun and Erskine paid a call on the famous painter Henry Raeburn. Two of his wards had been at the school, and the lawyers' visit was an "endeavour to procure information as to what had fallen under observation of the two young ladies."[28] The gambit was fruitless. Jane had said that the Misses Dunbar could corroborate her account, but they were disqualified.

Cranstoun and Erskine scored somewhat when they got James Hare, a medical doctor long resident in Calcutta but now living in Edinburgh, disqualified as a witness. One can understand why they did not want him on the stand: as Clerk and Moncreiff stated, they were calling him because he would swear that the Calcutta schools Jane attended were dens of iniquity.

Clerk retaliated for the loss of James Hare by raising objections to Jane herself being called to testify, on account of her relationship to and dependency on Helen. Had his objection been sustained, the defense would have lost its key witness. Cranstoun argued that the rule disqualifying a close relative from testifying in a case involving a family member only applied to lawful issue. Since Jane was illegitimate, there could be no legal objection to her testifying. Lord Hope ruled that her illegitimacy entitled her to give testimony, but it wasn't much of a victory. Given what had already been learned, it could be assumed that while her titillating story would compel interest, its trustworthiness was dubious.

The legal teams set about collecting evidence to be presented in court. The cards Helen sent the other parents telling them to withdraw their children from the school were retrieved from their recipients. The angry letters exchanged between the two schoolmistresses; the scheming letters between the teachers and their respective sisters; the reference letters testifying to Pirie's skills, her zealous attention to pupils, her keen temper, and her obsessive affection for Marianne; Pirie's hysterical, self-righteous letter to Helen's daughter asking for an audience with Helen; Pirie's erotically charged birthday note to Marianne—all these and other materials were in the possession of the court by early 1811. Either because they didn't know or chose not to cite the seventeen cases that came before the criminal court of Amsterdam between 1751 and 1798 in which women were charged with the crime of lying on another woman "in the way a man is used to do when he has carnal conversation with his wife," Cranstoun and Erskine submitted a multilingual list of Biblical and classical authorities testifying to the existence of passion between women.[29]

On March 14, 1811, Lord Hope, accompanied by Lords Meadowbank, Robertson, Newton, and Boyle "proceeded to the house at Drumsheugh." The first thing they did was check Moncreiff's statement about the keyholes. In the document they produced about their visit, the four judges noted that there was one door that had a keyhole lock, but, as Moncreiff had mentioned, the keyhole was on one side only and did not allow a person to see through into the room. Willing to give Jane the benefit of the doubt, they then looked for "holes or chinks in the door, through which a person could peep." They found none, but noted that if a person stood on a platform or chair by a particular window in "favourable light" they thought that a person "so placed can see as far as the couch"; Jane had said nothing, however, about seeing through a window.[30] Having verified for themselves the correctness of Moncreiff's observation, the judges already knew that any further statement to the effect that the teachers were observed through a keyhole making love on the sofa was a fabrication. If Jane stuck to that statement in the witness box, then they had some kind of keyhole into her character.

The judges saw the garden in front of the house, now an empty triangular space, but not that long ago a little beehive of activity in which Jane and her classmates confabulated. They commented on the walls of the drawing room: a paint job was in order. The notorious drawing room sofa was still there in its spot against the wall, as was the piano against the other wall, but the music stool, upholstered in worsted and worked in silk, was gone. Upstairs, the men saw the close-packed beds on which the teachers and the pupils had slept, but not the sheets, mattresses, blankets, and bolsters Ann Woods had purchased that had once covered them. The chests of drawers that Mrs. Woods had bought for the use of the teachers and scholars were gone as well. The drawing stands and the set of globes, the dumbbells and the looking glass, the chairs, the set of fire irons, the plates, dishes, tea jugs, wineglasses, and soup plates, even the books, were nowhere in evidence; these moveable items had all been sold at auction. If the judges speculated that the teachers had lost a lot of money, they were right. Woods and Pirie subsequently averred that from the sale of the furniture they recouped "scarcely one-third of its actual value . . . and suffered a positive loss of not less than £450," in today's terms, at least $431,000.[31] The ghostly house bore mute testimony to the devastation Jane's story had wreaked.

On March 15, 2011, five of the seven judges appointed to hear the case were sitting around the curved bench in their splendid robes: Lords Hope, Meadowbank, Robertson, Newton, and Boyle. Many a witness summoned to testify would have felt intimidated in the presence of such men, their humanity hidden under their garb, but the behavior of witnesses, women particularly, was unpredictable. Mrs. Helen Campbell found the experience agonizing when she came before the court on March 29. In a letter written on April 25 to James Balfour, an instructing agent of the teachers' defense team, she asked the court to "take into consideration that though I am now an old woman, I never before took an oath . . . and that through life I have ever had a degree of timidity that I never could shake off. . . . It will account to you for any embarrassment or stupidity that may have appeared when I was taken before that (to me) formidable Court."[32] More women than might have been expected, however, were not awed into silence or intimidated. They showed a sense of their own agency, speaking confidently, remaining adamant in the face of aggressive questioning, and returning gaze with gaze.[33]

First to be called on March 15 was pretty Janet Munro, possibly afflicted with hearing loss in one ear. The fifteen-year-old came across as simple and uncritical, a girl who did what other girls told her to do. She said she took as truth Charlotte's story about the teachers' lovemaking as espied through the keyhole.

Having joined the school only in September 1810, Janet had been the most junior girl there, yet was already known for being given extra lines to learn as punishment. Like Jane, she was frequently in the teachers' bad books, and because both had teachers as bedmates, Miss Woods for Janet and Miss Pirie for Jane, they had something else in common. Janet and Jane had talked to each other about the teachers, and it was she, probably egged on by Jane, who had told her childhood nurse about the teachers' sexual encounters; Janet had reported back to Jane that the nurse considered such women worse than beasts. Probably in the latter half of October 1810, in the presence of other girls, Jane gave Janet to understand that she wanted to go to bed with her. While Janet was apparently willing enough to plumb her old nurse for sexual information, she balked at this request. Janet recognized that Jane was propositioning her and reported it to Miss Pirie, who seems to have made sure Jane never harassed her classmate again. The two young persons had not seen each other since the school collapsed in mid-November, four months back. On that day, Jane had clapped when Janet took leave of Miss Woods.

Janet, like Mrs. Campbell, found testifying an ordeal. She blushed and cried. Lord Hope, physically imposing, fiercely partisan, and violently impetuous, noted for a voice so impressive that only the celebrated actress Mrs. Siddons's surpassed it, must have terrified her.[34] It was "difficult to get her to talk," he recalled, and she spoke so softly that he "hardly heard her voice."[35] The court note-taker heard her, though, and took her responses down. Janet's account from the witness box of the teachers' conduct was similar to the one Jane voiced earlier through Cranstoun and Erskine; the major differences were that Janet presented Miss Pirie as the sexual aggressor and that she didn't have complete control of her story. Under oath, Janet swore that on two occasions, once at the end of September and once early in October, Miss Pirie came into Miss Woods' bed while Janet was also in it. There might have been a third occasion prior to these days in which she sensed that there was somebody besides Miss Woods and herself in the bed, but she wasn't sure. On the occasions she claimed to be sure about, she "felt the bodies of one or both of them in motion."[36] Janet's sense was that Miss Pirie's clothes were off and that the teachers lay one on top of the other, Miss Pirie uppermost, but she also admitted that on the first occasion it was too dark for her to distinguish anything and she was not fully awake.

In the soft voice Lord Hope could barely hear, Janet divulged more. She had had conversations with Jane about the teachers' disturbing behavior in which Jane said that she too "was accustomed to being so disturbed" (49). Janet told the court that she had mentioned to Charlotte that she had slept badly, from which Charlotte intuited that she was really talking about the teachers' lovemaking, then shared with her the titillating keyhole story. Later in her testimony Janet averred that Charlotte had told her, Jane, and Eliza Stirling that she had caught the teachers before breakfast "in an improper situation" upstairs, and that at breakfast Charlotte "made faces at them" (48). She also said Charlotte had told them that when Miss Woods and Miss Pirie came down that day, they had been too embarrassed to look her in the eye. As Janet recalled the situation, it seemed to her that the teachers had avoided Charlotte.

While Janet presented Charlotte as a disrespectful servant and a purveyor of sexual knowledge, she depicted Jane as the clever girl at Drumsheugh, the one who devised just the thing to prove Miss Pirie's guilty desire for Miss Woods: a situation that would make her blush. Janet recalled the afternoon Jane sprang the trap. She, Jane, and Miss Pirie had just come back from a walk. On the walk, Jane told Janet that when they got back to the school, she would tell Miss Pirie that she was "excessively tired with being disturbed in the night time" (49). According to Janet, on their return, when Jane made the planned remark, "Miss Pirie's face grew very red and she turned her back, and soon afterwards went out of the room; and then Miss Cumming observed to the deponent [person testifying, i.e., Janet], 'Do you see how guilt is on her face?'" (49).

However, Janet could not confirm that Eliza Stirling noticed anything unusual about the teachers on the morning they supposedly avoided making eye contact with Charlotte. Nor could Janet be certain that on the first occasion in bed she had testified to, it was Miss Pirie's legs that she had felt. As for the second occasion, she said that there was enough light for her "to perceive that Miss Pirie was lying above Miss Woods" (52). But in response to questioning, Janet said she could not be certain Miss Pirie was even in the bed since "her own face was to the wall" (52) most of the time. The two teachers exchanged words, but the only snippets of conversation the girl caught had to do with dogs and Miss Pirie's brother-in-law Tom Ferguson. Picking up on her statement to the effect that Miss Pirie was not wearing clothes, Lord Boyle asked her if "it was their naked bodies, or only their shifts, which touched her" (62). She testified, "both" (62), an answer that put her credibility in doubt.

On Janet's second day on the witness stand, Clerk and Moncreiff got her to reveal that it was Jane who initiated the conversation about the teachers' improper behavior, and Jane who had planted the idea in her head that the teachers' "kissing, caressing and fondling each other" (49) signified more than ordinary female friendship. Janet's testimony, therefore, proclaimed rather loudly that Jane had coached her and taken advantage of her gullibility to hatch her plot to get back at the teachers. But the most important detail Janet divulged was not one Jane had coached her on: that Jane asked Janet to sleep with her. Coming after the exposure of the keyhole story as a fabrication, it added to the suspicion that if there was any female at the school who had openly expressed interest in initiating a sexual relationship with another female, it was Jane Cumming.

Jane Cumming was called to testify at ten o'clock on the rainy morning of March 11. Her trip to Parliament Square from Charlotte Square would have taken her along Princes Street, across the bridge over the now-drained loch, and very shortly thereafter onto the High Street. In the margin of his copy of "Additional Case for the Appellant," Moncreiff noted that Helen was not present on the days Jane gave testimony. So unless her aunt Louisa was sitting somewhere in the courtroom that morning when Jane entered, perhaps dressed in a plain, well-tailored, dark-colored silk dress with matching cloak and bonnet appropriate to the occasion and her status as the granddaughter of a respectable Scottish matron, there was no female family member to whom she could turn to for support. Instead, she saw four sumptuously robed and bewigged judges sitting at the bench. In addition to Lord Meadowbank, there was the terrifying Lord Hope, the thin-lipped and square-jawed Lord Robertson, and the obese Lord Newton, well-known for dozing at the bench and being one of the "profoundest drinkers" of the period, yet able to render perspicacious judgments under the influence.[37] She saw the counsel for the parties as well as their respective agents, and an official note-taker. If she had counted the men present in the room, the total would have been about fifteen or twenty. At various points of the day, thirty or forty eyes would have looked at, maybe roamed over, this buxom adolescent. However, she belonged to the camp of testifying women who were not intimidated by the courtroom setting.[38]

If what Jane wanted was to be the center of attention, she got her heart's desire. By the time she stepped down from the box, she had spent, over the course of four days, close to twenty-four hours in it, during which time she betrayed no fear, showed no embarrassment talking to men about sex, and rarely lacked for an answer. Except on her second day in court, when Lord Hope rattled her, her demeanor, insofar as can be gauged from the court note-taker's transcriptions, was controlled, steely, even icy. Though only sixteen, Jane defied the conventional stereotype of the meek, modest, powerless, voiceless female with downcast eyes. Resourceful and confident, she enjoyed the limelight, returning gaze with gaze and words with words.

March 22, 23, 24, and 25, 1811, were Jane's days in court. Over their course, she was asked question after question. The recording clerk captured a good deal of her speech, but sometimes rephrased her answers in indirect discourse.[39] When she paused or sat silent, he noted these breaks. Her testimony reveals her to be a woman of many moods, but always tenacious, always focused on presenting the teachers as "very improper, and very indecent" (80): morally filthy women. Depending on the questions hurled her way, she was open, animated, gushing, almost out of control verbally. Alternatively, she presented as defensive, laconic to the point of silent, strategizing, bitter, adamant, angry, distant, noncommittal—but never as cowed by the experience.

On the first day, she was voluble and forthcoming with details that appeared to have been seared into her mind. She repeated what Cranstoun and Erskine had already stated in the January condescendence but now added that she was disturbed by a particular noise. This she likened to the sound made "by putting one's finger into the neck of a wet bottle" (71). The sound, she said, lasted for a good five minutes. Intrigued by her comparison and perhaps awed by the duration of the implied performance, the judges decided to test her knowledge of sexual noises and imagery. Could the noise she had heard also be compared to the drawing of a cork, or to a person rubbing against another person, clapping or patting another on the cheek or shoulder, or dabbling a hand in water? Jane rejected all the comparisons except for the last, to which she gave slight assent. When asked if she had heard more than caressing and indistinct whispering, she shared the racy dialogue she claimed to have overheard on various occasions: Miss Pirie saying, "Oh, you are hurting me," while Miss Woods was above her, Miss Pirie saying to Miss Woods, "you are in the wrong place," Miss Woods clarifying that she was "in the wrong place . . . for fun," Miss Woods saying, "I would like better to have somebody above me," and so on. During cross-examination, Jane confirmed that the words she heard were "in the wrong place" and not "on the wrong place" (84).

In his 1755 *Dictionary of the English Language*, Samuel Johnson gave a number of definitions for "cant," including its usage by Jonathan Swift to mean "barbarous jargon." Somewhat further on, before he defined "fun" as "sport; high merriment; frolicksome delight"; he called it a "low cant word." Jane's placement of the word "fun" in the mouth of the genteel, polished Miss Woods must have shocked the judges, but her prepositional insistence really distressed them. They would have known that for their learned counterparts in the navy and High Court of Justiciary who heard sodomy cases, the distinction between the unquestionably penetrative "in" ("ejaculation offense"), and the non-penetrative "on" ("emission offense") was the difference between a felony possibly carrying a death sentence and a misdemeanor. Dismayed that what Jane was saying was that Woods and Pirie had achieved what another judge called "a crisis, like that of a woman in the embraces of a man," or, to use modern terminology, orgasmic release, the female equivalent of ejaculation, Lord Hope asked her about emission, if "she felt anything wet in the bed. . . .[if] "she ever perceived any stain upon the sheets" (91). She responded that she hadn't.

Without being prompted, Jane told the court that she had informed Janet Munro of the nocturnal visits Miss Woods paid to the bed Jane shared with Miss Pirie. She said that Janet, in turn, mentioned that Miss Pirie was in the habit of making the same kind of visits to the bed Janet shared with Miss Woods. On returning from a walk later that day, Jane said, Charlotte told both girls she had seen the teachers "at it" on two occasions "quite well" (72). once in the drawing room and once upstairs. Jane thus used eye-based information she claimed emanated from Charlotte to support and shared by confirm the ear-based account of the teachers' lovemaking that she shared with Janet. The next day, Jane went on to testify, Charlotte told the girls that they would be able to detect guilt on their teachers' faces. Jane followed Charlotte's advice and observed that Miss Woods's face turned red when she (Jane) shook hands with her teacher at breakfast that day. Jane confirmed that she was the author of the plan described in Janet Munro's testimony, by which Miss Pirie's red face confirmed *her* guilt as well. While this was basically the same information she had earlier conveyed in the privacy of Helen's house to Cranstoun and Erskine, it was now being delivered in a formal setting to a considerably larger audience. She delivered her lines flawlessly.

In the final segment of her first day in court, Jane's imagination took flight. Regarding the court as a performance space, with herself the star of the show and the assembled men an audience to be enthralled, she presented the last day of school as dumb-show theater in which Charlotte, stationed behind Miss Woods, and apparently for Jane's benefit, once more stuck her tongue out at Miss Woods. Then she piled up story after story of trysts featuring rumpled beds and a sexually aggressive Miss Pirie, well-known among the girls for taking "Miss Woods out of the school-room, as if against her consent, into the drawing-room when it was dark, and stay[ing] there a considerable time" but who also was a laughingstock for "coming out of Miss Woods' bed with her stockings on, and a red garter" (74).

If Jane felt she had scored on the twentieth of March, she was disabused of that perception on the twenty-second. The keyhole story had been discredited by Moncreiff some months earlier, but Lord Hope began to probe it as a way into Jane's thinking processes. After she was sworn in, he unleashed a barrage of questions. Why didn't you mention the keyhole on March 20? Did you never observe that the doors of the drawing room had no keyholes? What were you and Janet Munro talking about in the garden? What exactly did Charlotte say? The questions put Jane on the defensive. Feeling now that the less she said the better, her answers shrank to short disclaimers inconsistent with each other. Thus, she claimed that she forgot to mention the keyhole and that she did not know the doors to the drawing room lacked keyholes. With respect to information she claimed to have received from Charlotte, she now said Charlotte told her that she saw the teachers through the keyhole but not that they were lying on the sofa or kissing; Jane could not remember the time of day when Charlotte told her the story, either. More significantly, Jane no longer recollected the nature of the conversation she had had with Janet in the garden.

Apparently satisfied with the long shadow of doubt he had cast over her account, Lord Hope moved on to Jane's early years in Scotland. Did something happen to her in that time period that could account for her sexualized story? The information she provided about her six years at Miss Charles's school in Edinburgh indicated that Helen's ex-governess educated her pupils in the standard skills and accomplishments that marked a girl of the gentry class and also kept them safe and "pure." They never bathed and never played with the local girls, and when they went out to play, it was always on a little hill at the back of the house, in eyeshot of Miss Charles if she happened not to accompany them.

Not finding anything eyebrow-raising in Jane's account of her Elgin years, the judge interrogated her about her time at Drumsheugh. She admitted that the discipline was stricter, that she was "frequently exposed to the punishments of the school" (78), and that she kept "a book in which she wrote down the punishments she was exposed to" (79). He next turned to the environment in which she had spent her early years. As mentioned earlier, in Western Europe at that time, and with very few exceptions, "the Oriental female" was conceptualized as a cauldron of sexuality, both literally and figuratively overheated. It was believed that the climate in Asia so affected females' biology that they matured sexually much earlier than females born and raised in colder latitudes; it was taken as fact that Indian girls were capable of consensual sexual intercourse by the age of seven or eight. Ripened by the sun, so to speak, then initiated into sexual matters at an early age by the women around them, their imaginations became sexualized, their minds hypersexualized. All they could think and talk about related to sex.

Lord Hope wanted to ascertain if Jane's imagination had been polluted or perverted, her mind hypersexualized by the licentious manners and conversation the teachers' counsel claimed she couldn't have avoided being exposed to in India. He also asked questions about Coongee (referred to as "the maid" [77] in the proceedings) to find out if she could have continued to pervert Jane, since she came with her to Scotland. In response to these queries, Jane told the court that the women servants at the schools she had attended in Calcutta were "natives" (77) and that the schoolmistress at the first establishment was European; she wasn't sure about the ethnicity of the schoolmistress at her second boarding school. She also stated that she had not learned to speak English before she left India. Neither from the children at these schools nor from any people employed there did she ever hear of the practices she ascribed to the Misses Woods and Pirie nor did she ever hear in any Indian language words that would now strike her as "improper" (77).

As for Coongee, Jane spoke of her without affect, confirming that she was the woman who accompanied her from India. Jane added that she (Jane) was brought up north by Mr. Tulloch and that Coongee was sent away about six months after Jane was settled at Altyre.[40] If Helen's lawyers had coached Jane to speak of Coongee in that emotionally distant way to convey that a lower-class native of India had had no effect on her, they seem to have succeeded, because Jane was asked no more about her.

Lord Hope started to ask her how much English Jane knew when she arrived in Britain after her voyage on the *Bengal*, then stopped mid-sentence.[41] By dropping the subject of what knowledge she might have acquired on the ship, Lord Hope denied himself and the court the opportunity to learn what she might have been exposed to at sea and to consider the long-term effects of that voyage on her mind. Since Captain Cumine's log indicates that untoward incidents did take place, Lord Hope's decision was, in retrospect, a bad one. Yet it was an understandable one. The judges' contemporary legal brethren serving on navy courts would have taken Jane's insistence that Miss Pirie said "in the wrong place" and not "on the wrong place" to mean that a penetrative same-sex sexual act had occurred, and Lord Hope did not want to continue along that line of questioning. The thought that the behavior of white men might be responsible for the cast of Jane's mind was too frightening to pursue, whereas linking her admittedly improbable Edinburgh story to a sexualized upbringing in Calcutta at the hands of dark-skinned women was convenient, and exculpatory.

Lord Hope next turned his attention to Jane's outburst that had set the case in motion. What the judges assumed to be Jane's sexually charged first impressions seemingly had lain dormant for many years. What had caused them to erupt in the form of the stories she told her grandmother in November—what was the trigger? At the March 22 court session, it was established that Jane was chastised and punished frequently at the Woods-Pirie School. The dominant tone of the notebook she had kept was spiteful and resentful toward Miss Pirie; thus, it belied her statement that she didn't find the discipline of the school either "harassing or disagreeable" (78). Until the book could be reviewed, however, the desire for revenge as cause of Jane's actions could not be further investigated.

In an attempt to probe the solidity of her central point, that the teachers had been intimate, Lord Hope interrogated Jane on one of her supporting details: the curious noise, sounding like a finger inserted into a wet bottle, that she claimed to have heard on a number of occasions when the teachers were in bed together. In rapid succession, he (and perhaps other judges) asked her how many times she had heard the noise, what time of the day she heard the noise, how long the noise lasted. To these questions she could give no precise answer. She admitted that nobody else who claimed to have seen the teachers "at it" had ever heard the noise, nor had she shared this detail with her classmates. When she told Lord Hope that she had never heard the sound produced by a person putting a finger in a wet bottle, he asked her how she could describe a sound she never heard, Jane responded, "I thought it would be the same" (82).When he grilled her on what the teachers were doing in bed, it came out that neither her hearing nor her sight was involved; rather, her knowledge came from an inferred perception of touch. She told the court that she had sensed they were putting down their hands and pulling up their shifts, but that she couldn't really feel them doing so. There were pauses and silences in her answers. One of her silences lasted fifteen minutes, as if it were she who had been caught in a compromising position and was trying to figure out how to get herself out.

More backpedaling followed. Jane reneged on her earlier statement that Charlotte had stuck out her tongue at the teachers. Under questioning, she admitted that the teachers' behavior only began to strike her as indecent and improper in late August, about a month after the summer holidays—around the time Miss Woods was brushing off her little signals of affection, though that particular sequence was not noted. She finally admitted that the idea that the teachers were sexually suspect was her own construction. In conceding that the story she had said came from Charlotte and could be corroborated by Janet Munro was of her own making, she was acknowledging that it was she who had fantasized them into a sexually active couple. She had taken advantage of the reputation of servants as conduits of sexual knowledge to frame Charlotte and the gullibility of Janet to set her up as a second witness, but this engineering didn't hold up under pressure. At the very end of her grilling on March 22, she also abandoned the nakedness and night shift claims and now recollected that when Miss Woods climbed into the bed Miss Pirie "had on her stockings, etc." (85).

On March 23, her third day on the witness stand, Lord Hope continued his assault on her allegations, taxing her to recollect minute details from the incidents she had mentioned on her first day. How did Jane know Miss Woods was on top? Was she sure Miss Pirie was wearing stockings the night Miss Woods came into the bed? Could she be sure that they were kissing? When exactly did Miss Woods come into the bed? How many times did Miss Woods come into the bed after the summer holidays? What particulars about the teachers did she share with Janet Munro when they talked in the garden? To none of these questions was she now able to give definitive answers. The recording clerk, putting her responses into indirect discourse, consistently wrote words to that effect that she didn't remember.

Inconsistencies developed during the course of the March 23 examination. Now Jane said she was sure of only four times that Miss Woods came into Miss Pirie's bed while she was also in it because "on other occasions she just wakened, and heard them whispering and kissing, and fell asleep again" (86). This particular voyeuristic detail, what might be called the hearing/whispering/kissing/falling unconscious sequence, struck Lord Meadowbank as so significant that he underlined it in his copy. She also added another tryst to the ones she credited Charlotte with peeping at, saying that Charlotte observed the teachers lying on the sofa through a window from the external stairs. These new details suggest that Jane had been thinking of a way to save her case after the keyhole material was discredited. She apparently remembered what Lord Meadowbank had also concluded after visiting the house—that it would have been possible to see the sofa from that window if one stood on a platform or the external stairs and the light was favorable.

While Miss Pirie had previously said that she always requested Jane to keep as far away from her as possible in the bed they shared, and Charlotte, whose job it was to make that bed, confirmed that the two slept as far apart as possible, Jane now said that it was *her* custom to "lie near Miss Pirie." Who was to be believed, the teacher and the maidservant, or Jane? When the questioning homed in on what Jane felt or thought she felt when the two teachers were in the bed, first she said that she was "inclined to think that Miss Woods' leg was lying with Miss Pirie's" (86), but when the question was repeated to her eight or nine questions later, she acknowledged that she was no longer so inclined to trust her memory (88). How could she state that she was sure of only four occasions and in the next breath mention other occasions of which she seemed very sure? What was real, what fantasy?

On the other hand, Jane stuck to her contention about being able to sense the skin of shift-free legs up to the knee or just above it with her own leg and clearly distinguished between these sexually charged occasions and the innocent times when Miss Pirie had asked for her rheumatism-racked limbs to be rubbed. These lords of the law were experts in prying out information, but despite the attempts to shake Jane through their barrage of questions, despite her memory lapses, embellishments and dramatizations, falsehoods, constructions, ignorance, interpretations, her fantasies or fantastic representations, her manipulations and inconsistencies, at the end of the third day in the courtroom she continued to maintain that the teachers had been sexually intimate on several occasions, the first during the summer holidays at Portobello. Dismayed by the unswerving commitment of this sixteen-year-old to that position, she was called back for another day of questioning.

Had Mary Wollstonecraft sat on the curved bench alongside the judges, she might have given them some food for thought. If, as she wrote in the *Vindication of the Rights of Women*, the practice of bedsharing leads children of the same sex to experiment sexually with each other and develop a taste for it, why not consider that when two adult females chose to share a bed they did so because they also found such a relationship pleasurable and satisfying?[42]

March 25, Jane's last day on the witness stand, began with her testimony being read back to her. That formality completed, she was interrogated on the number of times she was certain the teachers were together and what exactly happened during these incidents. The number of occasions was now four. Jane's aural memory failed her. She could not recollect if on each occasion there was kissing and whispering and now said that she could only be sure that Miss Pirie was panting ("breathing high" [92]) on the last occasion. For the first time, she claimed that the reason she did not talk to Janet earlier about the teachers was shame and embarrassment. When asked about Miss Pirie's birthday note, a cornered Jane said she did not recollect it. Then, when shown the document, she stated in a "lady doth protest too much" tone that even if she had seen it, she wasn't possessed of that morally questionable curiosity that would have led her to read it.

Seemingly satisfied that holes that been had poked in Jane's account and that Jane herself was coming across as an unreliable witness, the judges turned their attention to the three main proofs sought in criminal investigation: means, motive, and opportunity. Jane handled the questions on means and opportunity well. Basically, she had had no means at her disposal for revealing the teachers' relationship. She couldn't inform by letter as the teachers read the pupils' letters. Her aunt Sophia, who was staying at 22 Charlotte Square, had told her that if she had anything to say about the school, she must wait until Helen came back. She couldn't report the teachers to Sophia's sister Louisa Forbes because that aunt was breastfeeding. There was no need to ask for clarification here: in keeping with the belief in the abiding power of first impressions, it was accepted that thoughts and impressions communicated to a nursing mother would affect the quality of her milk and put the baby's physical and emotional development at risk.[43] Thus, Jane had no recourse but to wait until Helen came back to Edinburgh in the second week of November before unbosoming herself.

With respect to motive, two were uncovered: scorned or unrequited affection and revenge, the former relating to Miss Woods and the latter to both Miss Pirie and Miss Woods. It became clear that not long after school resumed after the summer holidays, Jane became so fond of Miss Woods that she would hover around her at teatime, offering to serve her, or want to be near her whenever they went out walking. Jane acknowledged too that it was at this time that she expressed a desire "to sleep with Miss Woods" (94). Miss Woods handled this crush by making light of it. Lord Meadowbank certainly picked up on the sexual roots of Jane's desire. In the margin of his set of proceedings, he made notes to the effect that Jane was very fond of Miss Woods and asked to sleep with her when Miss Munro was not there. Perhaps he was thinking that Jane's eagerness to do kind service at tea masked another agenda.

Unfortunately for Jane, the lack of attention she received from Miss Woods was more than offset by the rebukes she received from Miss Pirie. In response to questions from the bench, Jane went over that fight she had with Miss Cunynghame over a decorum card, after which Miss Pirie told her that she wasn't good enough to speak to her classmate and had either a black heart or no heart, then ordered her to leave the room. She recalled a dispute with the Edgar sisters in which Miss Pirie again sided against her, and a quarrel with Miss Pirie over forgetting to put all her dirty clothes into the laundry bag for the washerwoman. She recollected, too, that during the summer holidays, Miss Pirie "censure[d] her feelings or her heart" (97–98).

The examination on March 25 revealed that before her November unbosoming to Helen, Jane's emotions were a mix of spite, resentment, feelings of rejection, and jealousy. She was in despair, and that dangerous state of mind had cultured in her a desire to strike back. On March 25, she revealed to the court that she had also shared her story with classmate Elizabeth Stirling, who didn't like the school either. Eliza had counseled caution, but Jane had told her, "I don't care who hears me" (97).

Jane's formal part in the suit ended late in the afternoon of March 25 when that day's testimony was read back to her. The note-taker recorded that she wanted it to be understood that when she said she saw "the pursuers in their night shifts, she meant the night things in general" (99). In light of her earlier remarks about the teachers' sexual behavior, it is difficult to understand why she thought this wiggle of a clarification worth making. Perhaps the clarification was the last gasp of a ploy whose inconsistencies had been exposed. That afternoon, as on the previous afternoons, she signed each page of testimony taken down by the court note-taker on long paper at the bottom center. Her bold and even script took up so much space that Lords Meadowbank and Hope, the two judges who also signed, had very little space to write their names. Her story was in tatters, but her squeezing of these judges into the left- and right-hand corners of the page not only speaks of her dominance and defiance of men old enough to be her grandfather. All told, her testimony ran to forty-nine pages in the note-taker's longhand.

Certain facts were now clear. Jane's problems began shortly after Helen left Edinburgh. The teachers had shared a bed in Portobello; they were tender friends who kissed, embraced, fondled, touched. Once classes resumed, Jane propositioned her classmate Janet Munro after Miss Woods dismissed her crush. Not only did she want to be physically close to this teacher during the day, she wanted to sleep with her in her bed at night. Miss Pirie, who had never liked Jane, censured her feelings often. Jane was extremely hurt by Miss Pirie's tongue-lashings. Her behavior in court proved she wanted to be heard and listened to, that she was uninhibited and didn't care who heard her.

Her account contained errors, inconsistencies, falsehoods, embellishments, and imaginative touches, as well as statements of fact and truth; she had a sexualized imagination that could create a voyeuristic scenario. Unquestionably, she was a fabricator and a plotter. She contrived, constructed, interpreted, reneged. However, though she had been interrogated and "industriously interrupted" for nearly six hours a day over four days by men trained in that brutal art, and forced to cede on specific supporting details, she did not renege on her basic point, that the teachers were in a sexual relationship and had had sex on a number of occasions.[44]

Following Jane in the witness box was Charlotte Whiffin. Charlotte denied everything that Jane had imputed to her, and confirmed that Jane, Janet, and Eliza conversed together and that the two Janes slept at a considerable distance in the bed they shared. She thought that the door to one of the rooms had a keyhole. She mentioned that shortly after the school collapsed, she met Jane and one of her Dunbar cousins by accident in Charlotte Square and, prodded by Jane, told her only two scholars—they would soon be picked up—remained at the school. Jane "seemed very glad" (105) to hear this piece of information.

The most interesting story Charlotte relayed had to do with how the school celebrated Miss Woods's birthday in October. She informed the court that, by way of entertaining teachers and pupils on this happy occasion, a pregnant servant named Nancy put on men's clothing over her own. If Charlotte made up the titillating story, it showed her as lacking in respect for the teachers, and possessing a rather coarse sense of humor. On the other hand, if she was telling the truth and such an entertainment was organized for the amusement of the teachers and students, then, precisely because cross-dressing challenges and complicates conventional understandings of sex and gender roles, it independently gave some credence to Jane's point that the teachers were more sexually knowing than they were letting on. The begowned men in the Edinburgh courtroom chose not to investigate Charlotte's story. Because of her age (nineteen), sex (female), class (lower), and position (servant), she was distrusted.

The next witness was Eliza Stirling. Much to the dismay of her mother, who had told Helen in January that it would be an act of cruelty on her part to make her daughter speak, Eliza was called on March 26. Eliza had written Jane on January 22, telling her that whatever she knew about the relationship between the teachers she got secondhand, either from Charlotte, Janet, or Jane herself; she "never witnessed any thing improper between the Misses Woods and Pirie" (154). On March 28, Eliza informed the court that she remembered Jane had been scolded once by Miss Woods for "passing one of the punishment cards, called the decorum-card, unjustly to another girl, and Miss Woods said Miss Cumming was very unfeeling, and that the other girl had a great deal more good in her" (110). When asked whether Miss Pirie had told Jane that Jane had no heart, she was reluctant to commit herself. Her response (put into indirect discourse by the note-taker), "she does think that she recollects Miss Pirie having used words to

Miss Cumming to that effect, at least to the effect of saying 'She has no heart'; but does not recollect her saying 'She had a bad heart'; and her recollection on the subject is not very decisive at all" (114), would seem to confirm that Miss Pirie had uttered those fateful words. Eliza did state that she thought her mother had made an unwise choice in sending her to this particular seminary. She recollected, as well, that she had told her mother "that one of the mistresses was not very good tempered" (109).

When questioned about Charlotte, Eliza presented the servant as disrespectful and improper, one who spoke to the pupils about the mistresses' "indecent behavior and quarrels" (112) and whose coarse sexual expressions, such as that they "might as well take a man at once" and they were "worse than beasts" (108, 115), horrified her. Though she depicted Charlotte as vulgar, Eliza also presented Jane as a source from whom she heard about the teachers' "nasty . . . improper behavior" (109). She herself had heard or seen nothing to support such an allegation. Distancing herself from Jane, she told the court that she only vaguely remembered telling her that "if you are speaking truth, you need not care who hears you" (114) and that it never struck her "at any time or since, upon reflection . . . that there was anything more warm or improper in their [the teachers'] manner than became any other two friends" and that she never noticed "anything improper take place on the bed where Miss Cumming and Miss Pirie slept" (112). She added that she personally never heard any of the dialogue that Jane said had passed between the two teachers when Miss Woods joined Jane and Pirie in the bed, even though her bed was no more than two and a half feet away from the purported ménage-à-trois.

Did the stories originate with Jane or with Charlotte? Who communicated what to whom? What was the connection between Charlotte and Jane? Could Charlotte have passed on the phrase "for fun" to Jane? Eliza's answers clarified or confirmed a number of points. With respect to the pupils, Charlotte had spoken disparagingly about the teachers to them. With respect to the teachers, Eliza had received information about them whose accuracy she herself could not vouch for. With respect to Jane, she had been berated in strong language by Miss Pirie. With respect to Miss Pirie, this teacher was failing at keeping the affection of the girls at the school. If the judges hoped Eliza would be able to identify the originator of the stories, they were disappointed, for all that their questions revealed was that Eliza got her information about the teachers' conduct from either Jane or Charlotte, and now wanted to disassociate herself from both of them and the mess they had gotten her into. When the court adjourned for the day, Eliza left in the company of her father.

Neither the defender, Helen, nor the pursuers, Marianne Woods and Jane Pirie, spoke in court, but witness and letters addressed their characters and personalities. With respect to Helen, Lady Mary Cunynghame stated that a few days after the school closed (but before Helen had been served with the summons that opened the case), she had a conversation with Helen in which Helen "enjoined secrecy . . . caution[ing[her not to mention it to a single individual, not even to Sir William" (130). Taking up cudgels for an endangered child was one thing, but this shamefaced defensiveness suggested Helen knew she had acted inappropriately. Moncreiff and Clerk produced an emotional letter from Helen to Mary Stirling, the mother of Jane's classmate Eliza Christian, in which she appealed for help as one mother to another. She pleaded with Mrs. Stirling to allow her daughter to testify, and to regard the case, what she called "this business," as a "common cause"(155) lest her (Helen's) reputation be impugned. A judge subsequently characterized Helen's note as "a very near subornation of perjury."[45]

With respect to the teachers, it became clear that Marianne was the pleasanter and the more balanced of the two. As revealed in the letter she wrote to her sister Martha in London after returning from the Portobello holiday, in which she compared herself to a boiled bean, she could poke fun at herself. Another letter, this one to Jane Pirie, showed that Marianne found unacceptable her colleague's prejudice toward an unnamed student we can strongly assume to have been Jane Cumming.

In person, on the stand, and by letter sent to John Clerk, Elizabeth Hamilton addressed Jane Pirie's character. Called to testify on March 29, Hamilton did not want to admit that she had judged her ex-mentee's character wrongly, so she tried to balance the negative against the positive. Her manner was unquestionably too fervent, Hamilton admitted, but she was most conscientious and her moral conduct was exemplary. Calling attention to Pirie's "uncommon zeal to perform her duty to her pupils" (120) was a calculated risk on Hamilton's part. It could be taken as praise by the Mrs. Campbells of the world, but if we remember Hamilton's earlier remarks about the good schoolteacher going about her job with "disinterested zeal," then it could be understood as signifying that she now realized Pirie's zeal was of the wrong kind. As it turned out, Hamilton had difficulty maintaining that her zeal was of the right kind, for she told about a time when Miss Pirie asked her advice about a student at the Drumsheugh school. Apparently the student's lack of progress made Pirie anxious and frustrated. Pirie had adopted an "Ossa upon Pelion" approach, piling book upon book on the student in the belief that that would enable the girl to reach the desired goal, and had visited Hamilton in the hope that she could recommend more books. Hamilton gave her a few titles but also warned her against this method. And then there was Pirie's disposition. In a letter she sent John Clerk the day after giving testimony, Hamilton defined it as "irritable," saying that when "anything occurred to call forth her censure, dislike or disapprobation . . . her imagination exaggerated the circumstance into a cause of real vexation, so as to agitate the whole frame of her mind" (132–33).

Though Hamilton was willing to critique Pirie on her disposition, she could not admit that the woman she had handpicked to work under her lacked the right temperament for a teacher. Rather than say that children were the victims of Pirie's irritable nature, with its out-of-proportion reactions to their behavior, she maintained that Pirie's tongue-lashings were "severe" but not so much so "as to prevent her from conciliating their [the pupils'] affection" once she calmed down (133). Janet Munro would have found Hamilton's assessment laughable. The oft-punished student she said that she liked to sit next to the fire during geography lessons, but—she was quite emphatic about this—"not in order to get near Miss Pirie" (60). Temper notwithstanding, Hamilton's conclusion was that "in every respect [she was] a safe person to have the charge of young ladies" (121).

Mrs. Helen Campbell, who also testified on March 29, defended Jane Pirie. Unhappy with her performance on the witness stand, she was more forthcoming in the letter she sent to the court the next month. While she accorded the highest praise to Jane Pirie as a teacher and said that even now she would "without hesitation place a child of my own under her charge," she also called Pirie's attachment to Marianne Woods "folly" and "nonsense." In suggesting that these proceedings would make her see the error of her ways, she was implying that they would cure her of an unhealthy inclination. She referred to Jane Pirie's verbal violence and her eyebrow-raising passion for Marianne as elements of her "ardent temper" (134).

Between Mrs. Hamilton and Mrs. Campbell, the court received an insightful glimpse into Pirie's disposition. What both Campbell and Hamilton were implying was that Jane Pirie was too invested in possessing Woods to be sensitive to the feelings of others. Though she was professionally qualified to be a teacher, she was too emotional. Ardent herself, she could do immense damage to a sensitive, ardent young person, a person like Jane Cumming, without realizing that her method of instilling knowledge rained such blows on the pupil's pride and self-esteem that she would find a way to retaliate.

Both Campbell and Hamilton, however, thought that Pirie's strengths outweighed her drawbacks. Campbell thought the legal proceedings would "cure" Pirie of her attachment. What weighed more heavily with Mrs. Campbell than Jane Pirie's extreme temperament was her strict morality and her indefatigability in the discharge of her duty. Nevertheless, what Campbell's testimony made clear was that despite her satisfaction with Jane Pirie as a teacher for her wards, Pirie's temper was a dangerous instrument, and her attachment fixed, possessive, and unhealthy in nature.

Also produced as proof for the pursuers was the November 16 letter to Mary Cumming. Though it uses the pronoun "we," its tone marks it as a Jane Pirie production. Making all allowances for her distress at students' withdrawals and circulating rumors, what comes out very strongly in the letter is a blinding self-righteousness and lack of self-control. This is a woman who lacks the ability to reflect and relate sensitively to others. So wrapped up in herself is she that she cannot conceive of the possibility that in "too freely telling her [Jane Cumming] of her faults" she might have cruelly hurt the girl's feelings. What she thinks is righteous anger comes across as mortified ego. Nor does she seem to realize that the Christian rhetoric she is employing to present herself as a slaughtered martyr is actually working against her; rather than impressing the reader with her piety, her references to showing pity and mercy are threatening, guilt-inducing, and demanding. Pirie's letter was self-incriminating, damning evidence that she was temperamentally unsuited for the role of teacher.

However, that is was not the offense Jane Pirie was charged with. The issue at stake was her sexual orientation. Her friend Mrs. Campbell's "folly [and] nonsense" assessment of her attachment to Marianne and her feeling that the humiliation of the case would cure her of them suggest that at the core of Jane Cumming's construction of this preceptress there was a kernel of truth.

Chapter Five

JANE AND THE LORDS OF THE LAW (2)

The testimony phase of the lawsuit over, the pages and pages of handwritten material taken down by the note-takers as well as the evidence or proofs submitted to the court by both sides, Janet's punishment-marked history book and Jane's "grudge" book being the notable exceptions, were sent to the printers. Judges and lawyers reassembled in court on June 10, 1811, for closing arguments. Henry Erskine spoke first, addressing his peers in the lovely voice that was his hallmark.[1] He made a number of points, arguing first that since his client's intent in informing the other parents about the teachers was to prevent damage, not to spread a malicious story, the pursuers had no grounds for suing her for defamation. On the topic of same-sex passion, he opined that as with males, so with females. "Lusts arise . . . in persons early in life—boys—in presence of one another—girls the same," he stated. He then added that so-called unnatural passion was nothing more than an odd taste. Just as he personally knew a man, otherwise perfectly unremarkable, "whose only delight was with deformed," so he begged the judges to consider that it was perfectly possible for "ladies of the best character" to find their delight in sexual relationships with each other.

In other words, Erskine was making the argument that moral character and sexual preference were independent of each other. Women could desire women for the same reason that men desired men, because of a natural inclination; the most that one could conclude about such an inborn predilection was that it was uncommon. The large point was that same-sex couples had sexual relationships that ended in mutual gratification, just like heterosexual couples. Like all circumstantial arguments, it was weak, for it did not prove that Woods and Pirie were in fact a sexually active lesbian pair.

Since the keyhole story had been exploded and there was no witness who could corroborate the Portobello tryst, Erskine had no direct evidence to support Jane's assertion that the teachers had been physically intimate. So he made the most of what nobody denied: that they had met at night. With a little help from Shakespeare, Erskine used their meetings to deduce the teachers into actual lovers. Alluding to a scene in *The Merry Wives of Windsor* in which Dr. Caius remarks, "What shall de honest man do in my closet? Dere is no honest man dat shall come in my closet," Erskine noted dryly that in his experience, no adult ever climbed into another adult's bed out of "platonic affection."[2] Erskine's conclusion, therefore, was that the teachers' nocturnal meetings were sexual in nature, and Jane more of a whistleblower than a fabricator or fantasizer.

His clinching argument, however, had to do with color—Jane's color. On the one hand, he pointed out that "virtue is of no color," meaning that the court should not make pejorative assumptions about Jane based on her color and background. On the other, he played the race card adroitly. Precisely because Jane, as a person of color, stood to lose too much by lying, she must be telling the truth. He then reminded the court that Jane was the only witness "on whose general credibility an attack was made."[3] Such an attack was a display of prejudice, a ganging up against a person who was being presumed guilty. Morally and legally, it did not become the Court of Session to engage in such behavior.

Speaking for the pursuers, John Clerk addressed the Court the next day, June 11.[4] Clerk's strategy to defend his clients and get them the £10,000 in damages they were demanding was two-pronged: poke holes in the arguments offered by Helen's counsel and take aim at the witnesses they called and the evidence they marshalled. What makes his closing speech compelling, however, is his complicated presentation of Jane. As might have been foretold, Jane Cumming was at the receiving end of his caustic wit. Nonetheless, the lawyer was not consistently vituperative. The hateful rhetoric won out, but there was a moment when Clerk reverted to the position he took when he and his colleagues were discussing among themselves Jane's admissibility as a witness. At that time, it occurred to him that she was like a child brought up in a brothel, innocent in herself but corrupted by the environment into which she had been placed. In the June speech, he again presented her as a victim. Born innocent but having been sexually touched by figures who shouldn't have had, but did have, access to her in her early infancy, he presented her as a victim of maltreatment, both neglect and sexual abuse. At this moment, he felt something like pity for the adolescent, and speculated about the shape her adult life would take.

At the beginning of his oration, Clerk characterized Jane as a "girl who wanted the instrument of thought," but during the course of his speech, he presented her as a clever and manipulative person, one who chose her collaborators carefully. She chose Janet because of her "most limited" ratiocinative capacities and Eliza because "her heart [was] full of bitterness against them [the teachers]"; she took advantage of Charlotte's status as "an ordinary servant maid" to make it look as if the story about the Misses Woods and Pirie's trysts emanated from her.[5]

Clerk sullied Jane Cumming's character by presenting her as a peeper and nasty rumormonger. While he acknowledged that "girls of 15, 16 and 17 know they can abuse their privy parts," he stated that her sexual knowledge began when she was in India. It was so well-known "what black or half-blooded females learn in India" that it needed no proving.[6] He then mocked Helen's defense team for dishing up a list of authorities to vouch for the existence and practice of tribadism by quoting a voyeuristic stanza from Jonathan Swift's "Corinna, A Ballad."[7] In this poem from 1712, Swift presents Corinna as a "subtle" girl, a "jade," who at the age of six

> Stole to the pantry-door, and found
> The butler with my lady's maid;
> And you may swear the tale went round,
> She made a song, how little miss
> Was kiss'd and slobber'd by a lad:
> And how, when master went to p—,
> Miss came, and peep'd at all he had.

Clerk inserted this stanza into his speech because of its parallels with Jane's story, but the stanzas that Clerk did not quote may reveal his private feelings about Jane. Jane lost her white father in early infancy and was placed at various establishments where oversight seems to have been lax.[8] In the first two stanzas of the poem, Swift makes reference to Corinna's tender infancy and refers to her pityingly. Apollo, the god of beauty, was her midwife and "endued her with his art," but his influence was erased when she was only a baby. While Corinna lay sleeping in her cradle, unattended by a family member or a nursemaid, she was corrupted by Cupid and his companion, a Satyr. These two figures are associated on Roman ceramics with sexual desire, but Swift presents the duo as an evil pair intent on physically molesting Corinna. Entering stealthily like thieves, they first "softly to the cradle creep," then "stroke her hands and rub her gums," robbing her of her innocence, perpetrating a fictive version of what is now called nursery crime or child sexual abuse.[9] Satisfied that their handiwork will have wiped all vestiges of innocence and goodness from her mind, Cupid declares that Corinna will "of love always speak and write" and the Satyr pronounces "the world shall feel her scratch and bite."

In the public space of the courtroom, Clerk besmirched Jane by drawing a parallel between her and the young, low-minded Corinna, but in the stanzas that he didn't quote, he gained through Swift a keyhole through which he could present an alternative image of Jane. He could feel sympathetic to her because she had been institutionalized in infancy. He could imagine that in one of those places where a culture of neglect obtained, she, while still as passively helpless as a sleeping baby, had been molested by figures who impressed sexuality and maliciousness on her; indeed, we watch her being molested through the Swiftian keyhole. As a result of the maltreatment in institutions that Helen in far-off Scotland believed were respectable, Jane was corrupted. Thus, though defending the teachers, Clerk was willing to grant, at least on a careful reading of his speech, that, like his clients, Jane held victim status.

The last stanza of Swift's poem may also shed light on Clerk's assessment of Jane's nature and her post-case future. Swift predicts little Corinna's future. She will grow up wanton and malicious. She will produce "of scandal a cornucopia," an image connoting fertility and abundance, albeit of a vulgar sort. She will become a second Delarivier Manley, identified in this poem as the author of *The New Atalantis* (1709), a work that describes the lifestyle of the members of a lesbian community and their passion for one another. All told, Swift imagines the adult Corinna as mischief-making, sexually uninhibited, and oriented toward women, but able to give voice to her feelings, to act and to act out.

Filtering Jane through Manley's text would have allowed Clerk to wonder privately about Jane's future, since Manley also made a tale of lesbian love go 'round. Did Swift's presentation of Corinna lead Clerk to wonder if the uninhibited and well-developed adolescent with marked sexual feelings was the "real" lesbian in the triangle formed by her and his two clients? As an adult, would her life involve sexual transgression and acts of malice? Would she, like Swift's Corinna, grow up to be "a wit and a coquette," a woman who would marry "for love, half whore, half wife," cuckold her husband, elope, run into debt, and produce "of scandal . . . a cornucopia"? How capable, tough, sexually imaginative, and transgressive would she become? Which social and behavioral norms would she flout? How buoyant would she show herself to be? How would her resilience manifest itself?

Clerk's livelihood depended on his winning the case for his clients. Realizing that this line of thinking was neither advancing the argument nor in the teachers' best interests, he changed tack. At the end of his speech, he put forward the idea that Jane was evil by nature, not by nurture, now comparing her to "the cobra capello of her native Ganges."[10] Referring to the killing effect that she had on her schoolmistresses, he posited that Jane, like the Indian cobra, was born with a disposition to strike and kill by poison and without the human emotions of pity, remorse, or mercy. Whatever pity the lawyer might have felt for this girl who might have been victimized at her Calcutta schools by real equivalents of Swift's Cupid and Satyr figures was replaced by hatred.

At the outset of his closing statement, Clerk had described Jane as a "girl who wanted the instrument of thought" but had shown herself to be clever and manipulative. What he meant by the earlier phrase was now clear: By likening her to the cobra that strikes out of instinct, because its nature is to strike, he provided his audience a powerful illustration of what it meant to be wanting the instrument of thought. Jane was inhuman, below the human.

Erskine's legal partner George Cranstoun delivered his closing statement to the judges a week later, on June 18.[11] He outlined two scenarios and asked them to consider which was more likely. Did Jane, who had been known to be a good girl, suddenly and unaccountably morph into a "malicious and false one," "a monster of iniquity," or did same-sex passion between women exist, in which case the allegation was true? Calling the punishments and rebukes Jane received "mere trifles" and downplaying the pursuers' color prejudice against her, Cranstoun dismissed revenge as a motive. While not rejecting the notion that India was a land of moral pollution, he reminded the judges that Jane had sworn she remembered "to have heard nothing improper" in India and pointed out that she had left when she was "only 7 or at most 8," too young to have been imprinted with any improper sexual notions.

Last, Cranstoun acknowledged that Jane's account had cracks and inconsistencies, but he used the "memory plays tricks" defense to build sympathy for the girl and argue that the problems with her story were really evidence of her overall credibility. Referring to the four days on which Jane gave testimony and was interrogated, he asked the judges to consider how improbable it would be for a "young woman in a most disturbing situation, kept hour after hour, day after day, harassed with a perplexing cross-examination," to remember everything correctly. Never did he broach the possibility that something untoward had happened to Jane on board the *Bengal*.

Cranstoun differed from Erskine in his attitude toward Miss Pirie. While Erskine held that moral character and sexual orientation were independent phenomena, Cranstoun was homophobic. It could be presumed that a woman like Miss Pirie, who directed her "raptures of love and devotion" toward another woman, was "lustful, abandoned, and addicted to an unnatural vice." With his string of descriptors, Erskine sought to render Miss Pirie guilty by adjectival insistence.

The judges began discussing the case among themselves on June 25.[12] While agreeing with Erskine that "accomplished persons have fallen into sodomitical practices," Lord Hope could find no taint of impurity in the minds and behavior of the pursuers in their correspondence or in their professional and personal deportment.[13] Apparently the fact that the setting in which they were behaving romantically was a school did not trouble him. He concluded, "I have no more suspicion of their guilt than I have of my own wife."[14]

With respect to Jane, Lord Hope was so struck by her prepositional surety that when he quoted Jane's words about "in the wrong place," the note-taker who was present underlined "in" (57). That Jane hated the teachers was indisputable. She spoke, he said, with "teeth and bitterness" (57), words that betoken a complex view of Jane's state of mind. By itself, "teeth" conveys the idea that Jane was metaphorically baring her teeth, showing her hostility and readiness to fight. If Woods and Pirie were in the courtroom, they too would certainly have grasped the magnitude of her hatred. "Teeth" also recalls *Matthew* 8:12 and 13:42. In these verses when God punishes wrongdoers either by throwing them into a fiery furnace or the outer darkness, they gnash their teeth as a sign of their despair and rage. Whatever the legal outcome of the case, Jane's future would now be closer to outer darkness than social acceptance. Was Jane, according to Lord Hope, projecting the rage and despair that life at the school and with the teachers had brought her to? On the other hand, could she be imagining herself as an instrument of justice by which the teachers would be severely punished for wronging her—the trial their fiery furnace, their future, outer darkness?

"Bitterness" is also allusively rich. Given the context, Lord Hope's use of the word recalls both *Ephesians* 4:31–32, which exhorts people to "get rid of all bitterness, rage and anger, brawling and slander, along with every form of malice," and an incident in *Samuel* 1:6–16 in which a malicious woman named Peninah, by means of her unrelenting verbal abuse, brings a good woman named Hannah afflicted with infertility to a breaking point, a state of despair and anguish described as "bitterness of soul" (1:6–16). Hannah's husband, a good but obtuse man, can't understand why she is miserable, since he maintains her comfortably, feeding her choice cuts of meat and giving her a seat at table. Hannah finds her way out of her morass through prayer. She is rewarded with a pregnancy; Peninah disappears from the narrative. If we apply the Biblical scenario to Jane's situation, Jane is a Hannah, acknowledged and maintained comfortably enough, but taunted by an unkind, jealous figure and not taken seriously by another important figure in her life. Though these allusions, Lord Hope suggested that Jane was an unsuccessful Hannah, a tormented girl whose bitterness and rage led to the slander she developed, essentially another morass. He could see how Jane's notebook functioned (or didn't function) as Hannah's prayer, why kind Marianne Woods couldn't fathom the depths of Jane's unhappiness, how Jane Pirie's verbal abuse led to her pupil's despair and anguish. But he didn't take any of these factors into consideration when passing judgment on Jane. He wanted to send her to jail for prevarication.

Her comparison of the sound produced by the teachers to a "finger in a wet bottle" also made a great impression on Lord Hope. It led him to conclude that Jane had not been penetrated but had acquired, at some unspecified point in time, in some unspecified locale, either through reading or overhearing, "a good deal [of information] of the intercourse of the sexes. . . . a pretty accurate idea of the act of copulation in its completion" (57). In terms of sexual knowledge, therefore, she was both "knowing" and ignorant," possessed of notional knowledge but physically still a virgin, "ignorant, as being innocent in her own person" (57).

At the same time, the judge believed that sexual relations started very early in India. He said that he had it on the highest authority that "princes get wives of 7 and 8, document states it as actual cohabitation." He presented the other judges with the "historical fact" that a "young man in India at 12 [had been] detected violating child 9 months old."[15] Lord Hope must have realized that his "historical fact" was grounds for thinking that Jane could have been a victim of child sexual abuse and her story a signifier of that violation, so he returned to the Orientalist argument. It could be taken for granted that a female raised in India would be not only more precocious and sophisticated sexually than European girls her age, but cleverer and more mendacious than European female servants. Since *Miss Marianne Woods and Miss Jane Pirie Against Dame Helen Cumming Gordon* was a defamation of character suit resulting from a respectable woman taking the word of a biracial child born and raised in India until she was almost eight, Lord Hope was all for Helen paying damages, as she had acted foolishly.

The proceedings had been agonizing for Meadowbank. He stated that in his "24 years practice at the Bar and 19 on the Bench [he had] never passed such painful hours as during the examination of these young persons."[16] Jane in particular excited his sympathy and pity because she was "deprived of" legitimacy and a European complexion and went through the ordeal of a prolonged examination. However, he acknowledged that her story was a flimsy fabrication, its falsehoods easily revealed. Eliza Stirling's testimony, for instance, proved that Charlotte never stuck out her tongue so that the girls would know what the teachers were doing. However, like all false stories, Jane's had "hair to make tether," meaning that it made connections but the connections themselves were weak.[17] As an example of a preposterous falsehood, he singled out the time at Portobello when Jane claimed the teachers went to bed in broad daylight while she and Charlotte walked together. Yet even though he called it a "false story . . . a collection of falsehoods," he was opposed to sending Jane to jail for lying.

Lord Robertson spoke next. He found it as improbable that two women lay with each other as that two sixteen-year-olds "combined to ruin 2 women," but basically he was sympathetic to Jane on account of the grilling she went through, which he called "unexampled in any case civil or criminal." He also thought that the pursuers' case would have been stronger if their lawyers had called girls whose testimony would have countered Janet's and Jane's about the teachers' lewd practices. While he admitted that the case was taking him into uncharted waters, he thought Helen's side the stronger of the two.[18]

Lord Boyle went through Jane's account meticulously. Because of its many inconsistencies, contradictions, and inventions, he opined that, on the whole, he could "lay no weight on Miss C—." As for Janet Munro, he thought there was "real evidence" that Jane had put the idea that the teachers were lovers in her head. However, the real reason he believed the teachers to be innocent had to do with a point that was never mentioned during the proceedings, namely, that in "other melancholy cases" where women conceived a passion for each other, "they took guilt to themselves." Turning to his fellow judges, he asked, "Any such thing here?" Lord Boyle understood that Jane's future was at stake and felt sorry for the defendant, Helen, but that the teachers' presence in the courtroom proved for him their innocence and the justice of their claim for damages.[19]

Lord Glenlee confessed his first thought was that the girls conspired to bring down the teachers with a concocted story, but as he reviewed the testimony and evidence, he changed his mind. He could accept that "in all ages and countries" women have found gratification in postures considered impossible, irregular, improper, and unspeakable and derived much pleasure, too, from fantasizing about such postures.[20] Thus he had no problem believing that women could engage in sexual relations with other women or that a woman could be a voyeur and develop fantasies from watching women make love. But he was disposed to believe Jane wasn't fantasizing because in her account the teachers seemed very much like women caught in an adulterous relationship. Therefore he felt that Helen was justified in acting precipitately. (Not entirely surprisingly, Glenlee's son Thomas married Helen's daughter Edwina in 1814.)

Lord Newton's wits were in no way impaired by his fondness for the bottle. Whether or not the teachers' behavior had crossed the line from the affectionately playful to the sexually intimate in bed, he considered displays of affection consistent with romantic friendship inappropriate in a school setting and Woods and Pirie "unfit for the superintendence of young ladies." On the other hand, he thought it a "monstrous improbability" that they would choose a bed occupied by another person as a site for their lovemaking.[21] Had he been a juryman forced to come up with a verdict on the teachers' sexual behavior, had lesbianism been a crime and the teachers charged with it, he stated he would have most probably returned a decision of not proven, that uniquely Scottish form of acquittal used in criminal cases in which the factual evidence to convict is held inadequate but those sitting in judgement are not strongly convinced of the accused person's innocence.[22] But as this was a civil case about awarding damages, what, if anything, the teachers did in bed was irrelevant.

What Lord Newton was not conflicted about was Jane, and Lord Hope's interrogation of her. He stated categorically that "nothing short of the spirit of the devil" could have induced her to fabricate such a story, and he did not believe that she had been possessed.[23] As for Lord Hope, Lord Newton regarded his colleague's examination as an ad hominem attack. Any evidence collected through a personal attack on a witness, however important and revealing, could not be taken into account, he argued. Newton interpreted the questions that the Lord Hope had flung at Jane as an attempt to prove "Miss C herself guilty of such practices."[24] Newton's stance precluded him reviewing her testimony to ascertain if it indeed supported the idea that frustrated sexual desire on Jane's part might have led to the story of sapphic love she told Helen.

The judges voted on June 28. The six who had participated in the deliberations were evenly split. Lords Hope, Meadowbank, and Boyle sided with the pursuers while Lords Robertson, Glenlee, and Newton sided with the defendant. Lord Polkemmet, who never attended a session, cast the deciding vote for the defendant. Helen must have been thrilled, as the determination meant she wasn't liable for damages—or, to be more precise, that she hadn't burdened her two sons with that huge expense. Jane, who in November 1810 had greeted the pursuers' ruin with joy, must also have been very happy in June 1811.

The case was far from closed, however. Three months later, on September 12, Clerk and Moncreiff submitted a petition asking for the decision to be reviewed. The petition to appeal was quickly granted. Within a month the two lawyers had another document ready to be perused by the judges.

The document—or, in Scots law usage, petition—that Clerk and Moncreiff submitted "unto the Right Honourable the Lords of Council and Session" on October 11 did not break new ground. The pursuers' team rehashed all the inconsistencies and contradictions in Jane's testimony in painstaking detail. They argued that "if a man and a woman are in bed together, venereal congress would be presumed," and that while "an unnatural intention" could be inferred if two men slept with each other, no such inference could be drawn if the pair in question were female.[25] Without directly referring to Erskine's application of the lines from *The Merry Wives of Windsor*, they challenged his interpretation, limiting it to heterosexual encounters, and upheld the notion that romantic female friendship was asexual. Even if two women engaged in erotically charged, sexually exciting displays of affection that would have been construed as foreplay if a heterosexual couple were involved, no such interpretation could be drawn on the basis of two women's behavior in bed.

To further diminish Jane' credibility, they put her under the Orientalist microscope—again. They argued that simply by living in India for so long and in the company of natives, her mind inevitably became contaminated. Such an upbringing would have corrupted any child, they maintained, but the impressions of lewd behavior that would develop into "licentious or libidinous propensities" ("Additional Petition," 50) later on would have sunk more deeply into a child of mixed race. Implicitly drawing support from Captain Thomas Williamson's *Vade-Mecum*, where it was stated (erroneously) that most children born in India to two white parents were sent to Europe by the age of four, Clerk and Moncreiff tweaked the facts a little and did not have Jane leave "till she was of the age of eight or nine" ("Additional Petition," 49).

Moncreiff and Clerk had to do more than play to Western unstated fear that unless a biracial child was brought to Britain at a very early age, her "black" blood inevitably trumped her "white" inheritance. They needed to identify the trigger, the event or situation that caused an adolescent Jane to manifest those so-called licentious propensities she had been impressed with. They located this trigger in the punishments Jane regularly incurred and the effect these had on her disposition. They did not connect her ardent, brooding, intense temperament to her Indian blood or breeding.

And, of course, since it would not have suited their clients and would have toppled their own Orientalist strategy, Moncreiff and Clerk did not point out that Jane Pirie had the same temperament as her pupil and nemesis, that the two Janes both desired Miss Woods, and that (as Mrs. Hamilton had explained) in situations where two people want the same object, it is very common for them to display anger, jealousy, and malice.

Instead, Moncreiff and Clerk tweaked the facts. They glossed over the sharpness of Miss Pirie's temperament and the prejudice the teacher manifested toward the pupil. They presented Miss Pirie's remark that Jane Cumming "had no heart or a bad one" as a trifle. They acknowledged but minimized the degree of resentment and spite radiating from Jane's notebook. They further dismissed Jane's feelings by claiming that the "malicious falsehood" she told was out of all proportion to her real motive, a very common one for a sixteen-year-old female: "to shake off the trammels of a school, and to begin to be treated as a woman" ("Additional Petition," 53).

Clerk had also implied in June that by nature Jane was not evolved. Her inborn disposition was that of a cobra; she lacked the instrument of thought and was endowed with the ability to strike. That being the case, it was only natural, Moncreiff and Clerk concluded in October, only to be expected, that at the age of sixteen this Gangetic cobra in girl's dress would construe the teachers' romantic friendship as "the gross fondling of wantonness": a lesbian relationship, something "never before heard of in [this] country" ("Additional Petition," 107).

Helen's counsel George Cranstoun, this time supported by James Mackenzie, responded to this presentation on February 22, 1812. They offered a portrait of Jane so radically different from the one painted by Clerk and Moncreiff that it seemed they were talking about another girl altogether. They claimed that both Jane and Helen had been the victims of ad hominem attacks by Moncreiff and Clerk, when the latter characterized Jane "as a monster, polluted, malevolent, insidious, and perjured beyond example" and Helen as "a rash and malicious calumniator." They stated that the pursuers' lawyers could find themselves sued for the same thing their clients were suing Helen for: defamation of character. In fact, Clerk and Moncreiff had everything reversed. If anything or anyone had done anything to harm Jane's mind, it was the teachers, who, "in violation of a sacred trust . . . endangered the purity of Miss Cumming's mind."[26]

Given that Jane had compared the noise the teachers made while pleasuring themselves to that of a finger inserted in a bottle, the defense lawyers' faith in the purity of Helen's granddaughter's adolescent mind was touching but unfounded. Cranstoun and Mackenzie were on surer ground when noting the race prejudice that had been openly expressed against Jane. They pointed out, for example, that her credibility as a witness was impugned largely on account of "her being a native of Hindustan" ("Answers," 44).

This point was a repetition of Erskine's earlier argument that virtue was of no color, yet the defense lawyers too believed whiter was better. Addressing Their Lordships, they reminded them that, as seen with their own eyes, "the tinge" was barely "perceptible" ("Answers," 5). In a similar vein, they reminded the judges that Jane had been placed at respectable establishments in Calcutta, that she had left India when she was seven and a half, and that "even the wildest theorists on the subject of Oriental precocity have not thought of extending it to children" of that age, particularly those "born of a European parent" ("Answers," 63). Jane therefore was credible because she had left India before her mind could have become polluted and, though she was not quite white and had a good bit of sexual knowledge, she was white enough to be taken as truth-telling.

In addition, Cranstoun and Mackenzie proffered common sense as a reason to believe Jane's testimony. Why would the girl want to tell such a story? It was not in her interest to tell it. The duo went over the by now well-trodden ground of how Helen had apprised Jane that good behavior at the school would be "the means of qualifying her to be introduced into society as a lady" whereas removal from the school would send her back to a life as a milliner or mantua-maker, a fate Jane "dreaded" ("Answers," 6). Why would she take such a risk?

Once again, Cranstoun and Mackenzie downplayed the punishments and rebukes she had received. They made light of Miss Pirie's saying that Jane had no heart or a bad one, dismissing it as the kind of remark that every girl receives from a schoolmistress at some point or other. Cranstoun also described Jane's grudge book as exhibiting "a most engaging picture of the perfect innocence of Miss Cumming, and the playful and easy temper of Miss Woods," who gave her the "task of learning a few lines of poetry by heart" ("Answers," 6).[27] Adroitly eliminating the irritable Miss Pirie from the equation, he asked the judges to consider why Jane would want to hurt sweet-tempered Miss Woods, since she was particularly attached to her. In their account, rather contradicted by the letter the teachers sent Mary Cumming, the teachers had not picked on her and she had taken their criticism in a good spirit. With revenge as well as the character flaws of malice and ardent brooding jettisoned as motives, there could be only one explanation for Jane's allegation and only one assessment of her character.

In keeping with that honest character, Jane was telling the truth about the teachers' sexuality. At age sixteen, she was still the amiable girl who had been boarded with Miss Charles.

This line of reasoning to prove that Jane's moral character as an adolescent was consistent with her moral character as a girl in Elgin was a bit of a reach, since Helen had derived her glowing assessment from a paid caregiver, but Cranstoun and Mackenzie continued to stretch the truth. As had already been established, Helen had not met Jane until 1803, when she was about eight. Within six months, she boarded the child in Elgin. Between 1804 and 1806, Helen was distracted by the illnesses and deaths of her husband and her daughter Charlotte. Despite all evidence to the contrary, Cranstoun and Mackenzie claimed Helen had known Jane from infancy and had personally "never seen the smallest deviation from innocence and truth" ("Answers," 6). Wasn't it more logical that Jane was telling the truth about the teachers than that she had "at once become an adept in a species of obscene knowledge," motivated by malice that was hidden under "sentiments of tenderness?" ("Answers," 6). Considering the stereotype of the female servant of the era as crude and knowledgeable, wasn't it more logical to consider Charlotte Whiffin the source of the story?

Turning to the teachers, Cranstoun and Mackenzie then compared "the situation of the petitioners in their boarding-school . . . to that of nuns in a cloister," where they maintained three kinds of sexual irregularities were frequently indulged in: "illicit but natural amours" (heterosexual relationships), "secret and solitary vice" (masturbation), and "disgusting and unnatural lewdness" (female homosexual relationships) ("Answers," 25). In reality, in Protestant Britain, nunnery was a loaded word. It could mean a respectable convent or cloistered religious community that operated according to rules; it could mean a whorehouse; it could refer to a place that exuded purity but within whose walls the denizens maintained sexual liaisons with men or engaged in lesbian sex with each other.[28] Cranstoun and Mackenzie were implying that Woods and Pirie chose to found a school for the same reason some women entered nunneries—because it provided cover for engaging in a transgressive sexual relationship.

Actually, much thought had been given to the potential for same-sex relationships to develop within cloistered religious communities for females. The founders of medieval convents made sure the nuns followed a strict routine that kept them occupied all day long. Not trusting to busyness to keep the women focused on serving God, Donatus of Besançon in the seventh century generated a list of rules controlling their social behavior. Attached to the commandments were the sanctions for breaking them. The rules prohibited nuns from taking each other by the hand, walking or sitting together, sleeping in the same bed, or paying nocturnal visits to each other. A woman caught in a carnal relationship with another woman was deemed to have committed the sin of fornication, punishable with three years of penance. The seventeenth-century rule governing the nuns of the Sacred Order of Our Lady of Mercy uses "sodomy" rather than "fornication" to describe a same-sex intimate act. Nuns convicted of sodomy were either permanently incarcerated or expelled from the convent. In the sixteenth century, St. Theresa of Avila prohibited Carmelites from embracing, touching, or becoming too agitated when speaking, lest their affection and emotions lead them into forbidden territory.

Particular attachments were even more worrisome to these founders as they caused the individuals involved to lose focus, with their special friend taking the place of God. Furthermore, these particular friendships had the potential for giving rise to scandalous talk outside the walls and destroying peace and harmony within, almost always because one of the women involved in the special friendship developed resentment, started feeling jealous, or felt insulted. In the thirteenth century, St. Bonaventure developed a checklist to determine whether a deep friendship between two nuns was spiritual or sexual. It was probably sexual if it appeared that they wanted always to be together, were obsessed with each other, suffered from a jealous anxiety that somebody was going to steal their partner, fought passionately, or complained with great bitterness that they were being mistreated and then made up afterward.[29]

Drawing on an entrenched understanding of cloistered religious communities as sites of vice, Helen's lawyers were implicitly establishing similarities between the behavior of the Protestant Woods and Pirie at their highly structured, rule-governed Drumsheugh seminary and that of some Catholic nuns living a regimented life within their convent. Like well-regulated, respectable nuns who had chosen their vocation, the two schoolmistresses stayed busy in the conscientious performance of duties. However, while they were living lives deeply committed to an admirable cause, they were not above suspicion. They engaged in behaviors that the founders of convents had prohibited, on grounds that they led (or could lead) to the commission of a sexual sin. Woods and Pirie were like those special friends whose behavior Saints Theresa and Bonaventure warned against. The two teachers visited each other at night and sometimes slept in the same bed—which the lawyers called attention to, even highlighted, by noting that "there was not the least occasion" for the bedsharing.[30] The teachers fought, then they made up. Pirie in particular suffered from rancor and resentment, was obsessively jealous, and felt she had been maltreated. These malignant emotions deflected her from her primary commitment, to treating the pupils equally; destroyed her peace of mind and inner harmony; and led to the dissolution of the friendship.

Saints Theresa and Bonaventure had predicted that at convents housing special friends, a state of hostility would come to reign within the walls, while outside them, rumors about the nuns' sapphic practices would be flying—both of which came to pass for the Woods-Pirie School. Theresa and Bonaventure's fear that special friendships at convents were not only unacceptable in themselves but potentially dangerous to the individuals and the institutions they were associated with certainly came true once Jane shared her story with Helen.

Since further documentation could not be submitted at the appeals stage, Helen's counsel could not provide the judges with the books containing these conventual rules, regulations, and checklists.[31] And though they assumed this centuries-old information was within the judges' ken, Cranstoun and Mackenzie might well have hoped Their Lordships also remembered more recent works on the theme of women who loved women. There were, for example, two pieces by Swift from the early 1700s that appeared in *The Tatler*. *Tatler* 32, written while the periodical was still under the direction of Joseph Addison, bore the title "A Satiric Treatment of Mary Astell's *A Serious Proposal to the Ladies*." It combined a self-chosen homosocial lifestyle on English soil, "unnatural" love expressed in religious rhetoric, and women who claimed to be pure and high-minded but whom Swift presented as voyeurs gazing longingly at male visitors through peepholes.

The other essay, in *Tatler* 5, Swift's contribution to the periodical after it was taken over by William Harrison (a poet, diplomat, and lifelong fellow of New College, Oxford), is a voyeuristic dream fantasy about lions that can distinguish between virgins and nonvirgins by smell, killing the latter and leaving the former unscathed on their wedding day. In the dream, the voyeur is told that in one parish many women have chosen to live in nunneries rather than risk being torn limb from limb. He is then taken to see a lion-sniffer at work. A woman enters the pit fearlessly but the lion attacks her. As she is being dismembered, she shouts, "*The Lion is just, I am no true Virgin! Oh! Sappho, Sappho.*" Swift's stance is clear: a woman who has had same-sex relations is no more virginal than women who have had sex with men, and a lot more hypocritical.[32]

Should the judges not recall these two pieces, the lawyers could hope that they remembered one of the three almost identical pieces about the Ladies of Llangollen that appeared, as already mentioned, in July 1790 in the *St. James Chronicle*, the *London Chronicle*, and the *General Evening Post*. Entitled "Extraordinary Female Affection," the author insinuated that the relationship between Butler and Pononsby was carnal, and offered evidence in support of his claim. The fictional women of *Tatler* 32 and 5 suggested that the tribadic practices Woods and Pirie were alleged to have engaged in were far from exotic and that women who engaged in these practices had had as sexual a relationship as any heterosexual couple. The articles about the Ladies of Llangollen suggested that to some minds the behavior of women such as Woods and Pirie, was, at the very least, sexually suspect.

The petition submitted by Clerk and Moncreiff on October 11, 1811, on behalf of their clients totaled 115 quarto-size pages. Cranstoun and Mackenzie's answer to it, submitted four months later on February 22, 1812, was longer by thirty-four pages. When the judges met on February 25 and 26, they had had four months to review the October petition and just a few days to look over the defense's answer. Since what they considered was the testimony they had heard in March 1811 and the material submitted by both parties in June 1811, it seems that the judges never read these hefty documents.

Notes and other material from the judges' second set of deliberations in 1812, when the case was reviewed on appeal, are also bound in the sets that once belonged to Meadowbank and Moncreiff.[33] Of particular interest are the points of view expressed by Lords Woodhouselee, Meadowbank, and Gillies, the last a recent appointment to the bench. Lord Meadowbank's friend William Tytler, Lord Woodhouselee, had not been swayed by Erskine's "virtue is of no color" argument, and stated that he found it most improbable that "two women of such education, principles, characters" could engage in "unnatural debauchery . . . and sacrifice all for beastly gratification."[34] In addition, since it had been proved that Janet Munro had gotten her story from Jane, that Jane's tale about the teachers being hooted at in the vicinity of the Water of Leith had been discredited, and that Jane had acknowledged that she concluded the teachers were intimate on the basis of her own reflections, the judge's position was that Jane had concocted the whole story.

For Lord Woodhouselee, it was a "painful" and incredible story, but not calumny or a planned malicious act.[35] Perhaps based on his experience raising a large family that included a son who liked to get into fights and a niece who was something of a tomboy, he took a "children will be children" approach to Jane's allegations.[36] Saying that Jane had put together her story because she found the "bondage of school irksome," was "anxious to come into [the] world," and had no idea that it would be taken so seriously, he did not consider her "first iteration [to be] of that black [a] nature."[37] Since one of the teachers censured her more than any other girl at the school, he could understand her desire to take revenge: it was the way human nature worked. Jane's story got darker and developed inconsistencies and contradictions over time and under pressure, as she was forced to invent details to support the charge while in the witness box. The malefactor in this case, therefore, was not Jane, but the mature Helen who swallowed this incredible story. She showed "gross negligence," according to Woodhouselee, in taking "no means to enquire" into the "tale of [a] girl of 16."

Lord Gillies argued that Jane's formative years in India were partly responsible for the story she told. He believed that Jane arrived in Britain with knowledge on the subject. Echoing the consensus that bedsharing by members of the same sex was a perfectly acceptable practice, Gillies maintained that no presumption of guilt should be drawn from the teachers' visiting each other at night and sleeping in the same bed. Alluding to a sentence from William Robertson's 1769 *History of the Reign of the Emperor Charles V* in which the author notes that the Roman chancery established a system of set taxes to be levied on those convicted of terrible crimes, even "shocking crimes as seldom occur in human life, and perhaps only exist in the impure imagination," Lord Gillies implied that the sexual crime Jane accused the teachers of existed only in her imagination, which was impure by virtue of her being Indian and having spent some impressionable years in India—yet that her fabrication of the tale was a punishable offense.

Lord Gillies then considered the nature Jane was born with. To impurity of mind he added weakness of intellect, a less harsh version of Clerk's idea that Jane lacked "the instrument of thought," and also a charge far harsher, that Jane was filled with something approaching pathological malice. Her objective was a trifling one—all she wanted was "to get rid of school." But people with "depraved minds with weak intellects," Lord Gillies argued, not being able to correlate means and ends, use excessive force to achieve "paltry ends."

In support of this thesis that a defective or bad nature, rather than nurture, was behind Jane's story, Gilles adduced a recent case that had appeared in the newspapers involving a domestic servant working in the south of Scotland. She had poisoned her master and mistress with arsenic-laced porridge, with fatal results. According to Lord Gillies, the servant's reason was either to "eat fowl and drink wine" at supper or "almost no reason at all."[38]

The murder by poisoning that Lord Gillies was referring to was that of Thomas Stothart and his wife by their servant Helen Kennedy in Dumfriesshire. It was reported in the *Caledonian Mercury* on December 28, 1811, and received a brief mention in *The Scots Miscellany* of January 1812, which added the information that while Stothart and his wife consumed the tainted porridge, Kennedy, "under pretence that that sort of food did not agree with her . . . breakfasted upon bread and beer." Kennedy, the daughter of a Dumfriesshire farmer and his wife, was now in jail. The case was heard later in 1812. The court did not look into any aspect of Kennedy's upbringing or the Stotharts' treatment of her to see if something in the way of nurturing lay behind the poisoning.[39] By bringing up the Helen Kennedy case, Lord Gillies was suggesting that if the poisonous story Jane spread had been the product of a Scottish lass, it would have been ascribed solely to the malignant nature she was born with.

Interestingly, the notes of Lord Gillies's presentation that ended up in Lord Meadowbank's set indicated that Lord Gillies also found Shakespeare helpful in thinking about the characters of the case. Janet Munro, he ruminated, was "in the situation of Othello so well described by Shakespeare," thus implying that Jane and Iago shared an evil nature. Just as the plotting, malignant, mendacious, clever, vengeful, seductive Iago had convinced Othello of sexual falsehoods, so Jane had "abused" the simple Janet by filling her mind with "erroneous impressions" about the sexual orientation of the Misses Woods and Pirie.[40]

Lord Meadowbank came to the 1812 deliberations with a lengthy prepared statement, substantial portions of which were strongly personal. "I felt myself more concerned for Miss Cumming than for any human being for I felt her dependent and an orphan," he wrote, noting that she was placed in an institution in infancy in Calcutta and then boarded in in an institution in Elgin.[41] He must have been troubled by the lacuna in the printed transcript that leaves blank the number of years Jane spent at Miss Charles's school even though she had testified that she had spent six years with Miss Charles. When he paraphrased her words, he filled in the number, changed a verb, and cut the reference to Miss Charles. He states that she "was left at Elgin for six years." His excision of Miss Charles and the substitution of "left at" for both "sent to" and "kept by" are significant.

"Sent to" and "kept by" connote maintenance and some degree of involvement; "left at," without saying with whom, indicates abandonment.

Upset through he was at, and to some extent, by the nurturing she received in Scotland, Lord Meadowbank thought Jane's upbringing in India the more important shaping factor. She was the product of an education by female servants who taught her the arts of seduction and the language she would be expected to employ as an adult. So casually was sex taken and so sexually active were the people in India, she would have seen lovemaking couples wherever she looked; just as "a Lady in this country [can't] avoid seeing the congress of common flies," so it would have been, he stated categorically, "impossible for any person to have lived in Calcutta for any length of time without seeing the congress of the sexes." He also opined that "in hot countries where [women were] shut out from men," they would either use dildos or have sexual relations with each other to satisfy their needs. Jane's presentation of the teachers as a lesbian couple was—he was quite emphatic about this—"a theory of foreign importation." He could not believe her statement that she had never heard or seen anything immodest in India. Since he did not consider the possibility that she might have read one of the many lewd books produced in England during the eighteenth century, he concluded that the only place she could have learned about sexual practices and learned to talk about them so immodestly, so shamelessly, was in India.[42]

Meadowbank did, however, return to her Scottish nurturing at the end of his statement. Chastising Helen in the tones of a paterfamilias for poor parenting skills, he stated that this heart-wrenching case could have been prevented if Helen had only practiced the rule he followed in his family. "We all know," he remarked, "that when you question children it teaches them immediately to invent, whatever may be the subject. One of my earnest injunctions to my family is never to question children nor to run the risk of suggesting inventions to them."

Not content with these pronouncements, he criticized Helen sharply for believing herself "entitled to demand" blind support from the mothers of some of Jane's classmates. There were no grounds on which he could excuse Helen's rashness, which was a form of foolishness; she was, therefore, liable for damages.

Immediately following these deliberations the judges voted. The 1811 determination was now reversed, with four judges—Lords Meadowbank, Boyle, Gillies, and Woodhouselee—favoring the pursuers and three—Lords Robertson, Craigie, and Glenlee—supporting the defendant. A functionary attached to the pursuers' defense team requested the judges revise the statements they had read out in court in which they announced their decisions. These revised determinations would then be sent to the printer.

Of particular significance are the revisions that Lords Hope, Woodhouselee, Gillies, and Meadowbank made. Lord Hope deleted his "historical facts" on Indian sexuality. Reflecting on his initial attitude, he now said he had been "swayed by too much respect for the family of Lady Cumming Gordon" in pressuring his judicial brothers to send Jane to jail.[43] And he now called Helen's attempt to get Mrs. Stirling to make common cause with her "very near subornation of perjury" (61).

As his use of italics indicates, Lord Woodhouselee recognized that Jane "*had* reason, and *good reason, too,* for bearing them [the teachers] no good will" (73), but he didn't condone her. In fact, he now called her decision to escape from school "wicked" (75). More important, he orientalized her, stating that her mind "was contaminated . . . by impure ideas, which she had imbibed partly from her Eastern education, and partly perhaps from that precocity of temperament which she owed to an Eastern constitution" (73). Rejecting his earlier conclusion that Jane had no knowledge of sex, he now maintained that she knew about "lascivious commerce between persons of the same sex" (74). And though he said that for her, a lesbian relationship "did not carry with it, either the idea of impossibility, or of that shocking criminality, which it would have excited in the breast of a young girl, born and bred in this country," he also seemed to be implying that Jane had spent enough time in the West and was, despite the conviction among some of his colleagues that she was intellectually defective, smart enough to figure out that tagging the teachers as lovers was as good as accusing them of a "shocking criminality" (74). Calling lesbianism "a thing perhaps impossible" (75) did not rule out its existence in the West, but if it did exist, Woodhouselee opined, it was so rare that almost no one born and bred in Europe would have suspected the teachers of being lovers. But the combination of the brainpower Jane was endowed with and the Eastern notions impressed on her as a child had enabled her to construe the teachers' behavior as evidence of a same-sex sexual relationship.

It was not Jane with her infected mind, however, who had perpetrated the real wrongdoing, said Woodhouselee; it was Helen. He had previously described Jane's grandmother as grossly negligent, and this strong critique became even stronger. Helen's conduct, he wrote, was "rash, inconsiderate and cruel. . . . If there was not malice in this conduct, there was a precipitancy, and a culpable negligence, for which it is impossible to find excuse" (84–85).

Lord Gillies scuttled the notion that "perhaps" Jane only imagined the teachers were sapphists. "I am happy to express my belief," he now pronounced, "that no such crime was ever known in Scotland or in Britain" (93). The consequence of cutting the reference to Kennedy and keeping the allusion to Iago was to present her as incomprehensible and abnormal.

Lord Meadowbank took the opportunity to make less personal the statement he had read out in 1812. He omitted his remarks on his parenting skills and modified his reading of Jane. Earlier, the mental picture he had formed of her, maintained at the Elgin boarding school so near and yet so far away from the family, made her an object of pity who evoked his "strongest sympathies." Now altering his previous wording about Jane's heritage, that she was "deprived of" legitimacy and a European complexion, by inserting the phrase "unfortunately wanting in" (1) before those two qualities the judge not only reduced the pity quotient but suggested that Jane be seen as deficient because of her Indian blood.

The argument by Moncreiff and Clerk about the impact of Jane's early upbringing among female Indians of the lower orders seems to have impressed Lord Meadowbank, for he also concluded that the Eastern environment best explained the contriving and sexualized cast of her adolescent mind. Speaking ex cathedra, he "held [himself] entitled to assume . . . that the language of Hindoo female domestics . . . turns chiefly on the commerce of the sexes" (16). He obviously had decided that Helen, who said Jane left India before she turned eight, was not a trustworthy source of information on her granddaughter; Jane was eight or nine, he wrote, by the time she left India. By that age, everyone in Britain agreed, an individual's mind had been indelibly imprinted—in the case of a girl raised in India, sexually and morally corrupted. By the same logic, nothing Jane said pertaining to the teachers' sexual orientation could be taken as true; due to her "*eastern* [Meadowbank's italics] imagination and education" (20), she both misinterpreted the teachers' affectionate relationship as sexual and knew how to seduce two of her classmates into going along with it. That was all there was to it. So the judge who in 1810–11 found himself "caught up in the thickets of messy human relationships . . . in [a case] fraught with ambiguities," could write in 1812, "my view of the case . . . is a very simple one" (19).[44]

Meadowbank's certainty that Jane had told falsehoods and misconstrued and misrepresented the teachers did not prevent him from opening up the "were they or weren't they" question. However, he rejected the possibility of the Misses Woods and Pirie being tribades when he declared that it was statistically impossible for two women with the same proclivity to find themselves in the same art class in the same year in Edinburgh's New Town. Apparently granting himself the license to fantasize sexually, he opined that their genitalia were unremarkable.

Now very much the judge who had freed himself from the agonizing personal aspects of the case, Lord Meadowbank realized the issue he had to decide was whether Helen had libeled the teachers. If the answer was yes, she was liable for damages and expenses. That Helen's motivation was not malicious was irrelevant. He now considered Jane's story as the consequence of an Indian education, rejected the existence of women who loved women in New Town, and refused to acknowledge that erotic implications could be drawn from an emotional attachment between two well-bred British women. Meadowbank joined Lords Woodhouselee, Gillies, and Boyle in determining in favor of the Misses Woods and Pirie.

The judges' deliberations did not stay private. On March 6, 1812, Colin MacKenzie, the principal clerk of the Court of Session and a Gordon Cumming in-law, wrote a letter to James Skene, a well-known artist, antiquarian, and friend of Sir Walter Scott, in which he called Lord Woodhouselee a "stupid body" for convincing the other judges to determine against Helen.[45] He also expressed his unhappiness that this judge had convinced, or tricked, other judges into believing that "poor black Jeannie had a polluted imagination."[46] He compared the success of the Orientalist argument as used by Lord Woodhouselee to that of the Eidophusikon, an entertainment invented by Philip James de Loutherbourg, an experienced designer of theater sets. At least one hundred spectators at a time could view in Loutherbourg's mechanical theater spectacles accompanied by special effects produced by smoke, mirrors, gauze, and colored glass. The illusions were very popular; the painters Thomas Gainsborough and Joshua Reynolds were impressed by Loutherbourg's techniques for making dramatic fictions come to life.[47]

In referencing the Eidophusikon, MacKenzie was critiquing Lord Woodhouselee's presentation. He thought the judge had used misleading, irrelevant, and meretricious information in the way Loutherbourg had used mirrors and colored light: to lead people away from the truth. MacKenzie's letter further indicates that he personally did not consider that Jane's youth, race, upbringing, or gender disqualified her as an accurate observer or discredited her testimony. His use of the diminutive "Jeannie" and of the adjectives "poor" and "black" in connection with her, seem to show that he felt rather sorry for this adolescent, in a patronizing sort of way.

At the time the adverse verdict was rendered on February 26, 1812, the case had already cost Helen's sons Sir William and Charles Lennox a few shillings under £712, or about $62,700 in today's money. This stupendous amount, to be paid to Mackenzie & Innes, covered the fees for Cranstoun and Erskine and their clerks for pleading the case in court, attending debate hearings, calling on potential witnesses, and taking care of all the chamber work the case engendered. Mackenzie & Innes was also prepared for an adverse determination. Two hundred out of the seven hundred-plus pounds was for a very important piece of chamber work: preparing the case for the Law Lords of the House of Parliament in the event that the Lordships of the Court of Session returned an unfavorable verdict and the case had to go to London on appeal.

Neither the mounting cost nor the bench's unfavorable decision deterred Helen, who reacted in much the same way Penrose had in 1804, when he pursued the Reverend John Macdonnell. Goaded by ego, blinded by passion, and with access to money, she believed that she would live to laugh her opponents to scorn. Her devoted sons Sir William and Charles paid for their mother to continue the case against the teachers.

Mackenzie & Innes immediately began the process of getting the decision reviewed at the Parliamentary level by the Law Lords of the House of Lords, whose function was to act as the highest and final court of appeal for domestic matters. They contacted a London-based Scottish solicitor named Chalmer about entering an appeal and sent him the necessary paperwork. Mr. Chalmer wasted no time; the appeals process was initiated in early March. The maneuver blocked the Misses Woods and Pirie from obtaining any money from Helen. By the end of July 1812, Helen's sons owed Mackenzie & Innes another £142, or $12,500.

The wheels of justice turn slowly. Both sides requested and received extensions from the House of Lords for submitting documents, so the Law Lords did not have all the materials until 1816. The first piece they considered was *The Appellant's Case*, the statement prepared by Helen's team and largely cobbled together from the documents put before the Court of Session. It stated that Helen was not guilty of slandering the teachers because she had confided the nature of Jane's charges to only one or two people, and that given the allegations' seriousness, she had cause for acting precipitately. While it was admitted that the air of Hindustan was "polluted," the document stressed that Jane had left India before she reached the age of eight.[48] Therefore, it was prejudice of the most contemptible kind on the pursuers' part "to take it for granted that her mind must have been polluted there" (*Appellant's Case*, 17).

While Helen's counsel felt compelled to acknowledge that Jane was more sexually developed than many other girls her age, what they strove to impress on the Law Lords was that Jane was but "a girl of sixteen" who had passed her life "almost entirely in female society" (*Appellant's Case*, 16). Her well-developed body notwithstanding, she could possess "very imperfect notions, if any notions at all, concerning sexual intercourse" (*Appellant's Case*, 17). In being subjected to "the gaze of a court" and questions of "the most painful and agitating kind" for hours at a stretch, it was implied, Jane had gone through a traumatizing experience (*Appellant's Case*, 16). She was, therefore, due sympathy and understanding.

The document went over the old ground relating to motive. Jane had no motive for ruining the teachers, it stated. Reviewing the entries in the journal she kept in her last three months at Drumsheugh, the lawyers focused on those relating to Miss Woods. They said the tone of these remarks was not bitter or vengeful, but quoted no examples. They did not bring up Miss Pirie's explosive temper or the system of punishments and chastisements, stating rather that the "whole system of education and discipline" as practiced at Drumsheugh bore "the semblance of play" (*Appellant's Case*, 17). Therefore, there was only one explanation that could account for the story Jane told her grandmother: it was the truth.

The lawyers representing Woods and Pirie shot back with *The Respondents' Case*, a document almost double the length of *The Appellant's Case*. Their first ploy involved stressing that Jane was damaged goods from the outset. To develop this position they were loose with the facts. For example, they stated that Jane "remained in India till she was of the age of *eight or nine* years."[49] Playing to the sexual fantasies and race prejudices of their audience, they painted a hypersexualized picture of Indian boarding schools, arguing that in schools where girls such as Jane were maintained, "the children had unavoidable opportunities of seeing and hearing the grossest obscenities" (*Respondents' Case*, 2). Giving this detail its own paragraph to indicate its centrality to their case, they informed the Law Lords that Jane's corruption continued even after she left India because she was accompanied by "a black woman who continued with her for six months after her arrival" (*Respondents' Case*, 2) and did not leave her until "she was past the age of nine" (*Respondents' Case*, 22). The important point they were making here is that if anybody did anything injurious to Jane on the ship, it was Coongee. Helen's sending her away, therefore, was too belated an act of damage control to have made any difference.

The teachers' legal counsel turned the tables on Helen. Helen had argued that she had done the financially struggling teachers a favor by offering Jane as a pupil. Moncreiff and Clerk countered by stating "it was the practice" of boarding schools not to accept any "young woman of colour" (*Respondents' Case*, 2) and argued that the teachers had actually done Helen a favor by taking in this undesirable young woman.[50] Then they turned their attention to Jane's body. In addition to being far more knowledgeable about sexual matters by virtue of her breeding, she was also far more physically developed than a British girl her age. For Moncreiff and Clerk, Jane Cumming's early sexual maturity was another source of her problems at the school.

It was "natural," Moncreiff and Clerk said, for girls of that age, even for "the best educated females," to "love gaiety" and feel "impatience with restraint" (*Respondents' Case*, 22), but because Jane had the mind and body of a woman, they opined that the discipline and controls of the school affected her more. She had felt she needed to be out in society, and took steps to free herself from the school, they said. Moncreiff and Clerk also introduced for the first time the notion that Jane had a jealous streak. In particular, they claimed, she was jealous of her cousins the Dunbar girls, who, though younger than herself, were to leave the school at Martinmas, November 11, 1810, while she was supposed to stay on until Whitsunday, May 15, 1811. Jealousy led Jane, little realizing that she would unleash a whirlwind, to construct a "story of the grossest indelicacy" (*Respondents' Case*, 8) so that she would not have to go back for the next term either.

For Moncreiff and Clerk, then, Jane was comprehensible. Like many other adolescent girls, she didn't want to be in school and she suffered from jealousy, in her case imagining her younger cousins going to balls and other social gatherings while she had to remain at Drumsheugh. In the way of all adolescents, the lawyers argued, she had gleaned some knowledge about intercourse from what she had read, heard, or overheard, and was curious to find out more—and because she was an Oriental, she had more knowledge and was more curious and more physically developed. Because of "the turn of her mind, created unavoidably by early impressions" (*Respondents' Case*, 23), she sexualized ordinary events and imbued innocent things like female friendship with impure meanings. Her Indian birth and "black" breeding had given her a facility for invention, a talent for embellishment, a familiarity with sexual deviance, and an aptitude for constructing filthy stories.

But the person who should bear most of blame in the case, they argued, was not the sixteen-year-old Jane—it was Helen, now in her sixth decade. Having accepted Jane's story without investigating its claims, a selfish fear of loss of face forced her to embark on a crusade to destroy the teachers by imputing to them a behavior that couldn't exist in Scotland.

Helen's counsel responded with an *Additional Case for the Appellant*. This document stressed the respectability of the institutions in which Jane had been placed. Responding to Clerk's remark from 1811 to the effect that Jane's mind was formed by her being brought up in a "bawdy house," the lawyers vigorously rejected any comparison of the Calcutta establishments with a brothel. They also attempted to excite sympathy for the adolescent who had had to testify for four long days. While admitting the inconsistencies in her testimony, they asked the Law Lords to bear in mind how amazingly well she had held up. "Indeed, the only thing to be wondered at," they wrote, "is that a girl of such years, under a trial so cruel and unrelenting, did not lose all command of her faculties, and become alike incapable of recollection, distinction, and expression."[51]

Helen's lawyers next critiqued Woods and Pirie on grounds that Saints Theresa and Bonaventure would have recognized: they were special or particular friends whose feelings and behaviors were inappropriate for their vocation and deleterious in the setting in which they lived. Unquestionably, the schoolmistresses were cultivated and possessed of many virtues, but they were the wrong kind of people to undertake "the sacred and delicate task of female education" (*Additional Case for Appellant*, 4). Over the course of the year that Jane spent at the Drumsheugh establishment, it had become clear that Woods and Pirie were role models "of inconstant temper, of bitter squabbling, of passionate reconciliations; of minds without regulation, yielding to every extreme of rancour or enthusiasm; and altogether devoid of that composure, steadiness and rationality which is so essential to success in the education of youth" (*Additional Case for Appellant*, 4). Miss Pirie, in particular, was especially deficient in the area of self-control. Her discourse was not "the language of rational and well-regulated affection"; she often gave vent to "tears, kisses, and passionate ejaculations, highly . . . unbecoming . . . and giving room to the worst constructions" (*Additional Case for Appellant*, 5). The conclusion of Helen's lawyers was that Miss Pirie's extreme declarations were not only "the ravings of distempered passion" but a "fit precursor to the consummation of any vicious indulgence" (*Additional Case for Appellant*, 5).

By looking at the teachers through the "special friends at convent" keyhole, Helen's counsel argued that Helen had not only not defamed the teachers but accurately diagnosed them. They maintained that Jane's testimony was as true as the allegations made about her early years were false. In an attempt to turn the tables on the teachers, they put forward the idea that Jane, branded as a "premeditated, malignant calumniator" (*Additional Case for Appellant*, 1) by the pursuers' lawyers, was the real victim of character defamation. While the lawyers would have liked this picture of the innocent Jane and the courageous grandmother coming to the defense of a cruelly libeled granddaughter to stick in the minds of the Law Lords, they also included a detail that could not work in their client's favor. For years, Helen had maintained that when she put Jane into the Woods-Pirie School, it was with the intent of subsequently introducing her to society as a Cumming girl. But in this document from 1816, she changed her stance, indicating that "she never intended to bring her out into the world on the same footing" as her daughters (*Additional Case for Appellant*, 8). This surprise revelation was not followed by any others.

Moncreiff and Clerk responded with an *Additional Case for the Respondents*, in which they repeated the old arguments about the lascivious practices that must have impressed themselves on Jane's mind. Leaving the "cause to the justice of your Lordships," they begged the Law Lords to "dismiss the appeal with costs."[52]

Nothing happened until July 12, 1819, when the Lords Spiritual and Temporal in Parliament announced their determination. Siding with the arguments put forward by Clerk and Moncreiff about Jane's contaminated imagination, they dismissed the appeal. However, even if Jane had been lily white, they would have most likely have come to the same decision. Helen's refusal to meet with the teachers without offering any explanation, her asking Lady Cunynghame to keep quiet, and her attempt to suborn Mrs. Stirling undermined her case and its appeal to *veritas convicii*.[53] On top of that, Helen's only "proof" was Jane's story, which none of the girls corroborated and which on closer examination was revealed to be full of falsehoods. Though the Law Lords had accepted the Orientalist perspective, they actually didn't need it to determine in favor of the teachers.

Now that the supreme arbiters had held her liable, the only question left was how much Helen was liable for. By January 1820 Moncreiff was back at the Court of Session with a condescendence (Scots: statement of facts), on behalf of the pursuers. In an attempt to get Helen to pay the £10,000 to the teachers for damages and *solatium*, he itemized some of their losses: £450 on furniture, rent, wages (£3000), and future profits. He pointed out, too, that in the intervening nine years, both teachers had suffered—Miss Pirie more than Miss Woods, as might have been expected.

Moncreiff noted that Miss Pirie had not been able to work since the school collapsed and had contracted debts, and, "in consequence of the agitation and affliction produced by the defender's calumny, suffered so severely in her health and constitution, as certainly to embitter the remainder of her days." And though Miss Woods, "from better fortune and a few friends, has not suffered so much personal injury, the same cause has been, and will be a source of perpetual unhappiness to her, probably for her whole life."[54]

If Moncreiff hoped that Helen's sympathy would be elicited by a description of the destitute teachers, he was mistaken. Trial by jury had come to Scotland in 1816, but she rejected the option of having the case sent to a jury court where twelve men would be charged with determining the amount she was liable for. On February 12, 1820, her legal team responded with her answers to the condescendence. She acknowledged that, having lost the 1812 Court of Session appeal, she very properly paid the teachers' legal expenses in full, "amounting to £943.0s.7d."[55] Because she had refused to settle at that time, the costs for continuing the case kept mounting. Between 1815 and 1820, Mackenzie & Innes sent Sir William bills amounting to £1,220, or $1,300,000.

If this case about "lust in action" was proving to be a great drain of time and money for the Gordon Cummings, it was also revealing itself as a Pyrrhic victory for the teachers.[56] On June 29, 1820, Moncreiff pressed for the teachers to receive "the sum of £2000 as a *solatium*" but reduced their demand for compensation to "the sum of £5000."[57] Helen refused to listen to this offer, but her sons, who were paying the legal fees, were more realistic about the eventual outcome of the case. On November 14, perhaps without informing her, they took out a bond in which they said they would "bind and oblige ourselves, our heirs, executors and successors, to content and pay each of us, one-half to the said Miss Marianne Woods and Miss Jane Pirie, their heirs, successors and assignees, of such sum or sums of money, as the said Dame Helen Cumming Gordon, or her representatives, shall be found liable in to them in the foresaid action, either in name of damages or of expences. . . ."[58]

Even though it was Mackenzie & Innes that stood to gain from Helen's obstinacy, they were the ones who recognized that continuing the case was an "expense of spirit in a waste of shame."[59] Behind Helen's inflexible back, though probably with the consent of her sons, Mackenzie & Innes began negotiating with the teachers' lawyers for an out-of-court settlement. On March 5, 1821, Sir William received a personal note from William Innes informing him that the case was over. Mackenzie & Innes had also thought about taking the case to a jury court but decided against it. Readying the case for presentation to a jury would be costly and most likely not result in a reduction of damages, so they concluded that an out-of-court settlement was the only sensible choice. Innes explained that "after negotiating and deliberating amongst ourselves and negotiating with our adversaries thro' the winter, for we began to treat with them in earnest in November last, this was considered the wisest thing we could do, I mean that it was thought more advisable to give them the £4000 than put the matter to trial in the Jury Court, and so at last ended it this way."[60] Innes was afraid Sir William might think the settlement, $19,3000 in today's terms, "a hard bargain," but since it provided closure and gave the teachers a fraction of what they had originally asked for, it is more than reasonable to assume that Sir William was heartily glad the case was behind him.[61]

Following the settlement, the teachers became daily visitors to the Queen Street chambers of Mackenzie & Innes. Innes wrote Sir William on June 19, 1821, telling him that he was going to be distributing the £2000, the half that Sir William was liable for, to the two women. Presumably, shortly thereafter Charles Lennox sent Innes the money he had bound himself to pay, for Innes's correspondence does not mention the teachers again. Thus, unless further evidence is uncovered, it seems that the last time the schoolmistresses appeared in public together was in Edinburgh's New Town in the summer of 1821. So, by the middle of 1821, the teachers received double the *solatium* they had asked for ten years earlier and not a penny for any of the losses they had incurred. By 1821, Sir William and Charles Lennox, to satisfy their mother, had spent ten years and about £7,000 on this case.[62]

Did any of the Gordon Cummings ever wonder if they made a mistake in not settling with the teachers at the outset?

Chapter Six

JANE AND WILLIAM TULLOCH

Uncle George, last seen in 1803 receiving the encumbrances Jane and Yorrick into his Berners Street house, was not a man to dwell on failure and its consequences. Once the children had been consigned to the Mr. Tulloch who brought them up north, they apparently dropped from his consciousness, for Uncle George's surviving letters in the Gordon Cumming Depository make no mention either of Jane or of Yorrick. In 1814, however, the specter of their father, his late and hitherto unlamented nephew George, briefly came back to haunt him. His second coming gave the now sixty-two-year-old uncle, losing his eyesight but still involved in profitable financial speculation and East India Company affairs, the opportunity to reflect on the harsh attitude and unkind words he had directed toward the young man who had not made it to his thirtieth birthday.

Sometime around June of that year, the uncle received a parcel containing George's nymph poems of 1794. He wrote George's brother Sir William on June 14, telling him that he was "putting the parcel in [his] trunk." The perusal of Colonel Lawtie's letter and the poems written by his "poor brother," he said, would give "pleasure (tho' a melancholy pleasure)"; he advised him to remember that they were written "more than 20 years ago, and wrote [sic] without the most distant idea of being seen by anyone, but to the person they are addressed."[1] Lawtie's letter has not survived, but Sir William, who had at best only the faintest memories of his elder brother, saved his brother's effusions.

In 1811 Lords Hope, Meadowbank, Robertson, Newton, and Boyle visited the house in Drumsheugh that the year before had been Woods and Pirie's boarding school. By 1816, when the Law Lords began reviewing the documents, the house had been demolished. Meadowbank and Newton were dead, as was Lord Polkemmet, who had cast the deciding vote without ever attending a session. So was Lord Woodhouselee, and one of the most articulate witnesses, Elizabeth Hamilton.

Helen was very much alive. In the winter of 1816, the sixty-two-year old was living at 22 Charlotte Square. Her four unmarried daughters, Emilia, Jane Marianne, Sophia, and Mary, together with her sons William and Charles Lennox and William's wife, Eliza Campbell, were living under the same roof. Also living on Charlotte Square was Elizabeth Grant, Jane's contemporary. In her *Memoirs*, she recollects the Gordon Cummings and paints a warmly glowing picture of the drawing room of 22 Charlotte Square on a winter evening.

Helen comes across as a strong and beckoning presence, a kind of queen bee, very much the materfamilias, never going out by herself but encircled by family and close friends who did her bidding. Knowing how much their mother loved to have her children around her, the unmarried daughters convinced their sister Louisa Forbes to spend her evenings at Charlotte Square. While Louisa seamed sheets, Sophia played the piano and Charles the violoncello. The shutters were opened, the drawing rooms lit. A card table was set up. Friends were invited to partake of a musical *soirée*. "There was always musick," Grant recalls.[2]

Yet Elizabeth Grant undercut her own presentation of this happy family when she remarked that "all the Cummings were queer" ("queer" meaning only "odd" at that time)—but only to a degree—by their "good blood."[3] And the family had cares and worries that winter. *Miss Marianne Woods and Miss Jane Pirie against Dame Helen Cumming Gordon*, now on the docket of the Law Lords of Parliament, *was* draining the family exchequer. On top of the £1,700 the case had cost them since 1811, in 1816 Mackenzie & Innes billed Sir William over £200 for readying the case for its presentation before the Law Lords of the upper house of Parliament.

A most immediate problem related to Jane. It appeared that she was not only deficient in the good blood that barely kept the legitimate Gordon Cummings from manifesting signs of queerness or oddness, but might be queer in the modern sexually nonnormative sense of the word. What was to be done with this family encumbrance? By the end of 1816 she was about twenty, around the age when girls of the gentry class got married. What kind of man would want to marry a woman who nursed grudges, had a vengeful and malicious streak and a dirty mind, was quick-witted, possibly read other people's mail, presented herself as a voyeur, lied, enjoyed the limelight, and was unafraid to talk about sexual matters to a large gathering?

The unmarked diagonal shortcut that Jane probably took in November 1810 to reach her grandmother's residence on Charlotte Square was either now a proper road called Charlotte Place or in the process of becoming the road that is today called Randolph Place. The notorious Tolbooth on the High Street that Jane passed on the way to Portobello was slated for demolition; by 1818 it would be gone. The neoclassical principles that made Charlotte Square so attractive were being replicated in public buildings and private localities as Edinburgh continued its transformation into the Athens of the North. But Jane would never see this new Edinburgh. A receipt for £1 15s for two yards of fine longe cloth, three yards of Welsh flannel, and six pairs of cotton hose for Miss Jane Cumming, directed to Sir William's factor David Falconer in Forres and covering the period December 23, 1811, through January 20, 1812, indicates that Jane was sent back to the country not long after she gave testimony in March 1811.[4] A receipt from Miss Charles in Elgin, acknowledging that she had "received from Sir William G. G. Cumming Baronet . . . the sum of Twelve pounds ten shillings sterling being in full of a half years board for Miss Jean Cumming as from first day of January 1815 to first day of July 1815," confirms that Jane was back in Elgin with her old schoolmistress.[5] As before, the family was treating her as an encumbrance, one they were duty-bound to provide for but kept at a distance. As a solution to the Jane problem, this had to be a temporary one. Miss Charles was now in her seventh decade.

How did Jane pass the time in Elgin? She must have visited people, and on Sundays gone to church in the company of Miss Charles. Perhaps one of the people they saw regularly was the Reverend Hugh Buchan, the long-serving minister of Elgin's Episcopal Trinity Chapel with whom Yorrick/George had been placed shortly after arrival. The business of dressing and dining would have consumed a portion of each day, and time would have been set aside for reading and writing letters. She might have visited the bookshop of Isaac Forsyth or walked to Elgin Cathedral, majestic though in ruins, and watched one man remove the debris of centuries from the nave, wheelbarrow by wheelbarrow.[6] Surely she shopped for fabrics to be turned into items of apparel. Perhaps she beguiled the hours practicing some of the social accomplishments she had learned. One hopes that she saw her brother, who, between 1811 and 1812, was in Elgin studying French, Latin, arithmetic, and geography with a private tutor.

This gentlemanly education came to an end in early 1813 when Yorrick/George fell sick and was taken to Aberdeen, some seventy-five miles distant and home to an old and highly-regarded school of medicine.[7] There, despite the "coals, candles and medicine" that were purchased for him, his condition deteriorated.[8] On April 28, Jane, accompanied by Miss Charles, traveled by the safest, newest, and most expensive public means available from Elgin to Aberdeen. This was the two-horse, four-seat, red-and-black mail coach from Inverness to Aberdeen; at the rear, guarding the mail and the passengers, stood a resplendently uniformed guard armed with pistols and a blunderbuss. Ironically, even though this mail coach was the premier service, it was considered "a slow conveyance," particularly from Elgin to Forres, as its two horses were ancient, one deaf, the other blind.[9] Mail coaches in general made no stops for the convenience of the passengers; horses were changed every ten miles. At the best of times, they went about seven or eight miles an hour.

The 1813 *Farmer's Magazine* describes the weather in the Moray area at the end of April as cold and dry, so once the two decrepit horses were changed the coach might have done the rest of the journey at a better clip. Still, it is altogether possible that when Jane and Miss Charles travelled posthaste to Aberdeen in 1813, they didn't arrive until the following day, April 29. The two stayed at a hotel, where they treated themselves to some creature comforts: half a pound of butter, bread, beer, beef, and a bottle of wine, and coals and a candle to keep their room warm and lit. They paid the chambermaid three shillings for her services.

Yorrick/George died on April 30 and was buried May 1. Graveclothes were made for him, and four porters carried the corpse to a churchyard where he was interred, the coffin covered with a mortcloth or funeral pall. Those invited to attend the funeral were served almonds, rum cake, and cheese. Wine, porter, and three bottles of rum were also provided. It was a very respectable send-off. By May 3, Jane and Miss Charles were on the same mail coach, heading back to Elgin. Addressed to Miss Jane Cumming at Miss Charles's house, the trunk containing the effects of the late Yorrick/George was sent separately. Once back in Elgin, mourning clothes were made for Jane. Within days she and Miss Charles presented the bills for the expenses they incurred as well as the bills for Yorrick/George's medical and other expenses during the last months of his life to Sir William's agent in Elgin. Between the sixth and the seventeenth of May, Sir William disbursed over £200, equivalent to $17,300 today, in payment of these bills. Had Jane's brother lived, one wonders what he would have become.

On a happier note, the girls from the ill-fated Drumsheugh establishment were getting married. Eliza Christian Stirling and Janet Munro, both of whom were born in 1795, got married in 1815 and 1816, respectively. Both made "good" marriages. Janet married a wealthy English industrialist named Daniel Maude, and Eliza, William Millikin Napier, later the 8th Baronet of Napier. Both had a number of children. By late 1816 the time was fast approaching when Helen had to make her decision about Jane's future. Would she carry out her threat and make a milliner or mantua-maker of her because of the trouble she had caused? Would she carry out her promise and introduce her to the world as a member of the family? Or would she bring her out, but not quite on the same footing as she had her own daughters?

In a document dated March 7, 1818, and witnessed by Helen's son-in-law, the father of Jane's cousins and classmates the Dunbar girls, Sir Archibald Dunbar of Northfield, and the Reverend Richard Rose, Minister of Drainie, "William Tulloch Preacher of the Gospel and Jane Cumming spouse" acknowledged receiving from "Sir William Gordon Gordon Cumming of Altyre and Gordonstoun . . . the sum of one hundred and fifty pounds sterling in full payment of the said Sir William's portion of three hundred pounds sterling payable by him to us in virtue of our contract of marriage."[10] Since William and his brother Charles Lennox always split family expenses, presumably in a document now lost, Tulloch acknowledged receiving an equal amount from Charles in early March. The parish register for Knockando records that on that March 7, 1818, Jane Cumming and William Tulloch, "parochial schoolmaster at Nigg in Rosshire were matrimonially contracted and married." At that time, "with consent of Dame Helen Cumming Gordon, widow of the late Sir Alexander Penrose Cumming Gordon," £350, equivalent to $34,000 today, was settled on Jane and an equal sum on Tulloch, in a sense compensating or thanking him for marrying her.[11]

The 1882 Married Women's Property Act (which would allow married women to own things in their own right) being decades away, Tulloch was entitled to invoke *jus mariti*. Such behavior, however, went against the spirit of the marriage contract in Scotland, whose purpose was to provide a modicum of financial protection and security to the woman in case things didn't work out between the couple. Furthermore, even though the husband had power over what was given to his wife, Scottish law prevented him from laying claim to her marriage portion if such appropriation would be injurious to her.[12] In any event, on receiving his portion of the settlement, Tulloch renounced his *jus mariti*.[13] Now, Helen could rest assured that Jane was financially protected in the event that Tulloch proved not to be a gentleman.

The contrast between what Jane received and what Helen's daughters Helen and Louisa received at the time of their marriages is striking. Helen's and Louisa's settlements were each £2,000, while their respective spouses were also granted £2,000. While not treated badly, Jane and her spouse had certainly received the shorter end of the stick.

It was now obvious which of the three options Helen had chosen. Since Jane was being married to a schoolmaster with the qualifications to be appointed a minister, Helen was not putting her acknowledged granddaughter on the milliner or mantua-maker path. On the other hand, she was not treating her as she had her own daughters. However, as a highly educated man, Tulloch was not without breeding, and when he became a minister, his social status would rise. He would occupy the manse and not the mere two rooms heritors were obliged to provide for schoolmasters per the 1803 Scotch Parochial Schoolmasters' Act.[14] As a minister, a full-fledged member of the clerical profession, he would be considered more or less on par with doctors and lawyers, the two other service professions with whom the landed gentry networked and to whom they often married their younger daughters.[15]

However, for Tulloch to rise from schoolmaster to parish minister, he would need support. Per the Church Patronage (Scotland) Act of 1711, that backing had to come specifically from a heritor or a patron.[16] Sir William was actually both: the patron of the Dallas church and one of the large landowners in the Area. If Tulloch helped the Gordon Cummings by taking Jane off their hands, he could feel pretty certain that in due course Sir William would exercise clout to get him installed as a minister. If marriage to Jane and indebtedness to her family was the price he had to pay for career advancement, so be it. Born in 1777, he was forty-one years old, in no position to be choosy. Jane's uncles sweetened the deal by settling £350 on him, a stupendous amount for a man whom the 1803 Schoolmasters' Act guaranteed an annual salary of only £22, stipulating that no salary adjustment was possible until 1828.

On his return to the Gaelic-speaking village of Nigg, Tulloch, who also served as session-clerk there, recording the kirk minutes and entering births, death, and marriages in the parish register, entered his own marriage in the book, centering each line and writing large. The Nigg entry was considerably more expansive than the one in the Knockando register. Tulloch spelled out Jane's pedigree and added the name of the minister who had joined them together, Richard Rose. Highlighting her distinguished lineage in bold, flowing script, he referred to Jane as the "only surviving child of the late George Cumming Esquire of the Honourable East India Company's Civil Service & Eldest lawful son of the late Sir Alexander Penrose Cumming Gordon of Altyre and Gordonstoun Baronet," thus also acknowledging the short life of Yorrick/George. With nobody monitoring what he wrote in the Nigg register, he identified himself as a "reverend" rather than a "schoolmaster," thus giving himself a title he wouldn't possess for six more years.

Who was this William Tulloch to whom Jane had been contracted and married? Though he was born in Cawdor in 1777, the family had ties to Cromarty, a prosperous seaport located on an arm of the Moray Firth.[17] If Tulloch was educated in Cromarty, it might have been briefly at the hands of the man who would later officiate at his wedding, for roughly between 1790 and 1793, Rose was the parochial schoolmaster in Cromarty.[18] In the late eighteenth century, Cromarty was a bustling English-speaking town with many educational establishments besides the parochial school. It did a robust trade in salted herring, exporting the fish to German, Baltic, and Scandinavian ports. The trade and family connections between Cromarty and towns on the other side of the Moray Firth were so strong that many ferries ran on Sundays.[19] These towns included Inverness, Nairn, Forres, and Elgin.

However, for a schoolmaster who did not measure success in sales of salted herring but in how soon he became a minister, Cromarty was but a way station. Rose, born in 1769 and thus not much older than Tulloch, could well have served as a mentor, role model, or "big brother" figure, for by 1794 his schoolmaster days were behind him. That year Penrose's uncle got him installed as a minister in a village that was part of the Gordounstoun estate: Dallas. Penrose became Rose's patron after he inherited Gordonstoun. As long as they stayed off the subject of repairs to the manse, which were Penrose's responsibility as heritor, the two got along well. After Penrose's death, Sir William became Rose's patron, and the relationship continued as before. Like his father, Sir William paid Rose's stipend and spent no money repairing the manse. By 1818 Rose had been transferred from Dallas to nearby Drainie, but Sir William was still the most important heritor in the area and continued to be his patron. That Rose officiated at Tulloch and Jane's wedding suggests the regard Sir William had for him and the trust and confidence he placed in him.

Tulloch followed in Rose's footsteps. In 1799 Tulloch received his degree from Marischal College, Aberdeen, and a license to preach the Gospel. In 1801 he signed a contract with the Rosshire heritors to become the village schoolmaster of Nigg, now just three and a half miles by road from Cromarty on the other side of the firth but then accessible only by ferry. Nigg, however, was no Cromarty. Its population of 950 souls consisted largely of illiterate, Gaelic-speaking farmers. Other than the Nigg minister, Tulloch would have found himself bereft of companionship. In 1794 the minister described Nigg as a place where the rain-soaked earth "ooze[d] forth in springs in winter."[20] Furthermore, the Rosshire heritors had scant respect for education. A retrospective account of Scottish parochial schools that appeared in *Tait's Edinburgh Magazine* in 1844 states that the educational supplies provided to the schoolmaster consisted of a blackboard and a ball frame. This latter was most likely a device for teaching children to count—something like an abacus, a frame within which wooden balls were strung so that they could they be moved in either direction.

In 1801, the year Tulloch became schoolmaster in Nigg, Rose had been minister at Dallas for seven years and Penrose was about to succeed to the Gordonstoun property. Probably sometime in the latter half of 1801, Penrose had been made aware of the existence of Jane and Yorrick. By March 1802 he had given orders for them to be sent. By September 1802 they were en route to Britain; by May 1803 they had reached London. By then Gordonstoun belonged to Penrose, so he was now Rose's patron. Who was to bring the children north? Penrose needed a chaperone who would be competent, discreet, trustworthy, and not charge a lot of money.

Given these circumstances, it would have been only natural if Penrose had asked his minister Richard Rose for advice. It could be coincidence, but since Jane stated that the man who brought her north was a Mr. Tulloch, it seems reasonable to conjecture that Rose suggested Tulloch as an appropriate person to conduct the children from London to Scotland. Who could be a better choice to take care of two children than a man known to the local parish minister? Who could be more responsible or deserving than a twenty-six-year-old bachelor parochial schoolmaster stationed in a backwater village?

The Principal Acts of the General Assembly of the Church of Scotland is, as its title suggests, a compendium of the decisions taken by the Church's highest governing body. An annual publication, in the timeframe covered by this book, it was full of notices about clerical figures whose conduct was a cause of scandal in the parish. Frequent charges brought against preachers in the early years of the nineteenth century included intoxication and contumacy but topping the list were sexual misdemeanors. These were divided into three categories: fornication, adultery, and indecent and scandalous familiarity with a woman. If proved, the punishment for ministers found guilty of sexual misconduct was dire: they were removed from office and lost their stipend. A similar publication, *The Annals of the General Assembly of the Church of Scotland Covering the Years 1752–1766*, for example, include the cases of five ministers so charged, three of whom were removed from office and two cleared. Of the two cleared ministers, one squeaked through, for he was "admonished at the bar and exhorted to behave with more circumspection."[21] Of the guilty parties, one was a predecessor of Richard Rose at Dallas.

Schoolmasters were also found on the rolls of the misbehaving, including the sexually misbehaving. Both the volumes of *The Principal Acts of the General Assembly of the Church of Scotland* and the autobiography of Hugh Miller, the self-taught geologist and product of Cromarty's educational establishments, point out that many impecunious, educated bachelor schoolmasters got themselves in serious scrapes that either ended or threatened to end their professional careers. Around the time that Jane was giving testimony to the Court of Session in Edinburgh, Hugh Miller encountered, in quick succession, three schoolmasters, all of whom were forced to resign. These were a "clever young man" who got "diurnally drunk, on receiving the instalments of his salary at term-days, as long as his money lasted"; a licentiate of the Church whose physical and mental health declined after some Baptists made him doubt infant baptism; and another licentiate who realized that connection to a woman of wealth and class might improve his lot. Miller described this third schoolmaster as "a person of a high, if not very consistent religious profession, who was always getting into pecuniary difficulties, and always courting, though with but little success, wealthy ladies who . . . had 'acres of charms.'"[22]

In 1811, at the age of thirty-four, in his tenth year as schoolmaster in Nigg, Tulloch joined this dubious company. *The Principal Acts* for that year indicates that the presbytery of Tain suspended "Mr. William Tulloch, Schoolmaster at Nigg, and Preacher of the Gospel" from "making use of his License."[23] Rather like Helen but with greater success, Tulloch obtained the services of a legal agent and appealed the decision to the church's highest body, the General Assembly, whose members overturned the presbytery's determination on the grounds that he hadn't received in writing a statement of the charges before being suspended. The General Assembly was furious with the presbytery of Tain, whose behavior they characterized as premature, unconstitutional, irregular, and unjust. The highest body then removed the lower body's suspension, restored Tulloch to the exercise of his license, enjoined the presbytery to follow procedure in future, and ordained that "any examination of witnesses already taken in this cause to be expunged from their Minutes."[24]

The Tain Presbytery apparently followed the order of the General Assembly to expunge any trace of the case from its records but the middle oversight body, the Synod of Ross, didn't quite.[25] In April 1817, the Synod informed the presbytery of Forres that though the charge against Tulloch was not proved and he was restored to his rights and privileges, they, the elders of the Synod, had unanimously passed a motion "cautioning him to future watchfulness and circumspection in every part of his conduct."[26]

Though he had escaped punishment this time, the Synod's language implies that the charge was sexual in nature and that Tulloch might not be so lucky next time.

Thus, by 1818 both Tulloch and Jane had libel suits in their backgrounds. Both exuded the aroma of scandal, sexual in Jane's case, very probably sexual in Tulloch's. In theory, they made a good match. Tinged Jane needed a man who would make a respectable woman of her. Sex-starved schoolmaster Tulloch needed a wife who would make a respectable man of him—and a heritor who could advance his stalled career.

Rose knew Tulloch and had a long relationship with the Gordon Cummings that grew more amicable over time as the main cause of conflict between them, the condition of the manse Rose occupied, was somewhat ameliorated. In fact, Rose would write about the manse in Drainie that "though old, it is in decent and comfortable condition."[27] Though he had been transferred from Dallas to Drainie in 1816, Rose would still have been in regular touch with Sir William, as the heritor continued to be his paymaster. It is reasonable to assume that Sir William, like his father, had confidence in Rose's judgment. Rose might (again?) have suggested Tulloch to Sir William and Helen as the right man for the task at hand, perhaps even given him the gist of the Synod's recommendation to Tulloch.

The Gordon Cummings were looking for a man who would be able to set Jane straight about the proper relationship between man and woman and inculcate the lessons in female submission to higher authority that she had apparently not learned at the Drumsheugh establishment. Who could be better at the task of straightening out this young woman than a preacher of the Gospel for whom *Ephesians* 5:22–23 ("Wives, submit yourself unto your husbands, as unto the Lord, for the husband is the head of the wife, even as Christ is the head of the church") was the living truth? If the two Tullochs were the same, then Jane might also feel kindly toward him. In any case, he was available and wouldn't cost a lot of money. In return for getting the young female encumbrance off the family's hands, all Sir William would have to do would be to exercise patronage and get Tulloch installed at one of the churches in the presbytery of Forres.

To persuade Tulloch about Jane, Rose might have pointed out to him that as a cleric in a denomination engaged in missionary work in India that focused on lifting Indian women out of the degraded conditions in which they lived, he would redeem the half-Indian woman by marrying her. As a Christian and a Scot, it was incumbent on him to offer her a companionate marriage. She would be his companion, supporter, and helpmate; he would treat her with respect.[28] In addition, Rose also might have counseled or directed Tulloch toward contemporary marriage manuals that advised those considering the wedded state "not [to] regard the outward shape or beauty . . . of the person to whom they . . . [were] to be joined."[29]

Of course, Tulloch might not have needed these appeals to think positively about a union with Jane. After his brush with professional death in 1811, he was probably afraid to have contacts with women. If he had any inkling of what the Synod of Ross had written about him in 1817, he knew he wasn't highly regarded. He probably thought worse of his Rosshire heritors. In 1844 a reviewer looking at the educational scene in Scotland thought that the lack of respect paid to teaching, combined with the low, slavish economic status of schoolmasters and their high educational qualifications inevitably made them start thinking about how to get out of this morass. The observer lamented, "We must not be surprised to find that the parish schoolmaster, finding his profession in such small estimation, is forced to regard it in the same capacity himself, and view the desk as a stepping-stone to the pulpit. He accordingly . . . is . . . anxious to secure the heritors' suffrage in helping him to a kirk."[30]

In 1818, after seventeen years in Nigg, three times longer than Rose had spent in Cromarty, Tulloch must have been desperate. He was poor, over forty, living meanly, and stuck there. Hugh Miller had described one of his failed Cromarty schoolmasters as a man who tried to court wealthy women with "acres of charms." The phrase comes from a 1796 Robert Burns song in which the pragmatic speaker announces that what he's interested in is not beauty but a "lass wi' the weel-stockit [well-stocked] farms." To this, the chorus responds with four lines of "hey, for a lass wi' a tocher [Scots: marriage portion]" and a concluding line of "The nice yellow guineas for me." A girl "wi' a tocher" whose uncle could settle on him some decent cultivable land was exactly what William Tulloch needed. The benefits of the connection were obvious. Because her uncle Sir William was a local heritor and the patron of the parish of Dallas, Jane would help him to the pulpit there and its nice-sized glebe, that income-generating piece of land he could farm when not attending to his clerical duties.

Tulloch's underwhelming character reference from the Synod did not trouble Sir William. It's just possible that the sexual conduct that had gotten him into trouble was a selling point for Sir William and Helen, since what they wanted was a man who was robustly heterosexual. During her four days on the witness stand, Jane had shown an interest in sleeping with members of her own sex. Schooling had failed to improve Jane, but Helen was ever-hopeful that her granddaughter could be, as Locke said, "mended." She may well have thought that what her same-sex-inclined granddaughter needed was a man professionally committed to others' improvement and their hewing to the straight and narrow, and with a record that as good as proved he had a strong sex drive.

Helen might even have seen Tulloch as a latter-day Petrucchio, the scholar who announced that he was the very man born to tame Kate and bring her from a "wild Kate to a Kate / Conformable as other household Kates."[31] Petrucchio made an obedient, submissive wife of Kate by tormenting her, but how would Tulloch fare with Jane?

Tulloch and Jane were married on March 7, 1818, nine months after the Synod's material was recorded in the Forres Presbytery minutes. On the same day his marriage was formalized at Knockando, Tulloch recorded his gratitude to Sir William for the outright gift of £150 ($675) on stamped paper and in the presence of two witnesses, Sir Archibald Dunbar and Richard Rose. If invested at five percent, the interest on the principal would bring him an extra £17 a year. He had just received a gift from his wife's family equivalent to six years of his annual schoolmaster's salary, and he would be getting extra income from the interest generated by the settlement.

The couple began their life together in the schoolmaster's house in Nigg. Jane had a lot to reflect on at this point. Marriage was a desideratum, but she had been married to a man about twenty years her senior who wanted her connections and some "nice yellow guineas." Marriage had cast her out to Nigg. In her new abode she was deprived of English-speaking society. The polite arts and social accomplishments she had acquired in Elgin and Edinburgh were of singularly little use to her here. Helen, on the other hand, must have been very happy. She had married her granddaughter off to a man whose heterosexuality was known; his desire would reorient Jane. He wasn't gentry, but he held a respectable and responsible position in society. After causing her sons to spend a large amount of money on Jane-related expenses, she had found a solution that would not stress the family exchequer further. She had fulfilled her objective of giving her granddaughter a decent position in society, though not equal to that of her own daughters.

Jane soon became pregnant. In his flowing handwriting, Tulloch entered his children's names in the parish register. Named after her great-grandmother, Helen Grant Cumming Tulloch was born on November 2, 1819. Their second daughter, Eliza Maria, named after Sir William's wife Eliza Maria Campbell, was born on April 4, 1821. Helen Tulloch's life was brief. Tulloch inscribed her name following that of Eliza Maria's in the

Nigg register, suggesting that by the time Eliza was born Helen had already departed; above the entry is the somber word "Dead."

Grandmother Helen's life had also been touched with disappointment since Jane's marriage. Her eldest daughter, Helen, died in March 1819. The Law Lords of the House of Lords had determined against her and the family law firm of Mackenzie & Innes went behind her back and settled with the teachers. Helen, however, was not one to stay down and stop machinating. By 1821, Jane had been in Nigg for three years.

Just around the time the lawyers were finalizing the settlement with the teachers, Sir William began communicating with the ministers comprising the presbytery of Forres concerning the transfer of Francis W. Grant, the incumbent minister at Dallas, and the installation of William Tulloch in his place. A letter to Sir William dated December 9, 1820, from Thomas Macfarlane, minister of the parish of Edinkille, makes clear that Sir William wanted Tulloch brought from Nigg before May 22, 1821, so that his stipend would not be prorated. Macfarlane assured Sir William that he was his man and would do all in his power to "have Mr. Tulloch settled at Dallas before Whitsuntide"; in 1821 that holiday fell on April 22. But he also pointed out that other members of the presbytery, particularly the Dallas incumbent, Francis W. Grant, "were not so keen to have Tulloch at Dallas so soon."[32] It is difficult not to see Helen's hand guiding her eldest son at this juncture.

Despite pressure from Macfarlane and Sir William, Grant stood his ground. In a letter dated December 11, 1820, he told Sir William that while he had no problem with vacating Dallas and becoming the minister at Dyke, he had no intention of doing so on Sir William's timetable.

In the end, Macfarlane thought it more politic to ditch Sir William than to incur the anger of his peers. When the presbytery met in early March 1821 to vote on "Mr. Tulloch's being settled at Dallas before Whitsunday," he was not present to argue on behalf of Sir William. In what looks like a classic example of a white lie, he informed Sir William on March 5 that he "was prevented by a severe cold from attending the meeting" and was regretful that "Mr. Tulloch will be disappointed in this instance." Rather disingenuously, he hoped Sir William would believe that he "did all in my power to forward his views."[33]

Sir William persevered. In January 1821, Sir William again presented Tulloch to the Forres Presbytery. The presbytery voted in favor of him but requested a character certificate. Tulloch produced a statement from the presbytery of Tain affirming that, since the General Assembly's determination in his favor had not been appealed, "there was nothing scandalous in Mr. Tulloch's life and conversation so far as known to them."[34] The Forres ecclesiasticate were satisfied; Tulloch was installed at Dallas on April 11, 1822, four years after his marriage to Jane. The couple would remain there for the rest of their lives. In Dallas they would have three more children, William Gordon Tulloch (b. 1823), named after her elder uncle; Charles Lennox Cumming Tulloch (b. 1824), named after her younger uncle; and George Cumming Tulloch (b. 1826), named after her brother and father.

As Tulloch had hoped, his wife's gentry connections enabled him to become a minister, and as a protégé of Rose, it was somehow fitting that he followed in his footsteps, ending up at the church where Rose had served and in close proximity to Drainie, where Rose was now the parish minister. Tulloch's life improved considerably. A manse was infinitely better than a schoolmaster's two-room house. His salary rose from £25 to £158 a year, or, in today's terms, roughly from $3,020 to $19,100. He farmed the ten-acre glebe that came with the position. As for Jane, she was now the minister's wife, a position that came freighted with obligations and responsibilities.

As the local minister's wife, it was expected that Jane visit the sick and dying and teach children. It was assumed she would use her position to influence the women of the congregation in a positive way and would serve as a link between the minister and the parish.[35] She was supposed to put aside all thoughts of or desire for a life of ease and selfish pleasure. Because of the importance of her husband in the community, her behavior was watched carefully. Whatever she was feeling, her conduct as wife and mother had to be above reproach lest she compromise her husband's standing among the parishioners. As the anonymous author of *Hints to a Clergyman's Wife: Or Female Parochial Duties Practically Illustrated* stated, "if the habits and principles of the Clergyman's wife and children contradict the pulpit instructions of the husband and parent, his doctrine and exhortations will only excite the ridicule of those opposed to the truth, and tend to confirm them in their corrupt practices."[36] Though nobody could stop her from having opinions and making judgments, in public her views were expected to echo her husband's. Judgments on her part that diverged from his were to be kept unbroadcast, lest both of them forfeit the community's respect.[37]

The demands placed on the minister's wife were onerous and time-consuming. The author of *Hints* acknowledged the difficulty of the responsibilities confronting her, the emotional strain they placed on her, the toll it took. To succeed at the task, "to preserve simplicity of purpose, singleness of mind, and a willingness to be the handmaid of all" would require "much prayer and watchfulness" on the part of the minister's wife, as "events will be continually occurring to try and vex her temper, and to tempt her to shrink from her elevated and responsible standard of profession."[38]

In 1965, William Douglas, an American married minister, published *Ministers' Wives*, a book based on data received from thousands of Protestant ministers' wives about their feelings toward their position. The data indicated that ministers' wives could be divided into several types depending on how they felt about certain issues. As in mid-twentieth century America, so in early nineteenth-century Scotland. The parsonage, or what Jane would have called the manse, was always in need of repairs that weren't forthcoming. Another problem was the need to set an example for the congregation; the pressure of living a life in which all eyes were on the minister's wife was intense. Yet another problem was limited social opportunities. A fourth issue was that the husband was to a greater or lesser degree also married to the church. A fifth had to do with finding ways to express oneself without undermining one's husband's standing. Douglas learned that many ministers' wives worked out solutions to these concerns that enabled them to feel happy and comfortable in their role, but a significant percentage did not. Within that group, some became withdrawn and detached, some sullen, and some rebellious.[39]

These negative responses are not a twentieth-century phenomenon. The life of Sarah Alden Bradford Ripley is a case in point. Sarah was born into an old Boston family in 1793, just a few years before Jane, and married Samuel Ripley, a Unitarian clergyman, in 1818, the same year Jane married Tulloch. As in Jane's case, it was an engineered marriage. Samuel Ripley was exemplary as a husband and highly regarded as a minister, but her duties as wife and mother left Sarah no time to pursue her own interests in the classics and science. She expressed her frustration with the role she had to play in letters to her confidantes. To one female friend, she wrote that she could not promise good behavior and that her husband's "foreboding voice is continually sounding in my ears." In a letter to her brother, she called her position "the most servile of situations," "a hole" out of which she wished she could "creep."[40]

Sarah and Samuel, however, respected each other. They had a wide circle of supportive and intellectually lively friends and family with whom they were in frequent contact. Samuel was somewhat in awe of his wife's learning and intelligence, which, since she couldn't go to university anyway, she funneled into preparing young men for admission to Harvard. The boarding school fees helped them lead a comfortable life. She seems to have been comfortable with pregnancy and nursing. While she found marriage to a minister limiting because it occupied much of her time, she took satisfaction in knowing that many of the young men she tutored in science and the classics did well at Harvard. Access to scientific literature kept her abreast of the latest developments in botany and physics; access to philosophical treatises enabled her to overcome religious doubts that developed from her reading in the sciences. In socializing, in motherhood, in reading, in teaching, in making money, in critical thinking, and in cathartic letter-writing, Sarah had or found socially acceptable ways to deal with the demands of her position.[41] Jane, as we shall see, was less successful.

In 1823, the year after his appointment to the Dallas living, Tulloch lost money in cattle speculation and missed three of the six meetings of the presbytery, at one of which was discussed "A petition relative to some misunderstanding between Rev. Tulloch and James Young schoolmaster." Since neither Tulloch nor Young were in attendance, both were summoned to a special meeting where terms of agreement would be set. Young told the assembled ministers that matters "had been settled in a friendly manner" so he withdrew his petition.[42]

On July 14, Jane gave birth to her third child, who was named William Gordon Tulloch. While she must have been nursing the newborn, her husband started clashing with Sir William's factor Robert Young, on whom Sir William had conferred the privilege of sitting in the seat reserved for him at the Dallas church. Apparently wanting to demonstrate his respect for Sir William, the beholden Tulloch forced the factor to vacate the seat one Sunday. On September 23, Rose informed Sir William that Tulloch had consulted him "on the most effectual measures for bringing Mr. Young to a due sense of his inferiority and nothing less would satisfy than Young's submission to public censure." Tulloch apparently thought that his obsequiousness would meet with Sir William's approval, but Rose knew better. Now describing the man whose career he had nurtured as a fool, possessing not even "the brains of an oyster" which would have led him to realize that by degrading Young he would be incurring Sir William's "marked disapprobation," Rose called Tulloch's demand "an exhibition of fury and nonsense" such as he had never seen.[43]

To protect Tulloch from himself, Rose pocketed the document in which Tulloch expressed his desire to see Young censured publicly so that Young would not have access to evidence that could allow him to get Tulloch publicly censured. At the same time, Rose wanted to help Tulloch out of this self-created morass before Sir William's disapprobation waxed even hotter. Rose informed the heritor that he had talked to Young and persuaded him not to do anything that would "render Mr. Tulloch contemptible" or aggravate him by sitting in Sir William's dedicated seat, even though he had the liberty to do so. As Rose pointed out in the same letter, if Young sat in Sir William's seat at this moment, it would be tantamount to "rebuking Mr. Tulloch in the face of his congregation."[44]

Rose's intervention in this truly senseless kerfuffle pacified everyone. The incident, however, revealed Tulloch to be a bully. Blustery and confident on the outside, quick to flex muscle and strike back, with little ability to see a situation from anybody's position except his own, he was in reality insecure, dependent, not terribly bright, and not harmless. His sense of inferiority, manifesting as officious servility, led him first to bluster and then, when spoken to sharply by a figure with authority, to back down and toe the line. That said, he was still dangerous. Rose had defused the situation, not changed Tulloch's basic disposition.

In June 1824 Jane gave birth to another son, who was named, as previously mentioned, Charles Lennox Cumming after Jane's other uncle. In the same year, Charles's one-year old brother William died and Tulloch missed four of the fifteen meetings of the presbytery, at one of which "several delinquents" had been summoned "in expectation of meeting Mr. T." The ministers in attendance were "astonished and displeased" with Tulloch's absence and ordered him to attend a special meeting.[45] (He did.)

Absenteeism may have been the lesser of Tulloch's problems that year, for the man was proving not to be skillful at making money. Mindful of her obligation to support her husband in difficult times, Jane wrote Rose asking for his help in negotiating a reduction in the rent Tulloch was paying her uncle Sir William for a piece of land. Before writing to Sir William, Rose assessed the land in question, Tulloch's competency as a farmer, and his need for the land. Writing the heritor on November 6, 1824, Rose noted that Tulloch had little by way of "floating capital" because he had speculated unwisely in cattle the year before, commenting dryly that Tulloch had "yet to acquire his skills as a couper" (Scots: buyer and seller) and suggesting that Sir William reduce the rent from £15 to £10.[46] With all Tulloch's deficiencies, his mentor still seemed to feel for him. "Considerable allowance must be made to him, if you wish to retain him as your tenant and to him the farm is in a great measure indispensable—as his possession of it secures his peace and tranquility against the encroachments and turbulence of bad neighbors."[47]

Though Tulloch was no longer as ill-paid as in his Nigg days and he and Jane each received their semiannual interest payments of £8 15s on their respective portions of the marriage settlement, the family was growing. With the birth of their son George in 1826, the manse housed a family of five. The following year, an aspirational Tulloch informed the presbytery, first, that he had proposed to his patron uncle-in-law that the manse be substantially expanded and improved, and second, that the proposal had been accepted. What he said Sir William had agreed to was, in addition to general repairs, conversion of the old kitchen into a nursery and some new additions. These included a replacement kitchen, a servants' sleeping room, and a milkhouse, for which Tulloch gave exact specifications and specified how the interiors should finished, the kitchen with wood, the milkhouse with flagstones. He also wanted the garret plastered. As heritors were notorious for not maintaining, let alone upgrading, their minister's homes, one wonders if Tulloch had used baby George and his two siblings, Helen's great-grandchildren, as emotional leverage.

Sir William, reverting to type, did nothing. Throughout the 1830s, Tulloch complained at such presbytery meetings as he attended that the Dallas manse was in need of repairs. His peers told him to take his complaints to Sir William. The tone of Tulloch's 1842 entry for the *New Statistical Account of Scotland* reflects the anger Tulloch might have been afraid of voicing face-to-face with his patron. About the condition of his accommodations, he wrote that "owing to the miserable state of the interior, a new one is required immediately."[48]

The same year George was born, Miss Charles died. Miss Charles had been Jane's teacher for six years. She had accompanied her to Aberdeen when Yorrick/George lay dying, and housed and taken care of her after she gave testimony and before she got married. Yet when Miss Charles died in 1826, she left £50 ($5,590) to Jane's aunt the musically gifted Sophia and £50 to the "eldest daughter of my much loved, respected and honorable friend Mrs. Forbes of Edinburgh as a very small mark of my gratitude," and nothing to Jane.[49]

After applying behind-the-scenes pressure to get her granddaughter back to the environs of Altyre, Helen seems to have withdrawn from Jane's life. Yet if a letter dated March 28, 1828, from Helen to her daughter-in-law Eliza is any indication, she was much the same as she had been as a younger woman. Her handwriting was somewhat more spidery, but she was as motherly and as committed to a boarding school education as she had always been. She confided to Eliza that in the summer she would have her seven remaining daughters with her, "probably a thing never to happen again," and then tutted, "It was time they [Eliza's children] should be sent from home" and placed at a good school.[50]

Physically, she may have entered the twilight of her life in 1830, for in that year she drew up her will. She had very little to bequeath in the way of material possessions, but distributed the few items of plate, china, books, linen, and glass equally. A coffee pot that she inherited from her grandmother went to her eldest son; a miniature of her beloved husband Penrose she left for her other son, Charles Lennox. She requested her daughter Emilia to burn all her letters and papers, and expressed the hope that her children would live in harmony and that God "would reward them for their great attention and duty to me."[51] Jane does not figure in the will, but neither do any of Helen's other grandchildren. Helen had a strong constitution and did not die until two years later, in 1832, a few months shy of her seventy-eighth birthday, in Forres. She was buried in St. Michael's Chapel on the Gordonstoun property. The procession from Forres to Gordonstoun, a distance of at least twelve miles, must have been slow and stately, as befitted this remarkable woman. Luckily, many of Helen's letters were not burned.

Jane had a lot to reflect on in 1832. In late July of 1829, the year before Helen made her will, a high-pressure system centered between Iceland and Scotland began moving southwestward. As the system moved, Arctic air swept over the North Sea. Meanwhile, a depression moved south from Iceland toward northeastern Scotland and met up with a series of cyclonic events. The confluence of all this meteorological activity was rainfall over Moray. As the air mass moved inland, the rain intensified. Rivers rose and caused catastrophic flooding in the Findhorn River drainage basin.[52] Over the third and fourth of August 1829, the "muckle spate" (Scots: large flood) inundated a narrow stretch of Moray that included Forres and Dallas. Fatalities were few but many families lost their homes and roads and bridges were washed away. Landowners' losses ran into the millions as arable and pasture land were covered with sand and gravel.

Altyre was badly hit. Between the damage caused at Altyre to his "groups of rare evergreens and shrubs of magnificent growth . . . among the extensive walks and shrubberies . . . and in the lower or kitchen garden" and the "damage done to [his] estate above the Church of Dallas," Sir William's not quickly recuperable loss was conservatively estimated at £8,000, $934,000 in today's terms.[53] This figure was calculated by Sir Thomas Dick Lauder, a local heritor, scientist, and eyewitness to the catastrophe whose book *The Great Floods of August 1829 in the Province of Moray and Adjoining Districts* was so popular that it went through two editions by 1830. Today it is considered "the best example of its kind in the UK, with scientific evidence skillfully interwoven with a compassionate assessment of the societal impact of the flood."[54]

According to Sir Dick Lauder, on the afternoon of the August 3, the Lossie, which flows one-fifth of a mile from Dallas's main street and about the same from the manse and church, burst its embankment. Normally a narrow stream, the Lossie swelled to 430 feet in width. At the manse, which stood on slightly higher ground, the river was "9 ½ feet above its usual level."[55] By the morning of August 4, Dallas's main street was a river on which a boat might have sailed and the thirty-two houses lining it had three feet of water in them. Poor people lost their entire stock of winter fuel as well as their standing crops. Women and children were pulled from upper-story windows. Many were taken to the manse, for though the Lossie "swept down the walls of the garden, and passed right through it . . . [and] ruined "an arable haugh [Scots: low-lying meadow] of several acres" that formed part of Tulloch's glebe, the manse itself was untouched. Tulloch and Jane "received the greater part of the people" dispossessed by the flood "at the school-house and the manse."[56] The agricultural damage caused by the spate would still be visible in 1832. Men from Dallas would be busy planting saplings on Sir William's estate above the parish church to replace the felled trees. The farmers of Dallas, Tulloch included, would still be suffering from the loss of arable land.

Though Dick Lauder's account must have appealed to those who lived through the rains and flooding, it is unlikely that it would have entirely appealed to William Tulloch. For while it publicized the damage done to his garden and glebe as well as his response to the plight of the people, the compassion came with a sly joke at Tulloch's expense. Dick Lauder rounds off the account of damages suffered at Dallas with an anecdote told him by a parishioner. "Our parson," said this parishioner, "had a great many more wives that morning than the Grand Sultan."[57]

Ironically, considering that Presbyterian missionaries in India were implying Scottish Christians were morally superior to "heathen" Indians because they were chaste and monogamous, Parson Tulloch was falling far short of the ideal. As the comparison between the Presbyterian Tulloch and the polygamous, harem-maintaining Grand Sultan insinuates, it was apparently a standing joke in the parish that Tulloch liked to be surrounded by women. Though the parishioner whom Dick Lauder quoted laughed off his parson's predilection, on January 12, 1835, five and a half years after the Lossie brought the many women to the manse, Richard Rose could confirm that Tulloch was a bold and shameless womanizer and that Jane was bent on ruining him. In a letter that has not survived, Sir William had written to Rose a few days earlier requesting him, as Rose put it in his reply, to "endeavour to put an end to the deplorable and disgraceful contentions existing and likely to exist in the Manse of Dallas."[58]

Sir William was referring to Tulloch's improprieties and Jane's equally inappropriate response to them. "For all his stupidity," Rose informed Sir William, Tulloch attracted women, and was parading around the village with "good looking tempting jades." Jane believed he was sleeping with the house servants. The servants protested their innocence, and perhaps they were innocent, perhaps the adultery was a figment of Jane's imagination, but even if so, why were they walking arm in arm with her husband?

Rose gave a graphic account of the situation in Dallas, relations between the Tullochs, and Jane's plight in his letter. Long past the state of resentment that many unhappy ministers' wives fell into, she was actively working to bring about his professional ruination by broadcasting his infidelity to his marriage vows. Tulloch, for all that he protested his innocence, realized that she was trying to destroy him; he hit back with a move designed to "kill" her. Instead of consulting Rose, he visited law agents in Elgin "who filled," in Rose's words, "his empty head with notions of his Jus Mariti," that is, his right to the £350 that constituted her portion of the marriage settlement, even though in 1818 he had renounced that claim.

The Elgin lawyers must have been on the unscrupulous side for, as mentioned earlier, Scottish law prevented the husband from laying claim to his spouse's portion of the marriage settlement if such an appropriation would be injurious to her—and Tulloch's purpose was exactly that. To destroy Jane, he was planning to take out an inhibition or writ that would have prevented her from putting her portion out of his reach by transferring it to the trustee who managed the principal. Apparently the fact that the lawyer told him an inhibition could be accomplished without "public notoriety" weighed more with him than the lawyer's statement that it was "a most ungracious measure," what might be called the tactic of a bully. However, when members of the presbytery wrote to criticize him for contemplating taking out an inhibition and threatened him with a "parochial visitation," he reacted like the coward he was: he came to Rose and let Rose persuade him to drop the inhibition and attempt to get himself back into the good graces of his ecclesiastical peers.

According to Rose, the minister and his wife were both inflicting "such desperate wounds on each other's honor, character and happiness that neither can forget and forgive." In a vivid simile, he compared the couple to two bats he had once seen tied "tail to tail—their strife was deadly—they tore hair and skin and flesh from each other." As the minister who had officiated at their wedding, he was, by analogy, the man who had tied the bats together, but as he told Sir William, just as the person in the story "durst not approach" the bats in their deadly struggle, so "no one can approach them [Tulloch and Jane] without being bitten or torn by the one or the other."

Was Tulloch guilty of unchastity as Jane charged? Rose knew that Tulloch was no innocent. He himself had seen Tulloch strolling with village women, but whether he had committed adultery according to the formal definition of the word, Rose didn't know, couldn't say. Jane was no innocent either. Rose thought that her jealous and unrelenting nagging had driven Tulloch to discuss matters with law agents in Elgin. The congregation, which had earlier laughed off Tulloch's womanizing, now discussed the scandalous behavior of both Tullochs. Rose reported to Sir William that half the parish thought Tulloch was guilty and the other half thought Jane was the "blacker of the two"; indeed, all they could agree on was that "never [were] two things so black." Yet Tulloch was still the parish minister and she the minister's wife, and Rose would only conclude that both husband and wife were conducting themselves in a manner unbecoming their positions.

Nevertheless, Rose's sympathies lay with Jane. Exceeding his brief to orchestrate a solution to the situation at Dallas, Rose suggested a solution that only Sir William could bring about. After calling Sir William's attention to the psychological suffering Tulloch was inflicting on her, humiliating her in public and threatening to pauperize her by laying claim to her marriage settlement, he told the heritor she didn't deserve what she was experiencing and implored him to take pity on his niece. As it was only fitting that Jane should "enjoy more happiness than she does in the Manse of Dallas" and he could see "no prospect of reconciliation or even possibility of [Jane and Tulloch] living together," Rose thought separation was the best solution "of what all must agree to be a bad bargain"—a pointed allusion to the 1818 marriage settlement. He then urged Sir William to provide Jane with an additional settlement so she could live independently.

Sir William chose not to provide her with more funds. He must have used his authority forcefully to get both of them to conform, for the shocking drama being played out in Dallas ended. The unhappy couple continued to live together in the manse. They, their three children, Tulloch's married sister Isabella Gair, Isabella's grown son John, the village schoolmaster, and two female domestic servants, as well as an agricultural laborer, were duly counted as residing at the Dallas Manse on June 6, 1841, when Britain carried out its first census.

L'affaire Dallas was similar to the drama that had played itself out in Edinburgh two decades earlier. In both cases, Jane rebelled against authoritarian figures. In both cases, she defied the cultural expectations of the well-behaved woman by making sexual allegations that had some basis but could not be independently proved. In both cases, Jane perceived herself as betrayed, rejected, and humiliated by figures who were supposed to care for her. In both cases, she made herself the center of attention and produced a cornucopia of scandal for her audience. In the first incident she revenged herself on the Misses Woods and Pirie by informing her powerful grandmother; here, though Jane doesn't appear to have specifically asked the presbytery for help, individual ministers provided assistance. As Rose's letter, provided in full in Appendix D, indicates, McKay and Aitken got a servant dismissed and Rose himself tried to move Sir William.

But Jane was less successful in Dallas. Her uncle, regarding her as an expense-generating encumbrance, did not take Rose's advice. By not increasing her marriage settlement, he forced Jane to drop the idea of a legal separation and continue living under the same roof as Tulloch. Her uncle's harsh response to her distress and her husband's emotional abuse, combined with the psychic energy she had expended recoiled, wounding her severely. She drew up her last will and testament eleven months after Rose reported on the couple—written at the manse, it was registered at Elgin on December 17, 1835. The testament begins conventionally enough, with Jane identifying herself as "Jane Cumming, alias Tulloch, residing in Manse of Dallas, spouse of Rev. William Tulloch, Minister of the Parish of Dallas," and in the way of conventional testamentary documents, makes provision for her children, her daughter Eliza and sons Charles and George, and appoints executors, in this case her uncles Sir William and Charles Lennox.[59] As her husband's portion of the marriage settlement would terminate with her death, she added his £350 to her £350 and divided the total among her three children, £400 to Eliza and £150 to each of her sons. Her next item was to leave Tulloch something lest he challenge the will on the grounds that it was made by an insane person, one who couldn't remember she had a spouse. Accordingly, she left him the trifling sum of "two Shillings and sixpence Sterling, payable within the twelve months after my decease," and declared this amount "to be in full of all he can ask, claim or demand in and through my death."[60]

Jane was right in thinking that she was sick, but instead of dying she seems to have had a breakdown. On February 15, 1836, she wrote a disorganized, repetitious letter to Sir William from the Dallas Manse, informing him that two local men been stealing wood from his forested property in Dallas for at least a year.[61] She mentions that she has watched cartloads of woods pass by the manse. This detail suggests that she has positioned herself as a watcher, an eyewitness who has now gathered sufficient information to transmit a damaging story that others might think unlikely. Through the repeated use of "daresay," she presents her accusation as truth, or so probable as to be taken as truth. She tells Sir William how he could be confirm the story for himself by giving him names and details of villagers, where they could be found and questioned; she even gives him tips on how he could have information pried out of them. Her confidence in her story, however, is combined with a deep distrust and fear of people and an inability to stick to her narrative. She begs her uncle "not to tell anyone that I am writing to you about anything" then rambles on about a man who could tell him about another man who was unlawfully sawing wood on the property.[62] The letter meanders on to a woman who would know how to extract information from the informant but has to be approached carefully as she is very distrustful. Jane advises Sir William to be suspicious of Dallas people in general and also to make inquiries about wood being taken away in carts from Altyre.

There are no documents in the Gordon Cumming Depository at the National Library of Scotland pertaining to the Gordonstoun estate confirming Jane's story about stolen wood. In any case, Sir William suffered such a significant loss of mature trees during the floods of 1829 that her story of cartload after cartload of wood being taken away over the course of the year seems implausible. Jane's vigilant scanning of the environment and the letter's suspicious tone suggest she was suffering from paranoia or, since hypervigilance is also characteristic of females who were sexually abused in childhood, perhaps seeing wood being carted away somehow led her to relive one of her experiences involving loss, separation, victimization, or other trauma.[63] As she is dead and I am not a clinician, these are guesses.

At the end of the letter, Jane begs Sir William to respond to her. Beneath that desire for a response is a desire for attention, to be taken seriously and focused on. The absence of any response in the Gordon Cumming Depository may indicate that after rolling his eyes, Sir William thought that the more effective way to deal with the family encumbrance's unquiet mind was to ignore it. Alternatively, he might have communicated to her either in person or through a responsible agent such as a factor or a trustworthy minister like Rose that he considered her a nuisance, wasting his time with yet another product of her contriving imagination, and she needed to modify her behavior.

Jane's next letter to her uncle, in which she asks permission to buy some dead firewood from his factor, offers some support for this latter scenario. We know Penrose wanted to crush an ill-paid minister who was supposedly poaching on his land; perhaps if it had come to his attention that a poor lady was picking up dead boughs on his lands for firewood he would have taken her to court too. Though he would be within his rights to do so, all he might have gained from the action would have been a reputation for meanness and persecution of an inferior. In *The Gamekeeper at Home*, a work written in 1878 that went into many printings, the gamekeeper narrator, who comes across as a good man, makes the point that shivering old women scavenging on a landlord's property were a pitiful sight but allowing them to get away with it would open the floodgates to more serious poaching and trespassing and generally lead to diminution of the value of the estate. At the same time, while the gamekeeper is silent on the subject of the punishment such women would receive, he implies that young men who cut live branches for the purpose of turning them into fashionable walking sticks were committing a far more serious offense and would be punished more severely than the old women.

Penrose's far less choleric son Sir William probably would have fumed over rather than fought a woman caught collecting firewood without permission, but how would he have reacted if Jane were that woman? He hadn't treated Jane with compassion, though her misery had been brought to his attention. He didn't increase her settlement, which would have made it possible for her to live as a single woman. On the other hand, even though he had done it grudgingly, he had made it possible for her and her husband to have a position in society. Like it or not, she was dependent on her uncle. He had facilitated her return to the Moray region from Nigg; in 1842, with the Disruption still a year off, he still had the power to pressure the presbytery into having Tulloch translated to some uncouth corner of Scotland. Recognizing his power over her life and his disapprobation of her and her husband's past conduct, the last thing she wanted to do was rile him further. Lest he accuse and prosecute *them* for stealing his wood, on January 26, 1842, she wrote a short note to Sir William begging him to allow his factor to sell them some wood. It was both the proper and the legal thing to do and a way for her to make him, living in comfort at Gordonstoun, feel guilty about their suffering in the damp manse he had never repaired. So when Jane wrote, "as the weather is very cold and we are very ill off for fire Mr. Tulloch has bid me write and say that he will be much obliged to you if you will allow James Smith sell us some dead trees for firewood," she was evoking yet distancing herself from the guilt-inducing image of the shivering, stealing crone to whom compassion was denied. She, Jane, was not poor, and she was taking exactly the right step to stay on the right side of her uncle.⁶⁴ That said, behind that correct decision lay fear and distrust.

Compounding her fear of her uncle was the knowledge that her husband still retained a lawyer in Elgin. She was so fearful in early 1843 that she asked for the principal settled on her at the time of her marriage. Fulfilling her request required a certain amount of paperwork on the part of Sir William's lawyers, now Mackenzie, Innes & Logan. They had to prepare letters and obtain a loan necessitated by her demand. In addition, they had to contact the trustees of the settlement and Tulloch's Elgin lawyer, who was requested to send them the Tullochs' marriage contract. The statement of accounts prepared by Mackenzie, Innes & Logan for services rendered from November 1842 through January 1843 indicated that Sir William was billed a little over £35. The statement indicates that Jane's £350 was remitted to her account at the Forres branch of the National Bank on January 28, 1843.⁶⁵

Jane and Tulloch were an ill-matched pair, but their marital difficulties in the 1830s and 1840s paralleled, and were no doubt exacerbated by, church politics of the time. The 1711 Church Patronage (Scotland) Act was never popular with clerics and congregations, but starting in 1834, the year the Tullochs began to sling mud at each other, and raging through 1843, the year Jane took possession of her £350, the controversy over the legislation divided the Scottish Presbyterian Church into those who accepted the right of heritors to install their candidates on congregations and those who regarded this right as secular interference.⁶⁶ The former were called the Moderates while the latter were known as the Evangelical, or the Non-Intrusionists. Though Tulloch owed his installation to patronage, James McCosh, the editor of the *Dundee Warder*, a newspaper that advocated the cause of the Evangelical party, wrote that Tulloch "professed the principles of non-intrusion . . . [and] generally voted in church courts [i.e., at meetings of the presbytery] with the Evangelical side."⁶⁷

In 1834 the Evangelicals won a victory when the General Assembly passed the Veto Act. Per this act, a heritor presented his choice to the congregation but the parishioners had the right to reject his designee. Challenges to the Veto Act began almost immediately, however. The Moderates gained control of the General Assembly and refused to uphold the ordination of ministers that congregations had chosen. When in January 1841 Parliament rejected the idea that the Scottish Church could function independent of heritors, the Disruption was a foregone conclusion. On May 18, 1843, one-third of the ministers of the Church walked out of the General

Assembly, giving up their position and the stipend and the accommodations that went along with it for the sake of their principles. Their act split the Church into the Residual Establishment and the Free Church. Tulloch was caught between loyalty to Sir William and the principles of non-intrusion. He chose the former.

Within months of the split, McCosh published *The Wheat and the Chaff Gathered into Bundles*. In it, he offered a statistical account in which he separated the ministers who supported the Residual Establishment into two camps, the wheat and the chaff, according to their essential moral integrity. Richard Rose fell into the "wheat" category, but his cowardly, hypocritical mentee Tulloch was "chaff."[68] Tulloch, who was beholden to Sir William for his appointment, his position in society, his stipend, his accommodation, and the land he rented at a special price, couldn't give up those material blessings. McCosh came down heavily on the Tullochs of the church, stating categorically, "it is impossible to entertain for them as a body any shred of respect or esteem."[69]

In 1914, seventy-one years after the Disruption, the Free Church minister W. W. Ewing compiled the two-volume *Annals of the Free Church of Scotland*. The book gives a parish-by-parish account of the Disruption. Since the ministers who came out forfeited their livings, Ewing is particularly complimentary of Free Church people who donated land and money. Many of these benefactors were women, and Ewing mentions them by name. However, he presents what happened at Dallas in 1843 in the hushed tones reserved for the telling of a scandal. Without giving Tulloch's name, he states that at Dallas, "the minister of the parish did not 'come out' at the Disruption, but his wife and family, with many of his people, adhered to the [Free] Church."[70]

Even the Free Church was shocked by Jane's disruption. There is nothing in the *Annals* that at all resembles what took place at Dallas, with the husband, who was a minister, remaining within the Established Church while his wife and children went over to the Free Church. It is the only account in Ewing's two volumes in which a woman who joined the Free Church and whose name is known is not mentioned by name, where the minister is not named either, and where the minister's son, who became a Free Church minister, is not held up for praise. It is the only account in which the Disruption caused the breakup of that quasi-sacred unit the minister's family, orchestrated by, of all people, the minister's wife, the minister being unable to enjoin order in his own household. Even seven decades after the event, with all the principals long dead and her husband already condemned as "chaff," the Free Church would not name this woman because she had made her husband look foolish and unmanly as she led his children and his congregation away from him.

Jane's mid-1830s eruption against her husband was outrageous but not very successful, while her 1840s revolt gained her two victories. Though in the earlier sequence of events she displayed resourcefulness by making a will that protected her estate from him, she seemingly had a breakdown and certainly wasn't able to separate. Her actions in the 1840s were far more successful. Because she came out of the Established Church along with their three children and the majority of the congregation at Dallas, she not only obtained a kind of separation but humiliated Tulloch as a minister and a man. Jane's joining the Free Church, an act of symbolic emasculation if ever there was one, was a gendered triumph so shocking that it couldn't be celebrated by the Free Church.

Within days of the formal splitting of the church, a deputation of Free Church parishioners of Dallas wrote Sir William in his capacity as patron of the parish and asked him for permission to build a house of worship near Dallas. Sir William was very upset by the request. In an undated letter, he told them he thought they were making a big mistake by challenging his authority over their lives. He said Dallas was too small a parish to sustain two congregations. He claimed that the permanent presence of a dissenting church would only lead to further dissention. Nonetheless, to avoid a permanent schism between him and the Free Church adherents in Dallas, he allowed them to build their church. The permission was given grudgingly, for he reserved the right to terminate the feu (Scots: lease) with six months' notice, his object being "to exercise the right of patronage as once more to collect the sheep into one fold."[71]

Sir William was disabused of his hope that the Free Church members would come to see the error of their ways and allow him to exercise patronage. The number of Free Church congregants increased while the numbers worshipping at the Established Church where Tulloch was pastor "considerably decreased."[72] As she had as a schoolgirl when she saw Janet Munro taking leave of Miss Woods, Jane might have clapped for joy, but she was in an anomalous position. Though she worshipped at the Free Church, she continued to reside at the manse with Tulloch.

Jane did not enjoy her triumph for very long. According to her gravestone in the cemetery attached to the Dallas church, she died at the manse on April 24, 1844. The *Forres Gazette*, the *Elgin Courant*, and the *Aberdeen Journal* carried the same spare announcement. Cause of death was not given. All the obituaries stated that she was in her forty-seventh year. If she was indeed forty-seven, then she would have been born in 1797. Was the girl who gave testimony in 1811 younger than everybody claimed she was?

Soon thereafter, Jane's sons, Charles and George, wrote Sir William and Charles Lennox, respectively, requesting them, per their mother's testament, to be the executors of her estate. Charles Lennox politely declined. In a note dated June 7, 1844 and now attached to her will, he explained to Charles Tulloch that he had "so much business on [his] hands" that it was "quite out of [his] power to act as an executor."[73] Sir William, whose patience Jane had sorely tried, didn't even attempt a social lie. In his letter dated July 19, also attached to Jane's will, he wrote to George Tulloch, "Dear Sir, Referring to your letter of the 16th, I beg to state that I decline acting as an Executor under your late mother's will."[74] Their responses made it clear Jane's uncles wanted nothing more to do with her, even deceased.

On September 17, 1844, Jane's estate was inventoried by the Elgin Sheriff Court. The inventory confirmed that Jane had withdrawn her portion of the principal in January 1843 but showed that by the time she died, only £200 was left. The Forres appraiser valued her trinkets and clothing at £7. Tulloch's portion of the marriage settlement had flowed into her bank account after she died, and since it already held the £200, her estate was valued at a little over £550, or $71,900.

Tulloch did not live long after his wife, dying suddenly and instantaneously in the manse on November 23, 1845, an inclement Sabbath evening. Residents believed he had foreseen his demise and for that reason chose to sing the paraphrase of *John* 14:25–28, "You must now hear my voice no more; My father calls me home," from the pulpit that morning.[75] The obituary that appeared in the *Elgin Courant and Morayshire Advertiser* on November 28 indicated that "for a considerable period the Reverend . . . had been laboring under symptoms of apoplexy." He died from this condition, for the writer of the obituary mentioned that Tulloch's daughter, hearing a "heavy thud" from the room, hastened there and found her father lying dead on the floor. The notice then quoted *Ecclesiastes* 12: 6–7 ("Or ever the silver cord be loosed or the golden bowl be broken, or the pitcher be broken at the fountain, or the wheel broken at the cistern. Then shall the dust return to the earth as it was and the spirit shall return unto God who gave it"). It then put into practice the Latin aphorism *de mortuis nil nisi bonum* (say nothing but good of the dead). "Mr. Tulloch," the author of the piece wrote, "was most useful in the parish. In visiting his parishioners—tendering advice in every point—in adjusting disputes where he was made the referee—and in overlooking the interests of all who came within his charge, he was eminently successful, and will be long remembered throughout the parish." The *Elgin Courier*'s piece was more restrained: "We have not learned what was the nature of this sudden attack, but it is an instructive lesson—of which we have had many to record this season—of the uncertainty of human life."

The Dallas session elders met on November 30, a week after the minister's death, and recorded his passing in their minutes. "The Session deem it proper to record the death of their late Pastor, the Revd. William Tulloch who suddenly departed this life on Sabbath last, the 23rd, and the Session also record their sympathy with his bereaved family."[76] In comparison with the newspaper obituary from the *Elgin Courant* and the generally fulsome obituaries of ministers recorded in church session minutes that speak to the great love the congregation felt for their minister and their sense of loss at his passing, the Dallas elders' perfunctory sentence suggests that Tulloch's death was a relief and he would not be missed. Tulloch was buried with Jane in the Dallas churchyard, the tombstone erected some years later by the parishioners whom he had served for twenty-five years. Its full inscription reads: "Erected by the Parishioners of Dallas in memory of the Rev'd WILLIAM TULLOCH, Minister of that Parish for 25 years, who died 23rd November 1845 aged 68 years. Also of JANE CUMMING, his wife, who died 24th April 1844, aged 47 years. 'When Christ, who is our life shall appear, then shall ye also appear with him in Glory.' Col: 111, &4." The simple tombstone is still standing in the neat, peaceful churchyard by the wall of the church.

Had Jane at some point filled her sons' heads with notions of grandeur based on her status as an acknowledged granddaughter of Penrose and Helen Cumming Gordon? Her sons thought the connection worth looking into. A month after their father died, one of the sons paid a visit to the office of Mackenzie, Innes & Logan. A representative of the firm informed Sir William on December 23 that he had "called to inquire as to any provision having been left to his mother by the settlement of the late Sir Alexander Cumming." After examining Penrose's Deeds of Settlement, the representative concluded that there was "nothing in them upon which his mother or he could found a claim."[77] The firm then sent Sir William a thirteen shilling bill.

At the time of his death, Tulloch owed money and was retaining legal counsel. A month after he died, on December 22, a notice appeared in the *Forres, Elgin and Nairn Gazette, Northern Review and Advertiser* advising all those who had loaned him money to "lodge their claims with the vouchers thereof and declarations of verity, in the hands of R. and A. Urquart,

Writers in Forres, Agents for the representatives [of the estate], within fourteen days from this date." Tulloch's estate was inventoried by the Elgin Sheriff Court on September 26, 1846. As there is no record of outstanding loans on the inventory, presumably these debts had been paid off in the interim. The value of his "household furniture, books, wearing apparel and watch, farm stocking implements of husbandry, corn and straw and whole other moveable effects" came to £127 or $16,000.[78] Sir William had not yet paid him his Michaelmas stipend; when that flowed posthumously into his estate, its value came to a little under £200. Tulloch and Jane's eldest son Charles Lennox Cumming swore to the court's evaluation of the estate.

Though not reconciled to the existence of the Free Church, Sir William had learned his lesson from foisting a candidate on a presbytery and a community. Shortly after Tulloch died, the heritor drafted a note to be read to the parishioners at the Dallas church. Written in the third person, the undated note declaimed: "Sir William G. G. Cumming as patron of the Parish of Dallas at present vacant by the death of the Revd Wm Tulloch, is desirous to meet the wishes of the people of Dallas in the settlement of a successor to their late pastor. For this purpose he has laid before the presbytery of Forres a list of seven persons—highly recommended to him as regards both talents and character; and the presbytery at his request has agreed to allow these candidates to preach in the Church of Dallas."[79] After hearing them, the parishioners "would have an opportunity of forming their own opinion on their respective merits . . . and after making such enquiries as they may deem proper to consider which of them they would wish to be settled among them as their pastor," they "would acquaint him with their decision; when he will be most happy to issue a presentation in favor of the individual most acceptable to them." "His sole wish," the note concluded, was "to have a useful and an acceptable minister settled in the parish of Dallas."[80] The parishioners acceded and chose John MacDonald as their next pastor.

Life resumed its normal course in Dallas. From time to time the Lossie overflowed its banks, but the story of the unprincipled minister and his tormented wife faded from memory. In an email I received from Lord Simon Woolton, a collateral descendant of Sir William, he stated that his mother (b. 1925), a sister of the sixth baronet, had not known about Jane until she was presented with a copy of Lillian Faderman's *Scotch Verdict* (1984), a creative recounting of the case, and that neither he nor his mother had never heard of Yorrick/George before receiving my email. For the Gordon Cummings, Lord Woolton wrote, Jane is a "family story that has been quietly buried."[81]

Chapter Seven

JANE, POSTHUMOUSLY

Except for two grandsons who moved in the circle of George Henry Lamson, an American doctor and drug addict executed in 1882 for poisoning his English brother-in-law, Jane's descendants led conventional, respectable, honorable lives of service. Her daughter Eliza, stayed single and became a schoolmistress; Jane's son Charles became a Free Church minister and her son George a Poor Law Officer in London. Charles's daughter, Jane Cumming Tulloch (later Arthur), volunteered with the British Red Cross during World War I. Two of Mrs. Arthur's sons enlisted; one died in battle. Other descendants went into banking, business, insurance, and medical practice.

Jane's uncle William was debt-ridden and had fourteen children to support and three mansions to maintain, but apparently shared his brother George's propensity for living above his means. On one day in August 1831, William spent over £114 in London on cologne, soap, tea, coffee, Carolina rice, and assorted condiments. In September, he spent over £36 at a shop in Soho on commodes, silver cups and saucers, a porcelain elephant and packing cases for the commodes. The next month he spent over £123, also in London, on earrings, a ring, a broach, an antique necklace and matching ring. In today's terms, he spent $18,800 in two months on luxury and consumer items.[1]

Penrose's lawful descendants maintained a connection with India. Three grandchildren and one great-grandchild spent time there. Louisa Forbes's second son, Alexander Penrose Forbes, joined the East India Company as a writer in 1837 and held several positions in the Madras Establishment before resigning in 1844. Sir William's second son, Roualeyn, entered East India Company service a year later as a cornet in the Madras Light Cavalry; he too resigned. In the late 1850s, Roualeyn's sister Constance Frederica spent some seasons there painting and socializing with friends. She published two books about her experiences in India, *From the Hebrides to the Himalayas* in 1876 and *In the Himalayas and on the Indian Plains* in 1884. The great-grandchild was also a William. He became the fourth baronet in 1866 but found time to engage in big game hunting in

India. In 1871, his vade mecum of hunting in India, *Wild Men and Wild Beasts*, appeared in print. It would have been surprising if Jane had rated a mention in any of these books, but their authors make no reference to the family members who served with the East India Company, either.

In addition, the Gordon Cummings were involved in two more defamation of character lawsuits. The famous one featured the India-returned fourth baronet and the Prince of Wales (later King Edward VII). In 1890 this Sir William alleged that the Prince of Wales had cheated at cards. When the Prince of Wales claimed that it was Sir William who had marked the deck, Sir William initiated a lawsuit against him. The Baccarat Scandal, as it was called, received extensive coverage in the press and ended with the jury deciding in favor of Victoria's son. Within days, Sir William was cut from the rolls of the clubs he belonged to and dishonorably discharged from the British Army. Shunned by his erstwhile friends, his career and reputation destroyed irreparably, Sir William spent the rest of his days in seclusion.

The second lawsuit involved Roualeyn. Though much less famous than the Baccarat Scandal, this one bore an uncanny resemblance to *Miss Marianne Woods and Miss Jane Pirie Against Dame Helen Cumming Gordon*. After spending years in foreign parts, Roualeyn returned to Scotland with many trophies. He then formed connections with two lower-class Scottish women, with each of whom he had a daughter. Almost forty years later, in the first decade of the twentieth century, his sister Constance found herself embroiled in a lawsuit with one of these daughters, Eleanora. Eleanora claimed that following her father's death in 1866, the Gordon Cummings had deprived her of money from the posthumous sale of Roualeyn's effects. To put pressure on the Gordon Cummings to pay up, Eleanora threatened to reveal a dark family secret to the Elgin press.

On November 28, 1903, in a letter marked "Private" and directed to an unnamed editor of an unnamed newspaper, Constance gave vent to her anger against Eleanora.[2] She forewarned this editor that he might be receiving "a most malignant representation of facts" from Eleanora, who would be presenting herself as "an innocent swindled orphan—swindled by her Father's brothers." In this letter, she remembered her niece as a ten-year old, "a singularly ugly very common-looking child . . . furious because the family did not adopt her" after her father's death. Constance acknowledged that while the Gordon Cummings had paid for her training at an art school, they had no personal contact with her for many years until she reintroduced herself to Constance.

Eleanora had married a minister and had two children, but the husband and children had died. She was now married to a Polish man named

Michael Nakeska (or Nakeski), whose various business ventures had come to nothing. Constance felt sorry for Eleanora and tried to help the couple financially. However, Eleanor repaid Constance's "really generous and considerate kindness" with "venomously insolent letters," in which she informed the already disgraced fourth baronet that she would proclaim his villainy to the press and simultaneously reveal "damning discoveries" she had already made.

Was Eleanora revenging herself on her father's family for their rejection and abandonment of her, followed by decades of silence? Was she a contriving liar, a blackmailing bluffer whose story of scandalous discoveries was fabricated but striking a sensitive nerve? Or had she somehow unearthed information about *Miss Marianne Woods and Miss Jane Pirie against Dame Helen Cumming Gordon*?

Underneath the scornful, haughty tone reminiscent of Helen's demeanor, fear runs strong in Constance's letter. Constance recognized that Eleanora suffered from her status as an illegitimate child and an orphan. She acknowledged that the family had regarded Eleanora as an encumbrance, paying for her education but maintaining distance from her, even to the point of losing contact with her. As Constance proceeded, Eleanora became Clerk's final image of Jane—a woman filled with venom and viciousness, whose chosen victims had only shown kindness to her. Constance construed her as a malignant liar whose purpose was to revenge herself on the Gordon Cummings.

In another eerie parallel with the early nineteenth-century case, Constance understood that what Eleanora wanted was a forum, a space in which she could make herself heard and have attention focused on her. *Woods v. Pirie* was held behind closed doors and the proceedings were supposed to have been disposed of and destroyed. Constance's "private" letter represents her attempt to silence and contain her niece so that her account, like the proceedings of *Woods v. Pirie*, would not enter the public domain. In the end, no damning revelations were published between 1903 and 1907, when Eleanora's claim was dismissed with an award of £5. While it seems likely that Eleanora was bluffing, it is just within the realm of possibility that if she submitted anything to the press, Constance's social standing would have led to this material being disposed of, destroyed, or, as in the case of Jane's notebook, just disappearing.[3]

Though Sir William married an American heiress immediately after he lost his suit against the Prince of Wales, the legal costs, combined with decades of lavish spending by the baronets who had followed Penrose, had decimated the family's wealth by the time Eleanora began her action.

Constance, who earned her living through writing, spent about £400 or $54,300 in legal fees to clear the family name, but coming on top of the Baccarat Scandal, it was something of a Pyrrhic victory. The fifth baronet was forced to sell Gordonstoun, causing the property acquired by Penrose after lengthy and costly legal battles to drop from the family title. Gordonstoun then became a public school. Members of the royal family have been educated there, and the school has been welcoming to students from the Asian subcontinent.

While Jane's line did not maintain any connection with India, it did undergo a diaspora. By 1875 all members of the direct family had left Scotland. A great-granddaughter spent a number of years in Taiwan associated with the Presbyterian mission there. Two branches left Britain, settling in Rhodesia and Canada, respectively. A Rhodesian descendant named Alan Scott returned to England as a Rhodes Scholar on the cusp of World War II. After receiving a double first at Oxford, he joined a Highlands regiment that was sent to Burma. He died in combat and was buried in a military cemetery in Imphal, in northeastern India.[4] His sister married a farmer in Rhodesia and they came with their daughter to England in 1959. Ancestry.com indicates that husband and wife returned to the farm; I have not been able to trace the daughter after the boat docked in Liverpool in 1959. A great-grandson named Charles Lennox Tulloch Arthur enlisted with the Canadian Army Medical Corps and fought in World War I. He was a medical student at the time, and like his Cumming ancestors, upwards of six feet tall. His son served with the Royal Air Force and took part in the Battle of Britain and the North African offensive. A third branch stayed in England and seems to have put roots down in the north. Published on October 16, 1998, *The Vancouver Sun* obituary of Charles Ian Rose Arthur, the pilot who took part in the Battle of Britain, states that he had two grandsons and two great-grandchildren, so the line started by Jane and William Tulloch may be flourishing on two, and possibly three, continents.

In her will, Helen enjoined her children to destroy her letters, but those she sent to Lady Grant were beyond their reach and now comprise some ounces of the twenty tons of Sir James Grant of Grant papers and correspondence archived at one of New Town's architectural gems, the National Records of Scotland (formerly known as the General Register Office and the National Archives of Scotland) on Princes Street. The Gordon Cumming papers were stored in a stable on the Altyre estate, then were moved to the National Library of Scotland in 1969 after a flood in that stable. The boxes in which the documents relating to Jane's life reposed were not damaged by water, damp, or other conditions in the stable. The Court of Session deposited such evidence as remained from the case at the National Records of Scotland, probably about twenty years after the final determination.[5] Folded tightly to fit into the box in the nineteenth century, it was not easy to get the pages to lie flat in 2015 when I looked at them. Many felt damp to the touch. The Scottish government has digitized its old wills and testaments. Jane's can be read online at www.scotlandspeople.gov.uk, as can those of many of the other people who figure in this book.

The unanimously agreed-upon decision taken at the Court of Session in 1811 that the papers printed during the course of the legal proceedings were to be destroyed or disposed of was treated cavalierly. Once the case was settled, unnamed individuals who were friends of the Scottish lawyer John Borthwick and had also been "engaged in counsel," perhaps on opposing sides of the suit, had no qualms about sharing with him details of *Miss Marianne Woods and Miss Jane Pirie Against Dame Helen Cumming Gordon*. The result is that the suit is mentioned in his 1826 *A Treatise on the Law of Libel and Slander, as Applied in Scotland, in Criminal Prosecutions and in Actions of Damages: With an Appendix, Containing Reports of Several Cases Respecting Defamation, which Have Not Been, Hitherto, Published*.[6] In addition, three of the documents that were submitted to the House of Lords fell into his hands. Recognizing their scandalous content and tacitly acknowledging that they shouldn't even exist anymore, Borthwick scrawled on the inside front cover, "A private copy—to be kept always private—this is hardly to be got—I received it originally from Dr. Campbell, solicitor in London—& had occasion to study it, in reference to my treatise on libel. JB To be sealed up to hand to my trustees—who when they think right may give it to my son." This copy is now at Smith College in Northampton, Massachusetts.[7]

Clerk, Moncreiff, and Meadowbank also treated the agreement as nonbinding. Their personal, handsomely bound sets, which are not identical, are now housed at the Signet Library and the Law Library of the Faculty of Advocates, both in Edinburgh, and the National Library of Medicine in Bethesda, Maryland, respectively. Lord Meadowbank's set, which traveled farthest from Parliament Square, seems to have arrived in the United States in the last decade of the nineteenth century.[8]

Disaggregated sets of printed papers from the case have been cropping up since the latter half of the nineteenth century. A copy of "The Additional Petition of Miss Mary-Ann Woods and Miss Jane Pirie" of October 10, 1811, was sold in New York City in 1877.[9] Acquired in 1890, the British Library still keeps its set of three papers in its collection of pornographic and erotic materials (the Private Case), though under a less restrictive pressmark than a century ago.[10] In a 1930 bequest from a Glasgow lawyer, the Signet obtained two documents from the case, but as of 2016 these were still in stackage, unindexed and uncatalogued.[11] The set that Harvard bought in 1904 was digitized by Thomson Gale Cengage in the first decade of this century as part of its series *Making of Modern Law Trials 1600–1926*.

William Roughead, who owned Clerk's set for about twenty-five years and came across Moncreiff's set in the Law Library of the Faculty of Advocates, used both when writing his account of the case, which appeared in a 1929 issue of the *Juridical Review* and then in his 1930 collection of essays, *Bad Companions*. First published by the Edinburgh house of William Green, *Bad Companions* reached an even wider audience when the American edition came out in 1931. The American dramatist Lillian Hellman used Roughead's account as the basis for her 1934 play *The Children's Hour*, which was twice made into a Hollywood movie, in 1936 and 1961.

In 1936 the Hays Production Code was in force. It forbade the depiction of homosexuality, so Hellman turned the melodrama into a lighthearted screenplay. She replaced the teachers' putative lesbian relationship with a heterosexual love triangle; the Jane Cumming character, a girl named Mary Tilford, is a spoiled brat. To distance it from the drama, the movie was called *These Three*. The eponymously named 1961 movie follows the play more closely. Miss Dobie, the character based on Jane Pirie, acknowledges her feelings for the other teacher.

In more recent years, the case has led to a musical based on *Scotch Verdict* that was performed in Iowa; a play titled *The Two Janes*, which was given a staged reading at the Court of Sessions' neighbor on Parliament Square, the Signet Library; and a performance art piece, *Venus Nefanda*, that premiered in Mumbai (modern-day Bombay).[12] An unproduced screenplay titled *Scotch Verdict* (but not based on Faderman's book), having won awards at international film festivals in 2013 and 2014, was given a staged reading in 2015 at the Royal Academy of Dramatic Arts in London.[13] In these creative works, Jane variously comes across as a watchful "black" child, a victim of persecution because of her race, and a girl born in Bombay to wealth and status whose adolescent sexuality now plays itself out in an Edinburgh courtroom. In sum, posthumously Jane has appeared in spaces the historical Jane may never have heard of, and in such guises that the historical Jane might not recognize herself.

The posthumous metamorphoses of Jane Cumming began with the Scotsman William Roughead. He bought Clerk's set of proceedings in the late 1920s from an unnamed Edinburgh bookseller and, after going through it and Moncriff's sets, reduced the thick volumes into the article that subsequently became the chapter on the case in *Bad Companions*. By training Roughead was a lawyer but, finding great satisfaction in courtroom drama, he gave up the practice of law. He spent many days at Parliament Square listening to cases where, on his way to the rooms off the Hall, he would have seen objects and architectural features that Jane saw on the days she gave testimony in 1811: the statuary and portraits, the oak ceiling rising from grotesque corbels, even the macer's widow, albeit without the macer, who had in the interim been replaced by a loudspeaker system. And it was for him, as it had been in Jane's day, an assembly point for advocates and their clients.

Roughead was a mild-mannered family man with a special-needs daughter whom he loved deeply, a voracious reader and a Calvinist who believed in the existence of evil and eternal damnation. Like many in the Victorian era—or indeed our own—he was fascinated by crime. He regarded it as an abomination and felt that deviance in general, being subversive of the social order, had to be punished.[14]

Roughead was also blinkered by the racial and sexual prejudice of his generation. The worst epithet Roughead could hurl against a white woman was "black bitch," but he would only use this phrase (or phrases of this nature) in personal correspondence with men, where he also indulged in coarse sexual humor.[15] Like one of his favorite authors, Joseph Conrad, Roughead correlated a nonwhite complexion with moral evil; he was unable to consider that a person he labeled criminal and black might have been warped by the dominant social order's prejudice. However, Roughead was judicious enough to acknowledge that just as wolves could don sheep's clothing, it was possible that the teachers were lying and "black girl" Jane telling the truth, which led him to admit that "one or other must be false as hell."[16]

He may even have insinuated that the teachers were unnatural or deviated from the natural order when he titled the section of *Bad Companions* that dealt with the school "Regiment of Women." That phrase is part of the title of the Scotsman John Knox's 1558 diatribe *The First Blast of the Trumpet Against the Monstruous Regiment of Women*. Using "monstrous" and "regiment" in their obsolete senses to mean, respectively, "unnatural" or "deviant" and "regimen" or "rule," Knox trumpeted against female rule over men and Catholic female rulers over Protestant souls, with special reference to Mary, Queen of Scots, and her regent-mother, Mary of Guise. Roughead left out "monstrous" from his title, but for those who knew their Knox, this was Roughead's blast from *his* trumpet against the

Drumsheugh school on account of its similarity to a Catholic convent, that hothouse for culturing *special* friendships between women. Roughead expressed a conviction that the charge brought against the teachers was false," and said that if he had thought the allegations of sexual deviance leveled against them had any substance, "nothing would have induced me to deal with" their case.[17] But Knox's phrase allowed Roughead's Calvinist evil-is-real mind and damnation-acknowledging soul to wonder if there was something deviant about the Misses Woods and Pirie, and if so, to plant the thought that there was a special place in hell for them. In much the same way Clerk left out stanzas from Swift's "Corinna" that reveal his private thinking about Jane, so Roughead's editing of Knox's title allows us to consider that despite proclaiming their innocence on paper, Roughead secretly kept open the possibility that they were unnatural women.

Roughead's Calvinism and his Victorian sensibility, however, made his mindset different from Clerk's. As discussed earlier, Swift's Corinna allowed Clerk to consider that Jane might have been molested in her Calcutta years, and to toy with the notion that she was the "real" lesbian in the triangle formed by her, Marianne Woods, and Jane Pirie. Clerk must have been pleased with himself for finding a literary parallel to Jane's voyeurism in Corinna, shown gazing at her master's private parts while he pissed. The analogy led Clerk to speculate that Jane's adult life would involve sexual scandal; if she followed Corinna's path, she too would produce a "cornucopia" of scandal and lead a deliciously pleasurable, albeit transgressive, existence similar to life in *The New Atalantis*. As events proved, Clerk was completely wrong in the latter speculation, but exactly right about the former. Roughead, who no doubt fathomed what Clerk was implying, was unwilling to uncloak Clerk's thinking for his readers. Wrapping himself in a Victorian concern for public decency, he claimed that Clerk's "muse is rather too racy for quotation" and imagined a bitter and barren future for Jane, in which he was, like Clerk, partly correct.[18]

In addition to the two volumes of printed case proceedings available to Roughead in Edinburgh, he had Clerk's over-the-top address in his own hand, the judges' notes, also handwritten, the papers that went to the House of Lords, and the determination of the House of Lords' Law Lords. The handwritten material tendered conflicting analyses and interpretations of Jane's behavior and personality. For reasons only he could divulge, Roughead did not look at the cache of materials deposited by the Court of Session building on Princes Street he would have known as the General Register Office for Scotland, a short walk from the Law Library of the

Faculty of Advocates. He did not know what happened to Jane after she gave testimony, nor did he know that the case ended in an out-of-court settlement in 1821.

Roughead both followed and amplified the racism of the court documents. In contrast to his sources, he did not believe that nurturing or the environment in which Jane spent her formative years had determined her nature. He seemed glad that the judges did not allow any evidence purporting to show that Jane was corrupted by the licentious natives of the Calcutta schools she attended to be presented, because no evidence of that kind meant Jane's behavior was entirely due to the "black" nature she was born with. Roughead also ascribed Jane's sexual knowledge to that original "black" blood. Thus he not only included the invidious references in his primary material to Jane's complexion but referred to her as "a black draught" that had to be swallowed, "a black girl" with a "heart . . . to match her complexion," and a "fawn[ing] black sheep." Apparently not satisfied with this, he also called her an "Indian [who] shot her poisoned bolt," and a "half-caste . . . with a fertile and infragrant imagination" who had "imported to the banks of the Water of Leith the bane which she had gathered by the Ganges."[19]

Roughead saved his most extreme invective for a July 19, 1929, letter to his American friend, the librarian and fellow crime writer Edmund Pearson, in which he referred to Jane as a "black bitch" and a "real live devil."[20] Even then, he claimed that in his portrait of her in *Bad Companions*, he had toned down her wickedness and "camouflage[d] the truth" so as to "reduce . . . this real live devil . . . to respectable proportions."[21] By comparing Roughead's version of the case to the proceedings, it becomes clear that the method he adopted to reduce his "devil" to "respectable proportions" involved omitting details suggesting that she was coming out as a lesbian. He makes no mention of Jane's clingy fondness for Miss Woods. Similarly, Janet Munro's statement that Jane propositioned her finds no place in his narrative. Roughead, who called himself a "conscientious explorer of the dark continent of crime," did not want to follow a sexual route into Jane's psyche.[22]

Roughead was enough a citizen of the twentieth century to know of the work of Freud, Krafft-Ebbing, and Havelock Ellis, and refers to all of them dismissively in his chapter. Having decided that "psychological sauce" or "Freudian ornature" was not required for understanding Woods, Pirie, and Cumming and their dynamic, he left out any reference to Mrs. Campbell's suspicions and veiled his own suspicions in an arcane reference to John Knox.[23] Thus he queered (in the sense of falsifying through omission) evidence so as to avoid discussing material that queered (in the sexual-orientation sense) Jane Pirie. And claiming that in an emotionally overwrought letter by Miss Pirie "there echoes the authentic accent of truth," he convinced himself that the teachers were the pitiable victims of the "black girl's blacker charge."[24]

For Roughead, unlike Clerk, pronouncing judgment against Jane did not require much thinking. The race prejudice he openly, casually espoused did the work for him. Jane was black, therefore she was evil, therefore she was guilty, and therefore had to be punished. In the note that concludes "Closed Doors," he declared that for spreading the story about the Misses Woods and Pirie, "she had to abide the reaping of the whirlwind," a phrase that recalls *Hosea* 8:7 ("For they sow the wind and they shall reap the whirlwind").[25] To the extent that Jane's three years in Nigg constituted a social outcasting and her marriage to Tulloch misery that led to a breakdown, Roughead's prediction came true. On the other hand, Jane's public raging unmasked her anguish for Richard Rose, arousing the senior minister's pity and concern. Jane showed resourcefulness, resilience, and a fighting spirit by making a will and by "walking out" on her husband and the Free Church. She obviously had a strong impact on her children, since they came out of the Established Church with her. Her Free Church minister son Charles Lennox Cumming Tulloch showed his respect by giving his eldest child the forenames Jane Cumming.

Roughead died in 1952, leaving his books to the Signet Library. Tucked inside the front cover of the case proceedings he had bought decades earlier is a letter dated April 23, 1936, from a Manhattan physician named John B. Solley. Solley, a life member of the New York Psychoanalytic Association, had written in response to Roughead's presentation of Jane Cumming, which he found fascinating but wanting. Solley's view of Jane was shaped by the conjoined fields of sexuality and anthropology—studies by Freud on the unconscious and Ellis on homosexuality, and the works of Margaret Mead and Bronislaw Malinowski on sexual relationships in non-Western societies: the kind of literature Roughead snubbed.

Based on Roughead's articulation of the case, Solley deduced that Woods and Pirie were engaged in a lesbian relationship in which Miss Woods was the "sexual aggressor." Solley also felt that Jane Cumming was motivated by sexual jealousy "against Miss Woods . . . Miss Woods being successful with Miss Pirie, while she, Jane, could only indulge her wishful thinking—desire for Miss Pirie."[26] Thus, while the conscious motivation for "Jane's satisfaction in defaming her schoolmistresses" would be the punishments she received, what Solley called her unconscious or "disguised" motivation for exposing their relationship would be her own sexual frustration and jealousy.

From Solley's perspective, Roughead's way of viewing the case had led him into a grievous misinterpretation of Jane's character. There was nothing evil about Jane. Rather, she was a young woman coming into sexual consciousness. Like many young people at this point in their lives, she was overwhelmed by conflicting and baffling emotions and lashed out at authority figures. That said, her coming into sexual consciousness was more complicated than that of many other adolescents because she had a crush on one of the teachers, was both jealous of and stimulated by the teachers' affection for each other, and had spent her early years in India.

Solley recommended to Roughead Ellis's *Studies in the Psychology of Sex* (1910), saying it was well worth reading for its insights into the poorly understood subject of sexual behavior. In the book, Ellis presents homosexuality as a predisposition that can be triggered into action. Solley took this idea and grafted it onto material garnered from Margaret Mead's *Coming of Age in Samoa* (1928), which he also recommended to Roughead. From Mead, Solley learned that in that non-Western society, adolescence for boys and girls was reasonably uncomplicated because casual sexual experimentation was culturally sanctioned. Females learned early in life that sex was enjoyable. Though the Samoans had become Protestants, homosexual attachments, even intense ones, were still not considered of great import, and adolescent males and females could engage in same-sex relationships without fear that they would be punished, ruined, or regarded as abnormal and in need of reorienting.

While the idea that "primitive" Samoa could be equated with a boarding school run by Westerners for the children of East India Company officers in the heart of British India reveals both Solley's ignorance about the British in Calcutta and an essentializing mind that divided the world into the West and the rest, the Samoan model led him to conclude that Jane's sexual precocity could be traced to her upbringing in a sexually permissive nonwhite culture. Like the lawyers involved in the case, Solley thought Jane acquired "homosexual proclivities in her environment in India through observation or hearsay, less likely through personal experience—homosexual seduction attempted upon her." He concluded that many years later this predisposition was activated when the adolescent mind inside Jane's mature body fantasized the "covert intimacies" expressive of the teachers' tender friendship into "homosexual activities." And like a Samoan girl (as rendered in Mead's book), Jane saw nothing wicked in the teachers' behavior or in wanting to engage in such behavior herself.

And though he thought it less likely that she had been molested, Solley speculated that if in her Calcutta years Jane had ever "experienced homosexual seduction and been physically aroused by it, it would be reasonable to assume that she would desire to seduce any girl at the school who attracted her and whom she could safely <u>woo</u> [underlining his] without danger of being exposed." Thus, though Solley was wrong to assume that Jane could be understood as a Samoan primitive, and Mead's Samoa in the early twentieth century as culturally identical to an early nineteenth-century Calcutta establishment for biracial children, the psychosexual interpretation enabled him to infer two facts Roughead did not include: that the teachers' behavior only struck Jane as improper after Miss Woods rebuffed her advances, and that Jane propositioned Janet Munro, the girl with the least seniority at the school.

Though Solley had come to the same conclusion as Clerk and Moncreiff, the stance he adopted would have had the Scottish lawyers turning in their respective graves. The lawyers saw her through a racist peephole: dark-skinned natives were lascivious, promiscuous, debauched. Solley's anthropological approach, shaped by Mead's work on the Samoans and Malinowski's on the Trobriand islanders, allowed him to see that in non-Western societies natives led happier, healthier lives because they had a more fluid understanding of sexuality. Melanesians had sexual freedom, making connections and exploring practices that in the West would be stigmatized and criminalized. In their happiness lay a lesson for the West to consider, Solley implied. As Malinowski's (probably homosexual) teacher Edward Westermarck put it in his *The Future of Marriage in Western Civilization* (1936), people in the West would be happier and healthier if they had "greater freedom to mould their own amatory life."[27] If we follow Solley's thinking to its conclusion, the problem underlying Jane's retaliation, Helen's hysterical response, and the argument that lesbianism didn't exist in the West was the unhealthy sexual prescriptiveness of Western culture. From Solley's perspective, the traumatizing case would never have happened if the wisdom and values of Mead's Samoa had obtained in early nineteenth-century Edinburgh.

Stressing the clarifying power of psychoanalysis, Solley told Roughead that reading Freud's *Three Contributions to the Theory of Sex* had given him insight into the unconscious motivations of his patients and himself, implying that a combination of anthropology and psychoanalytic theory might expose Jane's unconscious motivations in tagging her teachers as lesbians. Had Jane been living in Manhattan in the 1930s, Solley would no doubt have encouraged her to seek help from an analyst, get a job, and separate from her husband. Guided to an understanding of her sexuality, she could have used that knowledge to mold her amatory life and find the satisfaction and happiness denied her in the married state.

It is interesting that Solley recognized his clinical diagnosis of Jane's "disguised motives" might not be all that different from the diagnosis in Clerk's 1812 speech, when the lawyer compared Jane to Corinna and implied that she, like the characters in Mrs. Manley's *New Atalantis*, was lesbian. Indeed, Solley asked Roughead to send him a copy of Clerk's speech so that he could see to what extent Clerk "could fathom the disguised motives of Jane Cumming."

There is no evidence that Roughead responded to Solley's letter.

Buoyed by good reviews in the *Times Literary Supplement* and other papers, *Bad Companions* sold well in Britain and the United States. Solley would most likely have read about the case in its American edition. So too with Lillian Hellman, in 1931 a young writer who wasn't having much luck writing short stories; her partner Dashiell Hammett may have suggested to her that she realize the dramatic potential of Roughead's account in a play. However, on the afternoon of November 25, 1934, a few hours before *The Children's Hour* premiered on Broadway, Hellman wasn't prepared to acknowledge Roughead as her literary source and made it seem as if the character based on Jane Cumming, a troublemaker named Mary Tilford, was a product of her imagination. In response to a reporter from *The New York Post* who asked her how Mary Tilford came to be, Hellman airily replied, "The imp came out of my own head."[28]

Hellman's play was different from Roughead's version of the case.[29] Among the most obvious changes the playwright made were relocating the action to New England, adding a male love interest, a doctor named Joe Cardin for Miss Wright, the teacher based on Miss Woods, making the grandmother character more honorable and her problematic granddaughter white, moving the court proceedings offstage, and reversing the legal decision of the historical case. Perhaps recollecting the snippets of Clerk's peroration in Roughead's account in which Jane is compared to a cobra, Hellman included a comparison between Mary and a viper in a draft of the play—then excised the line.[30]

Hellman replaced the blatant racism and Orientalism Roughead carried over from the case proceedings with notions derived from eugenics that the play itself derides.[31] Mrs. Mortar, the character based on Ann Woods, is a spokesperson for good breeding, but she is presented as a vain, pretentious woman with a streak of malice. In a line cut from the final version of the play, the teachers poke fun at their students' mothers for giving "Eugenic lecture parties."[32] Most important, Hellman demolishes a eugenics-based explanation for Mary's otherness. In an attempt to account for Mary's behavior, Martha asks Joe if there are any idiots in the Tilford family tree. When he replies that they are "a proud old breed," she counters by saying that the Jukes are "an old family, too."[33]

The Jukes allusion probably needs a footnote today, but in the 1930s it was an easily identifiable reference to a poor white New York family, many of whose members were paupers, diseased, or in jail for criminal behavior. An 1875 sociological study of the clan concluded that the family's environment had produced habits that became hereditary. The Jukes study led to the notorious Supreme Court decision in *Buck v. Bell* (1927) authorizing the compulsory sterilization of an eighteen-year-old girl on grounds that, as Justice Oliver Wendell Holmes put it, "three generations of imbeciles are enough."

However, in 1933, while Hellman was working on *The Children's Hour* in New York, Hitler became chancellor of Germany, and Dachau, the first concentration camp, was opened. With the dawning realization of the Nazi agenda of extermination of whole classes of people deemed inferior, the eugenics argument that a country's population would be improved if "undesirable" individuals were taken out of the gene pool started to fall into disfavor in the United States. Yet Hellman, who was vehemently anti-Nazi and consistently revised the play over the course of its four editions, kept the Jukes reference. The only explanation I can come up with is that she was exposing the fallacy of eugenics by turning it against itself, in the process subverting Roughead's position. That is, while Roughead construed Jane's strongly marked sexuality racially, as something passed on to her from her "black" maternal side, Hellman played devil's advocate, teasing her unacknowledged source with the possibility that her character based on Jane acquired her same-sex sexual feelings from her impeccably white and Brahmin Bostonian father's side.

Those differences didn't seem to matter to Americans familiar with Roughead's text. They viewed her statement about the imp's immaculate conception as a brazen lie. Like Roughead's Jane Cumming, Hellman's Mary Tilford is a sexually aware, disaffected, mendacious, contriving, parentless adolescent being raised by a grandmother who had put her in a boarding school. Like Roughead's Jane, Mary too has a fawning streak, perhaps most in evidence when she tries to convince her grandmother to let her live with her. Like Jane, Mary has been frequently chastised by the two teachers who run the boarding school. The clinching piece of evidence that the play's material was filched was that Mary gets her grandmother to believe she saw the teachers making love through a nonexistent keyhole. As it was in the source, this lie is exposed in *The Children's Hour.*

The plot was also derived from Roughead. Hellman's drama deals with two hardworking female teachers who are best friends. They bring a libel suit against the rash grandmother of a problem pupil of theirs after the grandmother informs the parents of the other pupils that she has come to know from her grandchild that the teachers are sexually intimate. The accusations lead to the school's collapse and the teachers' ruin. Roughead's Marianne Woods and Jane Pirie were clearly the inspiration for Hellman's teachers, the reasonable Karen Wright and the intense Martha Dobie. Martha's suicide may have its roots in Roughead's chapter. Roughead had quoted Moncreiff as saying that the case had traumatized Jane Pirie so severely "as in all probability greatly to shorten her life."[34] Though the play suggests that self-loathing and internalized homophobia led Martha to take her life, by having this character commit suicide, Hellman turned a voiced fear of an untimely death into a dramatic event. Finally, despite exhibiting signs of remorse at the end of the play, Hellman's grandmother character, Amelia Tilford, is quite similar to the historical Helen Cumming Gordon. Both were imperious, quick to judge, of recognized social standing, took responsibility for a female grandchild, and put the girl into a boarding school.

Earle Walbridge, librarian of the Harvard Club in Manhattan, exposed Hellman's literary theft in a letter to the editor of *The Saturday Review of Literature*, published on March 16, 1935. As a riposte to Hellman's "'The imp came out of my own head" line, he punned, "It is my suggestion that she should have said the imp came out of my own Roughead.'" However, Roughead had learned about Hellman's appropriation a month earlier from his American friend Edmund Pearson, who had sent him a copy of *The Children's Hour* inscribed on the flyleaf, "To William Roughead, this piece of stolen goods . . ."[35]

Roughead was furious. Responding to Pearson's sending him the play and "other printed matter relevant to this literary rape," he wrote Pearson that his son was "keen that I should take legal proceedings against Miss Hellfire on the ground of infringement of copyright, my *Bad Companions* having been printed in the United States." He then added, "after consulting my friend the Lord Advocate, who strongly advised me against having anything to do with American law, as it would cost me a lot of money and I would likely lose the case, I decided to let sleeping dogs—and bitches—lie."[36] It seems that to Roughead, there wasn't much difference between Jane Cumming and Lillian Hellman.[37]

Though Roughead did not bring charges, Hellman may have been made aware that she had come close to being involved in a reputation-ruining lawsuit. She began to make small changes to distance her play from Roughead's account. With its monochromatic characters, color or race discrimination was the area in which her play was least likely to be attacked as "literary rape," yet Hellman conscientiously expunged details that had such markers. Between 1934 and 1971, she went through the play meticulously to expunge the word "black." Thus, in the first version of the play, the one that opened on Broadway in November 1934, as well as in the Modern Library version of 1942, Joe Cardin explains that on his way over to check on Mary, he stopped to look at a "black bull" a neighbor had bought.[38] In the 1952 Acting Edition, used for the play's revival on Broadway in December of that year, the bull's color has disappeared, but Karen tells Mary's grandmother that Mary is a "dark" girl.[39] However, in the 1971 edition of her *Collected Plays*, the bull is completely gone and Karen calls Mary a "bad" girl rather than a "dark" one.[40]

In an attempt to prove that she had constructed her character independent of Roughead, Hellman began to assert that Mary incorporated autobiographical elements. On December 16, 1934, she told a reporter from the *New York Herald Tribune* that "we translate everything and everybody in terms of ourselves" and that an individual's response to a character is directly related to "whatever parallel memories he can summon up. . . ."[41] She also mentioned that she had been "pretty good" at telling "elegant lies" when she was a child, further establishing her kinship with Jane Cumming.[42] She made a point of telling Margery Rex of the *New York Evening Journal* that she made Mary Tilford an only child because she, Hellman, was an only child.[43] In the introduction she wrote for the 1942 Modern Library edition of her plays, she doesn't mention Roughead at all. She ascribes Mary's sexual awareness to her own reading of Théophile Gautier's salacious novel *Mademoiselle de Maupin* in childhood and stresses that Mary "faked a heart attack" and twisted a classmate's arm because Lillian once faked a heart attack and "saw an arm get twisted."[44]

If not quite truthful, Hellman's position that Mary came out of herself rather than from Roughead's characterization of Jane is not false either. The lives of Jane Cumming and Lillian Hellman share many important elements. Like Jane, Hellman was a transplant and an outsider to the dominant culture. A Jew, Hellman was born in New Orleans and spoke the patois as a child; she was taken back and forth between New Orleans and New York until her father finally settled in Manhattan. Jane was an orphan, and Hellman was not only attracted to the orphans she played with in New

Orleans but wished she were one. Hellman had the equivalent of an Indian ayah in the form of a black nanny named Sophronia; the future author was luckier, though, in that Sophronia was a constant, wise caregiver. Both Jane and Lillian were the bane of their teachers; both were observant children with vivid imaginations. Hellman had a voyeuristic story in her background too. In her 1969 memoir *An Unfinished Woman*, Hellman says she used to listen to the residents of her aunts' boarding house in New Orleans from behind the closed doors of the parlor, and that she started fantasizing, with a degree of malice, about what they did in their bedrooms. As a result, she understood how "masked" and "complex" were the "first sexual stirrings of little girls."[45] Hellman's public feud with the writer Mary McCarthy established that Hellman, like Jane, was a hater who nursed grudges, sought revenge, and enjoyed being the center of attention.

Their similar dispositions and parallel experiences enabled Hellman to channel Roughead's Jane through herself, with the result that Mary Tilford looked a lot like Lillian Hellman, who looked a lot like Jane Cumming. Instead of being shocked or disgusted like Roughead, the adult Hellman could identify with the adolescent Jane and the sexually loaded charge she levelled against her teachers. However "masked" Jane's motives may have been to herself in 1810–11, they were not masked to Hellman. With her parallel memories, Hellman could relate to Jane's fantasized, sexualized story of her teachers' relationship as an example of the coming-of-age process by which girls turned into women conscious and expressive of their own needs and desires, and appropriate it for Mary. She could thus claim, as she in fact did, that Mary Tilford was dredged up and reconstituted from the "hodgepodge" memories of her subconscious, which she defined as "the world of the half-remembered, the half-observed, the half understood."[46]

In Hellman's dichotomized mental universe, Roughead belonged on the other side of the "half-remembered." In a 1968 interview with Lewis Funke, who asked her how *The Children's Hour* came to be based on a Scottish law case, she avoided answering the question. She claimed she had no memory of how she came to read about it; it was something she found in "a book I just picked up and read."[47] She then quickly shifted the conversation to how she "changed the whole plot" by "reach[ing] back into [her] own childhood for material."[48] In a 1975 interview with Jan Albert, Hellman was a little more forthcoming, grudgingly acknowledging that she had read about the "half Indian half Scotch" girl who made accusations of a sexual nature against her teachers in a book "by a man called William Roughead," and that she used the story as the basis for her play *The Children's Hour*.[49] But that was as far as she ever went.

In addition to these connections, Hellman had claimed that she too was of mixed race. In *An Unfinished Woman*, she brings up the time she found out that her father was having an affair. His infidelity so upset her that she ran away from home. After spending a night on the street, Hellman knocked on the door of a house in a black neighborhood in New Orleans. The address was not chosen randomly; the people who lived there were known to Sophronia. In order to be admitted, Hellman, all of thirteen, announced to the man who opened the door that she was "part nigger." The man realized she was lying and was unwilling to let her in, lest she get him in trouble, and he responded by calling this white girl "part mischief" and "trouble," but in the end Hellman was allowed to stay. That night she had her first period; she was retrieved the following day by her father and Sophronia.[50]

To the extent that Hellman in this episode defined herself and offered a definition of a biracial female at a sexual turning point as not only trouble-making but affected by other people's sexual behavior, she set up a personal, albeit masked, connection to the "part nigger" adolescent trouble-causing Jane who had been sexually stimulated by the behavior of Woods and Pirie. And if, as Hellman's biographer Alice Kessler-Harris suggests, the story is a fiction, "one constructed to capture her feelings of despair at the time," the connection between Hellman and Jane is even tighter.[51]

Yet even more important than Hellman's hidden racial identification with Jane is her (also masked) identification with Jane through her parentless or orphan status. As Hellman knew from Roughead's rude dismissal of Jane's parents, the father who "bequeath[ed] . . . a bastard" to his family in Scotland and the mother "a black woman," he had no sympathy for her because she was an orphan.[52] Hellman's attitude was more complex. Mary definitely was capable of exploiting her orphan status and psychologically arm-twisting her grandmother. In a draft of *The Children's Hour*, Mary tells her grandmother, Mrs. Tilford, who wants to send her back to school, "I'm afraid to go back. I'm an orphan, that's what it is—I read in a book that people are always mean to orphans. Nobody cares about me."[53] On the other hand, Mary genuinely fears separation from Mrs. Tilford, who is the only family she has, and the only person in the play who is attached to and cares about her.[54] That Hellman wished her audience to see Mary more as fearful child than as cunning manipulator after her "orphan" outburst is indubitable, for the playwright added in parentheses, "This speech has been in deadly earnest. . . ."[55]

In addition, Hellman appreciated things that seemed not to owe their existence to anybody. She considered Moscow's St. Basil's Church an architectural orphan. She admired it because its unique shape bespoke "the daring self-assurance of a great work" and "violate[d] all rules."[56] She was attracted to the orphans who lived down the block from her in New Orleans because they did not follow the rules. In open defiance of the conventional edicts of social behavior, the girls played rough, beating her up, stealing her allowance, cutting her hair, pushing her into the gutter. A boy's declaration of love sexually excited her. Instead of turning away from these predatory children, the young Hellman sought out their company.

Hellman saw that these orphans were mean and aggressive, but those qualities also made them daring and self-assured—positive role models, in her view. Their refractory behavior indicated to Hellman that they were "self-made piece[s] of independence."[57] Indeed, she craved that *sui generis* independence so much that in *An Unfinished Woman*, she said she wanted to be an orphan herself. Hellman's own life story proves she found this understanding of "orphanism," a mixture of rule-flouting defiance, self-assurance, and creativity, irresistibly attractive throughout her life.

No wonder, then, that Roughead's account of the Jane Cumming story not only attracted her but led her to conceptualize her Mary as a not very nice but also recognizably human character. Many members of her audience left the theater with the understanding that Mary Tilford was mentally ill; in letters Hellman received, some went so far as to say she was psychotic, or a psychopath. But for Hellman, Mary Tilford was "sly, neurotic . . . never outside life . . . not the utterly malignant creature which playgoers see in her"; she rejected a comparison between her character and Iago.[58] Those remarks come from a 1952 interview; in her character descriptions from the early 1930s, she let off more lightly her bullying, intimidating, lying, manipulating, blackmailing Mary, merely remarking that she was "slightly unable to adjust . . . vicious in result but not in character."[59] In the same 1934 interview in which she said she was adept at constructing "elegant lies," she described Mary as a child who "gets desperate . . . is lost and frightened and fighting hard."

Indeed, instead of punishing Mary, as Roughead punished *his* teenager from hell with social outcasting and a wasteland existence, Hellman gave her Jane-based character her heart's desire. Despite acknowledging the evil that her granddaughter accomplished, Agatha Tilford does not disown her or commit to institutionalizing her. At the very end of the third and final act, Agatha informs Karen (who broaches the idea of sending Mary away) that for the immediate future, and possibly forever, Mary will live with her, and that whatever Mary is, above all she is family, and to be treated as family. From Mary's point of view, this is a coup rather than a punishment since all she ever wanted was to live at her grandmother's house. Whatever damage it did to others, her allegation has enabled her to fulfill her deepest wish.

Hellman's condoning, sympathetic, "slightly unable to adjust . . . bad but not outside life" take on the character whom she erected on Jane Cumming's foundation has never been realized. The theatre critic for the *New York Telegram* said that Florence McGee, the actress who played Mary in the 1934 Broadway production, did a brilliant job in realizing "this poisonous child, this imp of Satan."[60] When the play was made into a movie in 1936, a Chicago-based critic wrote that the Mary of this film "was as ingeniously evil as Shakespeare's Iago."[61] The critic of a 1950 performance of the play at Bolton's Theatre in London noted that the actress who played Mary acted with such "relentless intensity" that the character came across as "not so much a human child as an incarnate fiend."[62] Nor was Mary's humanity brought out in the 1952 Broadway revival of the play. *The New York Times'* Brooks Atkinson called Iris Mann's portrayal of Mary "psychotic," while Louis Sheaffer of the *Brooklyn Eagle* felt that Mann's acting brought out the "psychopathic" element in the character.[63] The irony is that since Hellman herself directed the revival, the responsibility for bringing out the evil in the character was hers. For all that Hellman disavowed the influence of Roughead on her work, it is a version of Roughead's "black bitch/real live devil" understanding of Jane that has historically dominated the way actresses have performed the role of Mary Tilford.

When the play was revived in London in 2011, the director, Ian Rickson, tried to break free of this interpretation. He offered hormones and a "regiment of women" environment to account for Mary's accusation. Rickson added a dumb-show prologue that showed Mary reading a dirty book, soon read avidly by the other girls. According to the website The Feminist Spectator, the scene "establish[ed] the play's over-ripe atmosphere of teenaged sexuality and longing and the school itself as "a powder keg of emotion waiting to explode."[64] Rickson's conceptualization was not realized, however. Mary was played as evil rather than as sexy; it was Roughead's Calvinistic vision of Jane Cumming that infused Bryony Hannah's performance. Ben Brantley of *The New York Times* wrote that Hannah made Mary out to be "so showily, insanely evil that you can't believe that anyone would be taken in by her fictions."[65] Paul Taylor of *The Independent* seconded Brantley, pointing to this Mary's "unappeasable demonic hunger."[66] Consequently, though the reviewer for *The Guardian* noted that the play was based on a true story, Jane Cumming stayed buried, along with her psychosexual issues.⁶⁷ Roughead, who rejected psychologizing about sex, considered Jane a devil, and punished her with a bleak existence, would have considered Hannah's stage triumph a vindication of his perspective on Jane Cumming.

In her second volume of memoirs, *Pentimento* (1973), Hellman noted that in older paintings, over time, the original design sometimes becomes visible, allowing viewers to see the "original lines." The emergence of these "original lines," she continued, leads to a reinterpretation of events and makes possible "a way of seeing and then seeing again."⁶⁸ Reinterpretation was something she did not want for *The Children's Hour*.

When in 1948 Landres Chilton, the white director of Baltimore's short-lived integrated Greenwich Theatre, asked Hellman to grant him the right to mount a production of *The Children's Hour* with an interracial cast in which Mary and her grandmother would be black and the teachers white, she refused. Through an intermediary, Chilton was informed on August 10 that Hellman "does not want mixed players. Completely changes the play." Chilton, obviously unfamiliar with Roughead's account, begged her to reconsider, arguing in a telegram sent the following day that it was "not purpose of Greenwich Theatre to inject racial problems in a play where not intended by author" and that those who went to the Greenwich Theatre were post-racial, seeing talent rather than color.⁶⁹ Hellman, who knew her Roughead and was no naïf, understood that "racial problems" were central to the case. Aware that in the segregated city of Baltimore in 1948 Chilton's casting would expose the original lines and reveal race-based prejudice as a cause for Jane/Mary's lashing out against her teachers, she telegrammed back to Chilton, "Sorry must refuse request for Children's Hour in mixed colored and white cast. Perfectly willing for play to be performed with entire Negro cast or entire white cast but mixed people seems to alter the meaning of the play."⁷⁰

Hellman's refusal quashed Chilton's plan, but in 1953 the "original lines" issue cropped up again. Lillian de la Torre, an American mystery writer, in 1948 had visited Roughead, who recounted the case to her. De la Torre was touched by "his easy erudition, his lively mind, his generous heart," but appalled by the blatant racism of the case and Roughead's casual racism.⁷¹ Out of respect, she kept quiet, but a year after his death and while Hellman's *The Children's Hour* was playing on Broadway, she wrote a letter to *The New Republic* in which she pointed out that the drama was flawed precisely because race had been left out. De la Torre saw Jane as a "tragic figure . . . a victim of racial discrimination . . . a member of an oppressed race." To her, race prejudice explained why the Indo-Scottish pupil took revenge against her teachers. Jane had internalized the prejudice to which she had been exposed: her mind had become "warped by forces of evil" because of others' injurious treatment of her. De la Torre concluded that "the tragic lesson of the story, as it actually happened, is the inmost evil of discrimination . . . it degrades and dehumanizes persons who happen to be the wrong color. . . ."[72] Since Mary had Jane's malignity without having her history, in de la Torre's opinion Hellman's character was nothing more than a bit of stage machinery, a "mere *diabolus ex machina*" whose fiendish histrionics make risible the deep and lasting damage that people of one race inflict on those of another. The play itself, she wrote, was an object lesson in the "danger of using historical sources and bowdlerizing them."[73]

In 1953 the liberal readers of *The New Republic* were more concerned with McCarthyism than with a flaw in a play by a left-leaning dramatist, so de la Torre's critique sparked no dialogue. Lillian Faderman, whose mid-1980s *Scotch Verdict* rekindled critical interest in the case, makes no reference to de la Torre's letter but comes to the same conclusion, albeit with strings attached. At the end of her book, Faderman admits that though she still found Jane "despicable" for ruining the teachers, she realized that she was "a victim . . . of the prejudices of the master race."[74] As Judith Halberstam wrote in the foreword to the 2013 reissue of *Scotch Verdict*, Faderman "tries to empathize with the plight of this young girl in terms of the loss of her mother, the cultural transition from India to Scotland, and the treatment she received in school."[75] However, Faderman's sympathy is grudging. What Jane suffered was a "misfortune" rather than long-lasting trauma.[76] Faderman admits she feels more for the teachers than for the girl. That sympathy may explain why, in a work crosscutting between past and present lesbian relationships, she doesn't consider whether Woods's and Pirie's public demonstrations of affections were "appropriate in a school setting." And for a work that purportedly raises "a set of fascinating questions not only about the meaning of different forms of erotic behavior in the past but also about the sexual imagination and its limits," *Scotch Verdict* does not hazard any guesses as to the nature of Jane's sexuality or her sexual imagination.[77]

De La Torre may have come down a little harshly on Hellman. In insinuating that Mary would live life with her grandmother at her house after the case ended, Hellman may, without realizing it, have intuited Jane's deepest problem and need. From very early in life, Jane was treated, as

Penrose called her, "an encumbrance," a thing that could be moved about, and did not receive attention from a consistent, loving caregiver. Seen in this light, Jane's whispered words about the teachers' relationship as well as her clearly enunciated court testimony were *cries du coeur*, albeit masked ones, that called attention to her plight, her need for attention and affection, her desperation. Jane's behavior in the last weeks at the Drumsheugh establishment showed she had stopped caring about what could happen to her; Hellman's understanding of her Mary was that she desperate under the bravado. In picking up on that desperation at that moment, Hellman showed herself to be not a historical bowdlerizer but the opposite, a psychologically astute dramatist giving us yet another keyhole into Jane's psyche through her understanding of Mary Tilford.

CONCLUSION

Assessing Jane

What was behind Jane's outbursts? What led her to spin troubling stories? What led her to scream "sexual irregularity" when she perceived herself unwanted, humiliated, or scorned? These questions have perturbed all those who have ever studied her. After taking into account her post-case life, I decided that four factors, presented here in ascending order of long-term significance, are responsible: race-based prejudice, erotic sensitivity to situational and contextual stimuli, stress and anxiety, and child maltreatment.

The first factor contributing to Jane's outbursts, race-based prejudice, has received much attention in the course of this book. Lillian de la Torre was spot-on when she said, apropos of the Jane who destroyed the teachers, that exposure to this kind of discrimination warps the mind of the victim. However, racism doesn't seem to have been at the root of Jane's eruption against her husband. This is not to say that it couldn't have been a factor. Tulloch was furious with Jane, and in his fury he might have hurled race-inflected epithets at her. The villagers who sided with Tulloch opined that she was the blacker of the two. Was the comment also an invidious allusion to her complexion and birthplace? But there is no hard evidence, as there is in the case of Margaret Stuart Bruce Tyndall, that behind Jane's back the Dallas folk qualified their respect for their minister's wife with snide remarks about her complexion. In fact, circumstantial evidence suggests otherwise, as the majority of the Dallas parishioners followed her lead and joined the Free Church.

I turn now to the second contributing factor, that Jane had an erotic sensitivity to situational and contextual influences.[1] Because of her age, the cloistered environment in which she was living, and the teachers' affectionate conduct toward each other, I think she was aroused by the behaviors that romantic friends and sexual partners have in common. This resulted in her crush on Miss Woods and her propositioning of Janet Munro. Because something similar happened in the 1830s when she had been married to Tulloch for close to twenty years, I could not write her behavior off as a "lesbian until graduation" phenomenon. My sense is that the same sensitivity came into play when she saw her husband walking about with young women of the village. Rose characterized this conduct as inappropriate but reserved judgment on whether Tulloch had committed adultery. Jane, on the other hand, intensified the sexual element in the situation. Apparently, she was giving vent to her misery and anger in histrionic outbursts filled with graphic details about her husband's unchastity that dismayed and shocked the villagers of Dallas, her uncle, and Richard Rose.

A parishioner called Tulloch a "Grand Sultan" in 1829, and the remark suggests that Tulloch was engaging in inappropriate contacts with women considerably earlier than 1834/5, the period mentioned in Rose's letter. Rose provided the obvious and neither insensitive nor illogical reading of Jane's misery: she was suffering from jealousy approaching the pathological. Just as she had sexualized her teachers' conduct, so she did her husband's. She brought to the fore the sexual element in his inappropriate familiarity with other women, elevating it into that form of abandonment known as adultery and, as earlier, externalizing her feelings in the form of uninhibited outbursts before an audience.

But I keep wondering if the situation was also revealing something less obvious about her sexuality. To what extent was Jane jealous because *she* wanted the girls her husband was paying attention to? The thought has led me to wonder if she belonged to the group of people best described by the term "sexually fluid." According to psychologist Lisa Diamond, sexual fluidity refers to "a capacity for *change* in attractions which results from an individual's heightened erotic sensitivity to situational and contextual influences," the key word in this definition being "change."[2] Such individuals are nonexclusive in their sexual attractions, and the intensity of their responses varies according to the stimuli and the situation.[3] If we apply that perspective to the situation Jane found herself in with her husband and see Tulloch and the women as the stimuli, then Jane's jealousy and public misconduct, the defiant, aggressive behavior Rose noted, could also be signing deep, complex sexual frustration. Tulloch wasn't interested in her, his conduct with the women was exciting her, she wanted what she wasn't getting and what he was receiving, and her desire for these women was hopelessly unrealizable because she was the minister's wife. To some extent, then, the Dallas situation reprised the school situation. Perhaps it also reset, as it were, Jane's erotic clock. But I admit I am on firmer ground with the first explanation, that her jealous rage and allegations developed from being, once more, the unwanted woman in the triangle—this time formed by Tulloch, the village jades (seen collectively), and herself.

If stress is defined as a response to pressure or threat (a "stressor") and anxiety as an effect of stress that makes a person feel apprehensive or frightened, even though the stressor itself may not be apparent, may be dormant, or may have been removed, there is no question Jane lived her life under a heavy load of stress, which would have made her a very anxious person. When she was sent for in India, she would have had no idea how her father's family would react to her. Her grandmother was mercurial. Jane wasn't on the same footing as her Dunbar cousins, and there were strings attached to Helen's promise that she would introduce her to society. Helen had left her with the teachers over the summer of 1810, a situation that led Jane to think she was unwanted and irrelevant. Woods and Pirie were great stressors. The notebook didn't produce catharsis, Woods rebuffed her, Munro wouldn't sleep with her, Pirie screamed at her. Jane herself told the court that unless she was near Miss Woods she felt anxious. Since Helen was out of town and Jane either couldn't talk to her aunts or they wouldn't talk to her, there was no family member to whom she could unburden herself. As she put together her story, she couldn't even be certain Helen would believe it. Unrelieved stress and anxiety characterized her last three months at Drumsheugh. And though she seems to have enjoyed her first day in the witness box, the other days were extraordinarily stressful. The examination was hostile; the judges rained questions on her. Her short responses and long silences reveal that she knew she was under attack, cornered.

When Tulloch set down the details of his wedding to Jane in the Nigg parish book, he referred to her as the "only surviving child of George Cumming." For Jane that "only" would (or could) function as a remembrance of her late brother, and though oblique, the acknowledgement of Yorrick/George's brief life might have reduced her stress, but his behavior in Dallas would have elevated her stress hormones to an even more toxic level than they had reached in her adolescence and increased her anxiety over what would become of her. His inferior farming skills put her in the uncomfortable position of having to ask Rose to request a rent reduction from Sir William. Tulloch's attempt to get his hands on her settlement was emotional abuse; together with his open womanizing, these actions triggered Jane's fear of being abandoned, unwanted, left out, unprovided for. Stress and anxiety lay behind Jane's unrestrained, public venting of her anger and jealousy and her misery. Rose all but said Jane was not in her right mind when he described the situation in Dallas. Her "wood-stealing" letter seems to be the product of a paranoid mind. She appears to have had a breakdown from which she emerged unhealthily suspicious and overly fearful and anxious.

A number of clinical studies have argued that chronic, unrelieved stress and anxiety can alter the neurotransmitter systems and cause structural changes in the regions of the brain responsible for cognition and emotion.[4] Of particular relevance to Jane's case is, I think, the work of Shonkoff and Garner. Their research points to the "disruptive effects of toxic stress," which damage the brain's neural circuitry. An elevated level of stress hormones, they have found, impairs the functioning of the amygdala, which becomes hyperactivated, and the orbitofrontal cortex, which atrophies.[5] In the former case, the individual becomes more anxious, and in the latter case, mood control deteriorates. In later life, stressful situations elicit a hyperresponsive reaction, causing physical disease and more mental distress, fear and anxiety, or some combination of these.[6] This research, applied retrospectively, suggests that Jane's extreme outbursts were due to brain damage caused by unrelieved stress. I think there is enough evidence to allow for that possibility, though in the absence of a brain to study, it is ultimately an unprovable thesis.

Stress, however, can be positive as well as negative, in that it can encourage or force a person to solve problems and adapt to challenges—to develop resilience, which will be discussed later in this section. I think Jane felt this kind of positive stress as well. As a schoolgirl, she wanted to break free of trammels, to be free to act as she desired, but the means she employed were hurtful and counterproductive. In contrast, her writing of a will and joining of the Free Church illustrate how stress enabled her to achieve that same goal in socially acceptable and effective ways.

In its initial iteration, my fourth explanation for Jane, maltreatment as a child, was not linked to race-based prejudice. When Clerk broached the idea that she was like a child brought up in a brothel, innocent at birth but adversely affected by her environment, he was referring to the effect on the psychosexual development of any child who has witnessed sex acts. When he quoted from Swift's "Corinna," he was expanding his earlier point to include abuse. Any girl anywhere who has the misfortune of being the victim of childhood sexual abuse would be affected.

While there is no evidence supporting the notion that Jane was sexually abused, there are very strong grounds for thinking that she was neglected. The little that we know about the institutions where orphans or children separated from parents such as Jane were placed when very young indicates that the inmates were maintained but not nurtured. Food, clothing, shelter, and a modicum of education could be expected, but not much (if any) attention was paid to the emotional needs of these abandoned, vulnerable children. Unfortunately, the neglect continued after Jane arrived in Scotland. Within six months, Helen placed her with a paid caregiver. As already mentioned, Helen continued the pattern of foisting Jane on others when, leaving Edinburgh for Altyre in May 1810, she consigned her to the teachers and told her daughter to look after her. In handwritten notes, Lord Meadowbank came down heavily on Helen for keeping Jane at arm's length, and though he did not use the phrase, implied that she provided Jane with only "a kind of loving."

Lord Meadowbank connected that history of casual abandonment and neglect with Jane's development into an emotionally needy, very sensitive, very anxious, lovesick adolescent. A careful reader of the printed case proceedings, he noted in the margin of his copy the signs of Jane's unrequited crush on Miss Woods: her clingy affection, the anxiety she felt if the teacher wasn't near her, the little tokens of affection she showed her, her expressed desire to sleep with her in her bed whenever possible.

The term "attachment bond" would have sounded strange to him, but Lord Meadowbank picked up on the four characteristics or components of attachment: repeatedly seeking and maintaining physical closeness, turning to the loved one for comfort, experiencing distress when separated from her or him, and considering that individual reliable, dependable, and supportive.[7]

Because she had been neglected, Jane had a desperate need for physical and emotional closeness. The teachers were behaving romantically, in a relationship in which they gave each other companionship, security, and comfort. Their romantic friendship was an evolved version of the attachment bond that a caregiver forms with a baby or child, in which the caregiver makes the child feel secure by being physically present and offering comfort, reassurance, and support.[8] What Jane wanted above all was to feel how the teachers were feeling—loved, wanted, desired—and she wanted that to come through a close, physical, intimate bond with Miss Woods. That Jane Cumming, an erotically sensitive adolescent whose attachment needs were never satisfactorily met, was attracted to kind Miss Woods and then felt hurt, angry and vengeful when her overtures to initiate a bond were rebuffed, seems, in retrospect, a foregone conclusion.

Despite acknowledging Helen's maltreatment of Jane, Lord Meadowbank found Moncreiff's explanation for the sexualized cast of Jane's mind more compelling. Moncreiff's thesis was Clerk's racialized: Jane's upbringing at the hands of dark-skinned lascivious women in a harem-type setting explained her thinking processes. The majority of the judges on the Court of Session and all the Law Lords of the House of Lords went along with that rationale. However, if we strip Moncreiff's position of its racism, we are back to child maltreatment as the most reasonable explanation for the nature of Jane's outbursts and fantasies.

That neglect and abuse in childhood have long-term consequences is accepted now. The American Psychiatric Association (APA) affirmed that children exposed to adverse experiences in early life, including loss of a parent and repeated out-of-home placements, are at increased risk for developing anxiety and mood disorders later on. In a position statement published in 1991, the APA stated that "child maltreatment contributes to the development of lifelong anxieties, disturbance of behavior . . . and severe disturbances in personality formation. These disturbances may include social isolation, withdrawal, and alienation; antisocial, hostile and destructive character disorders; disruption of the ability to form or to sustain loving, caring relationships with others. . . ."[9] A data-driven 1999 study on the relationship between early abuse and adult sexuality noted a link between anxieties over abandonment and the fostering of sexualized ties. It also found a correlation, particularly strong among females, between childhood abuse and adult romantic and voyeuristic sexual fantasies, emotional maladjustment, and an inability to trust others, especially marital partners.[10] A 2004 study, "Childhood Abuse and Neglect and Adult Intimate Relationships," concluded that victims of early maltreatment, be it sexual abuse or neglect, "experienced more dysfunction in their marital relationships" and "reported significantly higher rates of relationship disruption than adults" without such histories.[11] That study also established that women who have been abused or neglected are less likely than those in control groups to establish and maintain healthy intimate relationships in adulthood, or to trust their partners and perceive them as "supportive, caring, and open to communication."[12] A 2010 study found that nonpenetrative sexual trauma predisposed an individual to develop voyeuristic tendencies or voyeuristic disorder in later life.[13]

All in all, if we look at Jane through the "child maltreatment" keyhole, it appears that we have identified the strongest single cause for the plethora of disturbing behaviors she exhibited at two points in her life.

Studies focusing on the subset Jane comes closest to belonging to, later-adopted international children, also confirm the negative residual impact of the early years on a small but statistically significant percentage of that population. A Finnish study indicates that at school, many were either victims or bullies, and the case proceedings reveal that Jane was both.[14]

Another study has indicated that children who before being adopted and taken from their natal country were living in institutional settings, "deficient primarily in the lack of warm, sensitive, and responsive caregiver-child interactions," never developed a sense of belonging or feel loved.[15] As a group, they had higher problem scores on the Child Behavior Checklist (CBCL), an instrument whose items include the following: disobedient, doesn't get along well with other children, doesn't seem to feel guilty after misbehaving, easily jealous, gets in many fights, punishment doesn't change his/her behavior, has a hot temper, wants a lot of attention, and lies. These behaviors become particularly noticeable, even severe, during adolescence.[16] Almost all of them characterize Jane.

Later-adopted international children who grow up in environments where they have multiple caregivers and do not have an opportunity to develop attachment bonds also run a higher risk of manifesting signs of reactive attachment disorder (RAD), a rare, severe condition associated with foreign orphanage upbringing and marked by inappropriate social relatedness. A 2011 study that reviewed previous studies of children diagnosed with RAD found that some children were resilient and overcame their early history of institutional neglect while others continued to manifest such characteristics as lack of remorse, aggressiveness, anxiety when feeling abandoned, and hypersexuality well into adulthood.[17]

The *Diagnostic and Statistical Manual of Psychiatric Disorders* postulates that for a child to be diagnosed with RAD she must have shown signs of inappropriate social relatedness before the age of five, and we know nothing about Jane until she was about eight, when it appears that she was an unremarkable girl. I rather doubt that any clinician would diagnose her as suffering from RAD, even though she grew up in an environment of neglect and her desire to sleep with Miss Woods indicates that she was trying to establish an inappropriate attachment bond. But *something* was wrong with her. The problems and behaviors these studies highlight and she manifested suggest that she was a psychologically and neurobiologically impaired human being. In hindsight, it appears that Clerk's employment of Swift's "Corinna, A Ballad" to imply a "maltreatment" reading of Jane's future was prescient.[18]

This research is helpful in understanding not only the transported Jane but also two of her contemporaries, sisters Eliza and Elizabeth Jane Raine. Like Jane Cumming, the Raine girls were separated from their mother at an early age, and separated from their natal country at a later age. Their father provided for them handsomely in his will but when they boarded the *King George* in 1796, he did not accompany them on that long voyage to

Britain; they never saw him again as he himself died at sea in 1800. Once they arrived in York, their father's friend Dr. Duffin took responsibility for them. Even though both girls were socially accepted, their fates were disastrous. Eliza, who was Anne Lister's first beloved, had a breakdown in her late teens and spent the rest of her long life confined in a mental institution. Jane Elizabeth made an underage marriage that didn't work out.

To understand the Raine sisters, I turned to Helena Whitbread, the decoder of Anne Lister's diaries. She informed me that she had consulted psychiatrists based at York's now closed Bootham Hospital. While it is generally assumed that Eliza's breakdown was caused by Anne leaving her for another woman, the doctors believe that the sexual rejection was closer to a precipitating blow than the cause of the mental collapse. According to Whitbread, the psychiatrists concurred that the separation from the mother, the death of the father, and the translation to an alien land and culture at a later age were the three most important factors putting both sisters at risk for mental instability. Despite being accepted in York society, their history of separation and loss would make coping with rejection difficult for them. Despite being heiresses, race-based anxiety over their position in society made it more likely that they would be unable to sustain relationships (Jane Elizabeth) or would form highly dependent ones (Eliza), and be vulnerable to depression as adults. The doctors concluded that both Jane Elizabeth and Eliza Raine developed and were destroyed by either bipolar affective disorder or schizoaffective psychosis.[19]

Compared to the Raine sisters, Jane fared considerably better. Despite the history of child maltreatment, all the stress and frustration she endured, the traumatic losses and separations she experienced, the "kind of loving" she received from a changing cast of caregivers, the endemic racism and "bad bargain" of a marriage she could not escape; for all that she acted out and developed voyeuristic fantasies, deep anxieties, and paranoid suspicions; despite all that, for long stretches of time Jane was absent from the historical record. Since history records the exceptional, this absence implies that for many years she was an unremarkable woman, stable, able to function normally and maintain her equilibrium. In other words, she was resilient.[20]

David Finkelhor, an expert on childhood sexual abuse, has argued that four dynamics account for its long-term impact: traumatic sexualization, betrayal, stigmatization, and powerlessness.[21] Traumatic sexualization occurs when, for example, children are rewarded for sexual behavior inappropriate for their level of development or, because of rewards proffered, learn to use sexual behavior in manipulating others to get their needs met.

Children feel betrayed when a person they trust disregards their feelings or when they come to the realization that the person they trust is actively working to harm them. In the case of girls, the third dynamic, stigmatization, comes into play when the girl is labeled "spoiled goods" or told or made to feel she is of no worth. With the fourth dynamic, powerlessness, in the aftermath of abuse these victims find themselves unable to control their lives or to make decisions that might help them live freer ones. The second and third dynamics, betrayal and stigmatization, are directly relevant to Jane's case, even though the evidence suggests the abuse was emotional and psychological rather than overtly sexual.

Betrayal is obvious. Jane's behavior started to change when Helen, who had always sent for her when school let out, kept her with the teachers. If, as was mentioned in one of the documents sent to the Law Lords, she was now not thinking of introducing her into society as she had her own daughters, Jane may have perceived that change of mind as a betrayal of a promise. Jane's first documented eruption was triggered by Miss Pirie, who stigmatized her, making her feel inferior and worthless, and was directed against Miss Woods, who disregarded her affection, and whom she betrayed with a kiss.

In addition, Jane must have been considered something like "spoiled goods," for in 1818 she was married off to a man with a dubious past who was rewarded for taking her off the family's hands. Yet if the Tulloch whom she married was the Mr. Tulloch who brought her from London to Scotland in 1803, when she was about eight and he twenty-six, she might have been quite happy with the arrangement in 1818. When she was eight, she would have had to have put her trust in him for the last lap of the journey from India. Remembering that long-ago journey might have made her very happy to put her trust in him again. If we grant her sexual fluidity and erotic sensitivity to situational and contextual influences, those factors too would have predisposed Jane to feeling happy at the thought of being married to him. She had been brought up to regard marriage as a desideratum, and marriage to a schoolmaster who would become a minister would give her what she never really had before: respect and social status. I think Jane must have been thrilled at the turn her life took in 1818. Consequently, Tulloch's behavior in the 1830s, when Jane was over thirty and had had five pregnancies and he walked around the village of Dallas with pretty young women, must have seemed like a double betrayal, not to mention a blow to her self-esteem.

A 2012 article in *The New York Times Magazine* about child sexual abuse at the elite Horace Mann School in New York City sheds light on the response to traumatic sexualization. It pointed out that when children who have been prematurely exposed to sexuality and learned that sex can be traded for affection, attention, or special privileges feel their caregivers have betrayed them, in some way hurt or harmed them, they do not initially lash out against the caregiver. Rather, they feel conflicted or confused because they are not getting "paid in kind" for the affection they have bestowed. To preserve the feeling of attachment, they may cling even more strongly to that person, their demonstrations of affection an attempt to win the person over or, to use Solley's sexualized phrase, "to woo" him or her back into caring. But if the attempt to woo failed, the children came to feel humiliated, enraged, and vengeful.[22] Certainly Jane's raging attack against her teachers was preceded by a failed wooing of Miss Woods. Perhaps she fired the maidservants in an attempt to reclaim Tulloch, with all his faults, for herself. Reading backward, perhaps there was a history of traumatic sexualization in her background.

The fourth dynamic of Finkelhor's thesis is that sexual victims are identifiable by their powerlessness, which leads to their being revictimized. That does not fit Jane. By taking arms against the seas of troubles that threatened her, what she showed was resourcefulness. One of her tactics was destructive, scurrilous, and exhibitionistic. Her use of the Edinburgh courtroom and the village of Dallas as performance spaces in which to render sexualized accounts of figures who scorned her, fall into this category. But others of her actions were socially appropriate. In committing her feelings to paper, in making a will to protect her estate from him, in joining the Free Church, we see her looking for help and taking advantage of available socially acceptable resources to free herself from individuals she saw as restricting her freedom.

A resilient person is not necessarily a nice person, however. As the research of George Bonnano shows, some of the coping strategies of people who have suffered traumatic events, while pragmatic, are mean, nasty, vituperative, malicious, destructive, retaliatory, vengeful; his word for them is "ugly." Jane manifests this ugly kind of resilience when she is desperate, on the defensive, and fighting hard to survive, but to such an extreme degree that I think it pathological.[23]

It needs to be remembered that resilience is different from recovery. Recovery implies that over a period of time an individual is healed, her psychopathological demons expelled for good. That was not the case with Jane. She was resilient, able to lead a reasonably healthy, unremarkable life for substantial stretches of time, but she had psychological issues stemming from earlier traumatizing events, and these, as I have suggested, had adversely affected areas of her brain related to the experiencing of emotions.

As Bonnano's research has also shown, there are times when new events trigger a flashback and reveal the limits of a resilient individual's resilience.[24] We see the limits very clearly in Jane's case. In the 1830s Jane's husband's behavior awakened her anxieties over being unwanted, undesired, unloved, left out. Her emotional distress disturbed Rose, who thought she deserved a legal separation, but it left her uncle unmoved. Sir William rejected Rose's plea to grant her more money, which would have made it possible for her to live independently. Forced to stay married, she had what I think was a mental breakdown so severe that she thought she was going to die. Though she did not die, she did not heal well. The note she wrote to Sir William about men stealing wood is the product of a confused mind, and the letter begging him for firewood the product of a frightened one.

There were moments in Jane's life when she was able to employ socially acceptable "pathways to resilience"—and achieve personal freedom from an abusive man.[25] In 1914 the Free Church minister W. W. Ewing expressed shock sotto voce at the means she used; she was the woman so dangerous to the patriarchal social order that she couldn't be named. A little over a century later, we find the idea of a woman refusing to conform to social expectations rather attractive. We particularly celebrate women who find ways to speak back to those in authority and challenge or defy figures who abuse the power vested in them.

This politically correct reading of Jane's defiant energy does not take into account its destructiveness. When threatened, she was extremely dangerous, to others and to herself. Speaking personally, while I understand that coping by striking back aggressively is a known strategy and a pathway for some victims to reasonable functioning and I also feel very, very sorry for Jane because I think she was deprived of the most basic of human needs, I would be uncomfortable, maybe even scared, having her as a friend.

Jane's adherence to the Free Church is her last act of defiance, for she died not long after she came out of her husband's church. She is buried in a green and tranquil cemetery on a slight rise overlooking the Lossie. However, that river is an ever-present reminder that nature can and does change shape and course, sometimes explosively, and that despite our advances in science, we are not always able to predict, see, or correctly interpret the warning signs.

I would like to think that at the end of her life Jane joined that select group of individuals who rise above their destructive energies, and that if she had had the gift of years, she would have maintained her resilience in life-affirming ways. However, while Tulloch's obituary allows us to hear the thud with which he fell lifeless to the floor, the newspaper accounts of Jane's death give us no clue as to her state of heath, mental or physical, in her last days. In death, if not in life, she slipped the trammels of identification.

ACKNOWLEDGMENTS

From the web resource FIBIS (Families in British India Society), I learned that the last will and testament of Jane's father, George Cumming, was housed in the British Library's Asia, Pacific and Africa Collections (APAC), formerly known as the India Office Records (IOR). An email to reference specialist Dorian Leveque led to my obtaining of a copy of his will on a CD my computer couldn't read initially. Over the years, I tasered Dorian with further requests, and he has been unfailingly helpful in responding to them. I am indebted to Miriam Laskin and Rhonda Johnson, librarians at Hostos Community College/CUNY, where I taught.

I have been a plague to many in the decade it has taken me to complete this book, but I have met nothing but courtesy, kindness, and invaluable aid. Kevin Berland and Rebecca Shapiro deciphered James Thomas Grant's scrawl. Stewart Brown helped me understand the 1843 Disruption. Jane Rendall graciously shared her knowledge of Scottish feminist issues in the long eighteenth century. Pamela Perkins fielded my queries relating to Elizabeth Hamilton. Deborah Cohen and Bruce Drurie patiently answered my requests for information relating to Margaret Stuart Bruce Tyndall. In dealing with the sexual identity and orientation issues that Jane's life raises, I have been the beneficiary of Chris Roulston's and Katherine Kittredge's insights. John Cairns helped me through the thickets and over the stiles of the peculiarly Scottish legal issues raised by the case. Daniel O'Connor and Olivera Jokic shared their knowledge of East India Company figures whose paths intersected with those of characters in this book. Stana Nenadic took time from a busy schedule to respond to my questions on a broad range of topics, from the reading habits to the breeding behaviors of the Scottish Highland gentry in the long eighteenth century. I am deeply indebted to James Hamilton who provided weather data and helped me visualize Parliament Square and Parliament Hall; his generosity of spirit, stream of well-wishes, and dry humor kept me going on the many days when ideas were just not jelling. Henry Noltie jollied me along, too. He took time off to not only identify the location of the ill-fated school on an early map but physically measure the distance between it and Charlotte Square. Stella Fraser helped me locate Captain Cumine's gravesite and searched for the final resting place of Jane's brother. Stella couldn't find it, but as more cemetery records become digitized, it may yet turn up. I have also had the good fortune of receiving support and encouragement from Lillian Faderman.

I am indebted to the two listservs to which I belong. C18-L, the eighteenth century interdisciplinary forum, has been on the receiving end of numerous queries from me on such subjects as testifying children, girls' reading, the makeup of the student body at boarding schools, "nunneries," elocution lessons, keyhole scenes, female poisoners, and the cost of funeral expenses, and I have been overwhelmed by the seriousness with which they were taken. I am particularly grateful to Nancy Mayer, Jenny Moody, Mary Ann O'Donnell, Howard Gaskill, Neil Hitchin, Mark Davidson, John Dussinger, James May, Jim Chevalier, Lise Huggler, Timothy Stunt, James Rovira, Scott Gordon, Olivera Jokic, Miranda Sprathurst, Christine Jackson-Hughey, Mary Seymour, Jeremy Chow, John Levin, Maurice Brenner, Harriet Linkin, James Woolley, and George Thompson. I will always be especially grateful to Jim May, who suggested homes for material that could not be accommodated within this biography. The nineteenth-century listserv Victoria enabled me to make contact with Leslie Katz and Karla Walters. Leslie answered many of my general legal queries. Karla not only introduced me to many genealogical databases, but went the extra mile to help me uncover and recover Jane and her unfortunate teachers.

Though I have kept my references to Jane's descendants brief, I must acknowledge the help of a number of people who helped me with this aspect of my research. Carl James Grindley and Kathy Chater combed the records forward to trace her descendants. My husband, Brijraj Singh, found Jane's Rhodesian-born descendant Alan Scott, who was a Rhodes scholar prior to serving in World War II, in the *Register of Rhodes Scholars 1903–1995*, a book occupying a spot on a shelf in our own basement. Kazue Mino supplied me with information about Jane's great-granddaughter Peggy. In this quest, I made the acquaintance of three of Jane's collateral descendants, Hugh Rod Gair, Kim Hansen, and Jane Macgillivray, who shared their personal family history data sheets with me. I am also grateful to Robert Solley, a collateral descendant of John Solley. Robert bore the brunt of my numerous inquiries about his great-uncle with goodwill.

When I was in Elgin in 2010, I benefitted from the support I received at the Moray Council Local Heritage Centre from Graeme Wilson; over the years, James Nock, Sharon Slater and Scott Reid have also helped me with the Elgin aspects of Jane's life. Elgin resident Keith Mitchell drove me to

Dallas. Another Elgin resident, Peter Wills, provided me with information about two of Elgin's residents in Jane's time, Isaac Forsyth and Christian Charles. To all of these people, I offer thanks.

Keith is the chairman of the Moray Burial Ground Research Group. A very short article in the group's 2010 newsletter about the life of Jane Cumming led Rosemary Wake to email me. Our shared interest in schoolmistresses and their pupils, the gossipy world of late eighteenth- and early nineteenth-century Edinburgh, and, above all, in unearthing and piecing together the shards of past lives, led us to support each other in our respective archaeological enterprises. Rosemary has always gone the extra mile for me—or, to be precise, gone many miles for me. In 2015, thanks to Rosemary's skill in driving a car with stick shift and reading paper maps, I was able to visit Nigg. In Edinburgh, Rosemary and I explored Portobello, where Jane said the teachers' bedsharing took a sexual turn. Rosemary also did some last-minute fact-checking for me at the National Records of Scotland, for which I am infinitely grateful.

Thanks to grants from the PSC-CUNY (Professional Staff Congress-City University of New York) and the American Society of Eighteenth-Century Studies, as well as subventions from the Office of Academic Affairs of Hostos Community College/CUNY, I was able to spend parts of the summers of 2010 and 2011 questing for Jane in Edinburgh; London; Bethesda, Maryland; and Austin, Texas. I am very grateful to all the librarians, reference specialists, and staff I met in these places during this period. They all went out of their way to facilitate my research. Even more importantly, the interest they showed in my project made me feel like I wasn't talking to myself. I would not have been able to complete my research in Edinburgh and London had it not been for the hospitality of Jan and Tom Conway, Mary Ann Julian, John and Bini Malcolm, Henry Noltie, Dan and Juliet O'Connor, Rosemary Wake, and Peter and Mary Hiscock.

An early reader of my manuscript suggested that I needed to place Jane among the half-Indian children who were sent to Britain and, specifically, to compare her to Anne Lister's first beloved, the biracial Eliza Raine. To do justice to this recommendation, I needed access to the passenger lists of the ships that plied between Calcutta and Britain. Kathy Chater and Mary Hiscock went through the tomes of those voyages and transcribed the children's names. Patricia Silman, a direct descendant of General Samuel Need (who makes a cameo appearance in this book) and his *bibi*, provided me with evidence that Need's second wife, Annie Grant (who makes more than a cameo appearance), was a caring stepmother to her husband's children with the *bibi*. Very late in this work's gestation I exchanged warm and supportive emails with Daniel Livesay, the subject of whose recent book, *Children of Uncertain Fortune: Mixed-Race Jamaicans in Britain and the Atlantic Family, 1733–1833*, parallels mine.

Parts of the book have been tried out in the form of conference presentations at meetings of the East-Central Eighteenth Studies Association, the South-Central Eighteenth Century Association, the American Society for Eighteenth-Century Studies, the Canadian Society for Eighteenth-Century Studies, the Scottish Society for Eighteenth Century Studies, and the International Congress for Eighteenth Century Studies. I am grateful to all these groups for giving me a platform, to friends and colleagues like Linda Merians, Linda Troost, Sayre Greenfield, Ellen Moody, Elizabeth Denlinger, and William McCarthy, who always asked tactfully how the book was coming along and gave me wise suggestions, and to Sondra Phifer, who helped me with the PowerPoint aspect of the presentations. I am especially grateful to Ted and Anne Braun, who seemed always to be in the audience when I presented at conferences they attended. And I am grateful to all the audience members who engaged in "Janetalk" with me. I tested my ideas out on classes in which I taught *The Children's Hour*, and I benefited greatly from the students' perceptions. Brijraj Singh and Christine Hutchins read drafts of the manuscript and gave me feedback, which, like the medicine of my childhood, tasted foul but once swallowed made for significant improvement. Many thanks to the anonymous press readers; to my meticulous and perceptive copyeditor, Alice Phillips; and to Sonia Kane, Julia Cook, Tracey Engel, and Rio Hartwell at the University of Rochester Press for their help and support in bringing this book into being. They dealt with my torrent of emails with immense patience. The debt I owe my husband and son is incalculable and beyond words. Such mistakes as remain in the book I acknowledge mine.

Parts of this book—or spin-offs from the research that didn't make it into the book—have appeared as articles in *Notes and Queries*, *Nineteenth-Century Contexts*, *Signet Magazine*, *The Journal of the Edinburgh Bibliographical Society*, and *Journal of Scottish Historical Studies*. My co-biography of Jane Cumming and her grandmother appears as a chapter in Sonia Kane and Temma Berg's 2013 collection of essays, *Women, Gender, and Print Culture in Eighteenth-Century Britain*. My entry on Jane Cumming appeared in *The New Biographical Dictionary of Scottish Women* (2018), and Susan Skedd and I collaborated on the entry on Jane Pirie that appears in the *Oxford*

Dictionary of National Biography. All are reprinted here with permission from the publishers. Sir Alastair Gordon Cumming, whose father had the family documents moved from Altyre to the National Library of Scotland, gave me permission to quote the two letters from Rose and Jane in the appendix.

APPENDIX A

Marianne Woods, Jane Pirie, and Romantic Friendship

The phenomenon of romantic or passionate friendship among female adolescents is well-documented. It has been described as an "unusually intense friendship . . . that appears as emotionally intense as [a] romantic relationship but lack[s] explicit sexual interest, sexual activity, or both."[1] Across cultures, adolescent females in such relationships exhibit emotional behaviors "characteristic of romantic relationships, such as preoccupation, jealousy, inseparability, cuddling and hand holding."[2] In her mid-teens, Mary Wollstonecraft exhibited some of these characteristics. In 1773/74 she wrote a letter to her then best female friend Jane Arden. "I have formed romantic notions of friendship," she declared. "I am a little singular in my thoughts of love and friendship; I must have the first place or none."[3] When she was twenty-one, she told Jane Arden that what she desired most was to live with Fanny Blood, who succeeded Jane in her affections. "To live with this friend is the height of my ambitions," she stated unequivocally in a letter dating from early 1780.[4]

On the surface, Marianne Woods and Jane Pirie looked like a textbook example of romantic friends. Female friends frequently used very romantic language in which to couch their feelings, and Jane's "dearest earthly friend" single-sentence note to Marianne has this characteristic. That Marianne asked Jane to destroy her letters suggests that Marianne's letters also brimmed with passionate intensity. The two engaged in public displays of affection, kissing, caressing, and fondling each other in front of the students. They visited each other at night and, at least on one occasion, shared a bed. Pirie, like Wollstonecraft, was jealous and obsessive and wanted to live with her beloved friend.

However, Marianne Woods and Jane Pirie became friends after adolescence. Between 1802, when they met, and 1810, when Pirie joined the school, life kept them physically apart. Though their romantic friendship, nurtured by epistolary exchange, deepened, they hardly knew each other. By the time they got together, they thought they did, but in reality what they knew was the self each had developed for the other in the letters. Neither had an idea how the other would react to real circumstances.

Romantic friendship has always raised eyebrows. Could the women involved in a tender friendship stay chaste? As discussed in chapter 5, the founders of medieval convents were against such affective relationships; it was their considered opinion that these friendships had the potential for turning sexual. They wrote very strict rules and charters to ensure that in the walled same-sex communities of their order the atmosphere would not become erotically charged and the nuns would not form "particular" or "special" friendships. From their standpoint, the behaviors Woods and Pirie displayed would have been symptomatic of nuns desiring same-sex intimacy. Pirie's obsessiveness, the intensity of her feelings for Woods, her desire to live exclusively with her, would, in addition, have signaled to St. Bonaventure and his ilk that she was sexually aroused and wanted more than friendship.

In her adolescence, Jane's American near-contemporary Sarah Bradford (later Ripley) developed an intense friendship with an older woman, her cousin Mary Moody Emerson. About 1809, the year Jane was placed at Mrs. and Miss Woods Boarding School, Sarah wrote a letter to Mary in which she described their friendship from her point of view. It was, she wrote, sanctioned by religion. Sarah considered her affection for Mary pure, heavenly, and devoted. Her feelings for Mary made her (Sarah) happy. Sarah's mother, Elizabeth, was not so sure that relationships such as this one were pure and heavenly—or if they were, that they could stay that way. In the same letter, Sarah reports that she was "bantered a little at tea about romantic attachments, and quotes her mother's position on them, namely that "violent romantic attachments. . . . [create] a delusion innocent as to [their] object, rather dangerous as to its effects."[5] Might Sarah's mother have been thinking along the same lines as Mary Wollstonecraft on the related phenomenon of same-sex bedsharing—that it could or would "render the marriage state unhappy"? If it could, romantic friendship was in competition with or mounted a challenge to the notion of conjugal rights.

About 1810, when Jane was going through her troubles at school, Sarah again protested that her attachment to Mary was innocent. It is obvious that she meant that the two had not had genital sex, because she simultaneously acknowledged that it was only the difference in age between her and Mary that prevented them from developing and "cement[ing] . . . a bond of union."[6] But if sex is not defined by the male model of penetration, who is to say that they didn't derive sexual satisfaction from their kissing, caressing, and fondling?

A recent study led by psychologist Jenna Glover found that heterosexual women involved in a romantic friendship did not consider the cuddling sexual, while women who identified as lesbian did.[7] However, some academics with backgrounds in the humanities consider this binary approach simplistic. They think that the strong desire to label the women as either heterosexual or lesbian points toward the anxieties of a heteronormative culture with respect to women whose sexual orientation resists easy categorization into heterosexual and homosexual.[8] Fiona Brideoake, the most recent biographer of Eleanor Butler and Sarah Pononsby, argues that there are some same-sex attachments, such as that between her two subjects, that resist an either/or categorization. To a same-sex relationship that cannot be reduced to a "single, stable signification" or that resists "identitarian containment" Brideoake applies the term "queer."[9] Because Butler and Pononsby became socially accepted and even celebrities in their lifetimes, many people—including Miss Pirie's mentor, Elizabeth Hamilton, who visited them—didn't think of them in sexual terms.

Marianne Woods and Jane Pirie were not so lucky as to escape that "identitarian containment," and if you perceive Jane's testimony as truthful or having some truth in it, then they were not queer like the Ladies but women sexually categorizable as lesbian. For if you accept at least one of the situations she described, the one at Portobello, when she was in a bed at the foot of theirs, heard the teachers moaning and kissing and noticed the movements of their bodies shaking the bed, then you believe Jane's allegation: they were having sex. On the other hand, if you believe Jane contrived this scenario plus the ones at Drumsheugh, where the two women were touching each other's private parts in a bed they knew was also occupied by a third person (Jane), then you are free to entertain no suspicions at all about the teachers' physical chastity and many suspicions about the chastity of Jane's mind.

So did they or didn't they? Were they or weren't they? From their perspective, they certainly didn't, they certainly weren't. They lived at a time when the definition of sexual activity was based on a male model of penetration and female–female petting not considered similar to heterosexual foreplay in intention or result. Thus, they may not have even considered their kissing, caressing, and touching of each other's erogenous areas as sexually arousing. My own guess? I think these almost thirty-year-old women were sexually stirred by their own behaviors, but because of the age in which they lived, wouldn't have identified the pleasure they were giving to and receiving from each other as physiological—that is to say, sexual. In an understanding of sex that takes into account other ways of reaching what the judges might have called a venereal climax, I think they consummated their partnership from time to time. As to having genital sex on occasion, I just can't believe that two people, two teachers, however aroused, would make love in the same bed in which an adolescent pupil of theirs was also sleeping. I think it just within the realm of possibility that the Portobello incident happened: that they made love in a bed at the foot of which was another bed in which sleeping the same adolescent, little realizing that they would wake Jane up. So I think there could be a grain of truth in Jane's allegation. Platonic relationships are difficult to sustain. Why should tender bedsharing female friends not become intimate at a moment when they were feeling happy in each other's company and act somewhat incautiously?

Scholars in the humanities have written extensively on romantic friendship, but I decided to see what data-driven social scientists had to say about this phenomenon. That of psychologist Lisa Diamond seems to me to shed light on the "did they or didn't they, were they or weren't they" issue with the teachers. Diamond interviewed contemporary women who identify as tender friends. A number reported that their friendships turned sexually intimate, but they then told Diamond that the sexual turn surprised them. While they acknowledged that they had made love, they also claimed that their "sexual activity . . . was an expression of emotional closeness rather than a manifestation of sexual desire . . . the only place left to go in the relationship"—they weren't in the relationship for the sex.[10] Applying these insights to the relationship of Woods and Pirie, I think it possible that the relationship could, on occasion, have turned genitally sexual, but if it did, the sex was, as it were, a physiological response to something else: the deep and reciprocal emotional commitment the pair were feeling at that moment.

My reading of the Woods-Pirie relationship is that it began as relationships often do: two strangers of the same age and sex meet in a class and "click" because they find they have some things in common. In the case of Woods and Pirie, that feeling of affinity was stoked into an affective commitment through epistolary exchange in the years they were separated. My guess, since these letters don't exist anymore, is that both women became attracted or attached to the personas the other put forward in her letters. In those letters, they would have expressed themselves in the language of romantic friendship. However, when the letters were replaced by the school, when the epistolary relationship was put to the test of reality, its fault lines became apparent.

The obsessiveness and possessiveness that Pirie displayed suggest to me that she was, without realizing it, one very frustrated lesbian. Marianne was happy having Pirie as a friend and could be physically demonstrative toward her, but the person she cared deeply about was her aunt. Pirie's goal was the queer one realized by Butler and Pononsby: "let's live together as a committed couple devoted exclusively to each other for the rest of our lives." Woods's goal was not related to sexual identity: what she wanted to do was make money so that she and her aunt could live in financial comfort. Pirie's start-up capital was the means to that end. Recognizing that Pirie genuinely adored her, perhaps Woods thought she could exploit her and get away with it. Her insertion of Mrs. Woods into the school without the knowledge (let alone consent) of Pirie and her naming of the school after herself and her aunt even though it was Pirie's start-up capital that got the school going argues in favor of such a hypothesis. So too do some of Jane's descriptions of their congresses. Jane, of course, had a vested interest in punishing Miss Pirie, and presenting her as being on the receiving end of Miss Woods's fancies no doubt gave her vicarious satisfaction, but in constructing the relationship as unequal and abusive, one in which the dominant figure was taking advantage of the submissive figure's neediness, she was spot-on.

Woods and Pirie soon realized how different they really were. Marianne was gentle with the girls; Jane yelled at them frequently. Jane seems to have been far more invested in their learning the tenets of religion than Marianne. Marianne got over her racism and Jane Pirie was particularly vicious toward Jane Cumming. This was intolerable to the more balanced Marianne. Then there was the Mrs. Woods issue. Pirie idolized Woods, but her judgment wasn't clouded when it came to professional misrepresentation. Mrs. Woods had presented herself as Miss Pirie's superior, and Marianne had gone along with this imposture. I suspect that Marianne, who had to accept that Mrs. Woods would leave the school, may have finessed the deal by which her aunt would have retired with a third of the school's profits. If the school hadn't collapsed, Marianne would have dealt Pirie a dirty blow. As all acknowledged, the teachers were in a hostile rather than a friendly relationship for quite a number of months before the school actually closed.

I think it was not sexual attraction but their age, their common desire to improve themselves, and the need to support themselves that brought them together. When they started to live together, it soon became apparent that they lacked mutuality on the most important issues. I think it perfectly possible that the teachers had sexual relations at moments when they were able to lay aside their differences and disagreements and reclaim the feeling of affinity that had brought them together, but there is no evidence to support this hypothesis. Indeed, the one piece of evidence that we do have—that they parted ways, with Pirie staying in Scotland and Woods moving south—suggests that they wanted nothing more to do with each other.

APPENDIX B

What Really Happened to Miss Marianne Woods and Miss Jane Pirie?

In the last few months of the school's existence, the two teachers were talking about breaking up, professionally and personally. However, eight years after the initial appeal, Moncreiff stated that "so great was the success which had attended their exertions, that they had come to the determination of taking a larger house against the following term of Whitsuntide, and of taking an increased number both of boarders and day scholars."[1] Like so many statements passed off as truth during the case, this one appears to be a deliberate misrepresentation, crafted to implicitly call attention to the failure of their high hopes and their current state of near-indigence.

The case took more of a toll on Jane Pirie than on Marianne Woods. In 1820 Moncreiff averred that Marianne had friends who enabled her "to earn a very scanty subsistence for herself and a near relative," presumably her aunt.[2] After the breakup of the school, Jane Pirie gave lessons two or three times a week for an hour or more to a Miss Anstruther, one of the former pupils, but by 1820 Moncreiff claimed that her working days were behind her. Though not without friends, she was "totally ruined . . . entirely disabled from employing whatever talents she may possess, and the acquirements of many years, either for her profit or for her bare sustenance" and had run up some debts.[3] These "debts" may be connected to another court case she became involved in. Sadly, it pitted Jane against her sister Margaret and Margaret's husband, Thomas Ferguson.

Pirie v. Fergusons, which can be dated to December 18, 1819, had to do with a substantial and valuable piece of property in Gladstone's Land, very close to Lady Stair's Close, where Jane Pirie had grown up.[4] It had originally belonged to Jane and Margaret's aunt, Euphemia Rixon, who had divided it between two of her nieces, Jane Pirie and another sister, also named Euphemia, in 1809. According to Jane, in October 1814, Margaret, who had not been given any land, pressured Jane into giving over her share of the property. Euphemia died in 1815 and left Margaret her share. As a result of these transactions, Jane, who in 1809 was heir to fifty percent of this property, now had nothing, while Margaret, who in 1809 had nothing, owned it all.

By late 1819, Pirie was having second thoughts about what she had done in 1814. Probably thinking that if she won back her share of this property she would be able to live the remainder of her years in financial comfort, she brought the situation to the Court of Session. Jane claimed that Margaret had acted in an illegal and most unkind way at a time when she, Jane, was under an extra-heavy burden of stress because *Woods and Pirie* was still an open case. Jane stated that "repeatedly with tears and protestations [she] beseeched and prayed [Margaret] that she might not be driven" into this "hurt[ful] and prejudicial" agreement, but that Margaret, totally unmoved by the tears and protestations, exploited her emotional vulnerability, "threaten[ing], menac[ing] and concuss[ing] her" into agreeing to the disposition of the property. Jane Pirie also pointed out that the document she signed in 1814 was not legal because it "wants the names and designations of the writer and witnesses, is not duly signed nor tested and is defective in the solemnities required by law."[5] However, on March 10, 1821, just around the time she was about to receive her £2,000 from Mackenzie & Innes, the court determined against her. Not only did she not get any of the property, but she had to pay for the expenses incurred by her brother-in-law Thomas in defense of his wife Margaret—a tad over £20. Euphemia Pirie did leave Jane something in 1815, when she died—"a gold ring with a stone in it."[6]

Despite her having sued the Fergusons, they, or at least Tom, did not turn his back on Jane. Her last will and testament, which is dated February 22, 1833, was made at Thomas Ferguson's centrally located residence on Glasgow's Rosehall Street. In this document, she identifies herself as "Miss Jane Pirie, lately residing in Edinburgh," and leaves her entire estate to him; since she had no estate to bequeath, this was a strictly pro forma exercise but the only way at her disposal to acknowledge her gratitude and indebtedness to her brother-in-law for taking her in. On the day the will was drawn up, she was suffering from sickness so "severe" that she could not sign her name to the document. The will was read and explained to her by the notaries; she handed them the pen "in token of her authority to do so."[7] She died two weeks later, on March 6, aged fifty-four, at Ferguson's residence.

Moncreiff had said that Marianne had left Scotland, but there is no evidence of her whereabouts until 1842. In that year her brother (or half-brother) William died, and left his sister Marianne Woods "of Regency Street, Brighton" the sum of £100 in his will, or $12,200.[8] Fronting the sea and with a central private garden, Regency Square was a posh address designed for the social elite, but whether William was maintaining her in elegant comfort or whether she was living there as a lady's companion or governess is anybody's guess. She is not enumerated in the 1851 or 1861 census. However, the January 16, 1870, death record of an eighty-seven-year-old woman named Marianne Woods residing at 17 Clarence Square in Brighton must surely be the same Marianne Woods mentioned in William Woods's 1842 will. Marianne died of pneumonia, but the servant who was there when she expired could provide no useful information to the registrar who filled in the record. Thus, under the column "Occupation," the registrar wrote "daughter of _____(blank) Woods, gentleman (deceased)." Clarence Square, though pretty enough and not far from Regency Square, does not face the sea and is nowhere near as elegant. In the 1870s, 17 Clarence Square was a boarding or lodging house.[9] Blessed with a strong constitution, Marianne lived longer than any of the other principals in the case I have been able to trace. She died of a typical winter illness in genteel poverty, far removed from the scene of the deviant acts of which she was accused. She left no will.

Like Jane Cumming, the teachers had an afterlife in the twentieth century. Because of the success of *The Children's Hour*, the play was soon made into a movie. Hellman had to redo the plot because the Hays Production Code proscribed films dealing with sexually taboo issues, of which lesbianism was one. Consequently, in *These Three* (1936), Martha Dobie, the Miss Pirie character, is presented as initially jealous of her friend's boyfriend but at the end makes it possible for her dear friend to get married. *The Children's Hour* (1961) was based on a filmscript that Hellman reviewed but that she herself did not write. By then, the Hays Production Code had been dismantled, so the lesbian element was foregrounded. As in the play, Martha acknowledges that her feelings for Karen are sexual, and then kills herself. Also as in the play, Karen, played with sensitivity by the luminous Audrey Hepburn, does not come out as such, but rejects marriage. Holding her head high, her chin at a defiant tilt, Hepburn walks away from the community after Martha's burial, symbolically and literally turning her back on the establishment. As a gesture, it is equivalent to the lone cowboy riding off into the unknown at the end of a western. After such a performance, how can we not hope that Karen will find happiness on this other path? But as with those cowboys whom we never see again, the historical record does little to suggest that Marianne Woods's future fulfilled that hope.

APPENDIX C

"Corinna, A Ballad"

This day (the year I dare not tell)
Apollo play'd the midwife's part;
Into the world Corinna fell,
And he endued her with his art.

But Cupid with a Satyr comes;
Both softly to the cradle creep;
Both stroke her hands, and rub her gums,
While the poor child lay fast asleep.

Then Cupid thus: 'This little maid
Of love shall always speak and write';
'And I pronounce,' the Satyr said,
'The world shall feel her scratch and bite.'

Her talent she display'd betimes;
For in a few revolving moons,
She seem'd to laugh and squall in rhymes,
And all her gestures were lampoons.

At six years old, the subtle jade
Stole to the pantry-door, and found
The butler with my lady's maid:
And you may swear the tale went round.

She made a song, how little miss
Was kiss'd and slobber'd by a lad:
And how, when master went to p—,
Miss came, and peep'd at all he had.

At twelve, a wit and a coquette;
Marries for love, half whore, half wife;
Cuckolds, elopes, and runs in debt;
Turns authoress, and is Curll's for life.

Her common-place book all gallant is,
Of scandal now a cornucopia;
She pours it out in Atalantis
Or memoirs of the New Utopia.

—*Jonathan Swift*

APPENDIX D

Richard Rose's Letter to Sir William Written from the Kinnedar Manse, Dated January 12, 1835

My Dear Sir William,

I intended to have been at Altyre last week, and for the very purpose you ask me, to endeavor to put an end to the deplorable and disgraceful contentions existing and likely to exist in the Manse of Dallas, but my hopes of being of any service are very slender. These contentions are now approaching to a crisis. Tulloch, instead of consulting me as usual has had recourse to law agents at Elgin who has [sic] filled his empty head with notions of his Jus Mariti. Ever since Mr. McKay and Mr. Aitken dismissed his chaste and godly maid, but who Mrs. T asserts was neither chaste nor godly—Mrs. T has been bent on a separation and Mr. McKay's last visit has driven him to desperation—but for Mr. Grant's letter, an inhibition would have been taken out against Mrs. T before this time. That letter lowered his courage—he feared his lawyer could be of little service to him in the event of a Parochial Visitation—and down he came to me. I at once perceived the friendly intentions of these [??] gentlemen and offered to stand between him and the Presbytery, if he dropped the idea of an inhibition which his lawyer told him was a most ungracious measure and might be accomplished without having recourse to public notoriety.

I had no great difficulty in persuading T that he must get himself clear of his Ecclesiasticate before he entered upon a civil process. The dread of a Visitation alarmed him, and I endeavoured to paint the possible consequences in the most glaring colours. It will produce a temporary calm and when a new hearing [??] begins it must again be suspended over his head. It has had one good effect, it put a damper on the inhibition which I no more could have done without it, than put a stop on the [??] or reason.

But my Dear Sir William, when and how is this disgraceful conduct on the part of Mr. and Mrs. T to terminate? There is no hope of a permanent reconciliation. They have mutually inflicted such desperate wounds on each other other's honor, character and happiness that neither can forget nor forgive. Nothing but wrangling and contention may be looked for. I once saw two bats tied tail to tail—their strife was deadly—they tore hair and skin and flesh from each other—he who tied them would have separated but durst not approach them. Just so it is with our friends at Dallas, the one will be the ruin of the other. No one can approach them without being bitten or torn by the one or the other.

Nothing provokes T so much as Mrs. T's constant suspicion and impeachment of his chastity. Maid after maid—Miss Shanks, Miss Laing and others have had their characters aspersed and fully as many will believe them guilty as will believe them innocent. T with all his stupidity has no back taste in flesh and blood—how he comes by them I know not, but I have seen some good looking tempting jades about him—and their good looks arouse Mrs. T's jealousy and confirms the general suspicion. Now this is most provoking. The kettle says to the pot, "O you are black." "I am not black," says the pot. "Yes," says the kettle, "you are black as hell." "You are the blacker of the two," says the pot. "I am not," says the kettle, "and I appeal to the Rev. Mr. Duncan Grant and to the Rev. Geo. McKay which of us two is the blacker." The reverend gentlemen are at a loss how to proceed. Pray, gentlemen, come a little nearer, touch them, handle them, there is surely some ground of difference, the one may be rough the other smooth. Touch them. No—we can't soil our fingers with them but we will order the Bellman to hang up both pot and kettle in the Church of Dallas that the whole congregation may decide this important controversy. The congregation meets. One end of the parish says that the pot, the other end says that the kettle is the blacker of the two. There is nothing like unanimity—the more they investigate the more they differ—and so would all the astronomers and philosophers on the face of the earth if both pot and kettle were being up for their decision as high as the moon. They could but say "Never were two things so black."

I was averse to a separation while there was any prospect of reconciliation or even a possibility of living together but there is now no more prospect of reconciliation nor of peace. Mrs. T is foolish and he is obstinate. He has had recourse to lawyers and they will put him on plans which will work his ruin. Make a settlement for Mrs. T while it is in your power. Poor will it be if she cannot enjoy more happiness than she does in the Manse of Dallas. I wish it had been thought of sooner, it would have put an end to bad example.

I will see you at Altyre some day next week if you are at home, or if you are taken up with Elections, any other day you may appoint, and will go with you to Dallas and try to make the best of what all must allow to be a bad bargain. Peace in the Manse of Dallas will last I hope till then.

I am, Dear Sir William,

Yours sincerely,
Richard Rose

APPENDIX E

Jane's Letter to Sir William Written from the Dallas Manse, Dated February 15, 1836, Regarding Wood Stealing at Dallas

Dear Sir William,
 I beg you will not tell any one that I am writing to you about any thing. John Forbes, a married man in the Village and Murduch Maclean a young man in the village also, are sawing a <u>whole year</u> here. It is as though you paid them though they are not working to you. <u>They</u> can tell you more about your wood than any other body. You ought to try them. John Forbes will tell you every thing I daresay you ask. Miss Maddie MacPherson knows him—his sister was long servant to her sister Mrs. Clark. I daresay he will be at the Forres Market on Wednesday and <u>if you think proper</u> you can ask Miss MacPherson to find him and try him first—it is likely he will tell her more than he would tell you because people feel awed when they speak to you and then they feel no liberty to speak—he I daresay can tell you about the place under ground. You should ask him and other people what cars from this <u>parish</u> took your wood to Findhorn. When you ask any thing at the Dallas people you ought to be <u>quite alone</u> with the person you speak to as they will then tell you every thing—but they will not do it if there is <u>any</u> person beside. Be sure to enquire about the <u>carts</u> and you can then trace your wood. You should do the same at Altyre for many a load went from that all night. It must have been the tenants carts there as your own must have been at work all day. People in this place sometimes paid with wood for sawing. I am afraid you will not be up soon so please tell the bearer when Alex Forbes goes off and send me the Majors address. I hear David Mackay Rafford is going to India—would you advise me to give him my letter? But I would not tell him what it is about. Dear Sir William have the goodness to send me some word. I hope you will try to get James Cameron into Dunphail. Please send me word of how Lady Cumming & family are. I am dear Sir William,

Your very grateful
<u>Jane Tulloch</u>

NOTES

Author's Note

1. The secondary literature that engages with romantic friendship is vast, and what follows is a highly selective list. See Carroll Smith-Rosenberg, "The Female World of Love and Ritual: Relations Between Women in Nineteenth-Century America," *Signs*, 1, no. 1 (1975): 1–29; Lillian Faderman, *Surpassing the Love of Men: Romantic Friendship and Love Between Women from the Renaissance to the Present* (New York: William Morrow, 1981); Lisa Moore, "Something More Tender Still than Friendship: Romantic Friendship in Nineteenth-Century England." *Feminist Studies* 18, no. 3 (1992), 499–520; Emma Donoghue, *Passions Between Women: British Lesbian Culture 1668–1801* (New York: HarperCollins, 1993); Betty Rizzo, *Companions Without Vows: Relationships Among Eighteenth-Century Women* (Athens: University of Georgia Press, 1994); Lisa Diamond, "Passionate Friendships Among Adolescent Sexual-Minority Women," *Journal of Research on Adolescence* 10, no. 2 (2000): 191–209; Valerie Traub, *The Renaissance of Lesbianism in Early Modern England* (Cambridge: Cambridge University Press, 2002); Martha Vicinus, *Intimate Friends: Women Who Loved Women* (Chicago: University of Chicago Press, 2004); Sharon Marcus, *Between Women: Friendship, Desire and Marriage in Victorian England* (Princeton: Princeton University Press, 2007); Leila J. Rupp, *A Global History of Love Between Women* (New York: New York University Press, 2011); Susan Lanser, *The Sexuality of History: Modernity and the Sapphic* (Chicago: University of Chicago Press, 2014); and Jenna Glover, Renée Galliher, and Katherine Crowell, "Young Women's Passionate Friendships: A Qualitative Analysis," *Journal of Gender Studies* 24, no. 1 (2015): 70–84.
2. Act 4, scene 3, ll. 2041–42.
3. Act 1, part 8.

Introduction

1. Christina de Bellaigue, "Behind the School Walls: The School Community in French and English Boarding Schools for Girls, 1810–1867," in *Paedogigica Historica* 40, nos. 1–2 (2004): 115–17.
2. According to Francis Hutcheson, one of the leading philosophers of the Scottish Enlightenment, these five qualities made for a good marriage. See Jane Rendall, *The Origins of Modern Feminism: Women in Britain, France and the United States, 1780–1860* (Chicago: Lyceum, 1985), 11.

3. Kate Barclay, *Love, Intimacy and Power: Marriage and Patriarchy in Scotland, 1650–1850* (Manchester: Manchester University Press, 2011), 126–44.

4. Rictor Norton, ed., "Extraordinary Female Affection, 1790," *Homosexuality in Eighteenth-Century England: A Sourcebook.* April 22, 2005. Updated June 15, 2005.

5. The term "lesbian" was not in use in the early nineteenth century, but for the sake of accessibility I use it, along with the older and now less familiar words "tribade" and "sapphist."

6. *Miss Marianne Woods and Miss Jane Pirie*, photo reprint (New York: Arno Press, 1975), 75, 2 ("Speeches"). Hereafter abbreviated as *MWJP*.

7. On adolescence, see Patricia Meyer Spacks, *The Adolescent Idea: Myths of Youth and the Adult Imagination* (New York: Basic Books, 1981), 16–26.

8. ABC TV Documentaries, *The Trouble with Merle*, www.abc.net.au/tv.documentaries/stories, accessed March 15, 2017. See also Maree Delofski, "Place, Race and Stardom: Becoming Merle Oberon," *Continuum: Journal of Media and Cultural Studies* 26, no. 2 (2012): 803–14.

9. P. J. Marshall, *East Indian Fortunes: The British in Bengal in the Eighteenth Century* (Oxford: Oxford University Press, 1976), 218. See also Philip D. Curtin, *Death by Migration: Europe's Encounter with the Tropical World in the Nineteenth Century* (Cambridge: Cambridge University Press, 1989).

10. Edward Said, *Orientalism* (New York: Random House, 1979), 190; Jane Rendall, *The Origins of Modern Feminism: Women in Britain, France and the United States, 1780–1860* (Chicago: Lyceum, 1985), 21–22; Carmen Nocentelli, *Empires of Love: Europe, Asia, and the Making of Early Modern Identity* (Philadelphia: University of Pennsylvania Press, 2013), 1–89. The allusion to men made of "iron or steele" being the willing sex slaves of Eastern women comes from a book by the Dutchman Jan Huygen van Linschoten, who spent five years in the Portuguese Indies in the late sixteenth century. Quoted in Nocentelli, 79.

11. Christopher Hawes, *Poor Relations: The Making of a Eurasian Community in India 1773–1833* (London: Routledge, 1996), 6; Durba Ghosh, *Sex and the Colonial Family: The Making of Empire* (Cambridge: Cambridge University Press, 2006), 68–77.

12. IOR/L/AG/34/29/13. The fate of the younger child is treated in chapters 1, 2, and 6.

13. GD 248/690/2/2/B.

14. Quoted in Kathy Fraser, *For the Love of a Highland Home: The Fraser Brothers' Indian Quest* (St. Kilda: Grey Thrush, 2016), 81.

15. Elizabeth Grant of Rothiemurchus, *Memoirs of a Highland Lady*, complete edition (Edinburgh: Canongate, 2001), 1:262.

16. Blaikie, "A Kind of Loving," 41–57.

17. *MWJP*, 4 ("Answers," February 22, 1812).

18. Stana Nenadic, "Military Men, Businessmen, and the 'Business' of Patronage in Eighteenth-Century London," in Stana Nenadic, ed., *Scots in London in the Eighteenth Century* (Lewisburg: Bucknell University Press, 2010), 230–32.

19. Quotations from Elizabeth Grant: Grant, *Memoirs*, 2:262, 261.

20. Ibid., 1:177–78.

21. DEP 175/161 (1).

22. Quoted in John Malcolm, *Malcolm: Soldier, Diplomat, Ideologue of British India* (Edinburgh: John Donald, 2014), 196.

23. Two important studies investigate the companionate relationships that developed between British men and Indian women: William Dalrymple, *White Mughals: Love and Betrayal in Eighteenth-Century India* (New York: Penguin, 2004); and Ghosh, *Sex*.

24. James Thomas died suddenly and intestate in 1804. His father wanted the children to be sent to Scotland, but his efforts to bring them across them were unsuccessful. See G. M. Fraser, *The Good Sir James: The Life and Times of Sir James Grant of Grant, of Castle Grant, Bart* (Kinloss: Librario, 2012), 208–9; and Frances B. Singh, "James Thomas Grant, George Cumming and Lewis Mackenzie: A Case Study of Three Scottish First Cousins in East India Company Service, 1792–1804," *Journal of Scottish Historical Studies* 38, no. 1 (2018): 160–77.

25. Victor Jacquemont, *Letters from India 1829–1832: Being a Selection from the Correspondence of Victor Jacquemont*. Trans. Catherine Alison Philips. (London: Macmillan, 1936), 314.

26. DEP 175/78/4354.

27. Quoted in Vyvyen Brendon, *Children of the Raj* (London: Weidenfeld & Nicolson, 1988), 55.

28. Deborah Cohen, *Family Secrets: The Things We Tried to Hide* (London: Penguin, 2014), 3.

29. Brendon, 56–59.

30. Charles Lushington, *The History, Design, and Present State of the Religious, Benevolent and Charitable Institutions Founded by the British in Calcutta and Its Vicinity* (Calcutta, 1824), 125–26.

31. Captain Thomas Williamson, *The East-India Vade Mecum; or Complete Guide to Gentlemen Intended for Civil, Military, or Naval Service of the East India Company* (London: Black, Parry, and Kingsbury, 1810), 1:337; Suresh Chandra Ghosh, *The Social Condition of the British Community in Bengal: 1757–1800* (Leiden: E. J. Brill, 1970), 85.

32. Williamson, 1:464, 459.

33. Princeton University Library Finding Aids, s.v. "George Alexander Thompson." http://rbsc.princeton.edu/databases/princeton-university-library-finding-aids.

34. Kate Teltscher, *The High Road to China: George Bogle, the Panchen Lama and the First British Expedition to Tibet* (London: Bloomsbury, 2006), 253.

35. H. E. Richardson, "George Bogle and His Children," *Scottish Genealogist* 29, no. 3 (1982): 74–75.

36. Cohen, 3–12.

37. Ibid.

38. Ursula Low, *Fifty Years with John Company: From the Letters of General Sir John Low of Clatto, Fife, 1822–1858* (London: John Murray, 1936), 62.

39. Cohen, 14–15.

40. Quoted in Margot Finn, "Anglo-Indian Lives in the Later Eighteenth and Early Nineteenth Centuries," *Journal for Eighteenth-Century Studies* 33, no. 1 (2010): 49–65.

41. Ibid.

42. On William Raine's unconventional and adventurous life in India and death at sea, see Dirom Grey Crawford, *A History of the Indian Medical Service 1600–1913* (London: Thacker, 1914), 20, 120, 205, 208, 241.

43. Personal email from Daniel Sudron, Archivist, West Yorkshire Archives Service Calderdale, dated September 20, 2018.

44. Personal email from Helena Whitbread, Anne Lister scholar, dated January 18, 2017.

45. All of these details come from his will. IOR/L/AG/34/29/205. See also Joanna Frew, "Scottish Backgrounds and Indian Experiences in the Late Eighteenth Century," *Journal of Scottish Historical Studies* 34, no. 2 (2014): 172–75.

46. Quoted in Marla Karen Chancey, "In the Company's Secret Service: Neil Benjamin Edmonstone and the First Indian Imperialists, 1780–1820" (PhD diss., University of Florida, 2003).

47. Quoted in Dalrymple, 387.

48. *List of Carthusians, 1800–1879* (Lewes: Fancombe, 1879), 143.

49. On the subject of families who developed a connection with India that spanned generations, see Elizabeth Buettner, *Empire Families: Britons and Late Imperial India* (Oxford: Oxford University Press, 2004).

50. Williamson, 1:457. See also Chancey, "In the Company's Secret Service: Neil Benjamin Edmonstone and the First Indian Imperialists."

51. Eliza Ann's maternal grandparents were John Shaw and a woman with a single name: Osannah. This name strongly suggests that she was an Indian convert to Christianity. On reasons children often followed in their father's footsteps and returned to India, generation after generation, see Buettner, 176–91.

52. Susan's protracted battle to claim her father's estate is detailed in Montague Chambers, Philip Twells, and Francis Towers Streeten, ed., *The Law Journal Reports for the Year 1852*, vol. 30 and vol. 21 (New Series) (London: Edward Bret Ince, 1852), 782–84 and 177–82.

53. "Slippers in Hand, Aussie Hunts for Princess," *Telegraph* (Kolkata), October 14, 2010.

54. Personal letter from Patricia Silman, a direct descendant of Johnstone Need, to author. Dated September 17, 2018.

55. Personal emails dated September 17, 2018, and October 30, 2018, from Patricia Silman.

56. Personal email from Kathy Fraser, author, dated September 4, 2018; Fraser, *Highland Home*, 345, 395.

57. Fraser, *Highland Home*, 338, 345.

58. Ibid., 345.

59. Thomas Starzl, *The Puzzle People: Memoirs of a Transplant Surgeon* (Pittsburgh: University of Pittsburgh Press, 1992), 3.

60. Hawes, 23, 32, 119.

Chapter One

1. M. E. Cumming Bruce, *Family Records of the Bruces and the Cumyns* (Edinburgh: William Blackwell, 1870), 468.
2. DEP 175/64/1.
3. P. J. Marshall, *East India Fortunes*, 217–18, puts the mortality rate at 57%.
4. DEP 175/175.
5. John Prebble, *Mutiny: Highland Regiments in Revolt 1743–1804* (London: Penguin, 1975), 291.
6. GD 248/515/13/11; Constance Frederica Gordon Cumming, *Memories* (Edinburgh: William Blackwood, 1904), 13.
7. GD 248/517/13/13.
8. Brendan Cassidy, "The Fate of a 'Missing Masterpiece': Gavin Hamilton's *Andromache Mourning the Death of Hector*." *British Art Journal* 10, no. 1 (2009): 11–13.
9. Robert Hay, *Lochnavando No More: The Life and Death of a Moray Farming Community, 1750–1850* (Edinburgh: Birlinn, 2005), 94.
10. GD 248/58/1/66.
11. Hay, 94.
12. DEP 175/77/4108.
13. On the cost of women's education, see P. J. Miller, "Women's Education, 'Self-Improvement' and Social Mobility—A Late Eighteenth Century Debate," *British Journal of Educational Studies* 20 (1972): 305.
14. Both quotations in this paragraph are from DEP 175/76/3748.
15. GD 248/706/3/1.
16. DEP 175/138.
17. DEP 175/59.
18. DEP 175/22.
19. DEP 175/77/3948.
20. The History of Parliament Online, s.v. "CUMMING GORDON, Alexander Penrose (1749–1806), of Altyre and Gordonstown, Elgin," https://www.historyofparliamentonline.org/volume/1790-1820/member/cumming-gordon-alexander-penrose-1749-1806, accessed January 12, 2019.
21. GD 248/683/1/3/7.
22. IOR/J/1/14/ Folios 238–41.
23. DEP 175/77/39AY.
24. "Necessary Expense of Fitting a Lad for the East Indies," *Hardwicke Papers*, vol. DLXX. *East India papers*, August 1769–1810, f. 222. Quoted in Holden Furber, *John Company at Work* (Cambridge: Harvard University Press, 1970), 338.
25. DEP 175/159(2).
26. Charles Gold, *Oriental Drawings Sketched Between the Years 1791 and 1798* (London: 1806), n.p. Quoted in Bernard S. Cohn, "The British in Benares: A Nineteenth-Century Colonial Society," *Comparative Studies in Society and History* 4 (1962): 183.

27. Stana Nenadic, *Lairds and Luxury: The Highland Gentry in Eighteenth-century Scotland* (Edinburgh: John Donald, 2007), 137–58, 205–7; Ghosh, *Social Condition*, 126.

28. These items are listed on the inventory of George's estate, IOR/L/AG/34/27/27.

29. IOR/L/AG/34/29/8.

30. *The Bengal Obituary, A Record to Perpetuate the Memory of Departed Worth. . . .* (London: W. Thacker, 1851), 81; IOR/L/AG/34/27/27.

31. DEP 175/78/4354.

32. IOR/L/MAR/B292C.

33. "James Cumming's Papers," India Office Library, *Home Miscellaneous Series*, vol. 525: 69. Quoted in Cohn, 186.

34. IOR/L/AG/34/29/13.

35. GD 248/3418/7/15.

36. GD248/690/2/2.

37. In 1805 William Fraser travelled by barge from Calcutta to beyond Moorshidabad. He described the experience in letters to his father in Scotland. He noted the *shikaras*, which he called "pagodas." See Fraser, *Highland Home*, 50–51.

38. Quoted in Purna Ch. Majumdar, *The Musnud of Majumdar* (Murshidabad: Saroda Ray, 1905), 297.

39. In 2004 Christie's sold a jeweled flask and other items that had been in the Clive family's possession for £4.7 million.

40. GD 248/690/2/2.

41. For a study of the political translation of sensibility and sympathy, see Lynn Festa, *Sentimental Figures of Empire in Eighteenth-Century Britain and France* (Baltimore: Johns Hopkins Press, 2006); and Juliet Shields, *Sentimental Literature and Anglo-Scottish Identity, 1745–1820* (Cambridge: Cambridge University Press, 2010).

42. Sayre Greenfield, "The Impact of Laurence Sterne upon Yorick's Skull" (paper presented at the South-Central Eighteenth-Century Society (SCECS), St. Simon's Island, February 18, 2011).

43. *Hamlet*, act 5, scene 1, l. 190.

44. DEP 175/161 (1).

45. Ibid.

46. GD 248/192/2/16.

47. *MWJP*, 77 ("State of the Process," June 14, 1811). There is much confusion about her year of birth. The lawyers for Woods and Pirie claimed that she was born before 1795, while the inscription on her tombstone implies she was born in 1797. Her age is discussed in chapter 4, 5, and 6.

48. DEP 175/78/4354,

49. A. W. B. Simpson, *Legal Theory and Legal History: Essays on the Common Law* (London: Hambleton, 1987), 156.

50. *Hamlet*, act 4, scene 1, ll. 199–201.

51. DEP 175 /78/4354.

52. On the desire of migrants to maintain primary relationships, even strained and conflicted ones, and particularly those between fathers and sons, see especially David A. Gerber, *Authors of Their Lives: The Personal Correspondence of British Immigrants to North America in the Nineteenth Century* (New York: New York University Press, 2006), 192–94; and Andrew MacKillop, "Europeans, Britons and Scots: Scottish Sojourning Networks and Identities in Asia, c. 1700–1815," in *Notes on a Global Clan: Scottish Migrant Networks and Identities since the Eighteenth Century*, ed. Angela McCarthy (London: Tauris Academic Studies, 2006), 21–24.

53. DEP 175/78/4434.

54. IOR/L/AG/34/29/13.

55. Ibid.

56. DEP 175/109(1).

57. Walter Harte, *Essays on Husbandry* (London: W. Frederick, 1764), 36–37. Quoted in Jenny Davidson, *Breeding: A Partial History of the Eighteenth Century* (New York: Columbia University Press, 2009), 63.

58. IOR/L/MAR/B/177B.

59. *MWJP*, 4 ("Answers," February 22, 1812).

60. Emma Roberts, *The East-India Voyager* (London: J. Madden, 1845), 2–4. Quoted in C. Northcote Parkinson, *Trade in the Eastern Seas, 1793–1813* (Cambridge: Cambridge University Press, 1937), 271–72.

61. See Arthur N. Gilbert, "Buggery and the British Navy, 1700–1861," *Journal of Social History* 10, no. 1 (1976): 72–98; Jan Oosterhoff, "Sodomy at Sea and at the Cape of Good Hope During the Eighteenth Century," *Journal of Homosexuality* 16, nos. 1–2 (1998): 229–31; Cheryl Fury, "'To Sett Down All the Villainie': Accounts of the Sodomy Trial on the Fourth East India Company Voyage (1609)," *Mariner's Mirror* 102, no. 1 (2016): 75.

62. Gilbert, 70–78.

63. Oosterhoff, 233. The premium placed on keyhole testimony is discussed further in chapter 4.

64. Oosterhoff, 229.

65. Seth Stein LeJacq, "Buggery's Travels: Royal Navy Sodomy on Ship and Shore in the Long Eighteenth Century," *Journal for Maritime Research* 17, no. 2 (2015): 103–10. See also Gilbert: 79–86.

66. LeJacq, 109.

67. *MWJP*, 70 ("State of the Process," June 14, 1811).

68. L/MAR/B/177B.

69. Parkinson, 275.

70. Ibid., 264–303. See also Hans Turley, *Rum, Sodomy and the Lash: Piracy, Sexuality and Masculine Identity* (New York: New York University Press, 1999), 15–17.

71. GD 248/3418/7/16.

72. "The Berners Estate: Berners and Newman Streets," chapter 30, https://www.ucl.ac.uk/bartlett/files/chapter 30_the_berners_estate.pdf, accessed October 30, 2016.

73. Ibid.

74. See Shelley King, "Portrait of a Marriage: John and Amelia Opie and the Sister Arts," *Studies in Eighteenth-Century Culture* 40 (2011): 31–34. Opie's tale is discussed at more length in chapter 2.

75. GD 248/517/13/15.

76. In *Memories*, Constance Gordon Cumming recollects that in the early years of the nineteenth century, her father travelled between home and London "by a slow sailing-smack, a mode of transit which, besides being wretchedly uncomfortable, cut largely into the holidays; as in foul weather the voyage to London might take three weeks or even four" (13).

77. DEP 175/122.

78. DEP 175/96.

Chapter Two

1. For a study of the lives of Georgian gentry women, see Amanda Vickery, *The Gentleman's Daughter: Women's Lives in Georgian England* (New Haven, CT: Yale University Press, 1998).

2. James Fordyce, *The Character and Conduct of the Female Sex. . . .* (London: T. Caddell, 1776), 8. Quoted in Rosalind Carr, *Gender and Enlightenment Culture in Eighteenth Century Scotland* (Edinburgh: Edinburgh University Press, 2014), 14.

3. Barclay, 126.

4. Linda Pollack, "'Teach her to live under obedience': The Making of Women in the Upper Ranks of Early Modern England," *Continuity and Change* 4, no. 2 (1989): 231–58.

5. Jane McDermid, "Conservative Feminism and Female Education in the Eighteenth Century," *History of Education* 18, no. 4 (1989): 313.

6. Hannah More seems to have had this verse in mind when she extended its implications to cover the family and domestic hierarchy: "The woman is below the husband, and the children are below the mother, and the servant is below his master." Quoted in McDermid, 311.

7. Carr, 94–104; Pollack, 23–58. See also Katharine Glover, "'Polite London Children': Educating the Daughters of the Scottish Elite in Mid-Eighteenth Century London," in *Scots in London in the Eighteenth Century*, ed. Stana Nenadic (Lewisburg: Bucknell University Press, 2010), 253–71; and Josephine Kamm, *Hope Deferred: Girls' Education in English History* (London: Methuen, 1965), 113.

8. On breeding, see Jenny Davidson, *Breeding: A Partial History of the Eighteenth Century* (New York: Columbia University Press, 2009).

9. GD 248/517/13/11/2. See also P. J. Miller, "Women's Education, 'Self-Improvement' and Social Mobility—A Late Eighteenth Century Debate," *British Journal of Educational Studies* 20, no. 3 (1972): 302–14.

10. John Anthony Harrison, *Private Schools in Doncaster in the Nineteenth Century. Part II: Efflorescence* (Doncaster: Doncaster Museum and Art Gallery, 1960), 51.

11. Gordon Cumming, 32; and Grant, 2:44.

12. Isaac Watts, *An Essay Towards the Encouragement of Charity Schools*. . . . (London, 1728), 37; J. L. Chirol, *Inquiry into the Best System of Education: or, Boarding School and Home Education Attentively Considered* (London, 1809), 30–31. Quoted in Kamm, 137, 149.

13. Arden Hegele, "'So she has been educated by a vulgar, silly, conceited French governess!': Social Anxieties, Satirical Portraits, and the Eighteenth-Century French Instructor," *Gender and Education* 32, no. 3 (2011): 331–34. See also Dorothy Gardiner, *English Girlhood at School: A Study of Women's Education Through Twelve Centuries* (London: Humphrey Milford, 1929), 335.

14. *Gentleman's Magazine*, 1797, vol. 67, part 2, 983.

15. Elizabeth Hamilton, *The Cottagers of Glenburnie: A Scottish Tale* (Edinburgh, 1898), 5. See also Claire Grogan, *Politics and Genre in the Works of Elizabeth Hamilton* (Farnham: Ashgate, 2012), 126–27.

16. Fletcher, *The Autobiography of Elizabeth Fletcher* (Edinburgh, 1876), 20–21.

17. Ibid.

18. Quoted in Gardiner, 337.

19. William Roberts, *Memoirs of the Life and Correspondence of Mrs. Hannah More*, vol. 1 (New York, 1834), 406–7.

20. Bedsharing is discussed at greater length in chapter 3.

21. Mary Wollstonecraft, *A Vindication of the Rights of Women and a Vindication of the Rights of Men* (Oxford: Oxford University Press, 1993), 205, 249.

22. Quoted in Kamm, 148–49.

23. Quoted in ibid.

24. Erasmus Darwin, *A Plan for the Conduct of Female Education, in Boarding Schools, Private Families, and Public Seminaries* (Philadelphia, 1798), 99–107.

25. Kamm, 148–49; Gardiner 351–52.

26. *All's Well That Ends Well*, act 2, scene 1, l. 145.

27. Valerie E. R. Anderson, "The Eurasian Problem in Nineteenth-Century India" (PhD diss., SOAS, 2011).

28. David Arnold, "European Orphans and Vagabonds in the Nineteenth Century," *Journal of Imperial and Commonwealth History* 7, no. 2 (1979): 104–27.

29. "The Educational Establishments of Calcutta, Past and Present," *Calcutta Review* 13, no. 26 (1850): 443–44. On the culture of neglect at nurseries and schools in the Dutch East Indies, and the deleterious effect on the characters of children educated in those institutions, see Laura Ann Stoler, *Carnal Knowledge and Imperial Power: Race and the Intimate in Imperial Rule* (Berkeley: University of California Press, 2002), 114–21.

30. "Educational Establishments," 442.

31. Arnold, 111.

32. *MWJP*, 77 ("State of the Process," June 14, 1811).

33. Lushington, 127.

34. "Lieut-Colonel B. G. Barbut," *Journal of the Dutch Burgher Union of Ceylon* 23, no. 4 (1934): 193; Parkinson, 294.

35. Lushington, 132.

36. John Locke, *Some Thoughts Concerning Education and the Conduct of the Understanding*, ed. R. T. Grant and N. Tarcov (Indianapolis: Hackett, 1996), 41.

37. Davidson, *Breeding*, 40–48.

38. Locke, 26.

39. Himani Bannerji, "Age of Consent and Hegemonic Social Reform," *Gender and Imperialism*, ed. Clare Midgeley (Manchester: Manchester University Press, 1998), 35.

40. These lines are a mash-up of the following sources: *MWJP*, 49 ("Additional Petition," October 10, 1811); HL, *In the House of Lords, Cumming Gordon v. Woods and Pirie, The Respondents' Case*, 1812, 22; HL, *In the House of Lords, Cumming Gordon v. Woods and Pirie, Additional Case for the Respondents*, 1816, 4. The HL documents are in Moncreiff.

41. *In the House of Lords, Gordon Cumming v. Woods and Pirie, Additional Case for the Appellant*, 1816, 8.

42. Williamson, 1:469. Williamson may have been exaggerating. The ships' passenger lists, discussed in the introduction, indicate that many stayed longer in India than that. However, the idea that European children born in Asia should be sent back early because climate would sicken them and the environment, would corrupt and 'nativize' them was common. Asian women, particularly female domestics, were seen as the agents of moral corruption. See Stoler, 112–39.

43. *In the House of Lords, Cumming Gordon v. Woods and Pirie, Additional Case for the Appellant*, 8.

44. Williamson, I:341. See also Brendon, 34, 164–65.

45. Davidson, 23.

46. Webster, 82.

47. *MWJP*, 4 ("Answers," February 22, 1812).

48. Interestingly, Elizabeth Grant later remarked that the "good blood" of the Cummings barely kept their "queer" streak under control.

49. *MWJP*, 5 ("Answers," February 22, 1812), 1 ("Speeches").

50. *MWJP*, 4 ("Answers," February 22, 1812).

51. Nenadic, *Lairds and Luxury*, 123.

52. Elizabeth Grant, 1: 176.

53. See John Wood, *Plan of the Town of Elgin from Actual Survey* (Edinburgh, 1822), available online via the National Library of Scotland, http://maps.nls.uk/towns/rec/342, accessed October 1, 2019.

54. *MWJP*, 4 ("Answers," February 22, 1812).

55. *MWJP*, 78 ("State of the Process," June 14, 1811).

56. *MWJP*, 4 ("Answers," February 22, 1812), 9 ("Additional Petition," October 10, 1811).

57. Henry Kett, *Emily, A Moral Tale, Including Letters from a Father to His Daughter, upon the Most Important Subjects*, vol. 1 (London: Rivington, 1809), 61.

58. Ibid., 1:17.

59. Ibid., 2:325.

60. Elizabeth Hamilton, *Letters on the Elementary Principles of Education*, 3rd American ed., 2 vols. (Boston: Samuel H. Parker, 1825), 2:10.

61. Elizabeth Benger, ed., *Memoirs of the Late Mrs. Elizabeth Hamilton, with a Selection from Her Correspondence, and Other Unpublished Writings*, 2 vols. (London: Longman, Hurst, Rees, Orme and Brown: 1819), 1:41–43, 148–49.

62. Claire Grogan, "Crossing Genre, Gender and Race in Elizabeth Hamilton's *Translation of the Letters of a Hindu Rajah*," *Studies in the Novel* 34, no. 1 (2002): 31.

63. Lord Clive's Speech in the House of Commons, on the Motion of an Inquiry into the Nature, State, and Condition, of the East India Company, and of the British Affairs in the East Indies, in the Fifth Session of the Present Parliament, 1772, 42.

64. Julie Straight, "Promoting Liberty Through Universal Benevolence in Elizabeth Hamilton's *Translation of the Letters of a Hindu Rajah*," *Eighteenth-Century Fiction* 25, no. 3 (2013): 613–14.

65. Hamilton, *Translation*, 129.

66. On the extensive social connections and high level of discourse of these women, see Jane Rendall, "'Women that would plague me with rational conversation': Aspiring Women and Scottish Whigs," in *Women, Gender and Enlightenment*, ed. Sarah Knott and Barbara Taylor (Basingstoke: Palgrave Macmillan, 2005): 328–89.

67. *Letters on the Elementary Principles of Education*, 1:98, 124, 158.

68. This understanding of resilience is derived from George A. Bonnano, "Loss, Trauma, and Human Resilience: Have We Underestimated the Human Capacity to Thrive?," *American Psychologist* 59, no. 1 (2004): 20–38. I return to Bonnano's distinction between recovery and resilience in the conclusion.

69. Milton, *Paradise Lost*, book 11, ll. 616–17. In the following lines, Milton develops the Orientalist paradigm, writing that they were "bred only and completed to the taste / Of lustful appetence, to sing, to dance, / To dress and troll the tongue, and roll the eye."

70. Hamilton, *Letters on the Elementary Principles*, 1:20.

71. Esther Breitenbach, *Empire and Scottish Society: The Impact of Foreign Missions at Home, c. 1790–c. 1914* (Edinburgh: Edinburgh University Press, 2009), 99–117.

72. Ibid., 107–8. On divorce and separation in the Scottish context, see Leah Leneman, *Alienated Affections: The Scottish Experience of Divorce and Separation, 1684–1830* (Edinburgh: Edinburgh University Press, 1998).

73. Hamilton, *Letters on the Elementary Principles*, 2:20.

74. Ibid., 2:28.

75. Ibid., 2:156.

76. Hamilton, *Letters Addressed to the Daughter of a Nobleman*, 34–35, xi, 57, 8, 23, 53.

77. Robert Burton, *The Anatomy of Melancholy*. 9th ed. (London, 1800), 1:134–35.

78. Ibid., 8, 13.

79. Hamilton, *Letters Addressed to a Nobleman*, xvi–xvii.

80. Hamilton, *Letters on the Elementary Principles*, 1:22, 2:240.

81. *MWJP*, 4 ("Answers," February 12, 1812).

82. *MWJP*, 6 ("Answers," February 12, 1812).

83. A. J. Youngson, The *Making of Classical Edinburgh 1750–1840* (Edinburgh: Edinburgh University Press, 1967), 59–97; Julian Small, "The Architecture of Robert Adam (1728–1792): Charlotte Square, Edinburgh," https://sites.scran.ac.uk/ada/documents/square/charlotte_square.htm, accessed August 7, 2019; Mary Cosh, *Edinburgh in the Golden Age* (Edinburgh: John Donald, 2003), 1–124.

84. See *Post-Office Annual Directory from Whitsunday 1809 to Whitsunday 1810* (Edinburgh: Abernethy & Wallace, 1809), 272, https://www.nls.uk/family-history/directories/post-office/index.cfm?/place=Edinburgh, accessed February 24, 2014. However, as the establishment is generally referred to as the Woods-Pirie School or the Drumsheugh school, I follow convention here.

85. "*View: Old and New Town of Edinburgh and Leith with the Proposed Docks*" (Edinburgh, 1804), available online via the National Library of Scotland, maps.nls.uk/towns/rec/415, accessed March 18, 2016.

86. I am indebted to Dr. Henry Noltie for help in reading Ainslee's map and pinpointing the house. In his emails of March 18 and March 21, 2016, Noltie estimates the distance between the school and 22 Charlotte Square as 170 paces, or about 425 feet. Unlike 22 Charlotte Square, the house was not to last. On Ainslee's map just to the left of the house, the area is shaded. This shaded area would become part of Melville Street; on the next extant map, which dates from 1812, the added slice is visible in the road, meaning the house is gone.

87. Ann's expenditures are itemized in an account book that is among the contents of CS235/W/26/2/33 ("Miss Marianne Woods and Miss Jane Pirie v. Dame Cumming Gordon: Damages and Reparation," 1812), a massive file consisting of fourteen bundles, held at the NRS. The material in the file is what is left of the documents that were reviewed by the Court of Session in 1811–12. For more on this collection, see Frances B. Singh, "Dispose or Destroy: The Textual History of Woods and Pirie Against Dame Helen Cumming Gordon," *Journal of the Edinburgh Bibliographic Society* 11 (2016): 14–15.

88. *MWJP*, 140 ("State of the Process," June 14, 1811).

89. Heather A. Weir, "Helping the Unlearned: Sarah Trimmer's Commentary on the Bible," in *Recovering Nineteenth-Century Commentators of the Bible*, ed. Christiana de Groot and Marion Ann Taylor (Atlanta: Society of Biblical Literature, 2007): 24–28.

90. De Bellaigue, 113–18. William Roughead, who brought the life of Jane Cumming to the attention of a wide reading public in the twentieth century, implicitly recognized the school's Catholic convent roots, for he titled his section about the school "Regiment of Women." The phrase itself was coined by John Knox, the sixteenth-century Scottish Protestant reformer, to attack rule by women, particularly Catholic queens such as Mary, Queen of Scots, and her mother Mary of Guise, who served as regent for her. Roughead's use of the phrase is further amplified in chapter 7.

91. *MWJP*, 25 ("State of the Process," June 14, 1811).

92. Fletcher, *Autobiography*, 22.

93. Janet Munro's book was submitted as evidence to the Court of Session and is to be found in CS235/-.

94. Fletcher, 21–22.

95. Milton, *Paradise Lost*, book 11, ll. 618–19.

96. *MWJP*, 22 ("State of the Process," June 14, 1811).

97. Fletcher, 85.

98. Ibid, 92.

99. *MWJP*, 5 ("Additional Petition," October 10, 1811).

100. *MWJP*, 5, 4 ("Additional Petition," October 10, 1811).

101. *MWJP*, 96 ("State of the Process," June 14, 1811).

102. This is how Mrs. Fletcher described her four years at Manor House in Fletcher, *Autobiography*, 20.

103. *MWJP*, 126 ("State of the Process," June 14, 1811).

104. *In the House of Lords, Cumming Gordon v. Woods and Pirie, The Appellant's Case*, 1812, 1.

Chapter Three

1. Julian Small, "The Architecture of Robert Adam: Houses and Shops in Leith Street," https://sites.scran.ac.uk/ada/documents/leithstreet/leith_street.htm, accessed August 10, 2019; .*A Biographical Dictionary of Actors, Actresses, Musicians and Other Stage Personnel in London, 1600–1800*, comp. Philip Highfill, Jr., Kalman A. Burnim, and Edward A. Langham (Carbondale: Southern Illinois University Press, 1993), s.v. "William Woods," in *Edinburgh and Leith Directory to July 1801*, 208, https://archive.org/details/edinburghleithd01aitc/page208, accessed November 9, 2018.

2. *MWJP*, 32 ("Additional Petition," October 10, 1811).

3. *MWJP*, 122, 22 ("State of the Process, June 14, 1811).

4. *MWJP*, 2, 31 ("Additional Petition," October 10, 1811).

5. *MWJP*, 142 ("State of the Process," June 14, 1811).

6. Katharine Glover, *Elite Women and Polite Society in Eighteenth-Century Scotland* (Woodbridge: Boydell Press, 2011), 103.

7. See William Perry, "Alexander Penrose Forbes: Bishop of Brechin, the Scottish Pusey" (London: Society for the Promulgation of Christian Knowledge, 1939), available online via Project Canterbury, http://anglicanhistory.org/scotland/apforbes/perry/chapter1.html, accessed September 30, 2019.

8. On elocution classes in Edinburgh in the latter half of the eighteenth century, see Roy Porter, "Science, Provincial Culture and Public Opinion in Enlightenment England," in *The Eighteenth-Century Town: A Reader in English Urban History 1688–1820*, ed. Peter Boursay (New York: Routledge, 1990), 252; Joan C. Beal, "Prescriptivism and the Suppression of Variation," in *Eighteenth-Century English: Ideology and Change*, ed. Peter Boursay (Cambridge: Cambridge

University Press, 2010), 23; Marina Dossena, "Scottishness and the Book Trade: Print and Scotticisms," in *The Edinburgh History of the Book in Scotland*, vol. 2, ed. Stephen W. Brown and Warren McDougall (Edinburgh: Edinburgh University Press, 2012), 545–50. The quotation is part of the title of a 1791 book, *The Young Gentleman and Lady's Monitor, and English Teacher's Assistant*; its author was the Edinburgh-born John Hamilton Moore, most of whose other works deal with aspects of seamanship.

9. As a writer, he could not plead (that is, argue a case) in the Court of Session—that privilege was reserved for advocates—but he could do chamber work (that is, give legal advice and provide legal services, such as draft contracts or prepare claims; today he would be called a solicitor. Explanation courtesy of John Cairns, professor of legal history, Edinburgh University, personal communication, August 21, 2018.

10. *MWJP*, 2 ("The Additional Petition of Woods and Pirie," October 11, 1811), states that Marianne is "the elder of the two"; however, it was the other way around. Genealogical databases reveal that Marianne was christened on October 13, 1781, and Jane on March 26, 1779.

11. *MWJP*, 134 ("State of the Process," June 14, 1811).

12. Elizabeth Hamilton, *Letters on the Elementary Principles of Education*, vol. 2, 3rd ed. (Boston, 1825), 222.

13. *MWJP*, 152–53 ("State of the Process," June 14, 1811).

14. *MWJP*, 4 ("Replies," June 29, 1820).

15. See Christine Walker, "Pursuing Her Profits: Women in Jamaica, Atlantic Slavery and a Globalising Market, 1700–60," *Gender and History* 26, no. 3 (2014): 478–501.

16. Quoted in Alexandra Shepard, "Minding Their Own Business: Married Women and Credit in Early Eighteenth-Century London," *Transactions of the Royal Historical Society* 25 (2015).

17. Ibid. See also Alexander Shephard, "Crediting Female Friendship," *The History of Emotions Blog: Conversations about the History of Feeling*, March 24, 2014, www.qmul.ac.uk/emotions.

18. On family-run schools, see Susan Skedd, "Women Teachers and the Expansion of Girls' Schooling in England, c. 1760–1820," in *Gender in Eighteenth-Century England: Roles, Representations and Responsibilities*, ed. Hannah Barker and Elaine Chalus (London: Routledge, 1997): 110–12.

19. Sarah Hackett is discussed in chapter 2.

20. "Female Boarding Schools," in *The Female Preceptor, Essays on the Duties of the Female Sex, Conducted by a Lady in the Years 1813 and 1814* (London: 1814), 192, 140, 384. See also "Educating Your Daughters—A Guide to English Boarding Schools in 1814," Susanna Ives blog, March 10, 2013, Susannaives.com/WordPress/?s=educating+your+daughters.

21. Benger, 1:148, 178.

22. Hamilton, *Letters Addressed to the Daughter of a Nobleman*, 2.

23. *MWJP*, 138, 134 ("State of the Process," June 14, 1811).

24. *MWJP*, 134 ("State of the Process," June 14, 1811).

25. *MWJP*, 120 ("State of the Process," June 14, 1811).
26. "Christmas," quoted in Benger, 1:41.
27. Sophie Haslett, "A Million Dollar Friendship! Meet the BFFs Turned Business Partners Who Have Made a Fortune by Launching Companies with Each Other—and the Secrets to Their Success," *Daily Mail Australia*, July 30, 2018.
28. *MWJP*, 56 ("State of the Process," June 14, 1811).
29. Glover et al., 71–76.
30. *MWJP*, 152 ("State of the Process," June 14, 1811). Subsequent citations of "State of the Process" in this section appear parenthetically in text by page number.
31. *MWJP*, 53 ("Additional Petition," October 10, 1811), 97 ("State of the Process," June 14, 1811).
32. *MWJP*, 53 ("Additional Petition," October 10, 1811); 97 ("State of the Process," June 14, 1811).
33. *MWJP*, 136 ("State of the Process," June 14, 1811).
34. *Memoirs of a Highland Lady*, 1:98, 97.
35. Ibid., 1:136.
36. Sasha Handley, *Sleep in Early Modern England* (New Haven, CT: Yale University Press, 2016), 178–80.
37. James Grant, *Cassell's Old and New Edinburgh: Its History, Its People and Its Places*, vol. 3 (London: Cassell, Peter, Galpin & Co., 1886), 143.
38. Ibid., 143–47; *Portobello Architecture Heritage Trail* (Portobello Heritage Trust and Amenity Society, 2011).
39. Handley, 176–78.
40. *MWJP*, 80 ("State of the Process," June 14, 1811).
41. See, for example, Brendon, 50–65.
42. HL, *Gordon Cumming v. Woods and Pirie, Additional Case for the Appellant*, 1816, 8. In Moncreiff.
43. *MWJP*, 147 ("State of the Process," June 14, 1811).
44. *MWJP*, 149 ("State of the Process," June 14, 1811).
45. On schoolgirl crushes, see Havelock Ellis, *Studies in the Psychology of Sex*, vol. 1 (New York: Random House, 1942), 368–84; and Martha Vicinus, "Distance and Desire: English Boarding-School Friendships," *Signs* 9, no. 4 (1984): 600–622.
46. The three preceding quotations are from *MWJP*, 94 ("State of the Process," June 14, 1811).
47. De Bellaigue, 116.
48. *MWJP*, 94 ("State of the Process," June 14, 1811).
49. *MWJP*, 57, 60 ("State of the Process," June 14, 1811).
50. Letter to Miss J.B., November 8, 1818. Quoted in Benger, 2, 15.
51. *MWJP*, 71, 64 ("State of the Process," June 14, 1811).
52. *MWJP*, 97 ("State of the Process," June 14, 1811).
53. This path can be traced easily on Robert Kirkwood, "This Plan of the City of Edinburgh and Its Environs" (Edinburgh, 1817). Maps.nls.uk/joins/416/html.

54. Jemima Mayers, "Construction Techniques of the 18th Century," 18th Century History Articles, www.history1700s.com.

55. The preceding two quotations are from *MWJP*, 7 ("Answers," February 22, 1812).

56. John Borthwick, *A Treatise of the Law of Libel and Slander: As Applied in Scotland, in Criminal Prosecutions and in Actions of Damages: With an Appendix, Containing Reports of Several Cases Respecting Defamation, which Have Not Been Hitherto Published* (Edinburgh, 1826), 194, 317.

57. *MWJP*, 135–36 ("State of the Process," June 14, 1811).

58. *MWJP*, 136 ("State of the Process," June 14, 1811).

59. *MWJP*, 136 ("State of the Process," June 14, 1811).

60. *MWJP*, 128 ("State of the Process," June 14, 1811).

61. *MWJP*, 2 ("Condescendence," January 28, 1820).

62. Anne Grant of Laggan, *Memoir and Correspondence*, ed. J. T. Grant (London: 1845), 2nd ed., 3 vols., 1:291–93.

63. *MWJP*, 21 ("State of the Process," June 14, 1811).

64. Theo Van Der Meer, "Tribades on Trial: Female Same-Sex Offenders in Late Eighteen-Century Amsterdam," *Journal of the History of Sexuality* 1, no. 3 (1991): 424–30.

65. *MWJP*, 1–2 ("State of the Process," June 14, 1811). Note that although the summons insinuates that Woods and Pirie were guilty of criminal conduct, this was always a civil suit.

66. Brodie was a cabinet maker from a well-respected family who led a double life, businessman by day and burglar by night. Smith was his accomplice. Stevenson's *Strange Case of Jekyll and Hyde* was inspired by the case.

67. Clerk's summing-up speech of June 11, 1811. In John Clerk, ed., *The Notorious Drumsheugh Case of 1810: Miss Marianne Woods and Miss Jane Pirie v. Dame Cumming Gordon of Altyre* (Edinburgh: 1810–12).

68. Jonathan Swift, "Corinna, A Ballad," l. 30.

Chapter Four

1. Personal emails from James Hamilton, Research Principal at The Society of Writers to Her Majesty's Signety, and John Cairns, Edinburgh University, both dated February 3, 2015. See also *Parliament House Portraits: The Art Collection of the Faculty of Advocates* (Edinburgh: Faculty of Advocates, 1999).

2. "Legal Costume—I," *Irish Law Times and Solicitors' Journal* 18 (1884): 161–63.

3. The young man was Alexander Maconochie (1787–1860); after leaving the navy, he distinguished himself as a geographer and a penal reformer.

4. *MWJP*, 3 ("State of the Process," June 14, 1811).

5. Lenanan, "Legitimacy," 56–57.

6. *MWJP*, 17 ("Answers," January 22, 1812), 16–17 ("Additional Petition," October 10, 1811).

7. *MWJP*, 7 ("State of the Process," June 14, 1811).
8. *MWJP*, 5–6 ("State of the Process," June 14, 1811).
9. *MWJP*, 7 ("State of the Process," June 14, 1811).
10. *MWJP*, 5, 35 ("State of the Process," June 14, 1811).
11. *MWJP*, 45 ("Answers," June 10, 1811).
12. L. Fleming Fallon and Tish Davidson, "Voyeurism," in *The Gale Encyclopedia of Mental Health*, ed. Kristin Key, 3rd ed. (Detroit: Gale, 2012), 2:1, 642–44. In *The Gale Virtual Reference Library*.
13. Laran Joseph, "Voyeuristic Disorder DSM-5 302.82 (F65.3)," in *Theravive*, https://www.theravive.com/therapedia/voyeuristic-disorder-dsm–5-302.82-(F65.3), accessed July 11, 2017.
14. John R. Clarke, *Looking at Lovemaking: Constructions of Sexuality in Roman Art 100 B.C.–A.D. 250* (Berkeley: University of California Press, 1998), 73–78.
15. Greta Olson, "Keyholes in Eighteenth-Century Novels as Liminal Spaces Between the Public and Private Spheres," in *Sites of Discourse—Public and Private Spheres—Legal Culture: Papers from a Conference at the Technical University of Dresden, December 2001*, ed. Uwe Böker and Julie A. Hibbard (Amsterdam: Rodopi, 2002): 159–62.
16. George E. Haggarty, "Keyhole Testimony: Witnessing Sodomy in the Eighteenth Century," *Eighteenth Century* 44, no. 2/3 (2003): 172.
17. Ibid., 177.
18. Barbara Benedict, *Curiosity: A Cultural History of Early Modern Inquiry* (Chicago: University of Chicago Press, 2002), 18–20, 49, 204–34.
19. Haggerty, 107.
20. Michelle Bobker, "The Shape of Intimacy: Private Space and the British Social Imagination, 1650–1770" (PhD diss., Rutgers University, 2007), 56.
21. Haggerty, 167–71. On sodomy trials and the navy, see Gilbert, 72–98; Oosterhoff, 229–35; LeJacq, 103–16; Fury, 74–80.
22. DEP 175/111.
23. *The Exhibition of Female Flagellants*, 2 vols. (London: 1777–85). See Julie Peakman, *Mighty Lewd Books: The Development of Pornography in Eighteenth-Century England* (Basingstoke: Palgrave Macmillan, 2003), 178–79.
24. In Lillian Hellman's play, Mary Tilford's encounter with an obscene book is offered as the source of her allegation about the teachers' sexuality. See chapter 7.
25. *MWJP*, 72 ("State of the Process," June 14, 1811).
26. "Advising Woods and Pirie Against Lady Cumming Gordon, June 28, 1811," in Moncreiff.
27. "Notes of Debate and Judgment on the Objections to Miss Jane Cumming as a Witness, 1811," in Moncreiff.
28. DEP 175/106.
29. Van Der Meer, 434–45.
30. *MWJP*, 157, 158 ("State of the Process," June 14, 1811).
31. *MWJP*, 2 ("Condescendence," January 28, 1820).

32. *MWJP*, 133 ("State of the Process," June 14, 1811).

33. See Jessica A. Gibson, "'What are you—A Woman I suppose': Women in the Eighteenth-Century British Court" (MA thesis, University of Oregon, 2013).

34. George William Thomson Omond, *The Lord Advocates of Scotland from the Close of the Fifteenth Century to the Passing of the Reform Bill* (Edinburgh: David Douglas, 1883), 1:205.

35. "Notes of June 18, 1811," in Moncreiff.

36. *MWJP*, 46 ("State of the Process," June 14, 1811). Subsequent citations of "State of the Process" in this section appear parenthetically in text by page number.

37. The description of Lord Robertson is based on a portrait now at the Metropolitan Museum of Art in New York City, while that of Lord Newton is derived from James Paterson, *Kay's Edinburgh Portraits*, vol. 1 (London: Hamilton, Adams, 1885), 145–47.

38. On actively involved women spectators at trials, see Linda Mulcahy, "Watching Women: What Illustrated Courtroom Scenes Tell Us About Women and the Public Sphere in the Nineteenth Century," *Journal of Law and Society* 42, no. 1 (2015): 66–68.

39. Her testimony forms part of the printed document called "State of the Process," June 14, 1811. Her testimony in the notetaker's handwriting is preserved in CS235/-. The two are not identical.

40. I checked the outward-bound passenger lists of East India Company ships heading toward Calcutta from late 1803 through 1804 but found nobody by the name of Coongee.

41. In the handwritten version of Jane's testimony, after Jane's statement that "she herself had not learnt to speak English before she left India," Lord Hope started to ask her about her knowledge of English when she arrived. The note-taker got as far as writing "when she arrived in this" before breaking off. The fragment is neatly lined through. Lord Hope then went back to the subject of her Indian upbringing, asking Jane "whether while she was in India at school or otherwise, she heard or observed among the children or others any such practices as she has described took place between the pursuers." Since the phrase that would have led Jane to talk about what might have happened on the boat was crossed out by the notetaker, it does not appear in the printed transcript.

42. See chapter 2 for a discussion of Wollstonecraft's critique of the practice of bedsharing in girls' boarding schools. The unwritten rules governing consensual bedsharing by friends of the same sex is discussed in chapter 3.

43. Davidson, 21.

44. Ibid., 73 ("Answers," February 22, 1812).

45. Ibid., 61 ("Speeches," 1811–12).

Chapter Five

1. Erskine's concluding speech was never printed. It exists only in gist form in handwritten notes bound in Moncreiff. Hereafter referred to as "Erskine, June 10."
2. *The Merry Wives of Windsor*, act 1, scene 4, ll. 76–78; "Erskine, June 10."
3. Ibid.
4. This speech exists in holograph only and is bound with his set of the proceedings (*The Notorious Drumsheugh Case*), now housed at the Signet Library. Roughead, who owned this set, quoted from the speech in his account of the case, discussed in chapter 7. Hereafter referred to as Clerk, June 11.
5. Ibid.
6. Ibid.
7. The full poem is given in appendix C.
8. See also Frances B. Singh, "More . . . Drumsheugh Scandal." *Signet Magazine* no. 5 (2013): 26–28.
9. On the subject of nursery crime, see, for example, David Finkelhor and Linda Meyer Williams, eds. *Nursery Crimes: Sexual Abuse in Day Care* (Newbury Park: Sage, 1988).
10. Clerk, June 11.
11. Cranstoun's summing-up speech, like that of Erskine's, is preserved in the form of notes bound with Moncreiff's set of papers. Hereafter referred to as Cranstoun, June 18.
12. The notes of their in camera deliberations from 1811 are in three places. A few were printed in *MWJP* and are to be found in a section of that book entitled "Notes of the Speeches of Lords Robertson, Glenlee, Newton and Polkemmet. . . ." Handwritten notes are found in Moncreiff's set, in a section entitled "June 25, 1811. Advising *Woods v. Pirie* agst Lady Cumming Gordon," hereafter referred to "Advising 1811." Meadowbank's handwritten personal reflections and notes from 1811 are also found in his personal set. The 1811 notes found in Meadowbank's set are referred to as Meadowbank 1811. Sentences in this set that were carried over into print are given the *MWJP* section and page reference. On judges' notes in general and how they reflect the mindset of the judges when they felt free to say what they really thought, felt and believed, see James Oldham, "Eighteenth-Century Judges' Notes: How They Explain, Correct and Enhance the Reports." *American Journal of Legal History* 31, no. 1 (1987): 9–42.
13. "Advising 1811."
14. *MWJP*, 55 ("Speeches"). Subsequent citations of "Speeches" in this section appear parenthetically in text by page number.
15. "Advising 1811."
16. Meadowbank 1811.
17. "Advising 1811."
18. Ibid.
19. Ibid.

20. *MWJP*, 8 ("Notes").
21. *MWJP*, 15 ("Notes").
22. Trial by jury would come to Scotland in 1816.
23. *MWJP*, 15 ("Notes").
24. "Advising 1811."
25. *MWJP*, 28 ("Additional Petition," October 10, 1811). Subsequent citations in this section appear parenthetically in text as "Additional Petition," followed by page number.
26. *MWJP*, 3 ("Answers," February 12, 1812). Subsequent citations in this section appear parenthetically in text as "Answers," followed by page number.
27. This description of the notebook is highly suspect. Of all the evidence offered for inspection during the case, Jane's notebook is the only item that was not in the box of materials deposited by the Court of Session at the National Records of Scotland some twenty years after the case concluded—or to be more precise, it was not in the box when I inspected the contents in 2015. While it is possible that the book merely got lost in that interval, Helen's meddlesome nature and in-law relationship with one of the judges (Lord Glenlee) and the principal clerk (Colin MacKenzie) suggests that she somehow made that book disappear.
28. The first recorded use of "nunnery" to mean "brothel" appears in Thomas Nashe's 1593 *Teares Over Jerusalem*. Its far more famous use is in *Hamlet* (1600), where Hamlet tells Ophelia three times to take herself to a nunnery. In the eighteenth century, the press often referred to brothels as nunneries and prostitutes as nuns.
29. Sherry Velasco, *Lesbianism in Early Modern Spain* (Nashville: Vanderbilt University Press, 2011), 90–104. When Helen's lawyers submitted their bibliography of lesbianism entitled *Authorities with Regard to the Practice of Tribadism*, none of the ecclesiastical figures mentioned by Velasco were cited.
30. *MWJP*, 25 ("Answers," February 22, 1812).
31. See *Report from Select Committee on the Supreme Court of Judicature in Scotland* (Great Britain: Parliament. House of Commons, 1840), 259.
32. Craft-Fairchild, 421.
33. Meadowbank's set includes not only his notes from 1812, when the case was heard on appeal, but also the notes of Lord Gillies's 1812 determination. This material is referred to as Meadowbank 1812. The 1812 notes bound in Moncreiff's set also include the notes of Lord Gillies's decision, but taken down by a different recorder. This material is referred to as *Advising of Petition and Answers*, 1812.
34. *Advising of Petition and Answers*, 1812.
35. Ibid.
36. Fraser, *Highland Home*, 11.
37. *Advising of Petition and Answers*, 1812. Further quotations in this section are from *Advising of Petition and Answers*, 1812.

38. The reference to the poisoning taking place in the south of Scotland and the detail about the case appearing in the newspapers is found in Meadowbank 1812. The Moncreiff note-taker took down the motive as wanting to eat fowl and drink wine, while Meadowbank's note-taker, rather than give a specific reason, implied that it was trifling.

39. The case records are at the National Records of Scotland. See AD 14/12/66 (Precognition Against Helen Kennedy for the crime of murder by poisoning). She received the acquitting "not proven" verdict. See Karen Jane Merry, "Murder by Poison in Scotland During the Nineteenth and Early Twentieth Centuries" (PhD diss., University of Glasgow, 2010).

40. The allusion made its way into print. See *MWJP*, 99 ("Notes").

41. Meadowbank 1812. Further quotations in this section are from Meadowbank 1812.

42. See Peakman.

43. *MWJP*, 58–59 ("Speeches"). Subsequent citations of "Speeches" in this section appear parenthetically in text by page number.

44. Leneman, "Legitimacy," 47.

45. MS. 20471.34, *Skene of Rubislaw Papers*, "Letter of Colin MacKenzie to James Skene." MacKenzie's wife was the sister of Louisa Forbes's husband.

46. Ibid.

47. *The Oxford Dictionary of Art and Artists*, s.v., "Eidophusikon, Eidophusikon.

48. HL, *The Appellant's Case*, 22. Subsequent citations in this section appear parenthetically in text as *Appellant's Case* with page number.

49. HL, *The Respondents' Case*, 2. Subsequent citations in this section appear parenthetically in text as *Respondents' Case* with page number.

50. The argument was specious. See, for example, the cases of Susan Cochrane Moorhouse and the children of Alexander Read, detailed in the introduction, and that of Eliza Raine, discussed in the conclusion.

51. HL, *Additional Case for the Appellant*, 10. Subsequent citations in this section appear parenthetically in text as *Additional Case for Appellant* with page number.

52. HL, *Additional Case for the Respondents*, 7.

53. On *veritas convicii*, see chapter 4.

54. *MWJP*, 2 ("Condescendence," January 28, 1820).

55. *MWJP*, 6 ("Answers," February 12, 1820).

56. William Shakespeare, Sonnet 129, l.2.

57. *MWJP*, 13 ("Replies," June 29, 1820).

58. Appendix to *Replies for Miss Woods and Pirie*, November 14, 1820, 2. In Moncreiff.

59. Shakespeare, Sonnet 129, l.1.

60. DEP 175/142.

61. Ibid.

62. The amount could well be higher. I totted up the figures based on surviving documents.

Chapter Six

1. DEP 175/161 (1).
2. Grant, *Memoirs*, 2:44–45.
3. Ibid.
4. Longe cloth is a soft muslin fabric used for shifts or nightgowns. Welsh flannel is a napped wool. As it was believed that Welsh flannel protected against colds and rheumatism, petticoats and undergarments were made from it. Cotton hose was pricier than woolen hose and probably less scratchy, but definitely not fancy like hose made of silk.
5. DEP 175/111.
6. This comment refers to John Shanks, former keeper of the cathedral, whose tombstone states that he removed "many thousand cubic yards of rubbish" from the cathedral.
7. On Aberdeen as a medical center, see J. D. Comrie, *History of Scottish Medicine to 1860*, vol. 1 (London: Ballière, Tindall and Cox, 1932), 139–59.
8. DEP 175/111.
9. Robert Young, *Annals of the Parish and Burgh of Elgin from the Twelfth Century to the Year 1876* (Elgin, 1870), 58.
10. DEP 175/128.
11. Mrs. Jane Tulloch, inventory of personal estate dated September 17, 1845, Elgin Sheriff Court Inventories, SC26/39/5.
12. See G. Campbell H. Paton, "Husband and Wife: Property Rights and Relationship," in *An Introduction to Scottish Legal History* (Edinburgh: Stair Society, 1958): 100; and Rebecca Probert, *Marriage Law and Practice in the Long Eighteenth Century: A Reassessment* (Cambridge: Cambridge University Press, 2009), 66.
13. The statement appears on the inventory of Jane's estate. The relevant phrase is as follows: "The said William Tulloch by said contract of marriage renouncing and making over in her the said deceased's favor his *Jus Mariti* to the said sum."
14. Lord Hope, in his capacity as Lord Advocate and MP, shepherded this act through the House of Commons; eight years later, he would be interrogating Jane.
15. William W. M. Jacob, *The Clerical Profession in the Long Eighteenth Century 1680–1840* (Oxford: Oxford University. Press, 2007), 157–58.
16. The act actually restored this right, which had been taken away from them in 1688.
17. Personal emails to author from R. Hugh Gair, a descendant of Tulloch's sister, dated December 29, 2011, and January 8, 2012.
18. On Rose's career, see Hew Scott, *Fasti Ecclesiae Scoticanae: The Succession of Ministers in the Church of Scotland*, vol. 6 (Edinburgh: Oliver & Boyd, 1926), 383.
19. Ian R. M. Mowat, "The Moray Firth Province: Trade and Family Links in the Eighteenth Century," in *Firthlands of Ross and Sutherland*, ed.

John R. Baldwin (Edinburgh: Scottish Society for Northern Studies, 1986), 69–88.

20. The Reverend Alexander Macadam, "Parish of Nigg (County and Synod of Ross, Presbytery of Tain)," in *The Statistical Account of Scotland 1791–1799*, vol. 13 (Edinburgh, 1794), 14.

21. *Annals of the General Assembly of the Church of Scotland, from the Origin of the Relief in 1752 to the Rejection of Schism in 1766*, vol. 2 (Edinburgh, 1840), 293.

22. Hugh Miller, *My Schools and Schoolmaster or The Story of My Education* (1854; repr. Edinburgh: B & W Publishing, 2002), 122.

23. *The Principal Acts of the General Assembly of the Church of Scotland* (Edinburgh, 1811), 46.

24. Ibid.

25. Personal email from Peter Mennie, Assistant Archivist at Highland Archive Centre, which houses the church minutes of the Tain Presbytery, to the author, November 25, 2011.

26. Presbytery of Forres—Minutes, CH 2/162/2/149.

27. Richard Rose, "Parish of Drainie," in *The New Statistical Account of Scotland*, vol. 13 (Edinburgh, 1845), 157.

28. Breitenbach, 99–117.

29. Michael Gordon and M. Charles Bernstein, "Mate Choice and Domestic Life in the Nineteenth-Century Marriage Manual," *Journal of Marriage and the Family* 32, no. 4 (1970): 667.

30. "Parochial Schools in Scotland," *Tait's Edinburgh Magazine*, vol. 11 (September 1844): 567.

31. *The Taming of the Shrew*, act 2, scene 2, ll. 266–68.

32. DEP 175/162(4).

33. Ibid.

34. CH2/162/5/291.

35. Martha F. Bowden, "Mrs. Yorick and the Midwife: Women's Roles in the Eighteenth-Century Church of England," *Dalhousie Review* 82, no. 3 (2002): 377–93.

36. *Hints to a Clergyman's Wife; or Female Parochial Duties Practically Illustrated* (London: Holdsworth and Ball, 1832), 34–35.

37. Lois A. Boyd, "Presbyterian Ministers' Wives—A Nineteenth-Century Portrait," *Journal of Presbyterian History* 59, no. 1 (1981): 5.

38. *Hints*, 41–42.

39. William Douglas, *Ministers' Wives* (New York: Harper & Row, 1965).

40. Quoted in Emily Mace, "In the Parsonage, In the Parish: Experiences of Nineteenth Century Unitarian Ministers' Wives," Unitarian Universalist Women's Heritage Society (February 2002), www.uuwhs.org/mace.php, accessed July 11, 2010.

41. For a comprehensive study of Sarah Ripley, see Joan W. Goodwin, *The Remarkable Mrs. Ripley: The Life of Sarah Alden Bradford Ripley* (Boston: Northeastern University Press, 1998).

42. *Records of the Presbytery of Forres—Minutes, 1794–1844*, CH2/162/5/305.

43. DEP 175/142.
44. Ibid.
45. Presbytery of Forres—Minutes, 1794–1844. CH2/162/5/305.
46. DEP 175/142.
47. Ibid.
48. William Tulloch, "Parish of Dollas or Dallas," in *The New Statistical Account of Scotland*, vol. 13 (Edinburgh: 1835–45): 200.
49. Christian Charles, will dated July 31, 1826. Elgin Sheriff Court Wills, SC26/38/1.
50. DEP 175/165.
51. Helen Cumming Gordon, will dated December 6, 1832, Elgin Sheriff Court Wills, SC26/38/2.
52. A. Werrity and L. J. McEwen, "The 'Muckle Spate of 1829'—Reconstruction of a Catastrophic Flood on the River Findhorn, Scottish Highlands," in *Paleofloods, Historical Floods and Climatic Variability: Applications in Flood Risk Assessment*, ed. V. R. Thornycraft et al. (Madrid: Centro de Ciencias Medioambientales, 2003), 128.
53. Thomas Dick Lauder, *The Great Floods of August 1829 in the Province of Moray and Adjoining Districts*, 3rd ed. (Elgin: R. Stewart, 1873), 83–85.
54. A. Werrity and L. J. McEwen, "The Muckle Spate of 1829: The Physical and Societal Impact of a Catastrophic Flood on the River Findhorn, Scottish Highlands," *Transactions of the Institute of British Geographers* New Series, 32, no. 1(2007): 85.
55. Dick Lauder, 85.
56. Ibid., 85, 86.
57. Ibid., 86.
58. DEP 175/162(5). See appendix D for the entire letter.
59. Jane Tulloch, will of Jane Tulloch dated October 11, 1844, Elgin Sheriff Court Wills, SC26/38/5.
60. Ibid.
61. DEP 175/144. The letter is quoted in full in appendix C.
62. Ibid.
63. See, for example, Luisa Fernanda Habigzang et al., "Cognitive Behavioral Group Therapy for Sexually Abused Girls," *Revista de Saude Publica*, 43, no. 1 (August 2009).
64. DEP 175/145.
65. DEP 175/107.
66. The history of the Ten Years' Conflict is the subject of many books. See, for example, Robert Buchanan, *The Ten Years' Conflict: Being the History of the Disruption of the Church of Scotland*, 2 vols. (Glasgow, 1849); Hugh Watt, *Thomas Chalmers and the Disruption* (Edinburgh: T. Nelson, 1943); John H. S. Burleigh, *A Church History of Scotland* (London: Oxford University Press, 1960); Stewart J. Brown, *Thomas Chalmers and the Godly Commonwealth in Scotland* (Oxford: Oxford University Press, 1982); A. C. Cheyne, *The Ten Years' Conflict and The Disruption* (Edinburgh: Scottish Academic Press, 1993).

67. James McCosh, *The Wheat and the Chaff Gathered into Bundles: A Statistical Contribution towards the History of the Recent Disruption of the Scottish Ecclesiastical Establishment* (Perth, 1843), 92.

68. Ibid., 93, 92.

69. Ibid., 11.

70. W. W. Ewing, ed., *The Annals of the Free Church of Scotland*, 2 vols. (Edinburgh: T & T Clark, 1914), 2:206.

71. DEP 175/162(4).

72. Ewing, 2:206.

73. Jane Tulloch, will dated October 11, 1844, Elgin Sheriff Court Wills, SC26/38/5.

74. Ibid.

75. Robert Douglas, "Annals of the Parish of Dallas" (unpublished manuscript), Moray Council Local Heritage Centre, Elgin, Scotland. This particular paraphrase of *John* 14: 25–25—which was "allowed by the . . . Kirk of Scotland, and appointed to be sung in congregations and families"—appears in *The Psalms of David in Metre, Translated and Diligently Compared with the Original* (Edinburgh, 1809), 11; cover.

76. CH2/1129/2, "Dallas Kirk Session."

77. DEP 175/107.

78. William Tulloch, inventory of the estate of William Tulloch, dated September 26, 1846, Elgin Sheriff Court Inventories, SC/26/39/5.

79. DEP 175/145.

80. Ibid.

81. Personal email from Lord Simon Woolton, a collateral descendant of Sir William Gordon Cumming, dated November 30, 2010.

Chapter Seven

1. DEP 175/113. Spending on luxury items was common among the Highland gentry. See Stana Nenadic, *Lairds and Luxury*. On Sir William's weak financial situation, see Hay, 169.

2. The letter is held at the Moray Council Local Heritage Centre, Elgin, Scotland, LMisc267. Further quotations in this section are from this letter.

3. Formally called *Gordon Cumming v. Nakeska* (Eleanora's married name), documents and other material relating to the lawsuit are held in Boxes 102 and 132 of the Gordon Cumming Depository.

4. Malcolm Page, *King's African Rifles: A History* (Barnsley: Pen & Sword Military, 2011), 152.

5. Personal email from Jane Jamieson, Historical Search Room archivist, National Records of Scotland, January 26, 2015.

6. John Borthwick, *A Treatise on the Law of Libel and Slander, as Applied in Scotland, in Criminal Prosecutions and in Actions of Damages: With an Appendix,*

Containing Reports of Several Cases Respecting Defamation which Have Not Hitherto Been Published (Edinburgh: 1826), vi.

7. I am indebted to Mary Ann O'Donnell, who deduced that "JB" was John Borthwick (personal email, December 16, 2013), and Barbara Blumenthal, Neilson Reference Librarian at Smith College, who kindly provided me a scan of the front pastedown and shared other helpful information about the book in an email of December 21, 2013. I have not been able to track down "Dr. Campbell."

8. The book appears in the 1893 catalogue of the U.S. Surgeon General's Office, the predecessor of the National Library of Medicine, under the title of *Trial of Marianne Woods and Jane Pirie Against Dame Helen Cumming Gordon* (Edinburgh, 1811–20). See *Index-Catalogue of the Library of the Surgeon General's Office*, vol. 14 (Washington: Government Printing Office, 1893), 752, 756. For a fuller treatment of the transmission of the proceedings and papers connected with the case, see my "'Dispose or Destroy': The Textual History of *Woods and Pirie Against Dame Helen Cumming Gordon*," *Journal of the Edinburgh Bibliographical Society* 11 (2016): 11–22.

9. *Catalogue of the Private Library of the Late P. Hastie and the Late E. H. Tracy Comprising Biography, History Club and Society Publications* (New York: G. A. Leavitt & Co., 1870), 550.

10. Personal email from Lynn Young, Corporate Archivist & Data Protection Manager, British Library, December 17, 2013.

11. Personal email from James Hamilton, Research Principal at The Society of Writers to her Majesty's Signet, February 9, 2016.

12. The musical, with lyrics by Cynthia Goatley and music by Rebecca Burkhardt of the University of Northern Iowa, was performed at UNI in 2006 and was subsequently revised to focus on the relationship between the teachers. Richard Stirling's play *The Two Janes* was given a staged reading at the Signet in 2013. Suzy Messerole, the creator of the performance piece *Venus Nefanda*, has very kindly shared the script with me.

13. Royal Academy of Dramatic Art, "Scotch Verdict: Reveal Nothing or Lose Everything," January 22, 2015, www.scotchverdict.com/londons-royal-academy-dramatic-art.

14. Richard Whittington-Egan, *William Roughead's Chronicles of Murder* (Moffat: Lochar, 1991), 156–58.

15. Whittington-Egan, 86, 157, 101.

16. William Roughead, "Closed Doors; or The Great Drumsheugh Case." In *Bad Companions* (Edinburgh: W. Green & Son, 1930), 126, 137.

17. Ibid., 127.

18. Ibid., 138.

19. Ibid., 116, 126, 121, 120, 127, 135, 136.

20. Quoted in Whittington-Egan, 86.

21. Ibid.

22. Roughead, 113.

23. The phrases are ascribed to Roughead by Whittington-Egan, 151.

24. Roughead 124, 126.

25. Ibid., 146.

26. Solley seems to have confused Woods and Pirie.

27. Quoted in Andrew P. Lyons and Harriet D. Lyons, *Irregular Connections: A History of Anthropology and Sexuality* (Lincoln: University of Nebraska Press, 2004), 125.

28. The "imp" sentence is quoted in Earle Waldridge, letter to the editor, *Saturday Review of Literature*, March 16, 1935.

29. Jenny S. Spencer, "Sex, Lies, and Revisions: Historicizing Hellman's *The Children's Hour*," *Modern Drama* 47, no. 1 (2004): 46–47.

30. Box 9, Folder 7, Lillian Hellman Papers, Harry Ransom Center, University of Texas, Austin. Hereafter referred to as LHP.

31. On the similarities between eugenics and racism, see Mikko Tuhkanen, "Breeding (and Reading): Lesbian Knowledge, Eugenic Discipline, and *The Children's Hour*," *Modern Fiction Studies* 48, no. 4 (2002): 1002, 1021–22.

32. LHP, Box 9, Folder 7.

33. *Lillian Hellman: The Collected Plays* (Boston: Little, Brown, 1971), 20. This is the definitive edition. All quotations, unless otherwise noted, are from this edition.

34. *MWJP*, 4 ("Condescendence," January 28, 1820), quoted in Roughead, 144.

35. Whittington-Egan, 112.

36. Ibid.

37. Roughead's remark about Hellman's literary rape, thrown off in white heat, proved uncannily accurate. In 1973 Hellman published *Pentimento*, her second volume of memoirs. Its opening chapter was about a woman Hellman said she had personally helped during World War II. It was soon discovered that the chapter was an appropriation of another woman's story. When Mary McCarthy called Hellman a liar on TV, Hellman sued her for libel—and gave further interviews that were a confection of lies and fantasies. Hellman gained a reputation as a liar, a fabricator, and a fantasist; even those sympathetic to her began to feel that she couldn't distinguish between truth and fiction. Once a lionized writer, Hellman's reputation began to sink in her own lifetime, and it has not shown much sign of rising since, despite *The Children's Hour*'s successful run in London in 2011 and Alice Kessler-Harris's well-written and well-reviewed biography aptly entitled *A Difficult Woman: The Challenging Life and Times of Lillian Hellman* (2013). In this sense, it may be said that Roughead prognosticated, more accurately than he did for Jane, that "Miss Hellfire" would reap the whirlwind.

38. Lillian Hellman, *The Children's Hour* (New York: Knopf, 1935), 19; *Four Plays by Lillian Hellman* (New York: Modern Library, 1942), 18.

39. Lillian Hellman, *The Children's Hour*, Acting Edition (New York: Dramatists Play Service, 1981), 48.

40. Lillian Hellman, *The Collected Plays* (Boston: Little Brown, 1971), 47. As far as I can tell, the only occasion that she let "black" stand was in act 3, where Karen exclaims, "It's like that dark hour of the night when, half awake, you

struggle through the black mess you've been dreaming" (55). Nonetheless, she realized that the "black mess" line was problematic. While it is there in the 1971 definitive text, she excised it from the 1952 Acting Edition. There are no references to color or race in either of the two movies based on the play.

41. LHP, Box 126, "Little White Lie May Grow Big, Says Authority."
42. Ibid.
43. LHP, Box 126, "Girl Scared, Hid as 'Hit' Opened" (undated article).
44. Hellman, *Four Plays*, viii.
45. Lillian Hellman, *Three: An Unfinished Woman, Pentimento, Scoundrel Time* (Boston: Little Brown, 1979), 29.
46. Hellman, *Four Plays*, viii.
47. Lewis Funke, "Interview with Lillian Hellman," in *Conversations with Lillian Hellman*, ed. Jackson R. Bryer (Jackson: University of Mississippi Press, 1986), 96.
48. Ibid.
49. Jan Albert, "Sweetest Smelling Baby in New Orleans," in *Conversations with Lillian Hellman*, 167.
50. *Three*, 35–36.
51. Kessler-Harris, 27.
52. Roughead, 116.
53. LHP, Box 9, Folder 7.
54. For a psychological assessment of Mary, see Tanfer Emin Tunc, "Rumours, Gossip and Lies: Social Anxiety and the Evil Child in Lillian Hellman's *The Children's Hour*," *Journal of Literary Studies* 28, no. 3 (2012).
55. LHP, Box 9, Folder 7.
56. *Three*, 148.
57. *Three*, 29.
58. "The Bigger the Lie," interview by Harry Gilroy, in the *New York Times*, December 14, 1952. In Hellman, *The Children's Hour*, Acting Edition, 4.
59. LHP, Box 9, Folder 10.
60. LHP, Box 126, Robert Garland, "Children's Hour, a Moving Tragedy," in the *New York Telegram*, November 21, 1934.
61. LHP, Box 128, Ashton Stevens, "'These Three' Pictures First Child Actress You Would Like To Kill," *ILL American*, March 27, 1936.
62. LHP, Box 50, "Bolton's Theatre Reopens," *Daily Telegraph*, November 11, 1950. Box 50, LHP.
63. LHP, Box 130, Brooks Atkinson, "The Children's Hour," *New York Times*, December 29, 1952; Louis Sheaffer, "*Children* Has Same Wallop but a Change of Emphasis," *Brooklyn Eagle*, January 11, 1953.
64. Unsigned review of *The Children's Hour*, *Feminist Spectator*, March 17, 2011, https://feministspectator.princeton.edu/2011/03/17/the-childrens-hour/.
65. Ben Brantley, "All Over London, Love Hurts," *New York Times*, February 22, 2011.
66. Paul Taylor, "First Night: The Children's Hour, Comedy Theatre, London," *Independent*, February 10, 2011.

67. Mark Cook, "The Guide: Theatre: The Children's Hour," January 22, 2011, *Guardian* (London).
68. *Three*, 309.
69. LHP, Box 50.
70. Ibid.
71. Letter from de la Torre to Whittington-Egan dated September 1984, quoted in Whittington-Egan, 130.
72. Lillian de la Torre, letter to the editor, *New Republic*, February 23, 1953.
73. Ibid.
74. Lilian Faderman, *Scotch Verdict: The Real-Life Story that Inspired "The Children's Hour"* (New York: Columbia University Press, 2013), 291.
75. Judith Halberstam, foreword to *Scotch Verdict*, xi.
76. Faderman, *Scotch Verdict*, 289.
77. Halberstam, vii.

Conclusion

1. On erotic sensitivity to environmental factors, see Lisa M. Diamond, Janna A. Dickenson, and Karen L. Blair, "Stability of Sexual Attractions Across Different Timescales: The Roles of Bisexuality and Gender," *Archives of Sexual Behavior*, 46 (2017): 193–203.
2. Ibid., 194.
3. Ibid., 203.
4. See, for example, C. Helms and C. B. Nemeroff, "The Role of Childhood Trauma in the Neurobiology of Mood and Anxiety Disorders: Preclinical and Clinical Studies," *Biological Psychiatry* 49, no. 12 (2001): 1023–39; J. Kaufman and D. Charney, "Effects of Early Stress on Brain Structure and Function: Implications for Understanding the Relationship Between Child Maltreatment and Depression," *Developmental Psychology* 13, no. 3 (2001): 451–71; B. S. McEwan, "Early Life Influences on Life-Long Patterns of Behavior and Health," *Mental Retardation and Developmental Disabilities Research Review* 9, no. 3 (2003): 149–54; C. B. Nemeroff, "Neurobiological Consequences of Childhood Trauma," *Journal of Clinical Psychology* 65 (2004): 18–28; Jack P. Shonkoff et al., "The Lifelong Effects of Early Childhood Adversity and Toxic Stress," *Pediatrics* (2012), https://doi.org/10.1542/peds.2011-2663; "Chronic Stress, Anxiety Can Damage the Brain, Increase Risk of Major Psychiatric Disorder," *ScienceDaily*, January 21, 2016, www.sciencedaily.com/releases/2016/01/160121121818.htm.
5. The amygdala are two clusters within each of the brain's temporal lobes; they are involved with the experiencing of emotions. The orbitofrontal cortex is believed to be involved with the cognitive processing of decision-making and with rational thought and reasoning in general.
6. Shonkoff et al.
7. Diamond, "Passionate Friendships," 195.

8. Ibid, 194–95.

9. "Position Statement on Child Abuse and Neglect by Adults," *American Journal of Psychiatry* 148, no. 11 (1991): 1626.

10. Cindy M. Meston, Julia R. Heiman, and Paul D. Trapnell, "The Relation Between Early Abuse and Adult Sexuality," *Journal of Sex Research* 36, no. 2(1999): 385–90.

11. Rebecca A. Colman and Cathy Spatz Widom, "Childhood abuse and neglect and adult intimate relationships: A prospective study," *Child Abuse and Neglect* 28, no. 11 (2004): 1146.

12. Ibid., 1133, 1146.

13. Kate M. Scott, Don R. Smith, and Pete M. Ellis, "Prospectively Ascertained Child Maltreatment and Its Association with DSM-IV Disorders in Young Adults," *Archives of General Psychiatry* 67, no. 7 (2010): 712–19.

14. Hanna Raaska et al., "Experiences of School Bullying among Internationally Adopted Children: Results from the Finnish Adoption (FINADO) Study," *Child Psychiatry and Human Development* 43, no. 4 (2012): 592–611; Marko Elovainio et al., "Associations Between Attachment-Related Symptoms and Later Psychological Problems Among International Adoptees: Results from the FINADO Study," *Scandinavian Journal of Psychology* 56, no. 1 (2015): 53–61.

15. B. Hawk and R. B. McCall, "CBCL Behavior Problems of Post-Institutionalized International Adoptees," *Clinical Child and Family Psychology Review* 13 (2010): 208.

16. Ibid., 199, 208.

17. Monica Pignotti, "Reactive Attachment Disorder and International Adoption: A Systematic Synthesis," *Scientific Review of Mental Health Practice* 8, no. 1 (2011): 30–45.

18. Among recent studies, see, for example, Sara Elizabeth Kay Hall and Glenn Geher, "Behavioral and Personality Characteristics of Children with Reactive Attachment Disorder," *Journal of Psychology* 137, no. 21 (2003): 145–62; Ashley L. Hill et al., "Profiles of Externalizing Behavior Problems for Boys and Girls Across Preschool: The Roles of Emotion Regulation and Inattention," *Developmental Psychology* 42, no. 5 (2006): 913–28; Brandi Hawk and Robert B. McCall, "CBCL Behavior Problems of Post-Institutionalized International Adoptees," *Clinical Child and Family Psychology Review* 13, no. 2 (2010): 199–211; Monica Pignotti, "Reactive Attachment Disorder and International Adoption: A Systematic Synthesis," *Scientific Review of Mental Health Practice* 8, no. 1 (2011): 30–49. The long-term effects of child abuse, psychological, emotional, and sexual, are further discussed in the conclusion.

19. Personal email from Helena Whitbread, author, dated January 20, 2017.

20. George A. Bonnano, "Loss, Trauma and Human Resilience: Have We Underestimated the Human Capacity to Thrive After Extremely Aversive Events," *American Psychologist* 59, no. 1 (2004): 20.

21. David Finkelhor, "The Trauma of Child Sexual Abuse," *Journal of Interpersonal Violence* 2, no. 4 (1987): 348–66.

22. Amos Kamil, "Prep-School Predators," *New York Times Magazine*, June 10, 2012: 26–34.

23. George A. Bonnano, "Grief, Trauma and Resilience," in *Violent Death: Resilience and Intervention Beyond the Crisis*, ed. Edward K. Rynearson (New York: Routledge, 2006), 39; George A. Bonnano and Anthony D. Mancini, "The Human Capacity to Thrive in the Face of Potential Trauma," *Pediatrics* 121, no. 2 (2008): 372.

24. Bonnano, "Loss," 20–21.

25. Ibid., 25.

Appendix A

1. Lisa M. Diamond, "Passionate Friendships Among Adolescent Sexual Minority Women," *Journal of Research on Adolescence* 10, no. 2 (2000): 191. See also Smith-Rosenberg, 25–27.

2. Diamond, "Passionate Friendships," 192.

3. Janet Todd, ed., *The Collected Letters of Mary Wollstonecraft* (New York: Columbia University Press, 2013), 13.

4. Ibid., 25.

5. Quoted in Goodwin, 63.

6. Quoted in Elizabeth Hoar, *Mrs. Samuel Ripley: A Sketch* (Philadelphia: Lippincott, 1877), 12.

7. Glover et. al, "Young Women's Passionate Friendships," 77.

8. Craft-Fairchild, 415–16. On the concept of heteronormativity, see Susan S. Lanser, "Of Closed Doors and Open Hatches: Heteronormative Plots in Eighteenth-Century (Women's) Studies," *Eighteenth-Century* 53, no. 3 (2012): 274.

9. Fiona Brideoake, *The Ladies of Llangollen: Desire, Indeterminacy, and the Legacies of Criticism* (Lewisburg: Bucknell University Press, 2017), xviii.

10. Diamond, "Passionate Friendships," 194.

Appendix B

1. *MWJP*, 2. ("Condescendence," January 28, 1820).

2. Ibid, 3.

3. Ibid, 2–3.

4. NRS CS40/36/94, Decreet absolvitor and for expenses, Margaret Pirie or Ferguson and Thomas Ferguson, her husband, for his interest v Miss Jane Pirie, April 9, 1821.

5. Ibid.

6. NRS. RD5/1815/79, Deed of settlement of Miss Euphemia Pirie dated September 25, 1815.

7. NRS, SC36/51/10.
8. Will of Sir William Woods. Prob 11/1967, The National Archives.
9. Personal email from Kate Elms, History Centre Officer, Brighton and Hove City Libraries, April 17, 2012.

BIBLIOGRAPHY

List of Abbreviations Used

APA	American Psychiatric Association
APAC	Asia Pacific and Africa Collections, British Library
BL	British Library
CBCL	Child Behavior Checklist
Clerk	*The Notorious Drumsheugh Case of 1810. Miss Marianne Woods and Miss Jane Pirie v. Dame Helen Cumming Gordon of Altyre.* Edinburgh, 1800–1812.
DEP 175	Depository 175, Gordon Cumming of Altyre and Gordonstoun Papers
DSM	*Diagnostic and Statistical Manual of Psychiatric Disorders*
HL	House of Lords
IOR	India Office Records, British Library
LHP	Lillian Hellman Papers, Harry Ransom Center, University of Texas at Austin
Moncreiff	Moncreiff Collection, Advocates Library, Edinburgh
MWJP	*Miss Marianne Woods and Miss Jane Pirie Against Dame Helen Cumming Gordon.* Photo reprint (New York: Arno Press, 1975)
NLM	National Library of Medicine, Bethesda, Maryland
NLS	National Library of Scotland, Edinburgh
NRS	National Records of Scotland, Edinburgh
WS	Writer to the Signet

Archival Sources (Listed by Library)

Advocates Library, Edinburgh
Miss Marianne Woods and Miss Jane Pirie Against Dame Helen Cumming Gordon, 1810–1821. Vol. 21. Moncreiff Collection.
British Library (APAC Collection), London
Hardwicke Papers. Vol DLXX. *East India Papers, August 1767–1810.* "Necessary Expence of Fitting out a Lad for the East Indies," no. 8, n.d. f. 222.
East India Company: General Correspondence (IOR E/)
India Office: Accountant General's Office c. 1601–1974 (IOR L/AG)
India Office: Marine Records c. 1600–1879 (IOR L/MAR)

Harry Ransom Center, University of Texas, Austin
Lillian Hellman Papers
Moray Council Local Heritage Center, Elgin, Scotland
Douglas, Robert. "Annals of the Parish Douglas of Dallas." Elgin, 1920?
Cumming, Constance Frederica. "Private Letter" dated November 23, 1903.
National Library of Medicine (NLM), Bethesda, Maryland
Trial of Marianne Woods and Jane Pirie Against Dame Helen Cumming-Gordon. Edinburgh, 1811–20.
National Library of Scotland (NLS), Edinburgh
Gordon Cumming of Altyre and Gordonstoun Papers (DEP 175)
Skene of Rubislaw Papers (MS. 20465–71)
maps.nls.uk (https://www.nls.uk/family-history/directories/post-office/index.cfm?place=Edinburgh)
National Records of Scotland (NRS), Edinburgh
Crown Office precognitions, 1812 (AD14/12/)
Records of Church of Scotland synods, presbyteries, and kirk sessions (CH2/)
Court of Session: warrants of the Register of Acts and Decreets, 3rd series, Mackenzie's Office, 1st Division (CS 40/)
Court of Session: Unextracted Processes, 1st Arraignment, Innes-Mackenzie office (CS 235/)
Sir James Grant's Papers and Correspondence (GD 248)
Register of Deeds, Third Series, March 2, 1812–March 17, 1812 (RD 5/)
Signet Library (Roughead Collection), Edinburgh
Clerk, John, comp. *The Notorious Drumsheugh Case of 1810: Miss Marianne Woods and Miss Jane Pirie v. Dame Cumming Gordon of Altyre.* Edinburgh, 1810–1812.

Databases

Ancestry.co.uk
Findmypast.com
Libindx.moray.gov.uk
Scotlandspeople.gov.uk
www.historyofparliamentonline.org
www.measuringworth.com
www.nationalarchives.gov.uk
www.oldbaileyonline.org

Primary Sources

Alphabetical List of the Honourable East India Bengal Civil Servants, from the Year 1780 to the Year 1838.... Edward Dodwell and Samuel Miles, eds. London, 1839.
Annals of the General Assembly of the Church of Scotland from the Origin of the Relief in 1752 to the Rejection of Schism in 1766. 2 vols. Edinburgh, 1840.
Asiatic Journal and Monthly Register for British India and Its Dependencies. London, 1829.
Asiatic Journal for July 1826. Vol. 22. London, 1826.
The Bengal Obituary: A Record to Perpetuate the Memory of Departed Worth.... London, 1851.
Borthwick, John. *A Treatise on the Law of Libel and Slander, as Applied in Scotland, in Criminal Prosecutions and in Actions of Damages: with an Appendix, Containing Reports of Several Cases Respecting Defamation, Which Have Not Been, Hitherto, Published.* Edinburgh: W. & C. Tait, 1826.
Bruce, M. E. Cumming. *Family Records of the Bruces and the Cumyns.* Edinburgh, 1870.
"Bruce of Earlshaw in the Parish of Leuchars, Co. Fife." *Genealogist* 7 (1883): 131–41.
Catalogue of the Private Library of the Late P. Hastie and the Late E. H. Tracy, Comprising Biography, History, Club and Society Publications. New York, 1870.
Conversations with Lillian Hellman. Edited by Jackson R. Bryer. Jackson: University of Mississippi Press, 1986.
Darwin, Erasmus. *A Plan for the Conduct of Female Education.* Philadelphia, 1798.
De la Torre, Lillian. Letter to the editor. *New Republic*, February 23, 1953.
Dick Lauder, Thomas. *The Great Floods of August 1829 in the Province of Moray and Adjoining Districts.* 3rd ed. Elgin, 1873.
Ewing, W. W. *The Annals of the Free Church of Scotland.* 2 vols. Edinburgh: T & T Clark, 1914.
The Exhibition of Female Flagellants. 2 vols. London: 1777–85.
Fletcher, Elizabeth. *Autobiography of Mrs. Elizabeth Fletcher.* Edinburgh, 1876.
"Female Boarding Schools." *The Female Preceptor: Essays on the Duties of the Female Sex Conducted by a Lady in the Years 1813 and 1814.* London, 1814.
General Register of the Hon'ble East India Company's Civil Servants of the Bengal Establishment. H. T. Prinsep, comp. Calcutta, 1844.
Grant, Anne (of Laggan). *Memoir and Correspondence.* Edited by J. T. Grant. 3 vols. 2nd ed. London: 1845.
Grant, Elizabeth (of Rothiemurchus). *Memoirs of a Highland Lady.* Complete edition. 2 vols. Edinburgh: Canongate, 2001.
Grant, James. *Cassell's Old and New Edinburgh: Its History, Its People, and Its Places.* 6 vols. London, 1881–83?

Hamilton, Elizabeth. *The Cottagers of Glenburnie: A Scottish Tale.* Edinburgh, 1898.

———. *Letters Addressed to the Daughter of a Nobleman on the Formation of the Religious and Moral Principle.* 3rd ed. London, 1806.

———. Letters on the Elementary Principles of Education. Third American Edition. 2 vols. Boston, 1825.

———. *Translation of the Letter to a Hindu Rajah.* Edited by Pamela Perkins and Shannon Russell. Peterborough: Broadview Press, 1999.

Hellman, Lillian. *The Children's Hour.* New York: Knopf, 1935.

———. *The Children's Hour.* Acting Version. New York: Dramatists Play Service, 1981.

———. *The Collected Plays.* Boston: Little Brown, 1971.

———. *Four Plays.* New York: Modern Library, 1942.

———. *Three: An Unfinished Woman, Pentimento, Scoundrel Time.* Boston: Little Brown, 1979.

Highfill, Philip A., Jr., Kalman A. Burnim, and Edward A. Langham, eds. *A Biographical Dictionary of Actors, Actresses, Musicians and Other Stage Personnel in London 1600–1800.* Carbondale: South Illinois Press, 1993.

Hints to a Clergyman's Wife; or Female Parochial Duties Practically Illustrated. London, 1832.

History of the Westminster Election . . . to which is Prefixed a Summary Account of the Proceedings of the Late Parliament so Far as They Are Connected with the East India Business. . . . London, 1785.

Jefferies, Richard. *The Gamekeeper at Home: Sketches of Natural History and Rural Life.* London, 1880.

Jacquemont, Victor. *Letters from India: Being a Selection from the Correspondence of Victor Jacquemont.* Trans. Catherine Alison Philips. London: Macmillan, 1936.

Kett, Henry. *A Moral Tale Including Letters from a Father to His Daughter, upon the Most Important Subjects.* 2 vols. (London, 1809).

The Law Journal Reports for the Year 1852. Edited by Montagu Chambers, Philip Twells, and Francis Towers Streeten. London, 1852.

"Legal Costume-I." *Irish Times and Solicitors' Journal* 18 (1884): 160–63.

"Lieut-Colonel B. G. Barbut," *Journal of the Dutch Burgher Union of Ceylon* 23 (1934): 191–97.

List of Carthusians, 1800–1879. Lewes, 1879.

Locke, John. *Some Thoughts Concerning Education and of the Conduct of the Understanding.* Edited by R. T. Grant and N. Tarcov. Indianapolis: Hackett Publishing Company, 1996.

Lord Clive's Speech in the House of Commons, on the Motion Made for an Inquiry into the Nature, State, and Condition, of the East India Company, and of the British Affairs in the East Indies, in the Fifth Session of the Present Parliament. 1772.

Low, Ursula. *Fifty Years with John Company: From the Letters of General Sir John Low of Clatto, Fife, 1822–1858.* London: John Murray, 1936.

Lushington, Charles. *The History, Design and Present State of the Religious, Benevolent and Charitable Institutions Founded by the British in Calcutta and Its Vicinity.* Calcutta, 1824.

Macadam, Alexander. "Parish of Nigg (County and Synod of Ross, Presbytery of Tain)." In *The Statistical Account of Scotland, 1791–1799.* Vol. 13. Edinburgh, 1794: 13–22.

McCosh, James. *The Wheat and the Chaff Gathered into Bundles; A Statistical Contribution toward the History of the Recent Disruption of the Scottish Ecclesiastical Establishment.* Perth, 1843.

Memoirs of the Late Mrs. Elizabeth Hamilton, with a Selection from Her Correspondence and Other Unpublished Writings. Edited by Elizabeth Benger. 2 vols. London, 1819.

Messerole, Suzy. "Venus Nefanda." Unpublished manuscript. Microsoft word file.

Miller, Hugh. *My Schools and Schoolmasters.* Edited by James Robertson. Edinburgh: B&W Publishing, 2002.

Miss Marianne Woods and Miss Jane Pirie Against Dame Helen Cumming Gordon. Photo reprint. New York: Arno Press, 1975.

Norton, Rictor, ed. "Extraordinary Female Affection, 1790." *Homosexuality in Eighteenth-Century England: A Sourcebook.* April 22, 2005. Updated June 15, 2005.

Opie, Amelia. *The Father and Daughter: A Tale in Prose.* London, 1824.

Omond, George William Thomson. *The Lord Advocates of Scotland from the Close of the Fifteenth Century to the Passing of the Reform Bill.* 2 vols. Edinburgh, 1883.

Parliament House Portraits: The Art Collection of the Faculty of Advocates. Edinburgh: Faculty of Advocates, 1999.

Paterson, James. *Kay's Edinburgh Portraits: A Series of Anecdotal Biographies, Chiefly of Scotchmen.* 2 vols. London, 1885.

Perry, William. "Alexander Penrose Forbes: Bishop of Brechin, the Scottish Pusey." London: Society for the Promulgation of Christian Knowledge, 1939. Available online via Project Canterbury. http://anglicanhistory.org/scotland/apforbes/perry/chapter1.html. Accessed September 30, 2019.

Portobello Architecture Heritage Trail. Portobello Heritage Trust and Amenity Society, 2011. Tourist Brochure.

The Principal Acts of the General Assembly of the Church of Scotland. Edinburgh, 1811.

The Psalms of David in Metre, Translated and Diligently Compared with the Original Text. Edinburgh: 1809.

Report from the Select Committee on the Supreme Court of Judicature in Scotland. House of Commons, 1840.

Roberts, William. *Memoirs and Correspondence of Mrs. Hannah More.* 2 vols. New York, 1834.

Rose, Richard. "Parish of Drainie." In *The New Statistical Account of Scotland.* Vol. 13. Edinburgh: 1845, 145–58.

Roughead, William. "Closed Doors; or The Great Drumsheugh Case." In *Bad Companions*, 109–46. Edinburgh: W. Green, 1930.

Royal Academy of Dramatic Art. "Scotch Verdict: Reveal Nothing or Lose Everything." January 22, 2015. www.scotchverdict.com/londons-royal-academy-dramatic-art.

Scott, Hew. *Fasti Ecclesiae Scoticanae: The Succession of Ministers in the Church of Scotland from the Reformation.* 10 vols. Edinburgh: Oliver & Boyd, 1915-

"Slippers in Hand, Aussie Hunts for Princess." *Telegraph*, October 14, 2010.

Starzl, Thomas. *The Puzzle People: Memoirs of a Transplant Surgeon.* Pittsburgh: University of Pittsburgh Press, 1992.

Todd, Janet, ed. *The Collected Letters of Mary Wollstonecraft.* New York: Columbia University Press, 2003.

Tulloch, William. "Parish of Dollas or Dallas." In the *Statistical Accounts of Scotland*, vol. 13, 194–201. Edinburgh: 1845.

Walbridge, Earle. Letter to the editor. *Saturday Review of Literature.* March 16, 1935.

Williamson, Thomas. *The East-India Vade Mecum; or Complete Guide to Gentlemen Intended for Civil, Military, or Naval Service of the East India Company.* 2 vols. London, 1810.

Wollstonecraft, Mary. *Thoughts on the Education of Daughters: With Reflections on Female Conduct.* London, 1787.

———. *A Vindication of the Rights of Women and a Vindication of the Rights of Men.* Edited by Janet Todd. Oxford: Oxford University Press, 1993.

Young, Robert. *Annals of the Parish and Burgh of Elgin from the Twelfth Century to the Year 1876.* Elgin, 1870.

Secondary Sources

Anderson, Valerie E. R. "The Eurasian Problem in Nineteenth-Century India." PhD diss., School of Oriental and African Studies (SOAS), 2011.

Arnold, David. "European Orphans and Vagrants in India in the Nineteenth Century." *Journal of Imperial and Commonwealth History* 7, no. 2 (1979): 104–27.

Bannerji, Himani. "Age of Consent and Hegemonic Social Reform," in *Gender and Imperialism*, edited by Clare Midgely. Manchester: Manchester University Press, 1998, 21–44.
Beal, Joan C. "Prescriptivism and the Suppression of Variation." In *Eighteenth-Century England: Ideology and Change*, edited by Raymond Hickey, 21–37. Cambridge: Cambridge University Press, 2010.
Barclay, Kate. *Love, Intimacy and Power: Marriage and Patriarchy in Scotland, 1650–1850*. Manchester: Manchester University Press, 2011.
Benedict, Barbara. *Curiosity: A Cultural History of Early Modern Inquiry*. Chicago: University of Chicago Press, 2002.
"The Berners Estate: Berners and Newman Streets." https://www.ucl.ac.uk/Bartlett/files/chapter 30_the_berners_estate. PDF.
Blaikie, Andrew. *Illegitimacy, Sex, and Society: Northeast Scotland, 1750–1900*. Oxford: Clarendon University Press, 1993.
———. "A Kind of Loving: Illegitimacy, Grandparents and the Rural Economy of North East Scotland, 1750–1900." *Scottish Economic and Social History* 14, no. 1 (2010): 41–57. https://doi.org/10.3366/sesh.1994.14.14.41.
———. "Scottish Illegitimacy: Social Adjustment or Moral Economy?" *Journal of Interdisciplinary History* 29, no. 2 (1998): 221–41.
Bobker, Michelle. "The Shape of Intimacy: Private Space and the British Social Imagination 1650–1770." PhD diss. Rutgers University, 2007.
Bonnano, George. "Grief, Trauma and Resilience." In *Violent Death: Resilience and Intervention Beyond the Crisis*, edited by Edward K. Rynearson, 31–47. New York: Routledge, 2006.
———. "Loss, Trauma and Human Resilience: Have We Underestimated the Human Capacity to Thrive After Extremely Aversive Events?" *American Psychologist* 59, no. 1 (2004): 20–38.
Bonnano, George, and Anthony D. Mancini. "The Human Capacity to Thrive in the Face of Potential Trauma." *Pediatrics* 121, no. 2 (2008): 369–75.
Bowden, Martha F. "Mrs. Yorick and the Midwife: Women's Roles in the Eighteenth-Century Church of England." *Dalhousie Review* 82, no. 3 (2002): 377–93.
Boyd, Lois A. "Presbyterian Ministers' Wives—A Nineteenth-Century Portrait." *Journal of Presbyterian History* 59, no. 1 (1981): 3–17.
Brantley, Ben. "All Over London, Love Hurts." *New York Times*, February 22, 2011. http://nytimes.com/2011/02/27/theater/27London.html.
Breitenbach, Esther. *Empire and Scottish Society: The Impact of Foreign Missions at Home, c. 1790–c. 1914*. Edinburgh: Edinburgh University Press, 2009.
Brendon, Vyvyen. *Children of the Raj*. London: Weidenfeld & Nicolson, 2005.
Brideoake, Fiona. *The Ladies of Llangollen: Desire, Indeterminacy, and the Legacies of Criticism*. Lewisburg: Bucknell University Press, 2017.

Brown, Stewart J. *Thomas Chalmers and the Godly Commonwealth in Scotland.* Oxford: Oxford University Press, 1982.

Buchanan, Robert. *The Ten Years' Conflict: Being the History of the Disruption of the Church of Scotland.* 2 vols. Glasgow, 1849.

Buettner, Elizabeth. *Empire Families: Britons and Late Imperial India.* Oxford: Oxford University Press, 2004.

Burleigh, John H. S. *A Church History of Scotland.* London: Oxford University Press, 1960.

Burton, Robert. *The Anatomy of Melancholy.* 9th ed. 3 vols. London: 1800.

Carr, Rosalind. *Gender and Enlightenment Culture in Eighteenth-Century Scotland.* Edinburgh: Edinburgh University Press, 2014.

Cassidy, Brendan. "The Fate of a 'Missing Masterpiece': Gavin Hamilton's *Andromache Mourning the Death of Hector.*" *British Art Journal* 10, no. 1 (2009): 11–13.

Chancey, Maria Karen. "In the Company's Secret Service: Neil Benjamin Edmonstone and the First Imperialists." PhD diss., University of Florida, 2003.

Cheyne, A. C. *The Ten Years' Conflict & the Disruption.* Edinburgh: Scottish Academic Press, 1993.

"Chronic Stress, Anxiety Can Damage the Brain, Increase Risk of Major Psychiatric Disorders." *ScienceDaily.* January 21, 2016. www.sciencedaily.com/releases/2016/-1/160121121818.htm.

Clarke, John R. *Looking at Lovemaking: Constructions of Sexuality in Roman Art 100 B.C.–A.D. 250.* Berkeley: University of California Press, 1998.

Cohen, Deborah. *Family Secrets: The Things We Hide.* London: Penguin, 2014.

Cohn, Bernard. "The British in Benares: A Nineteenth-Century Colonial Society." *Comparative Studies in Society and History* 4, no. 2 (1962): 169–99.

Coleman, Rebecca, and Cathy Spatz Widom. "Childhood Abuse and Neglect and Adult Intimate Relationships: A Prospective Study." *Child Abuse and Neglect* 28, no. 11 (2004): 1131–51.

Comrie, J. D. *History of Scottish Medicine.* 2 vols. London: Ballière, Tindall and Cox, 1932.

Cook, Mark. "The Guide: Theatre: *The Children's Hour.*" *Guardian* (London), January 21, 2011. https://www.theguardian.com/stage/2011/jan/22/this-weeks-new-theatre.

Cosh, Mary. *Edinburgh in the Golden Age.* Edinburgh: John Donald, 2003.

Craft-Fairchild, Katherine. "Sexual and Textual Indeterminacy: Eighteenth-Century Representations of Sapphism." *Journal of the History of Sexuality* 15, no. 3 (2006): 408–31.

Crawford, Dirom Grey. *A History of the Indian Medical Service 1600–1913.* London: Thatcher, 1914.

Curtin, Philip D. *Death by Migration: Europe's Encounter with the Tropical World in the Nineteenth Century*. Cambridge: Cambridge University Press, 1989.

Dalrymple, William. *White Mughals: Love and Betrayal in Eighteenth-Century India*. New York: Penguin, 2004.

Davidson, Jenny. *Breeding: A Partial History of the Eighteenth Century*. New York: Columbia University Press, 2009.

De Bellaigue, Christina. "Behind the School Walls: The School Community in French and English Boarding Schools for Girls, 1810–1867." *Paedogogica Historica* 40, nos. 1–2 (2004): 107–21.

Delofski, Maree. "Place, Race and Stardom: Becoming Merle Oberon." *Continuum: Journal of Media and Cultural Studies* 26, no. 6 (2012): 803–14.

———. "TV Documentaries: 'The Trouble with Merle,'" August 29, 2002. www.abc.net.au.tv/documentaries/stories.s657300.htm.

Diamond, Lisa. "Passionate Friendships Among Adolescent Sexual-Minority Women." *Journal of Research on Adolescence* 10, no. 2 (2000): 191–209.

———. "Sexual Identity, Attractions and Behavior Among Sexual-Minority Women Over a 2-Year Period." *Developmental Psychology* 36, no. 2 (2000): 241–50.

———. "Was It a Phase? Young Women's Relinquishment of Lesbian/Bisexual Identities Over a 5-Year Period." *Journal of Personality and Social Psychology* 84, no. 2 (2003): 352–64.

Diamond, Lisa, Janna A. Dickenson, and Karen L. Blair. "Stability of Sexual Attractions Across Different Timescales: The Roles of Bisexuality and Gender." *Archives of Sexual Behavior* 46, no. 1 (2017): 193–204.

Donoghue, Emma. *Passions Between Women: British Lesbian Culture, 1668–1801*. New York: HarperCollins, 1993.

Dossena, Marina. "Scottishness and the Book Trade: Print and Scotticisms." In *The Edinburgh History of the Book in Scotland*. Volume 2: Enlightenment and Expansion 1707–1800, edited by Stephen W. Brown and Warren McDougall, 545–50. Edinburgh: Edinburgh University Press, 2012.

Douglas, William. *Ministers' Wives*. New York: Harper & Row, 1965.

"The Educational Establishments of Calcutta, Past and Present." *Calcutta Review* 13, no. 26 (1850): 442–67.

Ellis, Havelock. *Studies in the Psychology of Sex*. 6 vols. New York: Random House, 1936–42.

Elovainio, Marko, Hanna Raaska, Jari Sinkkonen, Saana Makipaa, and Helena Lapinleimu. "Association Between Attachment-Related Symptoms and Later Psychological Problems Among International Adoptees: Results from the FINADO Study." *Scandinavian Journal of Psychology* 56, no. 1 (2015): 53–61.

Ewan, Elizabeth, Sue Innes, and Sian Reynolds, eds. *The Biographical Dictionary of Scottish Women from the Earliest Times to 2004*. Edinburgh: Edinburgh University Press, 2004.

Faderman, Lillian. *Scotch Verdict*. London: Quartet Books, 1983.

———. *Surpassing the Love of Men: Romantic Friendship and Love Between Women from the Renaissance to the Present*. New York: William Morrow, 1981.

Fallon, L. Fleming, and Tish Davidson, "Voyeurism." In *The Gale Encyclopedia of Mental Health*, 1642–44. Third edition. Vol. 2. Detroit: Gale, 2012.

Feminist Spectator. Unsigned review of *The Children's Hour*. March 17, 2011. Feministspectator.princeton.edu/2011/03/17/the-children's-hour/

Festa, Lynn. *Sentimental Figures of Empire in Eighteenth-Century Britain and France*. Baltimore: Johns Hopkins Press, 2006.

Finkelhor, David, and Linda Meyer Williams, eds. *Nursery Crimes: Sexual Abuse in Day Care Settings*. Newbury Park: Sage, 1988.

———. "The Trauma of Child Sexual Abuse." *Journal of Interpersonal Violence* 2, no. 4 (1987): 348–66.

Finn, Margot. "Anglo-Indian Lives in the Later Eighteenth and Early Nineteenth Centuries." *Journal for Eighteenth-Century Studies* 33, no. 1 (2010): 49–65.

Fraser, G. M. *The Good Sir James: The Life and Times of Sir James Grant of Grant, of Castle Grant, Bart.* Kinloss: Librario, 2012.

Fraser, Kathy. *For the Love of a Highland Home: The Fraser Brothers' Indian Quest*. St. Kilda: Grey Thrush Publishing, 2016.

Frew, Joanna. "Scottish Backgrounds and Indian Experiences in the Late Eighteenth Century." *Journal of Scottish Historical Studies* 34, no. 2 (2014): 167–98.

Friedman, Geraldine. "School for Scandal: Sexuality, Race, and National Vice and Virtue in *Miss Marianne Woods and Miss Jane Pirie Against Dame Helen Cumming Gordon*." *Nineteenth-Century Contexts* 27, no. 1 (2005): 53–76.

Furber, Holden. *John Company at Work*. Cambridge, MA: Harvard University Press, 1970.

Fury, Cheryl. "'To Sett Downe All the Villainie': Accounts of the Sodomy Trial on the Fourth East India Company Voyage (1609)." *The Mariner's Mirror* 102, no. 1 (2016): 74–80.

Gardiner, Dorothy. *English Girlhood at School: A Study of Women's Education Through Twelve Centuries*. London: Humphrey Milford, 1929.

Gerber, David A. *Authors of Their Lives: The Personal Correspondence of British Immigrants in the Nineteenth Century*. New York: New York University Press, 2006.

Ghosh, Durba. *Sex and the Colonial Family: The Making of Empire*. Cambridge: Cambridge University Press, 2006.

Ghosh, Suresh Chandra. *The Social Condition of the British Community in Bengal: 1757–1800*. Leiden: E. J. Brill, 1970.

Gibson, Jessica A. "'What are you—A Woman I suppose': Women in the Eighteenth Century British Court." MA thesis, University of Oregon, 2013.

Gilbert, Arthur N. "Buggery and the British Navy, 1700–1861." *Journal of Social History* 10, no. 1 (1976): 72–98.

Glover, Kathleen. *Elite Women and Polite Society in Eighteenth-Century Scotland*. Woodbridge: Boydell Press, 2011.

———. "'Polite London Children': Educating the Daughters of the Scottish Elite in Mid-Eighteenth Century London." In Nenadic, *Scots in London*, 253–71.

Glover, Jenna, Renee V. Galliher, and Katherine A. Crowell, "Young Women's Passionate Friendships: A Qualitative Analysis." *Journal of Gender Studies* 24, no. 1 (2015): 70–84.

Goodwin, Joan W. *The Remarkable Mrs. Ripley: The Life of Sarah Alden Bradford Ripley*. Boston: Northeastern University Press, 1998.

Gordon, Michael, and M. Charles Bernstein, "Mate Choice and Domestic Life in the Nineteenth-Century Marriage Manual." *Journal of Marriage and the Family* 32, no. 4 (1970): 665–74.

Gordon Cumming, Constance Frederica. *Memories*. Edinburgh, 1904.

Greenfield, Sayre. "The Impact of Lawrence Sterne Upon Yorick's Skull." Paper presented at the annual meeting of the South-Central Eighteenth-Century Society (SCECS), St. Simon's Island, GA, February 2011.

Grogan, Claire. "Crossing Genre, Gender and Race in Elizabeth Hamilton's Translation of the Letters of a Hindu Rajah." *Studies in the Novel* 34, no. 1 (2002): 21–42.

———. *Politics and Genre in the Works of Elizabeth Hamilton*. Farnham: Ashgate, 2012.

Habigzang, Louisa Fernanda, Fernanda Helen Stroeher, Roberta Hatzenberger, Rafaela Cassol Cunha, Michela da Silva Romos, and Helena Koller. "Cognitive Behavioral Group Therapy for Sexually Abused Girls." *Revista de Saude Publica* 43, no. 1 (2009).

Haggerty, George E. "Keyhole Testimony: Witnessing Sodomy in the Eighteenth Century." *Eighteenth Century* 44, no. 2/3 (2003): 167–82.

Halberstam, Judith. "Foreword" to *Scotch Verdict: The Real-Life Story that Inspired "The Children's Hour,"* by Lillian Faderman, vii–xii. New York: Columbia University Pres, 2013.

Hall, Elizabeth Sara, and Glen Gaher. "Behavioral and Personality Characteristics of Children with Reactive Attachment Disorder." *Journal of Psychology* 137, no. 21 (2003): 145–62.

Handley, Sasha. *Sleep in Early Modern England*. New Haven, CT: Yale University Press, 2016.

Harrison, John Anthony. *Private Schools in Doncaster in the Nineteenth Century. Part II: Efflorescence*. Doncaster: Doncaster Museum and Art Gallery, 1960.

Hawes, Christopher. *Poor Relations: The Making of a Eurasian Community in India 1773–1833*. London: Routledge, 1996.
Hawk, Brandi, and Robert B. McCall. "CBCL Behavior Problems of Post-Institutionalized International Adoptees." *Clinical Child and Family Psychology* 13, no. 2 (2010): 199–211.
Hay, Robert. *Lochnavando No More: The Life and Death of a Moray Farming Community, 1750–1850*. Edinburgh: Birlinn, 2005.
Hegele, Arden. "'So she has been educated by a vulgar, silly, conceited French governess!': Social Anxieties, Satirical Portraits, and the Eighteenth-Century French Instructor." *Gender and Education* 23, no. 1 (2011): 331–43.
Helm, C., and C. B. Nemeroff. "The Role of Childhood Trauma in the Neurobiological of Mood and Anxiety Disorders: Preclinical and Clinical Studies." Biological Psychiatry 49, no. 12 (2001): 1023–39.
Highfill, Philip A. Jr., Kalman A. Burnim, and Edward A. Langham, eds. *A Biographical Dictionary of Actors, Actresses, Musicians and Other Stage Personnel in London 1600–1800*. Carbondale: Southern Illinois University Press, 1993.
Hill, Ashley, Kathryn A. Degnan, Susan D. Calkins, and Susan P. Keane. "Profiles of Externalizing Behavior for Boys and Girls Across Preschool: The Roles of Emotion Regulation and Inattention." *Developmental Psychology* 42, no. 5 (2006): 913–28.
Hill, Bridget. *Women Alone: Spinsters in England*. New Haven, CT: Yale University Press, 2001.
Hoar, Elizabeth. *Mrs. Samuel Ripley*. Philadelphia, 1877.
Jacob, W. W. *The Clerical Profession in the Long Eighteenth-Century 1680–1840*. Oxford: Oxford University Press, 2007.
Joseph, Lavan. "Voyeuristic Disorder." In *Diagnostic and Statistical Manual of Mental Disorders, Fifth Edition: DSM-5*. 302.82 (F 65.3). In *Therapedia*. https://www.theravive.com/therapedia/voyeuristic-disorder-dsm-r-302.82-(F65.3).
Kamil, Amos. "Prep-School Predators." *New York Times Magazine*, June 10, 2012: 26–34. www.nytimes.com/2012/06/10/magazine/the-horace-mann-schools-secret-history-of-sexual-abuse.html.
Kamm, Josephine. *Hope Deferred: Girls' Education in English History*. London: Methuen, 1965.
Kaufman, J., and D. Charney. "Effects of Early Stress on Brain Structure and Function: Implications for Understanding the Relationship Between Child Maltreatment and Depression." *Developmental Psychopathology* 13, no. 3 (2001): 451–71.
Kessler-Harris, Alice. *A Difficult Woman: The Challenging Life and Times of Lillian Hellman*. New York: Bloomsbury Press, 2013.
King, Shelley. "Portrait of a Marriage: John and Amelia Opie and the Sister Arts." *Studies in Eighteenth-Century Culture* 40 (2011): 27–62.

Lanser, Susan S. "Of Closed Doors and Open Hatches: Heteronormative Plots in Eighteenth-Century (Women's) Studies." *Eighteenth-Century* 53, no. 3 (2012): 273–90.

———. *The Sexuality of History: Modernity and the Sapphic.* Chicago: University of Chicago Press, 2014.

LeJacq, Seth Stein. "Buggery's Travels: Royal Navy Sodomy on Ships and Shore in the Long Eighteenth Century." *Journal for Maritime Research* 17, no. 2 (2015): 103–16.

Leneman, Leah. *Alienated Affections: The Scottish Experience of Divorce and Separation.* Edinburgh: Edinburgh University Press, 1998.

———. "Legitimacy and Bastardy in Scotland, 1694–1830." *Scottish Historical Review* 80, no. 209, part 1 (2001): 45–62.

Lewis, Reina. *Gendering Orientalism: Race, Femininity and Representation.* London: Routledge. 1996.

Livesay, Daniel. *Children of Uncertain Fortune: Mixed-race Jamaicans and the Atlantic Family.* Chapel Hill: University of North Carolina Press, 2018.

Lyons, Andrew P, and Harriet D. Lyons. *Irregular Connections: A History of Anthropology and Sexuality.* Lincoln: University of Nebraska Press, 2004.

Mace, Emily. "In the Parsonage, In the Parish: Experiences of Unitarian Ministers' Wives." *Unitarian Universalist Women's Heritage Society* (2002). Occasional Paper Series. www.uuwhs.org/mace.php.

MacKillop, Andrew. "Europeans, Britons and Scots: Scottish Sojourning Networks and Identities in Asia, c. 1700–1815." In *Notes on A Global Clan: Scottish Migrant Networks and Identities Since the Eighteenth Century*, edited by Angela McCarthy, 19–47. London: Tauris Academic Studies, 2006.

Majumdar, Purna Ch. *The Musnud of Murshidabad.* Murshidabad: Saroda Ray, 1905.

Malcolm, John. *Malcolm: Soldier, Diplomat, Ideologue of British India.* Edinburgh: John Donald, 2014.

Marcus, Sharon. *Between Women: Friendship, Desire and Marriage in Victorian England.* Princeton: Princeton University Press, 2007.

Marshall, P. J. *East Indian Fortunes: The British in Bengal in the Eighteenth Century.* Oxford: Oxford University Press, 1976.

Maxwell-Start, P. G. "'Wild, filthie, execrable, detestabill, and unnatural sin': Bestiality in Early Modern Scotland." In *Sodomy in Early Modern Europe*, edited by Tom Betteridge, 82–93. Manchester: Manchester University Press, 2002.

Mayes, Jemima. "Construction Techniques of the 18th Century." *18th Century History Articles.* www.history1700s.com.

McDermid, Jane. "Conservative Feminism and Female Education in the Eighteenth Century." *History of Education* 18, no. 4 (1989): 309–22.

McEwen, B. S. "Early Life Influences on Life-Long Patterns of Behavior and Health." *Mental Retardation Developmental Disability Research Review* 9, no. 3 (2003): 149–54.

Merry, Karen Jane. "Murder by Poison in Scotland During the Nineteenth and Early Twentieth Centuries." PhD thesis. University of Glasgow, 2010.

Meston, Cindy M., Julia R. Heiman, and Paul D. Trapnell. "The Relation Between Early Abuse and Adult Sexuality." *Journal of Sex Research* 36, no. 4 (1999): 385–95.

Miller, P. J. "Women's Education, 'Self-Improvement' and Social Mobility—a Late Eighteenth Century Debate." *British Journal of Educational Studies* 20, no. 3 (1972): 302–14.

Moore, Lisa. "Something More Tender Still than Friendship." *Feminist Studies* 18, no. 3 (1992): 499–520.

Mowat, Ian P. "The Moray Firth Province: Trade and Family Links in the Eighteenth Century." In *Firthlands of Ross and Sunderland*, edited by John R. Baldwin, 69–88. Edinburgh: Scottish Society for Northern Studies, 1986.

Mulcahy, Linda. "Watching Women: What Illustrations of Courtroom Scenes Tell Us about Women and the Public Sphere in the Nineteenth Century." *Journal of Law and Society*, 42, no. 1 (2015): 53–73.

Nemeroff, C. B. "Neurobiological Consequences of Childhood Trauma." *Journal of Clinical Psychology* 65 (2004): 18–28.

Nenadic, Stana. *Lairds and Luxury: The Highland Gentry in Eighteenth-Century Scotland*. Edinburgh: John Donald, 2007.

———. "Military Men, Businessmen, and the 'Business' of Patronage in Eighteenth-Century London," in Nenadic, *Scots in London in the Eighteenth Century*, 229–52.

———, ed. *Scots in London in the Eighteenth Century*. Lewisburg: Bucknell University Press, 2010.

Nocentelli, Carmen. *Empires of Love: Europe, Asia, and the Making of Early Modern Identity*. Philadelphia: University of Pennsylvania Press, 2013.

Oldham, James. "Eighteenth-Century Judges' Notes: How They Explain, Correct and Enhance the Reports." *American Journal of Legal History* 31, no. 1 (1987): 9–42.

Olson, Greta. "Keyholes in Eighteenth-Century Novels as Liminal Spaces Between the Public and Private Spheres." In *Sites of Discourse—Public and Private Spheres—Legal Culture: Papers from a Conference at the Technical University of Dresden, December 2001*, edited by Uwe Böker and Julie A. Hibbard, 151–66. Amsterdam: Rodopi, 2002.

Oosterhof, Jan. "Sodomy at Sea and at the Cape of Good Hope." *Journal of Homosexuality* 16, no. 1 (1998): 229–35.

Page, Malcolm. *King's African Rifles: A History*. Barnsley: Pen & Sword Military, 2011.
Parkinson, C. Northcote. *Trade in the Eastern Seas, 1793–1813*. Cambridge: Cambridge University Press, 1937.
"Parochial Schools in Scotland." *Tait's Edinburgh Magazine* 11 (September 1844): 565–70.
Paton, G. Campbell. "Husband and Wife: Property Rights and Relationship." In *An Introduction to Scottish Legal History*. Edinburgh: Stair Society, 1958, 99–115.
Peakman, Julie. *Mighty Lewd Books: The Development of Pornography in Eighteenth-Century England*. Basingstoke: Palgrave Macmillan, 2003.
Perkins, Pamela, and Shannon Russell. "Introduction" to *Translations of the Letters of a Hindoo Rajah* by Elizabeth Hamilton. Peterborough: Broadview Press, 1999, 1–45.
Pignotti, Monica. "Reactive Attachment Disorder and International Adoption: A Systematic Synthesis." *Scientific Review of Mental Health Practice* 8, no. 1 (2011): 30–49.
Pollack, Linda. "'Teach Her to Live under Obedience': The Making of Women in the Upper Ranks of Early Modern England." *Continuity and Change* 4, no. 2 (1989): 231–58.
Porter, Roy. "Science, Provincial Culture and Public Opinion in Enlightenment England." In *The Eighteenth-Century Town: A Reader in English Urban History 1688–1820*, edited by Peter Boursay, 243–67. New York: Routledge, 1990.
"Position Statement on Child Abuse and Neglect by Adults." *American Journal of Psychiatry* 148, no. 11 (1991): 1626.
Prebble, John. *Mutiny: Highland Regiments in Revolt 1743–1804*. London: Penguin, 1975.
Probert, Rebecca. *Marriage Law and Practice in the Long Eighteenth Century*. Cambridge: Cambridge University Press, 2009.
Raaska, Hanna, Helena Lapinleimu, Sari Salmivalli, Jaako Sanna Makipaa, and Marko Elovaino. "Experiences of School Bullying among Internationally Adopted Children: Results from the Finnish Adoption (FINANDO) Study." *Child Psychiatry and Human Development* 43, no. 4 (2012): 592–611.
Rendall, Jane. *The Origins of Modern Feminism: Women in Britain, France and the United States*. Chicago: Lyceum Books, 1985.
———. "'Women that would plague me with rational conversation': Aspiring Women and Scottish Whigs." In *Women, Gender and Enlightenment*, edited by Sarah Knott and Barbara Taylor. Basingstoke: Palgrave Macmillan, 2005, 326–48.
Richardson, H. E. "George Bogle and His Children." *Scottish Genealogist* 29 (1982): 73–83.

Rizzo, Betty. *Companions without Vows: Relationships among Eighteenth-Century Women*. Athens: University of Georgia Press, 1994.

Roulston, Christine. "'A Thing Nearly Impossible': The 1811 Woods/Pirie Trial and Its Legacies." In *Developments in the Histories of Sexualities: In Search of the Normal, 1600–1800*, edited by Chris Mounsey, 125–44. Lewisburg: Bucknell University Press, 2013.

Rupp, Leila. *A Global History of Love Between Women*. New York: New York University Press, 2011.

Scott, Karen M., Don R. Smith, and Pete M. Ellis, "Prospectively Ascertained Child Maltreatment and Its Association with DSM-IV Disorders in Young Adults," *Archives of General Psychiatry* 67, no 7 (2010): 712–19.

Shepard, Alexandra. "Minding Their Own Business: Married Women and Credit in Early Eighteenth Century London." *Transactions of the Royal Historical Society* 25 (2015): 53–74.

Shields, Juliet. *Sentimental Literature and Anglo-Scottish Identity 1745–1820*. Cambridge: Cambridge University Press, 2010.

Shonkoff, Jack P. et al. "The Lifelong Effects of Early Childhood Adversity and Toxic Stress," *Pediatrics* 2012. https://doi.org/10.1542/peds.2011-2663.

Simpson, A. W. B. *Legal Theory and Legal History: Essays on the Common Law*. London: Hambledon Press, 1987.

Singh, Frances B. "Dispose or Destroy': The Textual History of *Woods and Pirie Against Dame Helen Cumming Gordon*." *Journal of the Edinburgh Bibliographic Society* 11 (2016): 11–21.

———. "James Thomas Grant, George Cumming and Lewis Mackenzie: Three Scottish Cousins in East India Company Service, 1792–1804." *Journal of Scottish Historical Studies* 38, no. 1 (2018): 160–77.

———. "More . . . Drumsheugh Scandal." *Signet Magazine* no. 5 (2013): 26–28.

Skedd, Susan. "Women Teachers and the Expansion of Girls' Schooling in England, c. 1760–1820." In *Gender in Eighteenth-Century England: Roles, Representations and Responsibilities*, edited by Hannah Barker and Elaine Chalus, 101–25. London: Routledge, 1997.

Skedd, Susan, and Frances Singh. "Pirie, Jane (1779–1833), Schoolmistress." *Oxford Dictionary of National Biography*, ed. H. C. G. Matthew. Oxford: Oxford University Press, 2004.

Small, Julian. "Charlotte Square, Edinburgh." The Architecture of Robert Adam (1728–1792), https://sites.scran.ac.uk/ada/documents/square/charlotte_square.htm. Accessed September 30, 2019.

———. "Houses and Shops in Leith Street." The Architecture of Robert Adam (1728–1792), https://sites.scran.ac.uk/ada/documents/leithstreet/leith_street.htm. Accessed September 30, 2019.

Smith-Rosenberg, Carroll. "The Female World of Love and Ritual." *Signs* 1 (1975): 1–29.
Smout, Christopher. "Aspects of Sexual Behavior in Nineteenth-Century Scotland." In *Bastardy and Its Comparative History*, edited by Peter Laslett, Karla Oosterveen, and Richard M. Smith, 192–216. Cambridge: Harvard University Press, 1980.
Spacks, Patricia Meyer. *The Adolescent Idea: Myths of Youth and the Adult Imagination.* New York: Basic Books, 1981.
Spencer, Jenny. "Sex, Lies, and Revisions: Historicizing Hellman's *The Children's Hour.*" *Modern Drama* 47, no. 1 (2004): 44–65.
Stewart, A. A. Grainer. *Portraits in the Hall of Parliament House in Edinburgh.* Edinburgh: William Green, 1907.
Stoler, Laura Ann. *Carnal Knowledge and Imperial Power: Race and the Intimate in Colonial Rule.* Berkeley: University of California Press, 2002.
Stone, Lawrence. *The Family, Sex and Marriage, 1500–1800.* New York: Harper & Row, 1979.
Straight, Julie. "Promoting Liberty Through Universal Benevolence in Elizabeth Hamilton's *Translation of the Letters of a Hindu Rajah.*" *Eighteenth-Century Fiction* 25, no. 3 (2013): 589–614.
Taylor, Paul. "First Night: *The Children's Hour*, Comedy Theatre, London." *Independent*, February 10, 2011. www.independent.co.uk/arts-entertainment/theatre-dance/reviews/first-night-the-children's-hour-comedy-theatre-london-2210027.html.
Teltscher, Kate. *The High Road to China: George Bogle, the Panchen Lama and the First British Expedition to Tibet.* London: Bloomsbury, 2006.
Thomson, Stephen. "Mixed Jurisprudence and the Scottish Legal Tradition." *Journal of Civil Law Studies* 7, no. 1 (2014). http://digitalcommons.law.lsu.edu/jcls/vol7/iss1/3.
Traub, Valerie. *The Renaissance of Lesbianism in Early Modern England.* Cambridge: Cambridge University Press, 2004.
———. "Setting the Stage Behind the Seen: Performing Lesbian History." In *The Queerest Art: Essays on Lesbian and Gay Theatre*, edited by Alisa Solomon and Framji Minwalla, 55–106. New York: New York University Press, 2002.
Tuhkanen, Mikko. "Breeding (and) Reading: Lesbian Knowledge, Eugenic Discipline and *The Children's Hour.*" *Modern Fiction Studies* 48, no. 4 (2002): 1001–40.
Turley, Hans. *Rum, Sodomy and the Lash: Piracy, Sexuality and Masculine Identity.* New York: New York University Press, 1999.
Tunc, Tanfer Emin. "Rumours, Gossip and Lies: Social Anxiety and the Evil Child in Lillian Hellman's *The Children's Hour.*" *Journal of Literary Studies* 28, no. 3 (2012).

Van der Meer, Theo. "Tribades on Trial: Female Same-Sex Offenders in Late Eighteenth-Century Amsterdam." *Journal of the History of Sexuality* 1, no. 1 (1991): 424–55.
Velasco, Sherry. *Lesbians in Early Modern Spain*. Nashville: Vanderbilt University Press, 2011.
Vicinus, Martha. "Distance and Desire: English Boarding School Friendships." *Signs* 4 (1984): 600–622.
———. *Intimate Friends: Women Who Loved Women*. Chicago: University of Chicago Press, 2004.
Vickery, Amanda. *The Gentleman's Daughter: Women's Lives in Georgian England*. New Haven, CT: Yale University Press, 1998.
Walker, Christine. "Pursuing Her Profits: Women in Jamaica, Atlantic Slavery and a Globalising Market, 1700–60." *Gender and History* 26, no. 3 (2014): 478–501.
Watt, Hugh. *Thomas Chalmers and the Disruption*. Edinburgh: T. Nelson, 1943.
Webster, Anthony. *The Richest East India Merchant: John Palmer of Calcutta 1767–1836*. New Delhi: Viva, 2009.
Weir, Heather A. "Helping the Unlearned: Sarah Trimmer's Commentary on the Bible." In *Recovering Nineteenth-Century Interpreters of the Bible*, edited by Christiana de Groot and Marion Ann Taylor, 19–31. Atlanta: Society for Biblical Literature, 2007.
Werrity, A., and L. J. McEwen. "'The Muckle Spate of 1829': Reconstruction of a Catastrophic Flood on the River Findhorn, Scottish Highlands." In *Paleofloods, Historical Floods and Climatic Variability: Applications in Flood Risk Assessment*, edited by V. R. Thornycroft, G. Benito, M. Barriendos, and M. C. Llasat, 125–30. Madrid: Centro de Ciencias Medioambientales, 2003.
———. "'The Muckle Spate of 1829': The Physical and Societal Impact of a Catastrophic Flood on the River Findhorn, Scottish Highlands." *Transactions of the Institute of British Geographers*, n.s. 32, no. 1 (2007): 66–89.
Whittington-Egan, Richard. *William Roughead's Chronicles of Murder*. Moffat: Lochar Publishing, 1991.
Youngson, A. J. *The Making of Classical Edinburgh 1750–1840*. Edinburgh: Edinburgh University Press, 1968.

INDEX

abandonment, 94, 154, 198; and adultery, 220; Lord Meadowbank on Jane's casual, 223; Oberon and, 10–11; and sexuality, 224

Aberdeen, Scotland, 52, 167–68, 182

Aberdeen Journal, 46, 192

Addison, Joseph: "A Satiric Treatment of Mary Astell's *A Serious Proposal to the Ladies*," 150

adolescence: and adopted children, 225; in India, 98; Jane as adolescent, xxiv, xxix, 1, 3, 5, 72, 76, 79, 91, 105, 114, 121, 139, 145–46, 156, 160; in non-Western societies, 206; and romantic friendship, 237–28

L'affaire Dallas, 2, 6, 10, 185–90, 221; and Jane will and testament, 3, 187; and Sir William, 186, 190, 229, 249–50; and Tulloch grab for marriage settlement, 6, 10, 185, 221

Albert, Jan, 212

Alphabetical List of the Honourable East India Bengal Civil Servants from the Year 1780 to the Year 1838, 38

Altyre estate, 28, 30, 188, 199; Helen as mistress at, 31, 47, 71; Jane at, 5, 52, 63, 79–80, 92, 125; and Moray flood, 183–84; Penrose as laird of, 2, 31–32, 33, 47, 55, 189; Penrose's bequeathing of, 34, 43, 46

American Psychiatric Association (APA), 224

Anna, 38, 41, 46

The Annals of the General Assembly of the Church of Scotland Covering the Years 1752–1766, 172

Anne, Queen, 8

Arabian Nights, 114

Arden, Jane, 84, 237

Arthur, Charles Ian Rose, 199

Arthur, Charles Lennox Tulloch, 199

Atkinson, Brooks, 215

attachment bond, 223; and reactive attachment disorder (RAD), 225

Austen, Jane: *Pride and Prejudice*, 56

Baccarat Scandal, 197, 198–99; and Prince of Wales, 197

Baillie, Alexander, 13–14

Balfour, James, 118

Baltimore, MD, 216

Barbut, Eliza Nixon, 59

Bath, England, 30

Battle of Plassey, 40

bedsharing: as boarding school practice, 57, 93; dangers foreseen in, 57, 149–50; Wollstonecraft on, 57, 128; at Woods school, 87, 89, 93, 96

Bell, Lydia, 84

Benares, India, 40, 42

Benedict, Barbara, 112

Bengal, 48–51, 59, 125

Bengal Establishment, 29, 35, 38

betrayal, 101; as factor in Jane's sexual outbursts, 226–27

Bible: *Ephesians* 4:31–32, 141–42; *Ephesians* 5:22–23, 174; *Hosea* 8:7, 205; *John* 14:25–28, 193; *Matthew* 8:12 and 13:42, 141; *1 Samuel* 1:6–16; voyeurism portrayed in, 111

biracial children and individuals, 10, 12–13, 16, 58, 145–46; case studies of, 17–27; female, 61, 98, 213; and Jane Cumming's identity, 4, 8, 27,

43, 51, 72; prognosis in India for, 17, 59; and Williamson, 61–62, 98. *See also* racial prejudice
Blaikie, Andrew, 13
blood: "black," 143, 145, 204; and bloodlines, 24, 58; as "good," 162; as Indian, 61, 143, 145, 156
Blood, Frances ("Fanny"), xxiv, 84, 237
boarding schools, 54–55, 71–72; bedsharing as practice at, 57, 93; Camden school, 85–86; domestic model of, 74–75; in Elgin, 62–64, 72; Erasmus Darwin plan for, 76–77, 84–85; female relatives as proprietors of, 84–85; health and food at, 57–58; in India, 58–59; lax supervision at, 56–57; life span of, 85; Manor House school, 21, 56, 76; Reading Ladies' school, 56, 84; teachers at, 55–56; of Wollstonecraft, 55–56, 84. *See also* Mrs. and Miss Woods Boarding School
Bobker, Michelle, 113
Bogle daughters, 18, 26
Bombay (Mumbai), India, 10, 16, 18, 23–24, 38, 46, 102
Bonaventure, Saint, 149, 150, 161
Bonnano, George, 228, 229
Borthwick, John: *A Treatise on the Law of Libel and Slander*, 200
Boulton, Henry, 21
Boyle, Lord, 110, 117, 118, 120; judicial voting record of, 144, 154; opinion of *MWJP*, 143
Bradford, Sarah (later Ripley), 238
Brantley, Ben, 215
breastfeeding, 129
breeding: in agricultural sense, 71; in educational sense, 70, 77, 79, 83, 104, 170, 208; and foppish behavior, 35; and India, 76, 95, 160; and lesbianism, 155
Breithaupt, Eliza, 18

Brideoake, Fiona, 239
Brighton, England, 244–45
Brodie, Deacon, 104, 268n66
Brontë, Charlotte, 95–96
Brooklyn Eagle, 215
Brown, Mary, 97
Bruce, John, ix, 19
Bruce, Peggy, 19
Bruce, Robert, 16, 18–19
Bruce Tyndall, Margaret Stuart, ix, 18–19, 26–27, 219
Buchan, Hugh, 52, 63–64, 167
Burke, Edmund, 103
Burns, Robert, 175
Burton, Robert: *Anatomy of Melancholy*, 70
Butler, Eleanor, xviii, 8, 103. *See also* Ladies of Llangollen

Calcutta, India, 37, 41–42, 58–59
Calcutta Review, 58
Caledonian Mercury, 153
Camden Boarding School, 85–86
Campbell, Dr., 200
Campbell, Eliza, 166
Campbell, Helen, 83, 86, 118, 134–35
Cardin, Joe (character), 208, 211
Carlyle, Thomas: *Sartor Resartus*, 23
Carnie, John and Alexander, 18
Carter, Elizabeth, 84
Castle Grant, 31
Chalmer, Mr., 158
Charles, Miss Christian, ix–x, 24; as Jane's schoolmistress and paid caregiver, 52, 55, 62–63, 64, 72, 167; relationship to Gordon Cumming family, 62–63; will and testament of, 182
Charles, Samuel, 18
Charlotte Square, 81, 105, 131; about, 73, 167; as construction site, 99, 105; Helen home in, 99, 129, 165–66
child abuse, x, 3, 111, 137–38, 142, 333, 224; sexual, 226, 227–28

Child Behavior Checklist (CBCL), 225
The Children's Hour (Hellman play), 2, 201; autobiographical element in, 211; Broadway premiere of, 208; draft of, 208, 214; eugenics notions in, 208–9; Jukes allusion in, 209; London revival of, 215, 279n37; Mary Tilford character in, 2, 201, 208, 209–10, 211, 212, 213, 214–16, 218; other characters in, xxi, 10, 201, 210–11, 245; plot of, 210–12, 269n24; and race question, 211, 213, 216–17, 279–80n40; revisions made to, 211; Roughead as source for, 201, 208, 210–12. *See also* Tilford, Mary (character)
The Children's Hour (1961 movie), 201, 245
Chilton, Landres, 216
Chirol, J. L.: *Inquiry into the Best System of Education*, 57
Church of Scotland, xxxvii; Disruption in, 2, 3, 5, 190–91. *See also* Established Church; Free Church
Church Patronage (Scotland) Act of 1711, 5, 170, 190
Churchill, Sarah, 8
Cleland, John: *Memoirs of a Woman of Pleasure (Fanny Hill)*, 112, 113–14
Clerk, John, x, 82, 110, 115, 120, 133, 203; appeal petition by, 145–46; closing arguments by, 137–40; and preparation of *MWJP*, 103–4; respondents' case documents by, 159–61, 162
Clive, Richard, 11
Clive, Robert, x, 11–12, 35, 40–41; address to House of Commons, 66–67
Cochrane, Peter, 24–25
College of Arms, 81
Comilla, India (now Bangladesh), 38

Conrad, Joseph, 202
convents, 75, 90, 148–49, 161, 203, 264n90. *See also* nunnery
Coongee, x, 59, 61–62, 125, 159
Cornwall, England, 28
Court of Session: about, 106–7; records of, 200–201. *See also Miss Marianne Woods and Miss Jane Pirie Against Dame Helen Cumming Gordon*
Cowper, William: *The Task*, 35, 38
Craig, James, 73
Craigie, Lord, 154
Cranstoun, George, x, 104, 107, 117, 146–47, 148, 151; closing statement by, 140; in initial *MWJP* hearing, 108–11; in pretrial hearings, 115, 116
Cromarty, Scotland, 171
Crommelin, Mary and Juliana, 18
cross-dressing, 95, 131
Cumine, Adam, x, 37, 48, 52
Cumming, Alexander (Jane's great-grandfather), 28
Cumming, Alexander Penrose (later Cumming Gordon) (Jane's grandfather): Altyre estate of, 2, 31–32, 33, 47, 55, 189; biographical information, xi, 28–30; and brother George, 32, 35, 45; death of, 32, 52; and parental responsibilities, 13–14, 33–34; parliamentary defeat of, 33; responsibility for Jane and Yorrick/George taken by, 52, 59, 61, 172, 217–18; as Rose's patron, 171, 172; and son George, 28, 34–36, 39, 43–44, 45, 46, 47; youthful hedonism of, 29–30
Cumming, Charles Lennox (Jane's uncle), xi, 34, 165–66, 169, 183; as executor of Jane's estate, 187, 193; and *MWJP* costs, 158, 164
Cumming, Charlotte (Jane's aunt), xi, 52, 53, 55

Cumming, Emilia (Jane's aunt), 165, 183

Cumming, George (Jane's father), xi; birth of, 30; career in East India Company service, 2, 11, 36, 38–39, 71; character of, 12, 35; death of, 38, 46; death announcements of, 46–47; debts of, 38, 39, 46, 47; education of, 34; and fop, 35, 38; and his father, 28, 34–36, 44, 45; and "Lady in the North," 15, 42–44; last will and testament of, 12, 38, 46; as letter writer, 40–42, 45; as poet, 15, 165; positions in India held by, 37–39; responsibility for children assumed by, 2, 12, 16, 46, 58; sending to India of, 2, 12, 35–37; sensibility of, 40; spending in India by, 37, 38, 39

Cumming, George (Jane's great-uncle), xi, 29, 51–52; estate of, 29; and house on Berners Street, 2, 57; in East India Company employ, 25, 35, 51; and nephew George, 34–36, 37–38, 165; as parliamentary candidate, 53; and Penrose, 30, 32

Cumming, Helen (later Dunbar) (Jane's aunt), 55, 169, 177

Cumming, Helen (née Grant; later Lady Cumming Gordon) (Jane's grandmother), xi–xii, 33, 53, 76, 77–78; at 22 Charlotte Square, 165–66; convinces parents to take children from Woods school, 3, 79, 100–101; death of, 183; Jane left with teachers during summer holidays by, 79–80, 92, 221; and Jane marriage to Tulloch, 9, 169–70, 175–76; and Jane's education, 2–3, 7, 62–63, 71–72, 77, 79, 148; Jane's race downplayed by, 4; and Jane's social position, 2–3, 94; Jane's story accepted by, 99–100, 103, 152; last will and testament of, 182–83, 199; marriage of, 30; as mother, 30–31, 154; *MWJP* filed against, 103–5; *MWJP* judgment against, 157, 158, 162–63; negligence attributed to, 152, 155–56, 223; personality characteristics of, 6–7, 9, 31, 53, 165–66; pursuers' lawyers on, 32, 133, 146, 161; responsibility for Jane and Yorrick/George accepted by, 47–48, 52, 61–62; Roughead on, 210; views on boarding school education, 55, 64–68, 182

Cumming, James, 38–39, 43

Cumming, Jane: and *L'affaire Dallas*, 2, 6, 10, 37, 184–90, 221, 229, 249–50; bedsharing by, 87, 89; betrayal feelings of, 101, 227; birth and age of, 43, 192–93, 258n47; brought to Britain, 48, 49–50, 51, 52, 59, 61–62; character traits of, 1, 9, 91, 95, 96, 97, 103, 137–40, 146, 152–53, 166; children born to, 176–77, 178, 180, 181; court testimony by, 3, 121–31; crush on Woods by, 3, 7, 95–96, 129, 219, 221; death of, 192–93, 230; as "devil," 144, 204, 215–16; in 1841 Census, 186; in Elgin, 62–63, 72, 167; and English language, 1, 59, 125, 270n41; Free Church joined by, 3–4, 5, 10, 191–92, 222, 228; grave and tombstone of, 194, 229; as Hannah, 142; Helen taking responsibility for, 47–48, 52, 61–62; Hellman's similarity to, 211–12; and illegitimacy, 16–17, 116; jealousy of, 130, 160, 205, 220, 250; judges' opinions on, 141–44, 151–54, 157–58; keyhole story of, 110, 113–15, 120, 121, 123–24, 136, 210; last will and testament of, 3, 187; lawyers' depiction of, 108–11, 115–16, 136–37, 140, 146–48, 160, 162;

marriage to Tulloch, 2, 5, 9, 169, 170, 174–75, 176; as minister's wife, 9–10, 178–79; motives behind story of, 129–30, 140, 152, 205–8; as neglected and excluded, 68, 94, 98, 222–23; in Nigg, 176–77, 205; notebook of, 96, 126, 142, 146, 147, 221, 272n27; paranoia and mental breakdown of, 187–88, 221; physical appearance of, 1, 62; Pirie hostility to, 3, 4, 6, 78, 79, 89–91, 96, 126, 130, 142, 146, 221; plot against Woods and Pirie by, 93–94, 97–100, 101; posthumous metamorphoses of, 4, 201–2; propositioning of Janet Munro by, 7, 96, 98, 119, 130, 219; race prejudice and Orientalism toward, 4–5, 8–9, 97, 115, 137, 145–46, 147, 216–17, 219; resilience of, 228–29; Roughead on, 201–8, 215, 216; schooling in India, 5, 46, 48, 59, 115, 161; and sexual knowledge, 1, 98, 138, 160; sexuality and sexual orientation of, 9, 98, 99, 159, 175, 219–20, 227; Solley on, 205–8; stress and anxiety in life of, 221–22; Tulloch's public humiliation of, 10, 186; value of estate of, 193; wood-stealing letter of, 188–89, 221, 251

Cumming, Jane Marianne (Jane's aunt), 165

Cumming, Louisa (Jane's aunt). *See* Forbes, Louisa

Cumming, Margaret (Jane's aunt), 55

Cumming, Mary (Jane's aunt), xii, 135, 147, 165

Cumming, Sophia (Jane's aunt), 55, 129, 165, 166, 182

Cumming, William (Jane's great-uncle), 37–38

Cumming, William (Jane's uncle). *See* Gordon Cumming, William Gordon (Sir William)

Cumming, Yorrick/George (Jane's brother), xii, 46, 47–48; brought to Britain, 48, 51, 52; death of, 167, 168; education of, 63–64; name of, 44–45, 52

Cunningham, John, 108

Cunynghame, Mary (daughter), xiii, 92, 93, 99, 129

Cunynghame, Mary (mother), xii–xiii, 101, 133

Dallas, Scotland: church in, 5, 170, 180, 191, 192, 194, 195; manse in, 182, 184–85, 186; and Moray flood, 183–84; Sir William as parish patron of, 170, 175, 192; Tulloch installed as minister in, 9–10, 171, 172, 177–78

Dallaway, Mr., 82

Darwin, Erasmus, xiii, 57; *A Plan for the Conduct of Female Education*, 76–77, 84–85

de la Torre, Lillian, xiii, 216–17, 219

Denby ("Jackson"), William, 19–20, 27

Denton, Diana, 18

Diagnostic and Statistic Manual of Psychiatric Disorders (DSM), 111

Diamond, Lisa, 220, 240

Dick Lauder, Sir Thomas: *The Great Floods of August 1829 in the Province of Moray and Adjoining Districts*, 183–84

Dickens, Charles: *Bleak House*, 25

Disruption, 2, 3, 5, 190–91

Dobie, Miss (character), 201

domestic female servants: prejudices against, 5, 262n42. *See also* Whiffin, Charlotte

Donatus of Besançon, 148–49

Donoghue, Emma, 8

Douglas, William: *Ministers' Wives*, 179

Drumsheugh, Scotland. *See* Mrs. and Miss Woods Boarding School

Duffin, William, 21
Duke of Dorset, 30
Duke of Norfolk, Charles Howard, 81
Duke of Gordon, Sir William, 32
Dunbar girls (Jane's cousins), 77–78, 83, 98–99, 110, 116, 160
Dunbar (of Northfield), Sir Archibald, 55, 169, 176
Duncan, Sandy, 14, 102–3
Dundee Warder, 190

Earl of Crawford, George Lindsay, 13
East India Company, 15–16, 25, 35, 40, 41, 42, 45, 49, 51, 66, 67, 165, 196–97, 231; children born to fathers and mothers in, 12, 17, 18–26, 58, 206; George Cumming (Jane's father) career in, 2, 11, 36, 38–38, 71
Edinburgh, Scotland: New Town in, 8, 73, 81, 101, 157, 164, 199; Old Town of, 72–73, 82–83; public buildings in, 106, 167
Edinburgh Magazine, 46, 171–72
Edmonstone ("Elmore"), Eliza, 22–23, 27
Edmonstone, Neil Benjamin, xiii, 12–13, 22–23
education: Erasmus Darwin on, 76–77, 84–85; Hamilton on, 68–71, 72; Helen Cumming views on, 55, 64–68; Jane's in India, 46, 48, 58–59, 115, 161; plans for Jane Cumming's, 2–3, 7, 59, 62–63, 71–72, 77, 79, 148; of women, 54–55, 67; of Yorrick/George, 63–64. *See also* Mrs. and Miss Woods Boarding School; United Free and Charity School
Eidophusikon, 157
Elgin, Scotland, 62–64, 72, 167; lawyers in, 185, 194
Elgin Courant, 192, 193, 194

Elgin Courier, 194
Ellis, Havelock, 204; *Studies in the Psychology of Sex*, 206
elocution, 82
Emerson, Mary Moody, 238
Encyclopedia of Identity, 111
Ephesians: 4:31–32, 141–42; 5:22–23, 174
erotic sensitivity, 219–20
Erskine, Henry, xiii, 104, 107, 117; closing arguments by, 136–37; in initial *MWJP* hearing, 108–11; in pretrial hearings, 115, 116
Established Church, 2, 3, 10
eugenics, 208–9
European Magazine and London Review, 46–47
Ewing, W. W., xiii–xiv, 229; *Annals of the Free Church of Scotland*, 191
Exhibition of Female Flagellants, 114
eyewitness testimony, 94, 113, 188

Faderman, Lillian: *Scotch Verdict*, 195, 201, 217
Falconer, David, 167
fantasizing: and childhood sexual abuse, 224; Hellman and, 212; Lord Glenlee on, 153. *See also* voyeurism
Farmer's Magazine, 168
The Female Preceptor, Essays on the Duties of the Female Sex, 85
female romantic friendship: asexual, 145, 146, 240–41; between Pirie and Woods, 83–84, 88, 89, 90, 93, 95, 97–98, 237–42; and sexuality, 125, 136–37, 149, 238–41. *See also* lesbianism
Ferguson, Margaret (née Pirie), 77, 83, 89, 90, 95, 243–44
Ferguson, Thomas, 83, 120, 243–44
Fielding, Henry: *Joseph Andrews*, 112
Finkelhor, David, 226, 228
Fitzjulius, William, 16

Fletcher, Elizabeth (née Dawson), xiv, 56, 75, 76, 77–78; *Autobiography*, 56
Forbes, Alexander Penrose, 196
Forbes, John Hay, 55, 100
Forbes, Louisa (née Cumming), xiv, 82, 100, 105, 129, 166; as Jane's guardian, 80, 116; marriage of, 55, 169
Fordyce, James: *The Character and Conduct of the Female Sex*, 54
Forres, Scotland, 2, 32–33, 52, 171, 173–74, 176–77, 183, 193, 195
Forres Gazette, 192, 194–95
Forsyth, Isaac, xiv, 62–63, 167
Forsyth, John, 26
Fraser, Amy (aka Young; later Surwen Forsyth), xiv, 26–27
Fraser, William, xiv–xv, 12–13, 15, 258n37
Free Church: creation of, 22, 191; Jane Cumming's joining of, 3–4, 5, 191–92, 222, 228
Freud, Sigmund, 204, 205; on primal scene, 114; *Three Contributions to the Theory of Sex*, 207
Funke, Lewis, 212
Furruckabad, India, 44, 61

Gainsborough, Thomas, 157
Gair, Isabella, 186
The Gale Encyclopedia of Mental Health, 111
The Gamekeeper at Home (Jefferies), 189
Gautier, Théophile: *Mademoiselle de Maupin*, 211
General Evening Post, 103, 151
The Gentleman's Magazine, 24, 46, 56
Gerrard, George, 50
Gibbon, Edward: *The Decline and Fall of the Roman Empire*, 41
Gillies, Adam (Lord Gillies), xv, 152–53, 154, 156

Glasgow, Scotland, xx, xxii, 18, 83, 201
Glenlee, Lord, 110, 143–44, 154
Glover, Jenna, 239
Godwin, William: *Caleb Williams*, 112
Goldwyn, Samuel, 10
Gordon Cumming, Constance Frederica ("Eka"), xv, 196, 197–99; *Memories*, 260n76
Gordon Cumming, Roualeyn, 196, 197
Gordon Cumming, Sir William: *Wild Men and Wild Beasts*, 196–97
Gordon Cumming, William Gordon (Sir William), xv, 34, 165–66; and *L'affaire Dallas*, 186, 190, 229, 249–50; and Church split, 5, 192; as Dallas church patron, 170, 175, 195; debts of, 196; as estate owner, 47, 52–53; as executor of Jane's will and testament, 187, 193; and illegal cutting of wood, 188–89, 251; and Jane marriage to Tulloch, 9, 169; Jane's fear of, 189–90; Jane's letters addressed to, 187–88, 189, 251; Moray flood losses of, 183, 188; and *MWJP* expenses, 158, 163–64; as Rose patron, 171, 172; and Tulloch, 9, 169, 170, 177, 180–81, 182, 190, 195; Yorrick/George's expenses paid by, 53, 64, 168
Gordon Cumming papers, 199–200
Gordonstoun, Scotland, xxxvii, 32, 33, 63, 64, 72, 171–72, 183, 188–89, 199
Graham, Maria, 15–16
Grant, Anne (of Laggan), xv, 102
Grant, Annie (later Need), xvi, 14, 25–26, 91
Grant, Duncan, 250
Grant, Elizabeth (of Rothiemurchus), xvi, 13, 15, 62, 166; on children, 14–15, 102–3; on teachers, 91
Grant, Francis W., 177

Grant, James (Sir James Grant of Grant, 8th Baronet), xvi, 34, 36, 39; papers of, 199
Grant, James Thomas, 12, 15, 255n24; children of, xvi–xvii; in India, 40, 42, 46, 61; and Jane-Yorrick/George trip to Britain, 50–51
Grant, Lewis Alexander, 33
Grant, Ludovic, 34
Gray, Richard: *Memoria Technica*, 74
The Guardian, 215

Hackett, Esther (La Tournelle), 56
Hackett, Sarah, 84
Halberstam, Judith, 217
Hamilton, Elizabeth, xvii, 77, 87, 165; allegory about pride by, 96–97; court testimony by, 133–34, 135; on education, 68–71, 72; on emotions and passions, 68, 79, 83; Pirie discussions with, 75, 84, 89; Pirie relationship to, 77, 85, 86, 90; on Pirie's character, 133–34, 135; prejudices against Eastern women of, 68–69; works: *The Cottagers of Glenburnie*, 56; *Letters Addressed to the Daughter of a Nobleman*, 66, 69, 70–71; *Letters of a Hindoo Rajah*, 66–67, 68, 102; *Letters on the Elementary Principles of Education*, 66, 68–69
Hamilton, Gavin: *Andromache Lamenting the Death of Hector*, 31
Hammett, Dashiell, 208
Handley, Sasha, 93
Hare, James, 116
Harris, John, 45
Harrison, William, 150
Hastings, Warren, 16, 66
Hatchett, Elizabeth, 84
Hays Production Code, 10, 201, 245
Haywood, Eliza: *Love in Excess*, 111–12
Hellman, Lillian, xvii, 2, 10, 201, 208–17; as eavesdropper, 212; feud with Mary McCarthy, 212, 279n37; and interracial casting, 216; Jane Cumming comparisons with life of, 211–13; on orphans and orphanism, 213–14; as "part-nigger," 213; reputation as fabricator, xvii, 209, 211, 213, 279n37; Roughead on, 210–11; and sexual awakening, 212–13; works: *An Unfinished Woman*, 212, 213, 214; *Pentimento*, 216, 279n37. See also *The Children's Hour* (Hellman play)
Hepburn, Audrey, 245
Hints to a Clergyman's Wife, 178–79
Holmes, Oliver Wendell, 209
homosexuality: Hays Production Code ban on depicting, 10, 201, 245; male, 49–50, 112; in navy, 49; in Samoa, 206; Solley on, 206–8; and voyeurism, 111, 113. See also lesbianism; sodomy
Hope, Charles (Lord Hope), xvii, 116, 118, 119, 144; interrogation of Jane Cumming by, 121, 122, 124–26, 270n41; opinion on *MWJP* by, 141–42, 155
Hort, William: *Mythology*, 74
Hosea 8:7, 205
House of Commons, 41, 66–67

illegitimate children, 12–27, 69, 108; and Jane Cumming, 7, 47, 78, 116
Imphal, India, 199
improvement through education, 54–55, 83–84; Penrose as improver, 31, 55; through transplantation, 47
India, 11–12, 15; Calcutta, 37, 41–42, 58–59; death and dying in, 29, 45, 61, 257n13; George Cumming in, 2, 12, 35, 36–39; James Thomas Grant in, 40, 42, 46, 61; Moorshidabad, 40–41; Patna, 42–43; portrayal of sexual activity

in, 12, 59, 60, 142, 147, 159–60; removing children from, 61; schools in, 58–59; underage sex in, 60, 142; women as lascivious in, 60–61, 207, 223; women as sexually voracious in, 12. *See also* Orientalism; women
Innes, William, xvii–xviii, 163–64. *See also* Mackenzie & Innes (Mackenzie, Innes & Logan)
The Independent, 215
Inverness, Scotland, 12, 33, 53, 167, 171

Jacquemont, Victor, 15
Jamaica, West Indies, 20, 28
James VI, King, 106
John 14:25–28, 193
Johnson, Samuel, 70; *Dictionary of the English Language*, 122
John the dentist, 33
jury trial, 163–64, 197

Keasberry, John Palmer, 18
Kennedy, Helen, 153, 273n39
Kessler-Harris, Alice: *A Difficult Woman: The Challenging Life and Times of Lillian Hellman*, 213, 279n37
Kett, Henry, xviii; *Emily, A Moral Tale*, 65, 100
keyhole story, 110, 113–15, 120, 131, 210; collection of evidence about, 117; discrediting of, 115, 121, 123–24, 136; in literary works, 111–12, 114
Khair-un-Nissa, Begum, 23
Kirkpatrick, James Achilles, 23
Kirkpatrick, Katherine ("Kitty"). *See* Phillips, Katherine
Kirkpatrick, William George, 23
Knockando, Scotland, 169–70, 176
Knox, John, 204, 264n90; *The First Blast of the Trumpet Against the Monstruous Regiment of Women*, 202–3
Krafft-Ebbing, Richard, 204

Ladies of Llangollen (Butler and Pononsby), xviii, 103, 151. *See also* Butler, Eleanor; Pononsby, Sarah
"Lady in the North," xviii, 15, 42–44, 45
Lamson, George Henry, 196
Lanser, Susan, 8
later-adopted international children, 224–25
Law Lords, House of Parliament, 9, 94, 158–59, 161, 162, 165–66, 177, 203, 223–24, 227
Lawtie, Colonel, 42, 165
Leckie, Robert, 23
Leckie, Robert Lindsay, 23–24, 27
lesbianism: in *The Children's Hour* movie, 201, 245; among cloistered nuns, 148–50; and Jane Cumming's sexual orientation, 9, 99, 205–8, 219–20, 227; Faderman on Woods and Pirie orientation, 217; Jane Cumming's presentation of teachers' sexual behavior, 83–84, 98–101, 108–10, 113–15, 116, 120, 123–24, 126–28, 131, 142–43, 152, 210; and judges' deliberations, 143–44, 155, 156–57; in literature, 8, 150–51, 203; and Pirie's orientation, 240–41; Solley on, 207–8; viewed as abomination, 60, 98, 202. *See also* female romantic friendship; homosexuality; queer; Sapphic; tribades; *venus nefanda*
Lister, Anne, xviii, 21, 226
Locke, John, 175; *Some Thoughts Concerning Education*, 60, 68
London, England, 29, 30, 31–32, 34, 35, 36–37, 39, 40, 50–51, 55, 56, 63, 73–74, 80, 81, 84–85, 87, 95, 133, 158, 172, 196, 200–201, 215, 227

London Chronicle, 103, 151
Loutherbourg, Philip James de, 157

MacDonald, John, 195
Macdonnell, John, 33, 52, 158
Macdowall Grant, Mrs., 85–86
Macfarlane, Thomas, 177
MacKenzie, Colin, xviii–xix, 157–58
Mackenzie, Henry ("The Man of Feeling"), xix, 1, 43–44, 107
Mackenzie, James, xix, 146–48
Mackenzie, Lewis, xix
Mackenzie & Innes (Mackenzie, Innes & Logan), 194, 244; hiring of, 104; payments to, 158, 163, 166, 190, 194; and termination of *MWJP*, 163–64, 177. *See also* Cranstoun, George; Erskine, Henry
Maconochie, Allan (Lord Meadowbank), 107–11, 117, 118, 165, 200, 223; biographical background, xix, 107; and Jane Cumming court testimony, 121, 129; judicial determination in *MWJP*, 144, 154, 157; opinions on *MWJP* given by, 142–43, 153–54, 156–57; Orientalist approach of, 9, 154, 156
Madden, Samuel, 55
Madras, India, 12 17, 22, 196
Malcolm, Anne, 23
Malcolm, Robert, 15, 23
Malinowski, Bronislaw, 205, 207
Manley, Delarivier: *The New Atalantis*, 8, 139, 203
Mann, Iris, 215
Manor House Boarding School, 21, 56, 76
marriage, 6, 7, 54–55; and contract, 169; dangers of same-sex bedsharing to, 238; and fidelity, 186, 220; manuals' advice on, 175

Married Women's Property Act (1882), 169
Masham, Abigail, 8
masturbation, 49, 148
Matthew 8:12 and 13:42, 141
Maude, Daniel, 168
Mausalipatnam, India, 15, 23, 49, 138, 148
Maynwaring, Arthur: "A New Ballad: To the Tune of Fair Rosamond," 8
McCarthy, Mary, 212, 279n37
McCosh, James, 190; *The Wheat and the Chaff Gathered into Bundles*, 191
McGee, Florence, 215
McKay, George, 249, 250
Mead, Margaret, 205; *Coming of Age in Samoa*, 206, 207
Meadowbank, Lord. *See* Maconochie, Allan
Miller, Hugh, xix, 173, 175
Milton, John, 76; *Paradise Lost*, 68, 263n69
ministers: and establishment of Free Church, 190; and heritors, xxxvii, 5, 170, 175, 182, 190; inappropriate behavior of, 172; salary of, 178
Miss Marianne Woods and Miss Jane Pirie Against Dame Helen Cumming Gordon, 1, 243; appeal petition in, 145–48; appellant's case documents in, 158–59, 161–62; closing arguments for pursuers in, 137–40; collection of evidence in, 117–18; cost of, 158, 166; damages awarded in, 162–63; defense closing arguments in, 136–37, 140; filing of, 103–4, 107–8; final verdict in, 154–55, 157; Helen Campbell as witness in, 83, 118, 134; initial hearing in, 108–11; initial verdict in, 144; Jane Cumming testimony in, 3, 121–31, 270n41; Janet Munro testimony in, 118–21; judges' deliberations on,

141–44, 151–54, 157–58, 271n12, 272n33; keyhole story discussed in, 113–15, 117, 121, 123–24, 131, 136; Orientalism as theme in, 8–9, 142, 145–46, 154, 156, 157; preservation of records in, 200–201; pretrial hearings in, 115–17; respondents' case documents in, 159–61, 162; termination of, 162, 163–64; witness testimony in, 118–34. *See also* Law Lords, House of Parliament
mixed race. *See* biracial children and individuals
Moir, John: *Female Tuition*, 56–57
Moncreiff, James, xix–xx, 103–4, 110, 120, 121, 133; appeal petition by, 145–46; on case's impact on Pirie and Woods, 162–63, 210, 243; Jane Cumming's narrative rebutted by, 115–16; racialized thesis of, 223–24; respondents' case documents by, 159–61, 162
Moorhouse, Henry, 24–25
Moorhouse, Susan (née Cochrane), xx, 24–25, 27
Moorshidabad, India, 40–41
Moray, Scotland, 29, 168, 171; floods in (1829), 3, 183–84, 188
More, Hannah, xx, 57, 260n6
More, Jacob, 57
Mortar, Mrs. (character), 208
Mrs. and Miss Woods Boarding School. *See* Woods-Pirie School
Mrs. Bolts School, 46, 58, 59
Mrs. Cole's Cookery, 43
Munro, Janet, xx, 76, 101, 110, 134, 168; bedsharing by, 87, 96; as collaborator in Jane Cumming's story, 97, 99, 120–21, 137, 143, 151; court testimony by, 118–21; Jane Cumming's propositioning of, 7, 96, 98, 119, 130, 219
Munro, Mary, xx, 20; marriage to Daniel Maude, 168

MWJP. See Miss Marianne Woods and Miss Jane Pirie Against Dame Helen Cumming Gordon

Nakeska, Eleanora (née Gordon Cumming), xx–xxi, 197–99
Napier, William Millikin, 168
Need, Caroline, 26
Need, Johnstone and Walter, 26, 27
Need, Samuel, 25–26
neglect: and abandonment, 223; as factor in Jane's behavior, 139, 222–24; and Helen Cumming, 152, 155–56, 223; impact on children of, 58–59, 68, 70, 72, 224
Nenadic, Stana, 14
A New History of England, 76
New Orleans, LA, 211, 212, 213, 214
The New Republic, 216–17
The New Statistical Account of Scotland, 182
New York, NY, 200, 205, 209, 211, 227
New York Evening Journal, 211
New York Herald Tribune, 211
New York Post, 208
New York Telegram, 215
New York Times, 215, 227
Newton, Lord, 110, 117, 118, 121, 144, 165; opinion on *MWJP* by, 144
Nigg, Scotland, 173, 175, 233; about, 171–72; Jane's life in, 176–77, 205; Jane's marriage record in, 170
Noman, Nancy Moor, 15, 23
Northern Review and Advertiser, 194–95
nunnery, 148, 150, 272n28. *See also* convents

Oberon, Merle, xxi, 10–11
Opie, Amelia, xxi, 102; *The Father and Daughter*, xxi, 51, 65, 66; "The Poor Hindoo," xxi, 51
Opie, John, 51

Orientalism, 11, 66–67, 208; Hamilton challenge to paradigm of, 66–69; of judges, 9, 154, 155, 156, 157, 162; sexual assumptions about Indian women from, 124–25, 142, 147, 156, 159–60; as theme in Woods-Pirie lawsuit, 8–9, 142, 145–46, 154, 156, 157. *See also* racial prejudice

orphans, 47, 213, 222; Hellman's attraction to, 211, 214

Ovid, 34

Paley, William: *Natural Theology*, 74
Palmer, Fitzjulius, 66
Palmer, John, xxi, 16, 46, 58, 61
Palmer, William, 16, 66
Patna, India, 42–43
Pearce, Grace, 28
Pearson, Edmund, 204, 210
Peligan, Noel, 50
penetration, 49, 238–39
Phillips, James, 23
Phillips, Katherine ("Kitty") (née Kirkpatrick), xxi–xxii, 23, 27
Pirie, James, 82, 266n9
Pirie, Jane: affection for Marianne, 7, 96; and Ann Woods, 87–88, 89, 94–95; bedsharing by, 87, 89, 93; biographical information, xxii, 72, 82–83, 244, 266n10; character and personality of, 78, 86, 133–35, 140, 161; conflict with sister Margaret, 243–44; and establishment of boarding school, 73–74, 84, 85; as governess, 85–86; and Hamilton, 75, 77, 84, 85, 86, 89, 90; Hellman depiction of, 245; hostility toward Jane Cumming by, 3, 4, 78, 79, 89–91, 96, 126, 146; and Jane Cumming story about, 83–84, 98–101, 108–10, 113–15, 116, 123–24, 126–28, 142–43, 152; last will and testament of, 244; losses and damages incurred by, 118, 163, 243; racism of, 4, 7, 78, 90–91; post-case life, 243–44; and religious education, 75; romantic friendship with Marianne, 83–84, 88, 89, 90, 93, 95, 97–98, 237–42; Roughead on, 210; temper of, 6, 83, 86, 146, 159; as tutee of Marianne Woods, 83–84; verbal abuse by, 3, 6, 130, 142, 221

Pirie, Margaret, xxii, 243–44
Pirie v. Fergusons, 243–44
Plato: *Phaedrus*, 34
Plumb, John Barker, 23
Pocock-Price school, 85
Polkemmet, Lord, 110, 144, 165
Pononsby, Sarah, xviii, 8, 103. *See also* Ladies of Llangollen
Portobello, Scotland, 94, 95, 98, 109, 128, 130, 133, 143, 233; about, 92–93
Prebble, John, 30
Prince of Wales (later King Edward VII), 197
The Principal Acts of the General Assembly of the Church of Scotland, 172, 173
punishments: on *Anna*, 50; for male same-sex sexual offenses, 122–23; at Woods-Pirie School, 76, 109, 124, 140, 145, 147, 159; for tribades in Amsterdam, 103

queer, 166, 239, 241

racial prejudice: against Jane Cumming, 4–5, 8–9, 97, 115, 137, 145–46, 147, 216–17, 219; of Moncreiff, 223–24; of Pirie, 4, 7, 78, 90–91; against Robert Lindsay Leckie, 24; of Roughead, 202, 204–5, 208, 209. *See also* Orientalism
Radcliffe, Ann: *Mysteries of Udolpho*, 114
Raeburn, Henry, 116

Raine, Eliza, xxii, 20–21, 225–26
Raine, Jane Elizabeth, xxii, 20–21, 225–26
Raine, Jno., 20
Raine, William, 20–21
Ramghur, India, 38, 43
Rattray, Miss, 77–78
reactive attachment disorder (RAD), 225
Read, Alexander, 21–22
Read, Harriet, 21, 22
Read, Helena, 21–22
Read, William Alexander, 21–22, 27
Reading Ladies' Boarding School, 56, 84
Reid, Alexander, 63
Residual Establishment, 2, 3, 10, 191
resilience, 228–29
Rex, Margery, 211
Reynolds, Joshua, 157
Rickson, Ian, 215
Ripley, Sarah Alden Bradford, 179–80
Roberts, Emma, 48–49
Robertson, Lord, 110, 117, 118, 121; determination in *MWJP* by, 144, 154; opinion on *MWJP* by, 143
Robertson, William: *History of the Reign of the Emperor Charles V,* 152
Robinson Crusoe (Defoe), 34
Rose, Richard, xxii–xxiii, 180–81, 191, 205; as advocate for Jane Cumming, 2, 6, 186, 229, 249–50; on Jane Cumming's character, 221, 229, 250; opinion of peers on, 191; Penrose as patron to, 171, 172; and Tulloch character, xxx, 180–81; and Tulloch-Jane Cumming "bad bargain" of a marriage, 169, 170, 174–75, 176, 185–86, 250; as Tulloch's mentor, xxii, 171, 181; and Tulloch's womanizing, 184–85, 186, 220
Roughead, William, 201–8, 216, 264n90; biographical information, xxiii, 202, 205; Calvinism of, 203, 215; and Hellman's "literary rape," 210–11; as Hellman's source, 201, 208, 210–12; material used by, 201, 203–4; racial prejudice of, 202, 204–5, 208, 209; as Solley source, 205–6, 207–8; works: *Bad Companions,* 201, 202–3, 208

same-sex relationships. *See* female romantic friendship; homosexuality; lesbianism; queer; Sapphic; tribades
1 Samuel 1:6–16
Sandford, Daniel, xxiii, 75, 105
Sapphic, 8, 101, 144, 150
Saturday Review of Literature, 210
schoolmasters: Hugh Miller on, 173, 175; salary of, 170; scant respect accorded to, 172. *See also* Scotch Parochial Schoolmasters' Act
Scotch Parochial Schoolmasters Act (1803), 170
The Scots Magazine, 107
The Scots Miscellany, 153
Scott, Alan, 199
Scott, Sir Walter: *The Lay of the Last Minstrel,* 92
Scottish Presbyterian Church. *See* Church of Scotland
sexual precocity, 60, 142, 147, 206
sexual preference, 136, 140, 240–41
Shakespeare, William (characters): Hamlet, 39–40, 41–42, 44–45; Iago, xxix, 153, 156, 214, 215; Petrucchio, 176; Yorick, 41, 42, 44
Shakespeare, William (plays): *All's Well That Ends Well,* 261n26; *King Lear,* 48; *Macbeth,* 48; *The Merry Wives of Windsor,* 136–37; *The Taming of the Shrew,* 275n31
Shand, Mr., 36
Sheaffer, Louis, 215
Sheridan, Thomas, 82
Sherwood, Mary Martha (née Butts), xxiii, 56

ships: discipline issues on, 49; lack of privacy on, 50; harassment of women reported on, 49; smell of, 50. *See also Anna; Bengal;* Cumine, Adam
Skene, James, 157
Smith, George, 104, 268n66
Smith, James, 189
Smith, Thomas, 50
Smollett, Tobias: *Roderick Random,* 112
sodomy, 122–23, 149; on ships, 49. *See also* homosexuality
Solley, John B., xxiii, 205–8, 228
St. James Chronicle, 103, 151
Starzl, Thomas: *The Puzzle People,* 26
Sterne, Laurence, 114; *A Sentimental Journey,* 40; *Tristram Shandy,* 112
Stirling, Eliza Christian, 110, 120; as collaborator in Jane Cumming's story, 97, 99, 137–38; court testimony by, 131–32, 142–43; marriage to William Milliken Napier, 168
Stirling, Mary, 133
Stirling, Richard: *The Two Janes,* 201, 278n12
Stothart, Thomas, 153
stress and anxiety, 221–22; effect on brain, 222; Helen unable to tolerate, 32
Swift, Jonathan, 8, 122; "Corinna, A Ballad," 138–39, 203, 222, 225, 247; *The Tatler,* 150, 151

Tain, presbytery of, 173, 177
Tait's Edinburgh Magazine, 171–72
Tanner, Eliza Ann, 24, 256n51
Taylor, Paul, 215
Ten Years' Conflict, 2, 3, 5, 190–91
Ternan, Richard Richards, 22
Theresa of Avila, 149, 150, 161
These Three, 10–11, 215, 245; and Hays Production Code, 161, 201
Thompson, George Nesbit, 18

Tilford, Mary (character), 2, 201, 208, 213, 218; comparisons of Jane Cumming to, 209–10; Hellman's attitude toward 214–15; Hellman similarities to, 211, 212; movie and play portrayals of, 215–16
The Times Literary Supplement, 208
Tindall, Martha, 88, 95
Tolbooth, 92, 166–67
Traub, Valerie, 8
traumatic sexualization, 226, 227–28
tribades, 103, 107
Trimmer, Sarah: *Sacred History,* 74
Tulloch, Charles Lennox Cumming, 178, 181, 187, 193, 195, 196, 205
Tulloch, Eliza Maria, 176, 187, 196
Tulloch, George Cumming, 178, 181, 187, 193, 196
Tulloch, Helen Grant Cumming, 176–77
Tulloch, Jane Cumming (later Arthur), 196
Tulloch, William: and *L'affaire Dallas,* 2, 3, 6, 10, 185–90, 221, 249–50; becomes minister, 9, 170, 177–78; biographical information, xxiii–xxiv, 170, 171–72; character and personality of, 181; death of, 193–94, 230; debts of, 194–95; humiliation of Jane by, 10, 186; inferior farming skills of, 180, 181, 221; Jane and Yorrick/George brought to Scotland by, 52; *Jus Mariti* renounced by, 169, 274n13; license to preach suspended, 173–74; and manse plans, 182; marriage to Jane by, 2, 5, 9, 169, 170, 174–75, 176; non-attendance at presbytery meetings, 181; opinion of peers on, 177, 181, 191; as Petrucchio figure, 176; relationship with Rose, 171, 180, 249; salary of, 178; seeks Jane's marriage settlement, 6, 10, 185, 221; sexual misconduct

accusations against, 6, 173–74, 175; and Sir William, 9, 169, 170, 177, 180–81, 182, 190, 195; and split in Church, 3, 5, 191; value of estate of, 195; womanizing by, 2, 3, 10, 184–85, 220, 227
Tulloch, William Gordon (son), 178, 180, 181
Tyndall, Onesiphorus, 19
Tytler, Alexander Fraser (Lord Woodhouselee), xxiv, 154, 165; opinion on *MWJP* given by, 151–52, 155–56; Orientalist argument of, 9, 155, 157

United Free and Charity School, 58–59

Vancouver Sun, 199
venus nefanda, 9, 108; Messarole play about, 201, 278n212
voyeurism, 111–14; and sexual fantasies, 127

Walbridge, Earle, 210
Westermarck, Edward: *The Future of Marriage in Western Civilization*, 207
Whiffin, Charlotte, xxiv, 92, 114; court testimony by, 110, 131; and Jane Cumming's story, 100, 127; testimony about, 119–20, 123, 132
Whitbread, Helena, 226
Williamson, Thomas, 16, 58, 61, 98, 262n42; *Vade-Mecum*, xxiv, 145
Wollstonecraft, Mary, xxiv; on bedsharing practice, 57, 128; boarding school run by, 55–56, 84; and romantic relationships, 237, 238; *Vindication of the Rights of Women*, 57, 128
women: biracial, 61, 98, 213; boarding schools for, 54–58, 62–64, 71–72, 74–75, 84–85; as business partners, 84–85;
conduct unbecoming of, 5–7; and education, 54–55, 67; Orientalist view of, 12, 68–69, 124–25, 142, 147, 156, 159–60; sexual exploitation of, 59; as witnesses in court, 118. *See also* female romantic friendship; lesbianism
Woodhouselee, Lord. *See* Tytler, Alexander Fraser (Lord Woodhouselee)
Woods, Ann, xxiv–xxv, 94–95; and opening of boarding school, 73–74, 86–87; Pirie jealousy and resentment toward, 87–88, 89
Woods, George and Hannah, 81
Woods, Marianne: and admittance of Jane Cumming, 7, 78; and Ann Woods, 88, 94–95; biographical information, xxv, 73, 81–82, 83, 244, 266n10; character of, 116, 133; death of, 245; and establishment of boarding school, 73–74, 84, 85; Hellman's depiction of, 210, 245; Jane Cumming story about, 83–84, 98–101, 108–10, 113–15, 116, 123–24, 126–28, 142–43, 152; Jane Cumming's affections for, 3, 7, 95–96, 129, 219, 221; losses incurred by, 118; romantic friendship with Pirie by, 83–84, 88, 89, 90, 93, 95, 97–98, 237–42; as teacher, 75, 82; treatment of Jane Cumming by, 3, 89
Woods, William (later Sir William Woods) (Marianne's brother), 81
Woods, William (Marianne's uncle), 25, 81
Woods-Pirie School: bedsharing and sleeping arrangements at, 75, 87, 89, 93, 96; books in, 74; conflicts at, 87–88; curriculum at, 74–75, 76–77; decorum cards at, 76, 95, 99, 129, 131; discipline and rules at, 74–75,

75–76, 264n90; establishment of, 84, 86–87; funding of, 73–74; Helen's choice of, 76, 77–78; items bought for, 74, 118; Jane's admission to, 7, 79; judges' visit to, 117–18, 165; naming of, 87; parents' withdrawal of students from, 3, 100–102; Roughead depiction of, 202–3; schoolhouse for, 73, 87, 165; similarity to convent, 203

Woolton, Lord Simon, 195
Wordsworth, William, xviii
Wright, Miss (character), xxi, 10, 208, 210

Yorke, Sir Charles Philip, 49
Yorick (character) in Sterne, 40
Young, James, 180
Young, Robert, 180

www.ingramcontent.com/pod-product-compliance
Lightning Source LLC
Chambersburg PA
CBHW051557230426
43668CB00013B/1878